Orson Welles

Orson Welles

*Six Films Analyzed,
Scene by Scene*

RANDY RASMUSSEN

McFarland & Company, Inc., Publishers
Jefferson, North Carolina, and London

LIBRARY OF CONGRESS CATALOGUING-IN-PUBLICATION DATA

Rasmussen, Randy Loren, 1953–
    Orson Welles : six films analyzed, scene by scene / Randy Rasmussen.
        p.   cm.
    Includes bibliographical references and index.

    ISBN-13: 978-0-7864-2603-4
    softcover : 50# alkaline paper ∞

    1. Welles, Orson, 1915–1985 — Criticism and interpretation.
I. Title.
PN1998.3.W45R37   2006
791.4302'33092 — dc22   2006012348

British Library cataloguing data are available

©2006 Randy Rasmussen. All rights reserved

No part of this book may be reproduced or transmitted in any form or by any means, electronic or mechanical, including photocopying or recording, or by any information storage and retrieval system, without permission in writing from the publisher.

Cover photograph: Orson Welles as Charles Foster Kane in the 1941 film *Citizen Kane* (RKO/Photofest)

Manufactured in the United States of America

McFarland & Company, Inc., Publishers
   Box 611, Jefferson, North Carolina 28640
   www.mcfarlandpub.com

Contents

Acknowledgments	vi
Preface	vii
Introduction: Fun House Mirrors	1
1. *Citizen Kane*: Man through a Prism	5
2. *The Magnificent Ambersons*: A House Divided	61
3. *The Lady from Shanghai*: Lethal Habits	104
4. *Touch of Evil*: No Man's Land	136
5. *The Trial*: Waking into Nightmare	179
6. *Chimes at Midnight*: Rough Winds	217
Selected Bibliography	265
Index	267

Acknowledgments

My thanks to Tony Houdek, Brian Baier, Richard Suggs, and Karen Cloud for technical assistance in my never-ending battles with HAL 9000. And to Michael Anderegg for sharing his expertise and resources on Orson Welles.

Preface

The ways in which to write about Orson Welles and his films are as varied as the talents of the man himself. In addition to the usual biographies, interviews, and critical studies, there are the more specifically focused approaches. Michael Anderegg wrote about Welles's multimedia adaptations of the plays of William Shakespeare in *Orson Welles, Shakespeare, and Popular Culture*. Robert Carringer's *The Magnificent Ambersons: A Reconstruction* attempts to fill the gaping holes in a great film ripped apart by studio bosses who took it away from Welles. *Despite the System: Orson Welles Versus the Hollywood Studios*, by Clinton Heylin, chronicles that battle and many others the writer, director and actor fought to make *his* kind of movies. Peter Conrad's *Orson Welles: The Stories of His Life* purports to draw analogies between the stories he told on screen and the myths he created and encouraged off screen about his own life.

My approach to the subject of Welles's movies is strictly viewer based—a view from the cheap seats, similar to Jed Leland's perspective of Susan Alexander Kane's opera debut in *Citizen Kane*. As in my previous book about the movies of Stanley Kubrick, I try to delineate the dramatic rhythms of specific movies as they unfold on screen and from the soundtrack. While doing so I draw frequent analogies to other movies, and sometimes quote from the impressions of other commentators, but always within the scene-by-scene progression dictated by the film under discussion.

Welles was a very self-conscious storyteller who often invited his audience to question the methods and veracity of what they see and hear. He was that rare magician who both pulled the wool over our eyes, for our delight, and unravelled the wool *before* our eyes, encouraging us to ponder the nature of the magic itself. Many of the characters in Welles's movies are also magicians of a sort, creating impressions intended to manipulate other characters, or even themselves, into moving in one direction or another. But unlike Welles, few of them voluntarily expose their tricks to the scrutiny of their victims.

By involving us so intimately in the foundations as well as the surfaces of what we see and hear in his stories, Welles struck an exhilarating, sometimes precarious balance between subjective and objective points of view. At the very least, his approach to making movies should inspire those of us who presume to analyze his work to acknowledge that we too, however modestly, are engaged in manipulating perceptions, and that our personal inclinations and capacities and motivations inevitably shape our efforts. As in Welles's adaptation of *The Trial*, it is important to keep in mind the *projector* as well as the image being projected.

Like those of Kubrick, the movies of Orson Welles unfold in symphonic fashion, with each new scene building and reflecting back in some manner, ironically or otherwise, on its predecessors. By approaching them in a detailed, linear, scene-by-scene manner, I can hopefully trace their dramatic development. As to why I chose to write about the work of Orson Welles, the answer is simple. Fascination and pleasure. Writing at length and in detail about movies to which I am not fundamentally attracted would be merely a chore, unless of course the movies were incidental to the promotion of something else.

My research too was simple: hour upon hour of watching Welles's films on videotape and DVD, wearing out the rewind buttons on several machines. Making notes. Writing. Revising. Returning to a particular scene to make sure I remembered the details or the sequence of events correctly. Reading articles and books to compare my impressions with those of other commentators who, though perhaps more qualified than myself to offer an opinion, often differed passionately from equally qualified colleagues.

My choice to write about *Citizen Kane*, *The Magnificent Ambersons*, *The Lady from Shanghai*, *Touch of Evil*, *The Trial*, and *Chimes at Midnight* rather than Welles's other films involved several factors. First, the matter of limited space. *Macbeth*, *F for Fake*, and *The Immortal Story* all now exist in more or less the form Welles intended, and are all worthy of inclusion in any study. There just wasn't enough space to include them without compromising my approach to the others. *Othello* is a great film recently restored and released on DVD. But much of the soundtrack was enhanced and altered too, including a newly recorded version of the original music score, and I was in no position to compare this released version with its predecessors. *The Stranger* suffered greatly from studio interference, and in some respects was the most compromised by Welles himself as he tried to tailor his work to conventional Hollywood expectations. *The Magnificent Ambersons* and *The Lady from Shanghai*, and to a much lesser extent *Touch of Evil*, also suffered from the unwanted interference of others. But Welles's potent ambitions for those works shine through so fiercely in spite of that interference that I had to include them.

Given the time, money, and opportunity, Orson Welles might have gone on tinkering with and revising his old movies until the end of his life, as he did in fact with the never finished, perhaps never intended to be finished, *Don Quixote*. Magic acts are always in need of a little fine tuning. Taking my cue from Orson Welles himself, I offer this incomplete but passionate interpretation of his movies. Ten years ago my scattered notes on these same movies probably read very differently than my current observations. Ten years from now, if I'm still around, they'll have probably changed again, though not, I hope, beyond recognition. That's the nature of the game, as Jed Leland, Mr. Bernstein, and Susan Alexander discover in my favorite movie.

Introduction: Fun House Mirrors

More years ago than I care to admit, a college buddy and I attended a campus showing of Stanley Kubrick's *A Clockwork Orange*. Afterwards we argued about the movie through half the night — those being the days when a good night's sleep seemed less imperative than it does now. We parted company on less than cordial terms. If anyone had asked us to describe the movie, we would no doubt have supplied two very different commentaries. And over time each of *those* commentaries would likely have undergone revision, because at any given moment each of us brings a unique set of experiences, inclinations, and sensibilities to any perception.

Telling and retelling stories is a common practice among characters in the films of Orson Welles: from five individuals and one newsreel telling the story of Charlie Kane in *Citizen Kane* to Falstaff and Prince Hal playacting a reunion between Hal and King Henry IV before it even occurs in *Chimes at Midnight*. Various colleagues of and commentators on Welles have supplied differing accounts of how his movies were made. Of who did what, when, and why. And then there are the critics, who in the course of explicating a Welles film describe in their own words the action from a scene or two.

To describe an event after the fact, or to imagine it before it occurs, is to interpret it. Details can be added or subtracted. Mood can be altered by changing descriptive terminology and emphasis. We are all storytellers, whether recollecting events from our own past or telling someone else what we read in a book or saw or heard at a school reunion, at work, at home, or at the scene of a car accident. The persuasiveness and veracity of such accounts varies from person to person. But no single account provides a complete picture. And even if one storyteller *could* paint a complete picture, who among his audience could absorb, comprehend and retain it all?

It is not surprising that a man who could show many different faces to so many acquaintances over the course of a lifetime would be so adept at dramatizing the vagaries of human nature, behavior, thought, and feeling. There is hardly any impression in a Welles movie that doesn't serve as a mask for something else often contrary to it. Not because his characters are frauds, but because each of them is eminently human, with multiple, contradictory, and changing needs, impulses, and perspectives. In *Orson Welles: One Man Band* Welles contends "there is a villain in each of us, a murderer in each of us, a fascist in each of us, a saint in each of us." A slight exaggeration perhaps, but it helps to account for the breadth of his artistic vision and the allowances he makes for the inconsistencies in his characters. Hank Quinlan is alternately a vicious bigot and a sentimental romantic. Miguel Vargas leans more towards saint than sinner, but he too slides perilously close to the latter. And Charlie Kane spans a whole spectrum of traits, according to his former acquaintances. Of all the characters in Welles's films, only Sir John Falstaff is sufficiently aware of his own complexity and mutability not to get lost in any one dimension of himself. Though deeply flawed, Falstaff often plays the fool but seldom *is* one.

The movies of Orson Welles are magical balancing acts in which we are alternately coaxed into and jerked out of a variety of impressions: impressions of characters, of places and times, and of events.

Fictional totems are erected and then cut down or recarved, not necessarily because they are false but because they are inadequate. Always searching for a new angle, a fresh perspective, Welles's mobile camera restlessly explores its surroundings, which in themselves seem more developed, more three dimensional, than what we experience from most movies. His frequent use of deep focus photography, staging in depth, overlapping dialog, and multiple sources of sound crowds our senses with information. Characters change position with respect to each other and their surroundings. Body language may contradict dialog. Images and sounds are often exposed as illusions—illusions sometimes independent of but sometimes manufactured and exploited by the characters themselves. Illusions that are potentially enlightening (art itself being an illusion) or dangerous. Everything in a Welles movie seems to be in motion, competing for attention and dominance. We can pick and choose impressions at random in order to construct a point of our own, or we can try to appreciate the parade of diversity that makes up Welles's magical worlds, which are a distilled reflection of our "real" worlds.

In a 1940 essay entitled "New Words," George Orwell wrote that "every at all individual man has an inner life, and is aware of the practical impossibility of understanding others or being understood" (Orwell, p.5). The character Marlow in Joseph Conrad's *Heart of Darkness* referred to that inner life as "your own reality—for yourself, not for others—what no other man can ever know" (Conrad, p.40). Characters in the films of Orson Welles cross paths with many other characters, forming alliances, disputes, romantic entanglements, and business relationships, or sometimes making no connection at all other than a brief physical proximity. The difficulty of reaching and sustaining mutual understanding is continuously on display. Not even newlyweds Miguel and Susan Vargas can sustain a united front against attacks from their enemies in *Touch of Evil*.

Welles's rather chaotic vision of human life is not necessarily pessimistic. In some ways it is oddly liberating, because it allows him to see a wide range of possibilities in every situation. The man who made *Citizen Kane* with the vast technical resources of RKO Studios later improvised *Othello* without studio sponsorship, in scattered locations and over the course of several years. A decade after that, again strapped for money, he transformed an abandoned railroad station into a nightmare of convoluted bureaucracy in *The Trial*. A little chaos can be a good thing. But then so can those vast technical resources. Orson Welles experienced the joys and headaches of both, and his movies reflect that experience.

In *The Lady from Shanghai* protagonist Mike O'Hara gets trapped in a carnival fun house full of mirrors that distort whatever they reflect. In a broader sense the films of Orson Welles seek to convey the vividness of those distorted, singular impressions while exposing their limitations. Truth, especially emotional truth, is not visible through a single lens or from a single camera angle. So Welles makes up for it by jumping from one perspective to another, tempering each one with others that modify or even contradict it. None of his characters is reducible to a single dramatic equation.

This book is a personal interpretation of some of Orson Welles's work in film. It is no more or less valid than any of the various interpretations of Charlie Kane's life offered by his former acquaintances. Like Kane's life, the artistic legacy of Orson Welles inevitably becomes a bone of contention among people who are either linked to or interested in it, but each of whom has unique, private motives for responding to it as he or she does.

1

Citizen Kane: Man through a Prism

"Citizen Kane" shouts out in bold white letters on a black background. Without music or the distraction of supplementary credits, the public presence of Charles Foster Kane is loudly proclaimed, in the manner of an inflated headline from Kane's own newspaper, the *Inquirer*. In a sense, he becomes a victim of the same sensationalist journalism he practices.

Citizen Kane begins and ends with a close-up of a "No Trespassing" sign hanging on a fence around the perimeter of Xanadu, the sprawling estate and last refuge of Charles Foster Kane. The sign is a utilitarian metaphor for the emotional barricades Kane erects around himself during the course of the story. And in a broader sense it echoes the fundamental privacy of every other major character as well. Though Kane is the story's focal point, the supporting players are not merely his orbiting satellites. Glimpses into their private lives, as lived prior to and after as well as during their acquaintance with Kane, affirm that the mystery of individual life is not exclusive to the film's extraordinary protagonist.

After an initial close-up of "No Trespassing," the camera climbs slowly up a black, forbidding, chain link fence. The sheer height of that fence, accentuated by its varied patterns of wire mesh, is one measure of Kane's isolation. Lap dissolves soften the visual transition between those patterns. Accompanied by Bernard Herrmann's brooding Xanadu motif, these and subsequent dissolves inject a feeling of stealth and mystery into the scene. In tandem with the camera, we creep over the barricade and roam around the private domain of citizen Kane, whose great wealth allows him to inflate his personal boundaries far beyond those of the average citizen. Despite its size, however, Kane's realm is not a happy place. Deserted and deathly still, like the ruins of an extinct civilization, it reeks of desolation and decay.

A big, elaborate iron "K" crowns a large iron gate. Juxtaposed with that "K," yet far in the background, is Kane's mountaintop castle, Xanadu. A single lighted window glows within the castle's otherwise dark facade. The smallness of that light, emanating from Kane's bedroom, counterpoints the boldness of the iron "K." Both are visual metaphors of their owner. Appearing side by side, they illustrate the contrast between his material power and his shrunken physical and emotional existence, as is soon demonstrated in other terms.

A lap dissolve juxtaposes the giant "K" with two small monkeys perched on the bars of what was once a tiger cage. Before the dissolve concludes, the monkeys briefly appear to be prisoners of the iron gate and its imperial monogram. After the dissolve they are merely bewildered occupants of a cage built for a much larger, stronger animal. Fitting metaphors for the sycophantic "friends" who populate Kane's estate at the end of his life. Not inclined to indulge in symbolism for its own sake, Welles draws these metaphors from real elements in Kane's world. The monkeys and absent tiger belong to Kane's private zoo. Both exemplify his passion for simultaneously collecting and neglecting things—including people.

Gondolas occupy Kane's private boat deck. Like zoo animals, bits and pieces of foreign culture are added to Kane's menagerie. His appetite for acquisition is large and omnivorous. Our next stop on the nocturnal tour is a golf course, adding sports to the collection. Like the gondolas and the tiger cage, it too is deserted. A mist drifts silently over the grounds, its minimal animation contrasting with and thereby illuminating the dead stillness of Kane's vast estate. This effect is repeated in *The Trial*, where a breeze-rippled shroud hanging over a statue counterpoints a motionless crowd of condemned prisoners at the base of the statue. Like a lonely sentinel, the black stone figure of a cat sits facing Xanadu, as though contemplating the fate of its owner. But it too is merely a lifeless echo of Charles Foster Kane. Another black structure to the left of the cat statue adds massive volume to that heavy impression of fate.

Xanadu is our destination. We inch closer to it with every passing shot. And it is visible *in* almost every shot. In one shot it appears as a quivering reflection in water—one of the film's many filtered and illusory impressions. Finally we reach the window outside Kane's bedroom, pausing on the verge of penetrating his inner sanctum. But the light in the window goes out before we can do so. The music stops. We are too late. Then, strangely, the light fades back in and the music resumes. A renewal of hope? Not quite. We have reversed perspectives, thanks to another subtle lap dissolve. We now look *out* the window from inside the bedroom. The light comes from inside. This won't be the last time Welles confounds our expectations. Dawn illuminates Kane (though not his face) lying on his deathbed.

Another lap dissolve fills the screen with falling snow. Have we jumped to a new scene in a different location? There was no snow outside Xanadu. A quaint cottage appears in the midst of that snow. The camera pulls back quickly to expose the cottage as part of an idyllic winter scene contained within a round glass paperweight, which is in turn held in the palm of Kane's trembling hand. We share his point of view. Our initial impression of the winter scene was, by objective standards, an illusion. That the snow appeared before the cottage did, and is visible outside the boundaries of the glass ball after the camera pulls back, despite being derived *from* the glass ball, is a visual distortion suggesting the influence of Kane's imagination on what we see. Snow triggers a nostalgic childhood memory that Kane refers to, in a dying whisper, as Rosebud. That word, which as yet means nothing to us, is spoken by anonymous lips in a huge close-up. By not showing us Kane's entire face, Welles does not distract us from and thereby emphasizes the mystery of whatever lies behind the spoken word. Herrmann's music gives us a clue to the mystery by playing the Rosebud motif, which recurs in a later scene featuring Rosebud's first appearance.

The omnipresent snow lingers into the next two shots, which show the paperweight drop from Kane's hand and shatter against the floor. Kane's deathbed reverie ends. The snow disappears. Then we see, from two different perspectives but roughly the same angle, Kane's private nurse enter the room. The first image of her is fuzzy, grainy, and oddly curved. Only with the next shot, taken from a little further away, do we realize that we were looking at the nurse through the distorting lens of a piece of broken glass from Kane's paperweight. Before plunging us into a series of flashback impressions filtered through the memories of various characters, Welles reminds us, in purely visual terms, of the potential distortions of perspective. That he made his point through a piece of curved glass is also a clever critique of his exciting new toy—the movie camera. In its simplest terms, film is light filtered through and sometimes distorted by a lens.

The faceless, anonymous nurse folds Kane's arms and pulls a bed sheet over his head. With a single word and a handful of images we are encouraged to feel the dramatic impact of a man's death before learning much about his life. Even before we get a clear look at his face. An earlier long shot of Kane lying on his bed returns. Outwardly there is no visible difference between the two shots. But we now know that for Charles Foster Kane *everything* has changed.

Smooth, slow lap dissolves are displaced by a sudden, direct cut. Visually, verbally, and musically, "News on the March" begins as a slap in the face, signaling a new and very different approach to the protagonist. As brash as the opening scene was subtle, the newsreel draws a portrait of Kane as distorted as was our first impression of Kane's nurse. Which simply means that it is incomplete, not necessarily false. In addition to being a satire on celebrity, newsreels, and shallow public perception, "News on the March" is a clever tool for supplying us with background information about Kane. Information to be tallied with and against impressions provided later by Kane's personal acquaintances.

"News on the March" looks and sounds like a typical 1940's newsreel so that we might more easily accept it as, in part, a critique of such newsreels. It contains scratches typical of archival film footage, missing frames resulting in unintended jump cuts, generic music that seems both crude and overdone, plus jarring juxtapositions and awkward transitions as it lurches from one episode of Kane's life to another—typical of a newsreel thrown together quickly and cheaply.

"News on the March" roughly follows the pattern of the rest of the movie, beginning with a portrait of Xanadu, then Kane's death, then jumping back in time to chronicle his life. That similarity, however, serves to highlight *differences* between the newsreel and other impressions we get of the same subject. In *Citizen Kane*'s first scene Xanadu appears as a dark, gloomy, largely deserted ruin. A reflection of its dying owner. But in the newsreel a fast montage of images, accompanied by vigorous narration, equates Xanadu with the legendary palace of Kubla Khan, as immortalized in the poem by Samuel Taylor Coledridge. It is a dynamic, sunlit kingdom full of new construction, news acquisitions, and happy guests. In short, a "pleasure dome." Kane, who is not shown during this part of the newsreel, is defined as the sum total of his possessions, which are inventoried in admiring detail. He is compared to Noah and the Pharaohs as well as to Kubla Khan. Viewed so metaphorically, Kane is more legend than flesh and blood person. Still, the narrator's description of Xanadu as nearly the "costliest monument a man has built to himself" is not far off the mark.

Accompanied by Bernard Herrmann's deliberately fatuous funeral dirge, Kane's death is presented in public terms. Pallbearers carry his coffin out of Xanadu and through a crowd of mourners, in contrast to the previous scene's image of Kane alone on his deathbed. A series of international newspaper headlines attest to his status as a cultural icon. Then, in an abrupt transition, imagery and music switch gears to tell the story of Kane's financial empire, from its humble beginnings to its vast and diverse holdings. Within that chronicle we glimpse an old photograph of Kane as a young boy, with his mother. Little of their emotional bond can be surmised from the photo alone. But in retrospect it seems significant that Kane's father is absent from that photo.

Of all the characters who appear in the newsreel and the film proper, Walter P. Thatcher is the only one who expresses an opinion of Kane in both. That is because one of those opinions is part of the public record. Appearing as a witness at a congressional committee hearing, Thatcher describes Kane as "nothing more or less than a communist." A passionate capitalist himself, he defines Kane as an enemy in the simplest terms he knows. His lack of insight and subtlety is as evident here as it is later in his diary.

Another impression of Kane is offered by the committee chairman, who recounts a story he heard about Kane as a boy attacking Thatcher with a sled. The chairman obviously wants to embarrass Thatcher, who is a hostile witness. Later in the film we get a very different view of what in this scene is nothing more than a passing joke. For Kane the sled attack incident is far more significant than the chairman, Thatcher, or anyone else will ever know. Matching the shallowness of Thatcher's view of Kane, but from the opposite end of the political spectrum, a speaker at a mass labor rally condemns him as a "fascist." The speaker's hesitant, awkward delivery adds to our impression of the inadequacy of his description. Kane will later be seen to lean both left and right politically, depending on his personal needs. A third verbal assessment of the protagonist is furnished by Kane himself, who for reasons as self-serving as Thatcher's and the union leader's paints himself as an American patriot. Undercutting that assessment is the saccharine newsreel background music that reinforces it.

Despite its broad strokes, the newsreel evokes something of the contradictory nature of its subject, especially in his public activities. Kane's opinions of other people and events were as divided and fickle as the public's opinions of him. Through his mouthpiece, the *Inquirer*, he supported America's war against Spain, then opposed participation in World War One. He supported, then denounced Adolf Hitler. Particularly striking is a shot of a smiling Kane standing with Der Fuhrer on a balcony while narration informs us of his later change of heart.

The instability of Kane's *personal* relationships is illustrated by his marriage to Emily Norton. Her social prominence as the niece of a United States president makes us question Kane's motive for marrying her. Was she to be a stepping stone for his own political ambitions? While we *see* the happy couple behaving like giddy newlyweds on the White House lawn, we *hear* about their eventual divorce, and of a second divorce to follow for Kane. The clash between visual present and verbal future is stark, and exacerbated by the further revelation that Emily Norton and her son by Kane will die in an automobile accident just two years after the divorce. This information intensifies our impression of Kane's desolation as, one by one, his other relationships disintegrate later in the film. And it is information provided only by the newsreel, which for all its superficiality serves a valid dramatic function beyond reminding us of the public's dubious understanding of the lives of celebrities.

The narrator's account of Emily's tragic death is visually counterpointed by a newspaper headline from a couple years earlier, celebrating Kane's nomination as a New York gubernatorial candidate and accompanied by a photo of Kane, Emily, and their son smiling together outside a convention hall. With hindsight we can pinpoint the exact moment that photo was taken (igniting flash powder marks it), and note the bitter irony of its image of domestic and political bliss. Only seconds after the photo is taken, we learn later in the story, Emily will send their son home and reveal knowledge of her husband's infidelity. In other words, Kane's marriage and political career were doomed even before the photo was taken.

The newsreel's next shot is of Kane and his second wife, Susan Alexander, immediately after their wedding. Narration informs us the event took place a mere two weeks after

Kane's divorce from Emily, giving us the impression that Kane's romantic commitments are shallow. But what the newsreel leaves out is the tentative, tender, intimate beginnings of Kane's relationship with Susan, which emerge later in the story from reporter Thompson's interviews with Susan and with Jed Leland.

As Kane and his bride head for their car, they are pushed to and fro by a mob of reporters and photographers. Kane lashes out at them with a cane—a striking illustration of celebrities at the mercy of the fame they crave, exploit, and sometimes resent. Narration informs us that Kane built a three million dollar opera house for his second wife. That sounds like an extraordinarily generous token of love. Shots of Susan's confident face suggest that she benefitted from that generosity. But that impression is undercut much later when we learn that Susan's opera career was Kane's selfish means of soliciting public approval after being rejected at the ballot box. And that for Susan a career in opera proves to be a hellish, humiliating experience.

Equally misleading is the description of Xanadu as being conceived by Kane for Susan. Starting with a shot of the couple lounging outside their castle, the camera irises out to surround them with convivial and presumably famous guests. That Susan left Kane before Xanadu was finished makes her seem particularly ungrateful. The newsreel fails to show us what her life with Kane was like *inside* the castle, when they were alone together.

Scratchy campaign film footage of Kane's 1916 run for political office culminates in the image of a newspaper headline trumpeting his love affair with Susan Alexander. Narration adds that this scandal resulted in Kane's "shameful, ignominious" defeat and set back the cause of political reform in the United States for decades. True. But as an iris shot emphasizes, the headline we read comes from the *Chronicle*, a rival to Kane's *Inquirer*. And the luridly heart-shaped front page photo of Susan Alexander depicts her as a sophisticated femme fatale rather than the naive young woman we later see her to be at the beginning of her relationship with Kane. The *Chronicle* story and accompanying narration tell only part of the story of Kane and Susan, and even that part not entirely accurately.

Somber imagery, music, and narration convey the impact of the Great Depression on Kane's corporate empire. Then, in a jarring change of mood, we are told that his public status and influence remained intact. Again perceptions of Kane are full of contradiction.

During a 1935 interview on board a ship returning from Europe, Kane replies to a reporter's questions. His answers are tailored to serve his own interests and help him maintain a tactical edge over the interviewer. He promotes his own newspaper at the expense of radio news. He pokes fun at the reporter's interviewing style and slow paced questions by contrasting them with his own dexterity when *he* was a reporter. He deftly avoids commenting on business conditions in Europe (no doubt grim in 1935) by transforming the reporter's inquiry into a joke, and finds his own cleverness very entertaining. Striking a deliberately serious pose for a moment, Kane takes advantage of another question to proclaim his patriotism. And finally, with smug self-importance undercut by historical events occurring after this interview but before the newsreel was assembled, he implies that as a result of his high-level discussions with the leaders of Europe there will be no war.

The next newsreel film clip portrays Kane in less flattering terms than he portrayed himself during the interview. Older now, he looks awkward and confused during a cornerstone laying ceremony. Cheerful music and narration counterpoint that negative imagery, as though mindlessly disconnected from what we see, then clumsily switch gears to now reinforce a second image of weakness—Kane in a wheelchair. We are told of Kane's dwindling public influence and of his seclusion within the "already decaying" Xanadu. But there is a contradiction within that portrait. "Never photographed" is belied by shaky, handheld camera footage of him shot through a fence and from high up in a tree. This press intrusion on Kane's privacy is, we later discover, a tactic Kane encouraged his own reporters to use during the *Inquirer*'s heyday.

Returning to where it began, "News on the March" concludes with a public portrait of Kane's death. Footage of an electronic sign flashing news of Kane's passing is accompanied by a brief rendition of Frederic Chopin's "Funeral March"—an example of a piece of music adopted into an institutional ritual, the way Edward Elgar's "Pomp and Circumstance" and Felix Mendelssohn's "Wedding March" from *A Midsummer Night's Dream* have been into commencement and wedding ceremonies.

Transition from the newsreel's "The End" card to a side view of the movie screen on which that card is projected and then to a shot of the projection booth from which that image emanates, accompanied by the mechanical shutdown of the newsreel's soundtrack, emphasizes the artificiality of "News on the March" and of all impressions we derived from it. When it no longer occupies the entire frame of Welles's larger film, the newsreel seems less magical and less convincing. Reinforcing that de-mystification is the subsequent conversation among the newsreel's producers and promoters gathered in the darkened projection room. Their dubious motives and methods undercut their creation's credibility. Fitfully illuminated by light from the same source that illuminated pieces of Kane's life moments earlier, these men are never fully revealed to us. Their private motives and perspectives remain largely hidden. Most of them light up cigarettes after the show, visually pinpointing their individual identities in the collective shadows. We cannot even tell which of them is the first to voice an opinion of the newsreel. But it is a mildly critical voice, suggesting that seventy years of Kane's life cannot be summed up in one short film. Overruling that opinion is the voice of another man, who is obviously the boss of this particular gathering.

The only figure standing and moving around, boss Rawlston tells the newsreel's creator, reporter Jerry Thompson, that the film needs an "angle," something new and different to pique an audience's curiosity and set itself apart from other news coverage about Kane. For a moment Rawlston seems to be on the right track, advising Thompson to get at the "who" rather than just the "what" of Kane's life. But his goal is not quite that noble. "Maybe he told us all about himself on his deathbed" is just another "angle," a gimmick with which to hype the newsreel. Ignoring mild objections from Thompson and other reporters, Rawlston's bullying behavior foreshadows or echoes, depending on your chronological point of view, Kane's own practices as a newspaper publisher. Both men shape the news for their own ends rather than merely report it.

Standing in front of the blank movie screen, Rawlston enthuses about his plan to fill it with a story that will set Kane apart from other iconic American tycoons. And the key to that plan is "Rosebud," Kane's dying utterance. Whatever Rosebud meant to Kane, it now has a very different significance to Rawlston. Standing between the camera and a beam of light from the projection booth, Rawlston looks like an abstract tyrant, black beams shooting out from his head and hands as he waves them around to make his point. Ordering Thompson to contact all of Kane's old associates, he ignores Thompson's moral qualms about prying into the protagonist's private life so soon after his death. In retrospect, we can say Thompson plays Jed Leland to Rawlston's less scrupulous Kane.

At the end of the scene Rawlston makes a flippant remark about Rosebud that by happenstance proves accurate. "It'll probably turn out to be a very simply thing" is an unwitting and ironic insight for a man who is not so much searching for the truth about Kane as he is selling a plausible facsimile of the truth to the buying public. Rosebud does turn out to be a simple thing, though the role it plays in Kane's life is not.

Among the anonymous reporters dimly visible in the background of this scene are several played by actors who play other, more important roles later in the film, though chronologically earlier in the story. Like ghosts from the past, they return as silent witnesses to the same kind of shoddy journalism practiced by their previous boss.

Startling transitions between scenes are a hallmark of *Citizen Kane*. From Rawlston's casual comment about Rosebud turning out to be a simple thing, we jump to the stormy and not so simple story of Susan Alexander, Kane's second wife and original owner of the object (the glass paperweight Kane held in his hand when he died) we currently associate with Rosebud. Lightning from a thunderstorm illuminates a smiling, pretty image of Susan's face on a billboard outside the El Rancho nightclub in Atlantic City. Broken brick walls and a cracked skylight soiled with bird crap are evidence of the establishment's humble economic status. Contrasting Susan's happy, public billboard portrait but matching the gloomy weather and El Rancho's shabby exterior is Bernard Herrmann's bleak, cold music.

The roving camera glides up over the nightclub's roof, through a glowing neon sign advertising Susan's performances, and down to a skylight through which we get a blurry, distant view of Susan herself. Like reporter Jerry Thompson, the camera sneaks up on her in her hour of despair, prying into her private thoughts and feelings about the protagonist. A quick lap dissolve completes our stealthy approach, bringing us inside the nightclub and sidling up to a table where Susan sits, head down in a drunken, coughing stupor. We arrive at the same time as a head waiter named John and reporter Thompson.

The El Rancho is decorated in a Mexican style. Latin flavored blues plays softly in the background. The tune is "It Can't Be Love," established later in the film as a kind of theme song for Kane and Susans' dysfunctional marriage. Within the gloomy, mostly deserted nightclub, each table is lit by its own lamp. And that visual impression of isolation is reinforced by the occasional rumble of thunder, which isolates the nightclub's interior from the inhospitable world outside. The El Rancho is Susan Alexander's sanctuary in the same way that Xanadu was Kane's in the movie's first scene.

John introduces Thompson to Susan. The waiter seems nervous. Did he accept a bribe for the introduction? Does he feel guilty about it? Thompson tries to join Susan at her table. She coldly informs him that he is not welcome. Her now uplifted face is very different from her smiling, confident, public image on the billboard outside. "Why can't you people leave me alone" implies that Thompson is not the first reporter to badger her since Kane's death. "I'm minding my own business. You mind yours" is a clear statement of the barricade she has erected around herself, in the same way Kane erected a "No Trespassing" fence around Xanadu. When Thompson fails to take the hint, Susan repeats it, loudly, disturbing the subdued atmosphere of the nightclub. He wisely withdraws.

Thompson contacts Rawlston from a nearby phone booth. In a beautifully composed shot, Thompson, John, and Susan appear in the same frame but at varying distances from the camera. Susan occupies the far background, isolated from everyone else. John leaves the middle ground to join Thompson in the foreground. Perhaps anticipating a payoff, he encourages the reporter not to give up. Moments earlier John instructed a subordinate to fetch Susan another drink, hoping to loosen her tongue for their visitor. When the call to Rawlston goes through, Thompson closes the phone booth door, virtually in John's face. He too wants privacy, concealing a conversation about his future investigation plans from the nosy waiter, who after all might, for a price, reveal those plans to a rival reporter. In this one sustained shot we get a strong impression of how three separate lives intermingle, sometimes clashing and sometimes harmonizing.

Hanging up the telephone, Thompson opens the phone booth door and invites John back into his confidence—for selfish reasons, of course. He bribes the waiter for any information about Rosebud. John eagerly accepts the payoff before revealing that Susan told him she never heard of Rosebud. Not much of a return for the money, but if true it informs *us* that even after years of marriage Susan didn't learn all of her husband's secrets. And in retrospect that point becomes ironic when we discover that Kane's dying word and thoughts were triggered by an object that previously belonged to Susan herself.

If our first impression of Susan Alexander, on the billboard outside the El Rancho, was misleading, our next impression of Walter P. Thatcher is even more so. And like Susan's it is a *public* facade. In a low angle shot we see a large statue of Thatcher looming above us, deliberately posed in a serious, thoughtful manner. The statue and the memorial library surrounding it are the deceased Thatcher's monuments to himself, no less than, as the newsreel claimed, Xanadu was a self-styled monument to Charles Foster Kane.

Herrman's music mocks the pomposity of Thatcher's carefully crafted public image. At the foot of the statue sits the guardian of that image—a librarian named Bertha, dressed in black, with short, straight hair pressed tightly against her head. She speaks in hushed tones, as though out of reverence for the library's namesake. She speaks with precise, fussy enunciation. She is the master of this little fiefdom, laying down the law to the suspicious intruder by placing strict limits around his access to Thatcher's private diaries. Refusing to pause for even a moment to consider Thompson's needs, which are both modest and modestly stated, Bertha makes clear her low regard for the press, echoing Thatcher's low regard for Kane's journalistic efforts. Turning her back on the reporter, she strides with stern gait to the library's inner sanctum—a large vault where Thatcher's private diaries are kept, like sacred relics.

Despite the playful background music that initially undercut the visual bombast of Thatcher's statue and the sobriety of its guardian, the Thatcher Memorial Library is, like the El Rancho and Xanadu, a temple of privacy—a repository of that fundamental, inviolable, fragile individuality which is perhaps *Citizen Kane*'s central theme. Voices and sounds echo through its cavernous rooms. Herrmann's music turns serious, intimate, even awestruck as we track slowly with Thompson into the sacred vault. Movements are measured and ritualistic as a uniformed guard named Jennings places one of Thatcher's diaries on a huge table, in front of a large chair. Bertha reiterates the time and page restrictions on Thompson's access to the divine text. Light streaming in through an unseen skylight illuminates the table, reflecting brightly off the pages of Thatcher's diary. Like the projection booth beams in an earlier scene, that light metaphorically represents a glimmer of emotional intimacy within the pervasive gloom of ignorance and obscurity. Thompson delves into the intimate details of a man's life which normally pass unnoticed in the glare of public perception and myth. However unrevealing and unsatisfying Thatcher's recollections of Kane prove to be for Thompson, they constitute a rare glimpse into the private lives of two famous men. On one level the Thatcher Memorial Library is a joke, but on another it proves a valuable resource in what for Thompson eventually becomes a more ambitious quest than the one Rawlston assigned to him. And if nothing else, the Library is a powerful, haunting reminder of a long life lived and now gone. Like Xanadu in the last scene of the movie.

With Bertha and Jennings on guard nearby, the camera closes in over Thompson's right shoulder and peers into Thatcher's diary. The magic of personal recollections recorded on paper is echoed by Herrmann's music, which sloughs off the aura of mystery and plunges headlong into the thrill of discovery as we read, in intimate close-up, about Thatcher's first encounter with Kane, back in 1871. That music, by the way, contains one of many variations on the Rosebud motif. Thompson is closer to discovering the object of his original quest than he realizes. In addition, the music echoes the carefree exuberance of young Charlie Kane playing with his sled in the snow outside his mother's boarding house in rural Colorado. He seems very happy, though it is interesting to note that in his (chronologically) first appearance in the film he is alone.

Like most boys his age, Kane fights imaginary battles before fighting real ones. Curiously, he launches a snowball at a sign on the boarding house bearing his mother's name. This scene contains no overt evidence of pre-existing tension between mother and son. But with hindsight we can imagine young Kane resenting and even rebelling against Mrs. Kane's smothering protectiveness. Perhaps the snowball is a token of such rebellion, which never develops further because mother and son are separated at the end of this scene. If so, the round snowball is the metaphorical antithesis of the round paperweight that for elderly Kane represents the carefree youth and motherly love of which he believes he was deprived. Alternate futures balance precariously on the point of one incident. Herrmann's music fades out and is displaced by the local sound of winter wind, which aurally foreshadows young Kane's impending desolation.

Pulling back from Kane's imaginary games and surrounding him with the separate interests of three adults whose decisions will profoundly affect his future, the camera retreats through a window into the boarding house, where Kane's parents and a dapper young banker named Thatcher discuss the boy's impending departure for New York, and a new life in the custody of a stranger. Throughout their discussion Kane remains visible in the background, framed by the window. Blissfully unaware of the plans being made for him, he is visually and figuratively boxed in by the needs and desires of others.

Charlie Kane's mother, Mary, is austere, almost puritanical in appearance — similar to Bertha from the Thatcher Memorial Library. And like Bertha, she dominates her territory. Unlike Bertha, however, she is an emotionally divided character, torn between love for her son and a burning need to send him away in Thatcher's care. But our *first* impression of the relationship between mother and son is of protectiveness as she repeatedly reminds him to bundle up and keep warm.

Echoing her dominance in this scene, the camera backtracks with Mary as, overriding the objections of her older husband, Jim, she sits down at a table to sign documents authorizing transfer of her son's care to Thatcher's bank. The foreground to background layering of characters, accentuated by deep focus photography, is reminiscent of the telephone booth shot at the El Rancho. Each character has a different perspective of and interest in the transaction underway.

Jim Kane's protests against losing the right to raise his son seem reasonable and compelling, at first. Thatcher's cruel disregard for them is based on the economic fact that it is Mary, not her husband, who inherited a fortune from a deceased former boarder. In Thatcher's book the wealthy call the shots. Mary too brushes aside Jim's objections, but for different reasons. While Thatcher spells out the terms of the deal, Jim makes a final, plaintive plea as a devoted father and husband. But upon hearing that the bank will pay him and Mary fifty thousand dollars a year for the rest of their lives, his protest softens. "Well, let's hope it's all for the best" seems a rather hasty and convenient surrender of his paternal rights.

Still grumbling about the loss of those rights, but with little passion now, Jim Kane trudges back to the window and closes it, silencing the playful battle cries of his son. Here again is contrast between word and action. Jim *talks* like a loving father, but his son's voice either annoys him or perhaps makes him ashamed of giving up the custody battle so easily, and under terms so financially beneficial to himself. By contrast, Mary Kane, who initiated the custody change, cannot bear to be out of earshot of her son's voice. She moves quickly to the window and re-opens it.

In a powerful close-up, with her head bracketed by Thatcher and Jim in the background, Mary is a portrait of suppressed and divided passions. Calling out loudly to her son, whom she rather formally addresses as Charles (Thatcher does the same after taking custody of the boy), she simultaneously attends to Thatcher's assurances about the boy's financial future. Facing away from the two men, who are incidental to her overriding concern for Charles, she is torn between a desire to raise her son and a desire to protect him. Agnes Moorhead's performance as Mary Kane, though brief, is wonderfully convincing, combining intensity of conviction with outward restraint. Background music returns in softly descending notes as Mary, almost in a daze now, speaks distractedly of having packed her son's trunk a week ago, in anticipation of his departure. This plan has obviously preoccupied her for some time. In this one-shot portrait, Mary Kane appears at once heartbroken, fiercely determined, and stoic. The men visible behind her and the boy off screen in front of her form the box in which *she* is trapped. In emotional terms she occupies a world of her own, which no other character in the scene comprehends. Inside the boarding house Welles's camera gives visual prominence to the ceiling, which seems to press down oppressively on Mary Kane.

The adults join young Kane outside the boarding house. Mary again expresses concern about his health in the cold weather. Whether because or in spite of that concern, he seems very fond of her. Thatcher, however, charges ahead of Mary and obtrudes his voice over the boy's as Charles addresses his mother. It is a clumsy attempt to befriend the boy, who reacts politely but warily. Jim Kane, the last to join this new gathering, tries to ease the encounter between his son and the stranger. And whatever Mary Kane implies later about strained relations between father and son, they seem friendly now. Charlie warmly calls out "Pa" and moves towards his father, until summoned back to his mother's side.

Despite bad relations between them, Mary and Jim act in concert, along with Thatcher, to persuade Charles that leaving home with the stranger will be an exciting adventure. The three adults surround the boy, who seems even more at a tactical disadvantage because the camera films this action at their eye level instead of his. But the alliance of convenience among the adults is fragile at best. Thatcher's phony enthusiasm antagonizes Charlie. Frightened, the boy turns to his mother, not his father. Jim's attempt to portray his son's impending departure as a good thing draws a contemptuous glance from Mary, who as though from long habit slips her body protectively between father and son. Caressing the boy with a soothing touch, she rudely interrupts Jim's rambling speech to assure Charles that he won't be lonely.

Thatcher's overeager attempt to win the boy's confidence backfires. Kane turns on him, pushing him to the ground with his sled. Mary, predictably, moves towards her son. Jim, on the other hand, is more concerned about the banker. He takes an angry swing at Charlie, but misses. Jim apologizes to Thatcher, further appeasing him by declaring that Charlie needs a "good thrashing." Mary, in the heat of the moment, betrays her *real* motive for sending her beloved son away. "That's why he's going to be brought up where you can't get at him." In a big close-up she looks away from everyone, as though focused on a distant, imagined scenario in which, perhaps, Jim attacks their son in a drunken rage. Has Jim attacked *her* in the past? Neither Thatcher's diary nor Welles's camera trace the story back that far. The matter remains, as intended, a mystery. One thread in the fabric of Charlie Kane's life. But whether Mary Kane's fears are valid or not, her determination to act on them is fierce and unyielding.

The camera tilts down past Mary's face to focus on Charlie's. Despite the hug that physically bonds them, mother and son are miles apart emotionally. Young Charles glares up in fear and hatred at the stranger who has come to take him away from his parents. He seems oblivious to Mary's fear of what Jim might do to him. As a result, he cannot appreciate the sacrifice Mary believes she is making on his behalf by giving him up. From Charlie's point of view, his mother inexplicably abandons him.

Throughout this scene Welles's camera moves among the characters as they continuously assume new relationships to each other and to their surroundings. We learn as much about them from what we see as from what they say. Imagery and music fill the dramatic space between the lines of Thatcher's diary in order to tell a story far richer than he ever could.

Two lap dissolves showing Kane's abandoned sled being slowly buried by snow, after the boy's departure for New York, simply and beautifully illustrate Kane's loss of a normal childhood, assuming he ever had a chance of such a childhood with Jim and Mary as his parents. The scene ends as it began, with a sled in the snow. But the boy has disappeared.

The natural whiteness of snow is displaced, via a lap dissolve, by the artificial whiteness of wrapping paper, which is then torn away to reveal a sleek new sled. Much fancier than its predecessor, it is held by young Charles Foster Kane, who is also outwardly much fancier than his old self, with slicked down hair and a frilly white collar. But inside he is as he was. And he is not happy with his new sled. He looks up to acknowledge Mr. Thatcher's stiffly formal Christmas greeting. The camera, beginning at Kane's eye level, tilts up to show the banker looming oppressively over the boy, and us. But even when subsequently viewed from Thatcher's domineering, high angle perspective, the boy is defiant. By contrast, a group of Thatcher's sycophantic employees stand silently behind Kane. The tenor of Kane's relationship to Thatcher is established in Colorado and never changes. Only Kane's *methods* of defiance change as he grows older and more sophisticated. And whatever those methods reveal about their differences in political outlook, events in Colorado are always at the heart of Kane's antagonism towards Thatcher. And whatever resentment Kane feels towards his mother for abandoning him is conveniently rechanneled towards the banker who carried out her wishes.

Snow and Christmas again form a bridge between scenes as we jump nearly twenty years into the future, to a time when Kane is on the verge of becoming legally and financially independent. Against a backdrop of snow visible through an ice-encrusted window, an older Thatcher paces his office while dictating a stern letter to his wealthy but irresponsible twenty-five year old ward. In business matters the banker is both thorough and uncompromising. Snow and cold are appropriate metaphors for his relationship with Kane, and more importantly for the emotional deprivation Kane experiences from childhood through early adulthood.

A direct cut, with no change in location, brings us to Kane's reply to Thatcher's letter of admonishment. The editing out of any delay between those two communications punctuates our impression of the conflict. Kane is again defiant, but with a comic twist that galls his guardian. Apparently indifferent to weighty matters of property and finance, Kane is interested in a little newspaper he now owns, because he thinks it would be "fun" to manage. Thatcher is so irritated at Kane's preference for self-indulgence to the serious business of making money that, accustomed though he is to having things done for him by underlings, he grabs Kane's letter out of an assistant's hands and finishes reading it aloud himself.

A couple things about the grown-up Kane can be gleaned from his brief letter. First, he has become part rebel and part spoiled brat. And second, he is more than willing to exploit the suffering of others in order to defy his despised surrogate father. The *New York Inquirer* was obtained for Kane, by Thatcher and Company, through a foreclosure.

The success of Kane's crusade to defy Thatcher is confirmed by a montage of one-shot scenes in which the banker, observed in a variety of routine activities, reads of the *Inquirer*'s relentless attacks on corruption and greed in big business. The impression we get is light-hearted, accompanied by Herrmann's raucous music and by Thatcher's violation of movie convention. Twice he looks directly into the camera and at us while venting his exasperation. We can't help but be attracted to the new, adult, as yet unseen Kane, who has driven his guardian to such indiscrete expressions of disapproval. The deck is stacked in Kane's favor. Only at closer range do we begin to see his flaws.

Welles keeps the adult Kane off screen while indirectly establishing the character's adult traits. He builds our anticipation by providing us brief glimpses of Kane's wit and solid journalistic achievements. Who is this smart, funny guy who thumbs his nose at the Thatchers of the world? We already like and admire him. Now we want to *meet* him. And what better way than to reunite him with Thatcher, picking up their private feud where it left off twenty years earlier.

The last *Inquirer* headline to infuriate Thatcher proclaims, "Galleons of Spain off Jersey coast!" In close-up that headline fills much of the screen. Thatcher then lowers his copy of the headline to reveal the man behind it. Charlie Kane, seated at his desk in the *Inquirer* offices, calmly sips coffee. He is dressed casually, in contrast to his guardian and to his own prior appearance (Christmas) as a boy in Thatcher's custody. The loudness of Thatcher's protest counterpoints the placidity of Kane's voice and demeanor. A placidity at odds with the *Inquirer*'s headlines, rife with exclamation points. Kane's flippant remark about not knowing how to run a newspaper, "I just try everything I can think of," is intended to provoke Thatcher. Kane knows very well how to run a newspaper, especially for his own ends. When Thatcher complains of Kane's lack of proof that the Spanish navy prowls off the Jersey coast, Kane retorts, "Can you prove it isn't?" A clear indication that the pursuit and publication of facts is not his primary goal as a newspaper man. Even when his friend and colleague, Mr. Bernstein, enters and reads aloud a cable from an *Inquirer* reporter stating that there is no war in Cuba, Kane delights himself and baits his former guardian by replying that he will *provide* the war. The shift in *Inquirer* headlines from exposing corporate corruption to manipulating the United States into a war with Spain suggests an ethical slip by its publisher. And yet the mastery with which Kane takes sweet revenge on the man he believes robbed him of his childhood lends him charm. He is also master juggler, simultaneously conducting newspaper business with Bernstein and fellow colleague Jed Leland, debating with Thatcher, and casually lighting his pipe. Incidentally, Bernstein and Leland differ in their reactions to Kane's arrogant remark about providing a war in Cuba. Bernstein expresses approval. Leland remains silent.

After Leland and Bernstein depart, the camera slowly closes in on the intensifying debate between Kane and Thatcher. Kane's initial tactic is to deflect the impact of every verbal blow struck by his opponent. Thatcher complains of Kane's journalistic crusade against the Public Transit Company. Kane calmly asks Thatcher for any information he might provide for that crusade, knowing the banker bitterly opposes it. Thatcher describes Kane as "still the college boy." Kane, ever contradictory, points out that he was thrown *out* of several colleges. Thatcher reminds Kane that he owns stock in the very company he now attacks. Kane demonstrates that, contrary to Thatcher's low opinion of his business savvy, he knows precisely how much stock he owns in Public Transit. But while baiting Thatcher for his own amusement, Kane paints a picture of himself as a divided man. In the manner of Thatcher, he cares very much about his personal finances and social position. Yet he also concerns himself with the plight of the common man, who is often a helpless pawn in the schemes of "money mad pirates" like Thatcher.

Turning serious, leaning forward in his chair, and then standing up, Kane passionately declares it his duty as well as his pleasure to look after the interests of the poor. But it is obvious he does so at least in part because their interests clash with Thatcher's. And it is Thatcher whom he wants to punish. Yet it is Kane's great wealth, nurtured for many years by Thatcher, that allows Kane to now attack the banker. As becomes evident later, Kane has difficulty distinguishing public duty from private pleasure. When the former stops serving the latter, he loses interest in it. The most misleading statement Kane makes in this scene is, "We have no secrets from our readers." On the contrary, Kane has *many* secrets, which he guards jealously from everyone, including both general public and his closest acquaintances. The fact that Kane's verbal duel with Thatcher in this scene occurs in an office open to the scrutiny of other newspaper staffers adds to our brief illusion that the protagonist is a man with nothing to hide.

Frustrated and outraged, Thatcher withdraws from the debate. Kane graciously helps him on with his coat while continuing his verbal attack. Raising their private conflict to an ideological level, Kane hints at the political danger of the underprivileged masses finding a champion, unlike himself, *without* money and property, raising the specter of class warfare. But his argument provides Thatcher with new ammunition to renew the debate. Kane's philanthropic crusade is costing him a million dollars a year, threatening the "money and property" that according to Kane makes it a politically safe crusade. Kane, as always, has an answer, replying with a smirk that such a loss would force him to end his crusade in sixty years. The scene ends with a tight shot of his smiling face accompanied by Herrmann's musical chuckle — a snippet of what later becomes Kane's gubernatorial campaign song.

We jump forward in time to 1929. And what a change there is in situation and mood. The scene begins with an ironic parallel to its predecessor. Bernstein reads from a legal document that fills the foreground of the scene's first shot, just as Thatcher read from an *Inquirer* headline that did so in the previous scene. The new document details, in legalese, Kane's concession of control over many of his financial holdings, including his publishing empire, to Thatcher and Company. A consequence of the Great Depression. The old *Inquirer* headline was, by contrast, evidence of Kane's power to shape public opinion and to defy Thatcher. Bernstein lowers the grim document to reveal Thatcher seated in the middle background, just as Thatcher once lowered the *Inquirer* headline to reveal an amused and confident Kane seated in the middle background. Thatcher now appears to be getting revenge for his earlier humiliation. But being a money grubber at heart, he is more glum than triumphant. After all, if Kane has lost money, so has *he*.

Kane is the last character to appear in the shot. With his back to the camera and his hands clasped passively behind him, he recedes into the background, looking small and vulnerable against a backdrop of high windows on the far wall. What a change from the cluttered but vibrant newspaper office over which he once ruled with impunity. Now he is visually dwarfed by and squeezed between Thatcher, who is again in a position to dole out an "allowance" to his former ward, and Bernstein, the bearer of grim tidings.

It is again winter. Relations between Thatcher and Kane remain frosty. They quibble over the fact that Kane still refers to Thatcher as "Mr." "You're too old to be called anything else," Kane explains. "You were always too old" implicitly criticizes the banker's unchanging, unimaginative, grubby view of life, against which Kane has struggled for many years. Unwittingly proving his opponent's point, Thatcher characterizes the country's economic setback as temporary, assuring Kane that he might yet die richer than his former guardian. Wealth is Thatcher's primary yardstick for measuring personal fulfillment. He goes on to criticize Kane for using money merely to buy things rather than to invest in them. Kane, now seated at the table with his companions while signing away control over much of his newspaper empire, ruefully pleads guilty to the charge. This could be a rare moment of reflection and self-doubt for the protagonist. But that moment is quickly lost in a resumption of bitterness towards Thatcher. Kane self-righteously bemoans the wealth he inherited, blaming Thatcher for that too, and fancifully speculates that he could have been a greater man without it. Thatcher asks him what he would like to have been. Kane fixes him with a glare and declares, "Everything you hate." His resentment of the banker still burns hot. And yet Thatcher has remained his financial partner all these years. Whatever Kane thinks of Thatcher's priorities and business practices, he is emotionally addicted to the wealth that Thatcher's financial wizardry provides him. Money and property, we discover later in the film, have become integral to Kane's method of coping with disappointment and loss.

Aside from its continuation of Kane versus Thatcher, this scene offers another dramatic impression when juxtaposed with its predecessor. The *Inquirer* office scene featured several vigorous young men debating about and shaping their world. By 1929 these same men are older, stiffer, balder men reduced to ruminating over their pasts. Preoccupied with what was and what might have been, they seem powerless to change anything about their current lives. Even the once dynamic Kane is resigned to being less than he believes he could have been.

We return to Thompson at the Thatcher Memorial Library. As revealing as the banker's dramatized reminiscences have been for us, his brightly illuminated diary proves a disappointment for the reporter, who discovers in them nothing about Rosebud, in spite of coming much closer than he realizes. A reverse angle shot brings Jennings and then Bertha into view and into Thompson's awareness. The librarian smugly informs him that his time with Thatcher's diary has expired. Jennings mindlessly echoes her. Petty dictatorships exist at all levels of power, from librarian to newspaper tycoon. In a further attempt to humble the reporter, Bertha reminds him of how rare a privilege he has enjoyed.

From the camera's low angle point of view a huge painting of Thatcher, in a stilted pose of self-conscious importance, looms over the three living figures gathered around his diary. Jennings reverently removes his cap while gazing up at it. Thompson somewhat disrespectfully asks the portrait, "You're not Rosebud, are you?," mocking the value of Thatcher's memoirs to his journalistic quest and perhaps of Thatcher to Kane. Bertha is puzzled and offended by the reporter's remark. Thompson avenges his earlier humiliation at her hands by then referring to *her* as Rosebud, mocking the idea that she could ever be anyone's secret, dying passion. Then, rudely interrupting Jennings in the same manner that Bertha interrupted him upon his arrival at the library, Thompson disrespectfully puts his hat on his head and abruptly departs. "Thanks for the use of the hall" reduces the sacred vault to the status of a storage room. Herrmann's "wah wah" music returns, reinforcing Thompson's departing insolence and counterpointing the imposing visual presence of the vault.

The next stop on Thompson's Rosebud tour is Mr. Bernstein's high rise corporate office. As with Susan Alexander at the El Rancho, the mood is one of gloomy solitude accentuated by a thunder shower outside. Bernstein looks childlike sitting in a high-backed chair behind a large, polished desk. He tells the reporter that as Chairman of the Board he has plenty of time to reminisce about Kane. He is wealthy yet obviously non-essential to the firm's daily operation. Another form of isolation. Photographs, no doubt of people, places, and events from his past, dot the wall behind him. A large painting of Charles Foster Kane looks down on him from higher still, reflecting the protagonist's importance to and dominance of Bernstein's adult life. Surrounded by reminders of the dead past, and by tokens of his privileged but empty present, including a warming fire in the large fireplace, Bernstein is only relatively less tragic a figure than was Susan Alexander.

As the camera slowly dollies in on Bernstein, visually isolating him from Thompson, he explains to the rather naive, skeptical, and young reporter how Kane's dying utterance might be the product of a brief, even trivial past encounter. Turning storyteller, as so may of Welles's characters do, the aged businessman recounts such an encounter in his own life, decades earlier, when he was crossing from New York to New Jersey on a ferry. Aboard a second, passing ferry was a girl in a white dress, carrying a white parasol. He saw her for only a moment. She didn't see him at all. Yet he has thought of and perhaps fantasized about her frequently in the years since. Visible in the shot of Bernstein telling this story is an empty chair — an unobtrusive metaphor for his unfulfilled dream of love and companionship. Bernstein does not elaborate on his persistent memory of the girl, but it is easy to speculate that he created a romantic myth out of their brief, anonymous encounter. We see no evidence in the film of his every marrying. It is natural that his unfulfilled desires would encourage him to speculate endlessly about the possibilities presented by the woman in white. She has become his gentle fixation. A slightly faded reflection of Bernstein visible on the polished surface of his desk echoes that second self — the self of speculative imagination rather than disappointing reality. Viewed in hindsight, Bernstein's haunting memory of the woman in white parallels Kane's fixation with Rosebud. Both characters generate personal myths out of their unhappiness.

Shaking loose from his private reverie, Bernstein grabs a cigarette for a pacifier, adopts a more extrovert tone of voice, and changes the subject. Thompson, currying favor with his cooperative witness, leans into the camera frame and lights that cigarette. When he withdraws, the camera closes in further on Bernstein, eliminating most of his reflection on the desk top. But the empty chair remains in view, perhaps now symbolizing the *other* important characters from his past who are now either dead or estranged. Bernstein tells Thompson he tried unsuccessfully to telephone Susan after Kane's death. Whatever his faults, Bernstein is a compassionate man. But Thompson is still a reporter on a mission, with little patience for such digression. He re-directs conversation back to Rosebud and Kane, remarking that Bernstein was with Kane from the beginning. "From *before* the beginning, young fella. And now, after the end," the older man corrects him. Bernstein's recollections exceed Thompson's range of interest in them.

Thompson's reference to Thatcher aggravates Bernstein sufficiently to get him up out of his chair. Or is it the sound of a ticker tape machine on the other side of the room, spitting out the latest stock market figures? While deriding Thatcher as a "fool" interested only in making money, Bernstein glances at the ticker tape. Is he deliberately using the tape as a metaphor of Thatcher's small-minded greed? Or is his interest in the tape an unconscious and therefore ironic echo of that same greed? My guess is the former, especially when Bernstein walks over to Kane's portrait on the wall and declares that Thatcher never understood Kane's real motivations. Bernstein admits not always understanding them himself. And he generously points Thompson's quest in the direction of Kane's other old friend, Jed Leland. Bernstein may have been Kane's loyal stooge in the past, but his attempted kindness to Kane's estranged second wife, Susan, and to Kane's estranged friend, Jed Leland, suggest that with age and time he has attained some emotional distance and wisdom.

While seated behind his desk, Bernstein participated in a somewhat formal interview with Thompson. Now he sits and leans back in the once empty chair that seemed to symbolize his current lack of companionship. Reminiscing fondly about Leland, Kane, and exciting times at the *Inquirer*, he recaptures a bit of the old comradery. Lost in nostalgia, the Chairman of the Board now ignores the renewed tapping of the ticker tape behind him. There are more meaningful things in *his* life than making money.

Robert Carringer, in *The Making of Citizen Kane*, has written at length about how Welles and his skilled crew at RKO used camera magic to give the film a much bigger look than its fairly modest budget would have otherwise allowed. Kane's arrival at the *New York Inquirer* begins with a low angle shot of the newspaper building's facade set against a backdrop of much taller buildings circa 1890. The camera then tilts down to show Kane and Jed Leland pulling up in front of the *Inquirer* in a horse-drawn carriage. A lap dissolve occurs midway through that downward tilt, allowing a painted image of dated architecture to mesh seamlessly with live action characters. Art is an illusion, though not necessarily a lie. Welles appreciated that fact as much as any film maker.

Dressed in dapper attire of the period, the two young men appear to be the best of friends and very confident of their new venture. But Kane is clearly the senior partner. From the camera's oblique angle we sometimes see Leland and sometimes not, but we always see Kane, along with his reflection on the carriage window. For a moment Kane seems to be accompanied by his second self rather than his best friend. And in time Leland will feel the pressure of that egotism. Predicting big changes for the *Inquirer*, Kane is the first to jump out of the carriage and charge into the newspaper's offices, enthusiastically followed by Leland. Bringing up the rear of the invasion is their junior partner, Bernstein. Arriving in the back of a baggage wagon, modestly in charge of transporting Kane's surprisingly meager belongings, Bernstein nevertheless asserts his own authority by silencing the impudent remarks of the wagon's hired driver. It's all presented in a lighthearted and comic manner, like the disputes between Eugene Morgan and Isabel Amberson at the beginning of Welles's *The Magnificent Ambersons*. But the hierarchy of Kane's adult world is evident in this chronologically early scene, and is a hint of darker things to come.

Standing together at the threshold of the *Inquirer* newsroom, Leland yields to Kane despite being offered the chance to enter first. He will follow Kane's lead in many other matters as well, before finally defying his boss and setting his own course. They pass on opposite sides of one of the room's many thin support posts: Kane to the right, Leland to the left. Whether or not intended by Welles as a metaphor of their political inclinations, Leland deliberately retraces his steps in order to follow Kane on the right, as though superstitious of contradicting his dynamic friend.

The newsroom is a moribund place at the time of Kane's arrival. Reporters sit quietly at their desks, like timid schoolchildren. A printed sign commanding "Silence" hangs on the wall over their heads. A low ceiling, accentuated by a slightly low camera angle, seems to press down on them. Shades block the sun from shining through a skylight. When Kane speaks to one of the reporters, the man signals his boss, editor-in-chief Herbert Carter, with a whisper, as though afraid to break the rule of silence. Adding to the headmaster/pupil flavor of the scene by ringing a little bell signaling his reporters to stand in honor of their new boss, Carter steps down from the slightly elevated platform on which his desk sits and cheerfully yet diffidently greets the *Inquirer*'s new owner.

Communication is always tricky business in a Welles movie. The perceptions of different characters are often mismatched. The surprising shyness with which Kane greets the *Inquirer* staff results in a moment of confusion for everyone. He, Carter, and Leland behave like out-of-sync musicians as they exchange introductions. Identities are jumbled. Handshakes are mistimed and awkward. But as with actions in the street moments earlier, the results are amusing and inconsequential. A deceptively superficial taste of more serious lapses in communication to come.

Kane's show of humility makes him an appealing character at this stage in his life. He is not yet a selfish tyrant. But he has the makings of and means to become one, as we witnessed in an earlier incident that occurs later in his life: his newsroom confrontation with Thatcher. Contributing to his softer image in the present scene, Kane respectfully acknowledges Leland's desire to be a drama critic, tells the reporters to sit back down, and confesses to Carter that as yet he has no idea how to run a newspaper. Carter, less egalitarian than his new boss initially appears to be, re-states Kane's request of the staff in more formal, declarative terms. "You may resume your duties, gentlemen" is less an invitation to relax than a command to get back to work.

By dollying in on Kane, Carter, and Leland, the camera visually sets us up for an *aural* surprise coming from outside that trio. Bernstein tumbles loudly into the room after losing control of the Kane luggage he was carrying. This brief, comic disruption seems to jog the protagonist out of his uncertainty. In a firmer voice than earlier, Kane takes control. He calls out to Bernstein, who as viewed from behind runs towards his boss like a child summoned by a parent. Then, in an action reminiscent of the *Inquirer* office confrontation between Kane and Thatcher, Kane relishes his mastery of the overall situation by simultaneously attending to different tasks. Walking away from the other three men, he introduces Carter to Bernstein. In effect he uses Bernstein as a diversion while maneuvering to appropriate Carter's private office for his own living quarters. The prim, proper, and orderly Mr. Carter is befuddled. He doesn't even know to whom he is talking from one moment to the next. And unlike the confusion that occurred between Kane and Carter moments earlier, this time it is deliberately caused by the protagonist.

Blustering and babbling, Carter positions himself defensively between Kane and his private office. But from a low camera angle we see Kane looming over his shorter, older rival. And while their debate continues, Kane's soldiers visibly occupy Carter's sanctuary. Their entrances and exits, while transporting Kane's belongings, constantly interrupt Carter's feeble protests. Kane, meanwhile, slyly reverses positions with Carter. Now *he* stands closer to the office door. And as an excuse for appropriating Carter's office, Kane reveals his plan to transform the *Inquirer* from just a morning newspaper to a twenty four hour a day news gathering dynamo. Quite ambitious for a man who only moments earlier claimed to have no plan at all. Obviously Kane lied—a fact easy to overlook in the dramatic context of his amusing takeover of the *Inquirer* from his befuddled, overmatched foe. Herr-mann's playful dance music accompaniment highlights the fun and conceals the darker undertones of this early consolidation of power by the protagonist. Welles and co-writer Herman Mankiewicz acknowledge the enormous appeal of an American archetype of ambition, inventiveness, optimism, and humor before transforming their protagonist into a great American villain. And how can one watch a scene like this without thinking of Welles's own enormous ambition and ingenuity as he forged *Othello* out of chaos and transformed *Touch of Evil* from a studio programmer into a thing of beauty.

The same giddy atmosphere pervades the next scene, where Kane presides over a strategy session in his new office/home. There is no distinction between private and professional endeavors here. The place is cluttered with Kane's belongings, which at this point in his life are quite modest. Such is not the case, however, with his ambition to redefine the *Inquirer*'s journalistic mission and standards. Kane sits at his small desk. Against the wall behind him is the metal headboard of his bed. The camera angle contributes to a two-dimensional illusion that the headboard forms the back of his chair, giving it the appearance of a throne, which is more in tune with his true ambitions. Jed Leland comments disapprovingly on Kane's voracious appetite for food. "I'm still hungry," the protagonist replies. Food is only one of many ways Kane compensates for what he believes he was deprived of as a child. It is fitting that Leland is the only one of Kane's cronies to complain, since he is the only one to retain a measure of objectivity about his boss. But it is a feeble, indirect sort of criticism. Leland's willingness to subordinate his own desires and opinions to Kane's is evident from the start of the scene, when he entered Kane's office/home whining about his lack of talent as a cartoonist while holding up a poorly drawn caricature of a robber baron. Jed wants to be a drama critic, but accepted the political cartoonist assignment at Kane's request. Amused by Jed's incompetence, Kane accedes to his friend's wishes. The tension between them is negligible, for the time being.

Kane's duel with Herbert Carter is less friendly. The old editor-in-chief, his frazzled hair matching his frazzled nerves, objects to Kane's "scandal sheet" brand of journalism, which transforms a missing person investigation into a lurid accusation of spousal homocide. As in the previous scene, Kane keeps his opponent off balance by attending to more than one matter at a time. Carter compounds the confusion by accidentally bumping the back of a chair occupied by Bernstein, who is working diligently and unquestioningly on an assignment for Kane. Further diminishing our opinion of Carter is a trace of antisemitism in his pointed mispronunciation of Bernstein's name.

The debate on journalistic ethics continues. Carter's arguments are sound, but because of his opponent's charm and superficial egalitarianism we root for Kane instead. "If the headline is big enough, it makes the news big enough" is a despicable way to run a newspaper. And so is Bernstein's enthusiastic endorsement of that sentiment. And yet aesthetically Carter loses this contest. His flustered demeanor betrays him. Kane, by contrast, looks cool, calm, even roguishly elegant. A bottle of champagne on ice sits on his desk. The rapidity and self-assurance of Kane's speech are intoxicating, partly obscuring the arrogance of what he says. With vocal support from his morally seduced colleague, Leland, Kane orders Carter to threaten the suspected wife killer with arrest by the *Inquirer* if he fails to produce his spouse alive.

Kane stands up. Leland, as usual, follows his lead. The diminutive editor-in-chief is surrounded by taller, younger, more dynamic figures. Kane deflects Carter's continued objections by shifting conversation to an unrelated topic and then bidding Carter goodbye in a civil yet dismissive tone of voice. Carter indignantly withdraws.

Happy, jaunty music concludes the scene, as it did the previous one, glossing over the more disturbing aspects of Kane's takeover and transformation of the *Inquirer*. The same music carries over into the next scene, outside the *Inquirer* building, where a disgruntled Carter takes his final leave from the newspaper. A newspaper vendor on the street hawks copies of the latest *Inquirer* to the now former editor-in-chief, shouting out the scurrilous headline which Carter fought to suppress. The pomposity of Carter's disapproval undercuts the validity of his ethical stance.

The camera cuts to a broader view of Carter's departure. He looks tiny when pictured against the *Inquirer* building as he walks out of the camera frame, out of Kane's life, out of Bernstein's reminiscences, and into obscurity. In the context of the film's broader theme about the mystery and isolation of individual lives, one can't help but wonder whatever became of him. The *Inquirer* building, in turn, appears dwarfed by larger structures surrounding it, reminding us of the relative insignificance of Kane's activities and life in the same shot that depicts his victory over someone still less significant — at least by any public measure.

The camera moves forward into a tighter shot of the *Inquirer* building, then lap dissolves closer yet to show Kane already at work on a scheme to magnify the social and political importance of his small newspaper. The building's dingy, sooty, antiquated facade, plus the flickering flame of gaslight, yield a powerful sense of time and place. This is a *working* environment from the past. A world of struggle, triumph, and defeat. Not a quaint, tidy evocation of nostalgia, where tidy human motivations resolve themselves in a tidy manner. Overlapped by the fading voice of the street vendor is a somber piece of background music that helps shift our mood from amusement to reflection. We close in on Kane and Leland through an open window. They seem figuratively at odds with one another. Kane, standing, busily writes something on a large piece of paper. Leland, smoking a cigar and gazing out through the open window, is more pensive, and therefore more in tune with the subdued music. A portion of the window frame visually divides them. Even at a time in their lives when they are close friends and collaborators, these two young men, for a moment, differ greatly in their outlook and sensibilities.

Cut to an interior shot. Leland pulls away from the window and reconnects with Kane's world. Bernstein never left it. The reflective music lingers for a moment, counterpointing conversation among the characters, then fades out. But in an odd way Kane himself picks up on its note of discontent by referring to a "wasted" day of hard work preparing their first issue of the *Inquirer*. Brushing aside the protests of his two friends, and aesthetically backed by subdued twilight visible through the window behind him, Kane unveils his plan to greatly increase his journalistic clout and, by implication, overturn the earlier metaphorical image of the *Inquirer* dwarfed by its neighbor buildings. And he introduces that plan with a visual metaphor of his own choosing, drawn from the antiquated world that seems so alive in this part of the film. He intends to make the *Inquirer* as important to the people of New York as the gas in a light fixture on the wall next to him. By extinguishing that light to make a point, he oddly contradicts himself. Instead of being illuminated by the gas flame while proclaiming his journalistic principles for the first time, he is veiled in shadow. Appropriately, since the motives behind those principles are obscure and suspect. Still, despite the playful jibes of his friends, those principles are proclaimed so soberly by Kane that we are convinced of their sincerity. Leland slyly points out that Kane's frequent use of the word "I" betrays egotism. But Kane effectively transforms that challenge into an endorsement. "People have got to know who's responsible."

Kane's Declaration of Principles promises the truth, delivered quickly, simply, and entertainingly, without interference from special interests: e.g. Walter P. Thatcher and his cronies. But how does that promise square with Kane's blatant distortion of the few known facts in the case of the missing Mrs. Silverstone? Kane also promises to champion the rights of ordinary people. But we have already seen, in a later incident (derived from Thatcher's diary) shown earlier, how Kane will use the *Inquirer* to promote a war with Spain. Thanks to *Citizen Kane*'s unusual narrative structure, the protagonist's promises are undercut by both prior and future events. Yet in the passion of the moment, divorced from other perspectives, Kane's Declaration is convincing. It impresses Leland so much that he asks Kane for the original Declaration after it is printed in the *Inquirer*. He tries to mock its importance to him by comparing it to his first report card at school. But he cannot hide his admiration for and faith in Kane. The idealist in Leland in not entirely joking when he compares Kane's manifesto to the Declaration of Independence and the Constitution of the United States.

Adding to the charm of the scene is Kane's brief dialog with an assistant named Solly. By instructing the young man to print the Declaration on the front page of this morning's edition, he creates a load of new work for Solly and the other printers. But the grinning good humor with which Solly accepts the bad news suggests a strong sense of common purpose between management and labor. Something we did not see earlier during brief glimpses of Thatcher and *his* employees. On the other hand, Solly's eye-rolling expression of contempt for Leland's excessive admiration of Kane's Declaration brings a subtle, comedic balance to the scene. Of course, Solly cannot know at this moment how misplaced Leland's faith in the protagonist will turn out to be.

Prior to making *Citizen Kane*, Welles issued a Declaration of Principles on behalf of his Mercury Theater troupe in the August 29, 1937 issue of the *New York Times*. One bit of evidence that Welles himself was one model for Charles Foster Kane.

A close-up of Kane's Declaration of Principles in print, accompanied by a vibrant variation on Herrmann's power/ambition motif, pulls back to reveal many bundles of the new *Inquirer* waiting for distribution. This image dissolves to a shot of Kane, Leland, and Bernstein, all grinning broadly, looking out through a large window in the *Inquirer* building at street vendors, visible as reflections in that window, carrying away the Declaration to all parts of the city. Emblazoned on the window, like a frame around those three happy faces, is the *Inquirer* name and its current circulation — 26,000. But Welles is setting us up for a big reversal that gives us another measure of Kane's boundless appetite for success and power.

Another dissolve substitutes the rival *Chronicle*'s front window for the *Inquirer*'s. Three once happy faces are now somber. Reflected in the window glass, Kane, Leland, and Bernstein now look *in* from the outside rather than out from the inside. The emblazoned *Chronicle* circulation figure of 495,000 explains the reason for their pilgrimage. The previous impression of triumph is put into humbling perspective. But Kane is determined to reverse that reversal. Leland comments, "The *Chronicle* is a good newspaper." Kane modifies that statement of respect into something more practical and mercenary. "The *Chronicle* is a good *idea* for a newspaper." Image often counts for more than substance. And Kane is willing to cultivate either, if it gets him what he wants.

The camera dollies in on a photo of the illustrious *Chronicle* staff, displayed in the window. While Bernstein woefully points out that it took the *Chronicle* twenty years to assemble such a staff, the camera slips past the photograph's frame, eliminating one layer of detachment. Suddenly the reporters in the picture acquire motion, posing live for a *new* photograph. Another layer of detachment gone. A smiling Charlie Kane strolls into this new image and explains, to an off screen audience, that it took him six years to lure this group of reporters from the *Chronicle* to the *Inquirer*. Thus a clever transition device between scenes is also used by Welles to convey the as yet unstoppable ambition of the protagonist, who seems magically empowered to alter reality itself.

After a new photograph of the reporters is taken, Kane punctuates his victory by ordering a copy of it sent to the *Chronicle*, and by announcing that the *Inquirer*'s circulation has reached 684,000, surpassing its rival's old figure. Released from their pose, the reporters follow their new leader across the room. Ever the child in need of something more, Kane refers to them as his "candy." But notice that he is more conservatively dressed now than he was in the previous two scenes, which occurred six years earlier. In fact, he dresses like the *Chronicle* staff he acquired. Maybe *he* is the one who has changed loyalties.

A reverse camera angle shows the *Inquirer*'s old staff seated at a long, richly furnished banquet table. With Kane in the foreground, the small figure of Bernstein stands at the far end of the table and gleefully corrects Kane's rounded down circulation figure to 684,132. A giant "K" carved in ice decorates Kane's end of the table. At the opposite end sit Bernstein and Leland, bracketed by their own profiles in ice. Each of the three original colleagues has been given an affectionate public nickname. They have progressed from obscure but ambitious novices to prominent veterans and public icons in six short years, made to seem even shorter by the preceding scene transition. Not bad.

Announcing plans for a European vacation, Kane banters affectionately with Bernstein about Kane's growing collection of European art. Perhaps Kane's secret yearning for childhood, home, and mother manifests itself on a broader level as America's nostalgia for the Old World. At Bernstein's urging Kane promises to add to that collection, then jokingly reverses himself by questioning Bernstein's faith in that promise. Laughter erupts around the table. But when Kane fails to live up to his Declaration of Principles, the joke won't be so amusing.

Summoning a marching band and chorus girls to rally his new reporters to his journalistic crusade, Kane freely mixes ballyhoo with a serious political effort to foment war with Spain. Like a cheerleader he yells encouragement to his seated employees, who are spectators at a theatrical production designed to entertain and seduce them into devotion. Kane's tactics against his new enemy, Spain, are even more childish than his tactics against the *Chronicle*. But the scale of his ambition has grown. Previously it embraced only the *Inquirer*. Now it embraces the entire United States, which must be defended against all foreign rivals, real or imagined.

Kane repeats his question about declaring war on Spain, but this time directs it specifically at Jed Leland. Obviously they have disagreed over the matter. But theirs is still a good natured dispute. Targeting Kane's arrogance, Leland replies, "The *Inquirer* already has," presumably without public or government support. Kane retaliates affectionately, "You long-faced, overdressed anarchist." The charge "anarchist" targets Leland's rebellion against Kane's authority. Leland, typically self-effacing, pokes fun at himself by denying the charge "overdressed," as though fashion were more important to him than politics, which it is not. Kane, who must always have the last word, attacks even that mock defense, citing evidence that his friend is indeed overdressed. This semi-private debate takes place against a moving backdrop of pretty, prancing women, their white-stockinged legs and sparkly costumes incandescently illuminated by footlights. The visual effect is dazzling, as Kane intends.

Kane joins his captive audience in a front row seat to be entertained by a song about himself in which he is described as "good old" Charlie Kane. Laughing, grabbing a reporter around the shoulders and playfully punching the man's bald spot, the publisher of the *Inquirer* appears to be just one of the guys. A man of as well as for the people. And it is that dual appeal that the song and dance number celebrates. He could have written the lyrics himself. When the reporter locked in Kane's brotherly embrace removes the Teddy Roosevelt style hat (a symbol of pro-war sentiment) that was placed on his head moments earlier by one of Kane's dancing girls, Kane himself puts it back. This is *Kane's* production, right down to the costuming of his audience. But when Kane is lured away by the dancing girls, the reporter removes the hat again. Loyalty is not deeply felt here, especially by the new *Chronicle* acquisitions. Note also a slight continuity error here. In successive shots before the man removes his hat, he has it on, then he doesn't, then he does again.

With less reluctance than he pretends to feel, Kane allows himself to be drawn into the dance that celebrates Charlie Kane. He is everywhere in this scene: in the show, in the audience, in a semi-private debate with Leland. Movement, costumes, editing, and music infuse the spectacle with infectious enthusiasm. Prompted by the master of ceremonies and chorus girls, the reporters too sing the praises of their new boss. Two shots of Bernstein and Leland illustrate their slightly different reactions to the spectacle. The first is a medium shot in which Bernstein, wearing his Teddy Roosevelt hat, waves his arm and sings along with great enthusiasm. Leland, meanwhile, wears no hat, does not sing, and appears less than thrilled with the proceedings. Two shots later we see the same two characters isolated in close-up. Bernstein continues to participate in the song with uncritical vigor. Leland, closer to the camera because his reaction is more complicated and therefore more interesting, begins to bob his head in time to the music. Finally he yields to its seductive rhythm, singing along with uncharacteristic and awkward passion. But after awhile he regains a measure of composure and skeptical detachment.

While Kane dances with and romances the chorus girls, Leland and Bernstein carry on a private debate in the midst of the loud celebration. The camera, shooting from behind and between the two men, reduces Kane's musical extravaganza to a distant curiosity. Yet Kane unwittingly manages to intrude himself into their private conversation, tossing his jacket to them for safekeeping. Leland neatly folds and places it in his lap. Despite his objections to Kane's politics, he remains Kane's servant. The camera reverses angle, reducing Kane and his dancing girls still further by showing them only as a reflection in a window behind Leland and Bernstein. Nevertheless, Kane's presence continues to be felt even as Leland soberly points out to his old friend that the new reporters Kane hired were once just as devoted to the *Chronicle*'s policies as they are now to the *Inquirer*'s, suggesting a mercenary attitude on their part. Bernstein sees no problem with that, because their skills will now be put to better use. He is momentarily distracted by Kane's raucous activities in the distance. Our eyes too are continuously drawn to Kane's reflection in the window.

Prancing around the room's support posts with his girls, Kane is now fully integrated in their chorus line. Could he just as easily adapt to a contrary political philosophy? Leland draws Bernstein's and our attention back to the debate, insisting that fundamental differences exist between the *Chronicle* and the *Inquirer* philosophies. Bernstein, exhibiting infinite faith in his boss, insists that Kane will soon change the new *Chronicle* recruits into his kind of reporters. Leland raises the possibility of the reverse occurring, without Kane realizing it. At this point the scene ends with an exuberant Kane posing with his chorus girls for a photograph. This visual reminder of the photo of the *Chronicle* reporters, who sold out to Kane's *Inquirer*, foreshadows Kane's sellout to greed and a desire for power.

After Kane's departure for Europe, Bernstein rushes into the *Inquirer* office to tell Leland they've received a letter form him. They experience a moment of confusion while shouting at each other through a window — another example of flawed communication. Leland invites Bernstein to join him inside a room full of art objects purchased by Kane and mailed from Europe. A striking deep focus shot pictures Leland at background left, uncrating another piece of art. At foreground right is the shipping tag attached to yet another crate. The tag reads, "From CFK" and "To Charles Foster Kane"— a practical and clever metaphor for the protagonist's self-centered outlook. Most of what he does is to bring *himself* happiness, regardless of his public declarations to the contrary. But in a broader sense the film suggests that each of us carries through life a private agenda that can never be fully known by other people — or, over time, even by ourselves. Kane's private agenda is more interesting than most because it wears so many different masks, made possible by his wealth, power, and dynamic personality. Which is not to say the film portrays human beings as mere selfish brutes. Kane is often kind and generous, when it suits his private needs to be so. But whether by upbringing or by natural inclination, he is often a prisoner of those needs.

While attending to Kane's new acquisitions, Leland sings to himself his favorite lines from the Kane theme song heard in the previous scene. Putting "traction magnates on the run" suits *his* agenda. It is the Kane mask that Leland likes best. Bernstein, on the other hand, looks uncomfortable as he weaves his way through Kane's art collection. This is not *his* milieu. As they discuss Kane's letter, we get a glimpse of Leland's conscientiousness. The result of his ability to see beyond his own selfish needs once in awhile. Leland tells Bernstein he declined an invitation to accompany Kane to Europe because he wanted Charlie to have some fun. Taking to heart Kane's remarks from the previous scene, he asks Bernstein, "Am I a stuffed shirt? Am I a horse-faced hypocrite? Am I a New England schoolmarm?" He suspects Kane's good-natured accusations are true. Bernstein deadpans, "Yes," then admits he wouldn't have contradicted Kane even if he disagreed with him. That reveals something of *Bernstein's* character. Leland shrugs off the matter. He and Bernstein differ in their views of the protagonist, but not in their mutual affection for him. All differences between them are smoothed over as they share a smile while reading, between the lines of Kane's letter, about their boss's romantic involvement with a woman of means. Only with hindsight do we appreciate the irony of Bernstein's description of that romance. "He's collecting somebody that's collecting diamonds" is an unwittingly accurate critique of Kane's selfish motive for pursuing Emily Norton, and possibly of hers for accepting him.

Only Charles Foster Kane would get a trophy simply for returning to work after a long vacation. A close-up of that glittering prize, surrounded by the smiling faces of the *Inquirer* staff, tells us that the affection of employees for employer is genuine. Someone off screen loudly announces Kane's arrival. A vigorous rendition of the Kane power motif erupts on the soundtrack. Walter P. Thatcher would never have gotten such a greeting from *his* employees.

Kane charges into the room looking somehow both boyish and dapper, moving awkwardly while dressed stylishly in a white suit, with his hair slicked back. His admiring staff follow in his titanic wake. A backtracking camera captures his irresistible forward momentum. Shooting from a low angle, it also shows us the skylight we saw in an earlier scene. No longer shaded by the gloom of Herbert Carter's stifling reign as editor-in-chief, it now lets in sunlight more appropriate to Kane's inspired leadership, and matching his bright clothes. Kane's informal, shy manner as he hands a written announcement to the newspaper's society editor adds to his egalitarian charm. He interrupts Bernstein's formal presentation of the "Welcome Home" trophy to rush back out of the office. But in a wonderfully comic touch he returns briefly to retrieve his prize, which after all represents to him the affection and respect of his employees. Even in the midst of his first romance such a thing is important to him. He is a collector of symbols. But the fact that the trophy is worth a momentary delay in his departure while Bernstein's speech is not hints that symbols are more important to Kane than are people.

Kane's parting, stammering instructions that his "little social announcement" be treated the same as any other may well be a product of genuine rather than false modesty. He seems giddy and unsure of himself rather than calculating and cynical. Shown from a high window in the *Inquirer* office, Kane looks small and clumsy as he waves back at his staff, flops onto the seat next to his fiancee in a horse drawn carriage, and is driven away. From the window above, Leland and Bernstein are delighted by their old friend's newfound happiness with the niece of the President of the United States. Bernstein comments, optimistically, that Emily Norton may soon be a President's *wife*. But when the camera cuts to two successively wider shots from the same angle, we see Kane's happy, waving employees through a giant *New York Inquirer* sign attached to the side of the building. They look like captives in a zoo—like the monkeys we saw at Xanadu in the film's first scene. They may adore Kane now, but we are visually reminded that they are as much his property as his friends, to be manipulated according to his whims.

When the camera returns us to the present, in Bernstein's high-rise corporate office, the "Welcome Home" scene is undercut in yet another way. Bernstein informs Thompson that as things turned out, "Miss Emily Norton was no Rosebud," adding that a second romantic relationship also turned sour for Kane. Part of Welles's great skill as a dramatist was his ability to inject great energy, joy, and charm into a scene like "Welcome Home" while simultaneously making us aware (the trapped zoo animal metaphor) of its ephemeral nature and eventual decay.

Scenes in Bernstein's office are like somber bookends surrounding mostly vibrant glimpses of Kane's young adulthood and meteoric rise to fame and power. The second bookend, however, foreshadows Kane's downfall. Bernstein's recollection of the protagonist's marital failures prompts him to speculate that the mysterious Rosebud may be something Kane lost. More somber and reflective now than in the first office scene, Bernstein adopts a more critical perspective of Kane. Echoing Jed Leland's old complaint, if belatedly, he admits that the Spanish-American War was more Kane's fight than the nation's. He advises Thompson to seek out Leland for a keener insight into Kane than Bernstein himself can supply. But old loyalties still smolder. Backed by a flickering fireplace and the large portrait of the man who brought so much excitement and purpose into his life, Bernstein hedges his criticism by insisting that the Panama Canal was one positive consequence of Kane's war.

Shown in long shot, Bernstein and Thompson are dwarfed by the portrait and memory of Kane, as well as by the office itself, which is Bernstein's lonely outpost. The Chairman of the Board admits to losing touch with Leland. He doesn't even know if his old friend is alive or dead. "A lot of the time they don't tell me these things." "They" are presumably his business associates, trying to shield their old boss from pain. Another example of isolation. Thompson informs him that Leland resides at Huntington Memorial Hospital in the same city. Bernstein is delighted to hear it. But when the reporter adds that the only thing wrong with Leland is old age, Bernstein grimly observes, from personal experience, that it's the only disease of which we don't look forward to being cured. A simple truth, perhaps, but conveyed here with powerful dramatic impact. *Citizen Kane* is about many forms of human isolation, not the least of which is the inevitability of growing old and feeble, losing touch with old friends, old enemies, and even memories.

Three things mark the passage of time between the first and second scenes set in Bernstein's office: the rain has stopped, the blinds over the windows are now partly shut, and we see the remains of a meal, perhaps a *shared* meal, on a small table between the two men. The act of telling his life story, even if only the parts dealing with Kane, is therapeutic for Bernstein. A brief respite from the loneliness of old age. Whether young Thompson can yet appreciate the older man's point of view is questionable. At one point during the scene Bernstein walks away from the reporter and towards the fireplace. When Bernstein mentions the word Rosebud, Thompson quickly reappears in the camera frame, eagerly anticipating a scoop for his newsreel. It will take him more time and experience to understand the broader ramifications of his initially narrow quest.

The heavy mood of Bernstein's remark about the unwelcome cure for old age carries over, via Herrmann's background music blending with the low blast from the whistle of a ship on a river in New York City, into the next scene. Following the direction of Thompson's gaze, the camera slowly tilts up from the river to the distant sun deck of the Huntington Memorial Hospital. The word Memorial implies that the hospital was named in honor of a once prominent person, now dead. Who was Huntington, and what is *his* story. Did he too have a Rosebud? Rising oppressively above and behind the hospital is a massive bridge spanning the river, and diminishing in significance the last refuge of the man Thompson has come to interview. What a stark contrast there is between the three confident, energetic young men we saw in Bernstein's flashback and the images we get of their old age. That contrast between youthful vitality and decrepitude recurs in later Welles movies: notably *The Magnificent Ambersons*, *Touch of Evil*, and *Chimes at Midnight*. It is curious that someone as young as the director of *Citizen Kane* was so acutely aware of the physical and emotional effects of getting old.

Seeing Jed Leland as an old man only minutes after seeing him in the full bloom of youth is a shocking consequence of Welles's juxtaposition of different time periods. Wrapped in a robe for warmth, wearing dark glasses and a visor to shield his feeble eyes from the light, Leland is physically a shell of his former self. And in place of the two vibrant comrades with whom he used to raise hell we see, far in the background and out of focus, two wheelchair-bound figures. Grim harbingers of Leland's inevitable future. Motionless, silent, anonymous, and oblivious to one another (they face in slightly different directions, just as Leland faces away from *them*), each appears wrapped up in his own private thoughts and memories while Leland reminisces about Kane. The camera slowly closes in on Leland, eliminating Thompson from the frame, as it did when closing in on Bernstein at a similar moment, while the old man delves deeper into his recollections of the past. He describes his acute memory as a curse, probably because it reminds him of what he has lost and what he regrets. Things he is powerless to change but cannot forget.

Aware of the contradiction, Leland recalls Charles Foster Kane as a friend who behaved like a swine. He laughingly critiques himself as Kane's "stooge" while removing his sunglasses and leaning forward towards Thompson to close the distance between them. The reporter is less interested in Leland's life story than in Kane's. He prods the old man back to their main topic of conversation. But Leland stubbornly persists in asserting his own needs by asking Thompson for a cigar—forbidden to him by his doctor, just as Bernstein's caretakers, presumably for *his* own good, concealed from him information about Leland. Both men have experienced a significant decrease in their power to control their own lives.

Thompson has no cigars to offer. Leland, ever the gentleman, pokes fun at his own selfishness, describing himself with exaggeration as a "disagreeable old man." Sitting back in his chair, but not retreating back behind his sunglasses, which previously served as an emotional and well as physical shield, Leland returns to the subject of Kane. Validating Bernstein's high opinion of his insights, Leland accurately describes the protagonist as a man of contradictions: generous yet not a giving person, highly opinionated yet lacking conviction, and thoroughly self-centered.

Leaning forward once more to re-establish intimacy, Leland again intrudes his personal desires into the interview, unwittingly proving that he too, if to a lesser degree, is self-centered. Failing again to obtain the cigars he craves, he politely returns to the topic of Kane. Throughout this scene Leland stresses his independence from the protagonist, compensating for what with hindsight he regards as too many years of base subservience. In a manner too glib to be totally convincing, he points out Kane's many faults. And his witty dismissal of the Rosebud mystery ("I never believed anything I saw in the *Inquirer*," which is not true) amuses himself more than it does Thompson.

Recollecting that he attended dancing school with Kane's first wife, Emily Norton, Leland briefly looks away from Thompson and adds, more for his own benefit than for the reporter's, "I was very graceful." In view of his present lack of mobility, that memory is understandably bittersweet. He is again addressing his own concerns, based on his unique perspective. We all do it. How long has it been since Leland had anyone with whom to share his memories of the past? And who can blame him for indulging himself now? But the considerate gentleman in Leland reasserts itself. Returning his gaze to the reporter, he clears his throat by way of an apology and in a more matter-of-fact tone of voice resumes his discussion of Emily Norton, whom he now refers to more formally as "the first Mrs. Kane" rather than as his own former dance partner.

Leland's description of Emily as "a very nice girl," perhaps even "a little nicer" than most, hints that *he* might have once had romantic ambitions about her. We learned from Bernstein that Leland's family fell rather suddenly from wealth and social prominence to relative poverty and disgrace. Maybe Emily Norton is Leland's version of Bernstein's fleeting encounter with the woman in white. If so, the matter is too personal to share with Thompson. Leland clears his throat again and moves on to the subject of Emily's marriage to Kane. "It was a marriage just like any other marriage" implies that many marriages end up as badly as the one we are about to see enacted on screen.

Herrmann's melancholy, ruminative background score plays throughout the hospital scene, reinforcing our impression of Leland's isolation. Foghorns from distant, unseen ships mark the transition from that scene and that music to a breakfast table montage involving Kane and Emily, with accompanying music more evocative of their immediate happiness than of Leland's brooding reminiscence. But for a few seconds the image of Kane and Emily at breakfast replaces that of the two wheelchair-bound patients in the background, while Leland's image lingers on screen. What a relief it must be for him to look back on the past, even if it involves the break-up of an old friend's marriage, instead of looking forward to his own decline and approaching death. For a little while Jed Leland is not alone.

The first scene of the breakfast montage depicts marital harmony in a setting of wealth and privilege. Both characters are elegantly dressed. Kane behaves gallantly as he enters from off screen, kissing Emily softly on the forehead and sitting close beside her. The camera dollies in slowly to participate in their intimacy. Kane "adores" his beautiful bride. And under his tutelage Emily has learned how to have fun, staying up until dawn and attending several parties in one night. The only sour notes in this love duet, accompanied by a delicate Herrmann waltz suitable for two lovers moving in emotional tandem, are negligible. Emily worries about the propriety of their behavior the previous night. Kane dismisses her concern. Emily doesn't want her husband to leave for the office, so Kane puts off his dedication to the *Inquirer* until noon — a remarkable concession for a workaholic. This potential conflict of interest between the newlyweds is easily resolved, *this* time. Kane's loyalties are divided, as they always are. But for now romance trumps work. When Kane comments on the lateness of the hour, Kane contradicts her, as he often does people close to him. But this time it is a congenial contradiction. Insisting "it's early," Kane flashes Emily a leering grin. Sex trumps politics, for now.

A zip pan takes us past many more breakfast encounters, stopping at one several months, if not years, later. The work versus romance dispute makes another appearance. But this time Kane has stayed at the office longer than he said he would instead of cancelling appointments to spend time with Emily. Attire and setting are no less elegant than in the previous scene, but romantic passion between the characters is missing. Background music too has sacrificed romance for light comedy. Still, the married couple can joke about their differences. Kane insists that Emily's only rival is the *Inquirer* rather than another woman, as though that fact should put her mind at ease.

The third installment of the breakfast montage picks up where the second left off, with a mild quarrel about Kane's preference for work over home. But a new dimension to their growing split is introduced. Politics. Kane has dared to criticize Emily's Uncle John, the President of the United States, in the *Inquirer*. Echoing her earlier concern about propriety, Emily implies that the President should be above criticism. Kane, as usual, has the final word in this still good-natured domestic debate, hinting at an impending change of administration in the White House. Meanwhile, Herrmann's background music shifts gears to something less comic and more frenetic, almost martial.

By the fourth breakfast scene the setting's elegant ambience turns cold and formal, along with the characters' hair styles and clothing. Adding to their previous notes of discord, Kane and Emily now argue about Bernstein. Emily disapproves of Bernstein's taste in gifts for her and Kane's young son. And she pointedly refers to him as "your" Mr. Bernstein. No longer amused by their differences in perspective, Kane insists that Bernstein will continue to visit them. Emily complains about that, clearly objecting to more about Bernstein than his taste in children's toys. There is a hint of antisemitism in her references to Bernstein, as there was in Mr. Carter's back in the early days of the *Inquirer*. Kane, by contrast, seems at this moment a stout defender of fair play. Late events will suggest otherwise.

In the fifth scene of the montage all traces of affection and tolerance are gone. Both parties are now entrenched in rather than flexible about or even amused by their differences. "Really, Charles. People will think..." is yet another complaint by Emily about some violation of propriety. Her sense of right and wrong is determined by the edicts of polite society. Kane, on the other hand, no longer bothers to disguise his arrogance behind liberal values. "What I tell them to think!" he rudely interjects. Visibly middle-aged now, he has become the petty tyrant that always lurked in his character. The music accompanying this stage in Kane and Emily's disintegrating marriage is grim and menacing.

Verbal communication between husband and wife ceases altogether by the sixth and final breakfast scene. The two combatants sit in stony silence, eyeing each other with hostility while reading their morning newspapers: the *Inquirer* for him, the rival *Chronicle* for her. After the camera's initial approach to the happy newlyweds in the first breakfast scene, all subsequent interaction was shown in alternating medium shots. Now the camera withdraws to its original position at the beginning of the montage. Instead of sitting near each other at one end of the dining table, Kane and Emily now sit at opposite ends. A heavy crossbeam dividing two hemispheres of the ceiling above them has become a visual metaphor for their divided marriage. At the start of the montage it carried no such meaning. Herrmann's thin, sorrowful music now mocks the happy waltz heard in the first breakfast scene.

The final image of Kane and Emilys' breakfast montage slowly dissolves back into the last image we had of Jed Leland on the hospital sun deck. For a lingering moment he visually overlaps and usurps Kane's position at the breakfast table — perhaps a subtle hint that Leland secretly envied his friend's marriage to Emily, with whom he shared little in a political sense but whose old school grace and charm he admired. Which begs the question, could Jed and Emily have sustained a happy relationship any better than did Emily and Kane? For Leland she remains, like Bernstein's woman in white and Kane's Rosebud, an unfulfilled fantasy. Perhaps a further analogy could be drawn between Leland/Emily and Eugene/Isabel in *The Magnificent Ambersons*. No one can be certain how unfulfilled dreams might have turned out. But because they *are* unfulfilled, they become fixed points of regret and bittersweet speculation in the minds of the dreamers.

Leland tells Thompson that in spite of their eventual break-up, Kane married Emily for love. Extending his hypothesis further, he claims that the need for love motivated *everything* Kane did, including his venture into politics. But then he tempers our sympathy for Kane by insisting that Kane possessed no love to give in return. Thompson points to Kane's second marriage, to Susan Alexander, as evidence to the contrary. Leland rebuts by quoting Kane's description of Susan to him as a "cross-section of the American public." In other words, for the protagonist Susan was merely a symbol of the *public* affection he craved. Yet the ensuing scene between Kane and Susan, even though rooted in Leland's secondhand recollection, reveals more substance in that relationship than is credited by Leland's cynical remark, which may be tinged with and distorted by his bitterness towards Kane.

A close-up of cobblestones feeds the convincing illusion that we are on a New York side street circa 1916. The unevenness of those stones distinguishes this set from the excessive neatness of period sets in many Hollywood movies circa 1941. Streets wet from an earlier rain shower, high contrast lighting from a street lamp, and the clip-clop of a passing horse drawn carriage add to our sense of authentic time and place. And by staging this scene at night, with few pedestrians and little street traffic to distract our attention, Welles contributes further to the emotional intimacy of Kane's first encounter with Susan. An intimacy rare for the now famous and middle-aged Charles Foster Kane.

The camera pans to show Susan Alexander exiting a drug store while dabbing medicine on an aching tooth, about which Leland informs us. Momentarily distracted from her pain, she laughs at something off screen. The camera pans with her gaze to Kane standing at the curb, smoking a pipe, his face and clothes splattered with mud kicked up by the passing carriage which we still hear receding in the distance. How much less effective this scene would be if Welles had revealed all at once its diverse elements. By staggering our exposure to those elements (the passing carriage, then Susan, then Kane), he emphasizes their individuality and the happenstance way in which they intersect and affect each other.

The great man is humbled — something he is not accustomed to take lightly. But the woman laughing at him has a problem of her own, which diminishes his annoyance. Kane vents his irritation indirectly, by correcting her inaccurate description of *his* problem (mud, not dirt). He always has to have the last word. Kane snaps at Susan's soft-spoken, not entirely innocent invitation to accompany her to a nearby apartment for some hot water with which to clean himself. But she is so unthreatening to him that he quickly changes his mind and accepts. The double meaning of "hot water" becomes clear later, during Kane's campaign for the governorship of New York. The point in *this* scene is that Susan is the first to hint at a romantic interest between them. To her Kane is a well-dressed, handsome stranger, though she has no idea who he is or that he is married. And Kane's acceptance of her gently disguised romantic invitation is motivated by more than just sexual desire. They are two very different people who meet by chance at a moment of vulnerability for both.

The quiet melancholy of Herrmann's score, as the two characters proceed indoors, echoes the loneliness felt by both. Our first view of them inside Susan's apartment is a long shot through an open door, shot from a dark hallway outside. Blackness surrounds the bright interior of Susan's apartment, rendering it a warm, cozy retreat from the cold, wet inhospitality of the outside world. But that coziness, as conveyed by the music, disappears momentarily when Kane closes the door while suggestively promising to takes Susan's mind off her painful toothache. So sex *is* one of his motivations, as well as hers.

From behind the closed door Susan calls out "Hey!" in surprise. What is Kane doing to her? The camera, responding to *our* curiosity, moves forward in hopes of catching a glimpse. But then Susan re-opens the door, claiming that her landlady demands such propriety. Background music returns, and with it the sentimental subtext of this encounter. Kane, with sex now out of the question for the time being, generously offers to distract Susan from her pain by entertaining her with a few tricks. He loves an appreciative audience. Via the camera we now join them inside the apartment. In one particularly striking image we see a portion of Kane's body looming over Susan, who gazes up at him while seated. He commands her to look at him, for her own good of course. Later in the film we encounter a similar image under far less congenial circumstances. But for now Kane commands attention in order to soothe Susan's pain by wiggling his ears and poking fun at himself by telling her that it took an expensive education and a socially prominent acquaintance to teach him that trick. Susan laughs. Delighted with his success, Kane does too. Herrmann's music subtly shifts from melancholy, echoing various types of pain that brought these two characters together, to a sense of the contentment they now feel.

Susan's laughter carries us through a lap dissolve from one scene to the next, later that same evening. Kane continues to amuse her, this time with shadow puppets on the wall of her apartment. By now the characters are seated next to each other. Susan inquires if Kane is a professional magician — another link to Welles's life rather than Hearst's. The camera slowly moves into a tight medium shot of them. If Kane has charmed the pain out of Susan's tooth, she unwittingly captivates him with her naivete, her open affection, even her ignorance. He is especially touched that she likes him without knowing who he is. "I'm so glad you do," he says so quietly, while Susan continues to speak, that we barely hear him. The feeling behind Kane's words is genuine, in spite of Leland's cynical comment about the nature of his relationship with Susan. To Susan, Kane is not yet Charles Foster Kane — newspaper tycoon. He's just a nice guy who gallantly helped her when she needed it. Her comment," I don't know many people" is strangely complemented by Kane's contradictory reply," I know *too* many people. I guess we're both lonely." They form common cause out of very different experiences of the same phenomenon.

Few scenes in any Welles film are without the tension of contradiction. The growing empathy between Kane and Susan is disrupted for just a moment as he is about to reveal to her a pain of his own, hoping perhaps that she can return the favor by relieving it. But his painful narrative about being headed to a warehouse to look at some of his deceased mother's possessions being stored there is interrupted by Susan's unwelcome reference to his apparent wealth — a reference ironically triggered by Kane's own reference to having muddied his *best* clothes. "I was just joking [about them being my best clothes]" is Kane's gentle rebuke of Susan for disturbing the magical intimacy of the moment. Then he resumes his story, coming as close to sharing an emotional truth about himself as he will with anyone. A beautiful close-up of Susan, eyes sparkling, mouth smiling and silent, captures everything Kane sees in her. She appears to him, and to us, warm, compassionate, and guileless. A subsequent close-up of Kane conveys his passionate if genteel reaction to that image of Susan. In Welles's most intimate tone of voice Kane tells us about his disrupted journey to a Manhattan warehouse, "in search of my youth." The revelation of his mother's death "a long time ago" draws a voiceless "Oh" of sympathy from Susan's lips. We can only guess at what inspired Kane to take his solitary, sentimental journey into the past. A passing whim? The anniversary of Mary Kane's death? Growing estrangement from Emily? The possibilities are many and Welles wisely does not specify one. But it is interesting that Kane's sentimental journey and diversionary dalliance with Susan occurs at the height of his political popularity and power, suggesting that politics and public adulation cannot alone make him happy.

Whatever the reason for Kane's discontent, Herrmann's music echoes it by turning melancholy again.

The moment of intimacy passes quickly, as though Kane will not allow Susan, or anyone else, to get too close to him. He changes the subject and the mood by *formally* introducing himself to her, with typical false humility, as a man who runs a couple of newspapers. Then he brashly asks about Susan's age and profession. A humble music store clerk, she reveals her dream, or rather her mother's dream *for* her, of becoming an opera singer. It is an understandable gesture, revealing something private about herself in response to Kane's revelation about his nostalgic warehouse quest. Still very aware of her limitations as a singer at this point in the story, Susan half apologizes,"Well, you know what mothers are like." Kane's pallid affirmative indicates to us, though not to Susan, that he does *not* know what mothers are like. Ironic in a bitter sort of way, Susan will soon experience the darker side of parental attention that Kane never got a chance to experience, unless we count the paternal abuse hinted at by Mary Kane. Without hesitation Kane launches Susan on her singing career, if at first only for an audience of one, and confined to her own parlor. Perhaps it is another example of Kane bribing someone's affection. But initially there is kindness too in his effort.

Susan Alexander's apartment is cluttered and quaint, in the fashion of the period, with carved wood furnishings and elaborate wallpaper. It is also full of personal bric-a-brac. Dresser tops and shelves are crowded with possessions. In the shot of Susan seated while laughing at Kane, who stands over her wiggling his ears, we see along the edges of the camera frame, though prominently in the foreground and in sharp focus, many of her private treasures, beautifully lit in a manner that highlights every surface detail. Among them are a framed photograph. Of Susan's mother? Or Susan herself as a young girl? The point of showing them is to give us a powerful sense of Susan's life — its mysterious past and accumulated emotional baggage — prior to and separate from Kane's. Among her possessions is the glass paperweight that Kane held, then dropped and broke, in the film's opening scene. By the end of *Citizen Kane* we have some idea of what that paperweight signified to the protagonist. But lost to time and obscurity is what, if anything, it meant to its previous owner, Susan Alexander. The tragic richness of Kane's private life is an elaborate reflection of the less grandiose but no less complex lives of the film's supporting characters.

Like Susan's "hot water" invitation to Kane, his "Let's go to the parlor" contains sexual innuendo. But when we segue to the parlor, there is no sex. Kane, looking very comfortable and domestic seated in a chair, listens contentedly to Susan play the piano and sing. To *our* eyes and ears her performance is mediocre and heavy-handed. Susan's music forms a bridge to the next scene, where the positions of both characters remain similar while the setting changes significantly. Kane has installed Susan in a much larger apartment. Her hairstyle and manner of dress are now more modern and stylish. Her singing, relatively speaking, is more confident and her playing lighter, more lyrical. Susan's personality and modest musical talents have blossomed under Kane's encouragement. At the conclusion of her performance she turns eagerly towards him, awaiting his reaction. He dutifully applauds. So long as their relationship remains independent of other aspects of Kane's life, it reaps emotional rewards for both. But the ticking cuckoo clock on the wall reminds us that time eventually unravels everything.

Applause forms a transition from Kane and Susans' private happiness to Kane's political crusade for the governorship of New York, a *public* endeavor that will ruin and be ruined by that idyllic relationship. Kane's applause for Susan becomes the applause of a small crowd of laborers for Jed Leland's stump speech on behalf of Kane. Voicing none of the skepticism about Kane's political convictions that he did to Bernstein at the *Inquirer* party several scenes ago, Leland supports his friend's campaign without reservation. "Fight-

Citizen Kane. Susan Alexander (Dorothy Comingore) plays and sings for Charlie Kane (Orson Welles) in the apartment he has rented for her. But their private contentment is about to be destroyed by public exposure.

ing liberal" and "friend of the working man" is how he describes Kane. His enthusiasm grows as the camera closes in on him. But it cannot equal the microphone enhanced bombast of the protagonist himself as Kane picks up the thread of Leland's speech at a much larger rally in a huge auditorium.

The first shot at the big rally is of a giant poster depicting the candidate as a confident, larger than life figure, perfectly suited to the larger than life voice that accompanies it. Think of the false or at misleading image of Susan Alexander depicted on a poster outside the El Rancho nightclub. The camera slowly tilts down to show us the real, much smaller Kane, speaking from behind a podium. The visual contrast between poster and man is striking, but the big, sonorous voice of Welles, electronically inflated, makes the character's presence and force of will seem superhuman, even when the camera cuts to an extreme long shot from the back of the auditorium.

The camera dollies forward towards Kane, through a lap dissolve that skips over much of the intervening space. As he speaks of his improving prospects for getting elected and, conversely, of his opponent's diminishing prospects, the camera comes to rest looking up at him and the huge Kane poster behind him. Never has he seemed more powerful in a public forum. But while he speaks of all the polls and straw votes that register his lead, the camera cuts away to Emily and their son in the audience. The boy, impulsive like his father, is standing up. Emily, dressed like the patrician she is, discretely tells him to sit down. In more forceful terms she will soon tell her husband to do the same.

The camera returns to Kane, gazing up at him in the same respectful manner as before. As he launches into a series of vague political promises, it cuts closer. Party bosses, looking like the former *Chronicle* reporters he lured to the *Inquirer* years earlier, are visible behind him. Reaction shots show Kane's son proudly waving to his father, a reverent and idealistic Jed Leland watching from among a group of cigar and cigarette smoking party hacks at the back of the auditorium, and an enthusiastic Bernstein clapping along with yet more party hacks in the gallery. Declaring his intention to champion the "underprivileged, the underpaid, and the underfed," Kane briefly steps out from behind his podium, seeming to close the emotional distance between himself and his supporters. The crowd cheers its approval. Even a brief aside between Emily and her son add to our impression that Kane's election is inevitable.

Typical of Kane's speech, and of American political rhetoric in general, is an amusing remark saying nothing specific but implying much in the way of action. "I'd make my promises now, if I weren't too busy arranging to keep them." The crowd loves it. Even Leland laughs and applauds on cue. Kane is enormously pleased. But to our surprise he does not conclude his speech on that conveniently vague note. Instead he makes a bold and specific promise to indict, prosecute, and convict "Boss" Jim Gettys, his opponent, for crimes of corruption. The camera cuts back to its original high angle long shot in order to begin another admiring run at the candidate, stopping in medium shot as he reaches the climactic end of his speech.

The auditorium erupts with cheering. Kane's self-appointed theme song is played by a band. But as party bosses gather round him to offer congratulations, the camera cuts to a high angle extreme long shot taken from a private box far above the boisterous crowd. Observing unseen from that perch, as though casually watching a movie on a distant screen, is the target of Kane's campaign against government corruption. Though visually surrounded by images of his enemy, on the stage to his left and on a campaign poster hanging on the wall to his right, Jim Gettys calmly dons his hat and departs.

Descending from the stage to the auditorium floor, Kane is happily surrounded by party bosses shaking his hand and congratulating him, and press photographers generating favorable publicity for his campaign. Outside the building he strides towards the backtracking camera, with supporters on both sides telling him he is unbeatable. He own image, on a large campaign poster, guards his rear. He looks particularly dashing in his dark suit, top hat, and long white scarf. A silver "K" hangs on a chain around his neck. The whole world seems to be turning *into* Charles Foster Kane. This backtracking shot is similar in effect to an earlier shot of his return to the *Inquirer* offices after a vacation. He stops to pick up his son (like his trophy, just another extension of himself), then launches another verbal jab at Gettys.

Visually made up of dark-attired admirers, Kane's world is suddenly invaded by the white-attired Emily. She quietly takes charge of the proceedings, sending their son home in a taxi and then, without explanation, leaving Kane's side to enter one herself. Puzzled at her disruption of his triumph, Kane follows her. Visually supported by his campaign portrait in the background and by the silver "K" on his chest, Kane nevertheless loses a *verbal* skirmish with Emily, who announces her departure for an address he knows to be that of Susan Alexander's apartment. Stunned by the implication of her invitation to join him, he meekly submits to her.

Just after Emily joined her husband outside the auditorium, and while Kane still held his son in his arms, the camera cut away to a long shot to show us a press photographer taking a picture of the family. Joseph McBride (McBride, p.41) points out that this is the same photograph we saw earlier on the front page of a newspaper heralding the candidate's triumph, as reproduced in "News on the March." In the present and following scenes we see and hear some of the human drama behind that photo—drama left out of the newsreel. And what a difference there is between the two versions.

Standing outside the door to Susan's apartment building, Kane criticizes Emily's "flair for melodrama." But his sarcasm is undercut when a housemaid opens the door from inside and cheerily greets Kane by name. Obviously he has been there before. And that incriminating evidence is compounded at the top of the stairs by Susan, who also greets him by name. The rest of the scene is a tactical ballet by four characters. The camera's low angle point of view amplifies their expressions. So do the patches of light and shadow through which they pass as they maneuver around each other. Even mundane elements such as stair railings, wallpaper, and curtains seem aesthetically charged with their emotional conflicts.

Susan makes the first tactical move—a pre-emptive strike in her own defense. Moving into the open doorway of her apartment, she hastily explains to Kane that she was forced to send a letter to Emily by a threat of scandal. Her excuse is cut short by the appearance of Jim Gettys in the doorway behind her. Their period of splendid isolation clearly ended, Kane and Susan are visually bracketed by Emily and Gettys, whose separate interests threaten the no longer secret lovers. Emily reluctantly but politely accepts Gettys' invitation to enter the apartment and begin negotiations. The only character attired in white, she is the only character who has not contributed directly to the present mess, though she certainly made an *indirect* contribution to Kane's unhappiness, which encouraged his connection to Susan. As Emily enters the apartment, Susan glances at her elegant dress and bearing as though awed by them.

Gettys corroborates Susan's claim about the letter. Susan turns to Kane to defend her actions. He ignores her and confronts Gettys in the doorway, threatening physical violence. Emily faces the camera, her brightly lit figure positioned between and behind the shadowy combatants. Gettys insolently dismisses Kane's threat and walks back into the apartment. Kane follows, determined to carry out that threat. But just as Kane cut short Susan's initial protest of innocence, Emily stops him in his tracks by reading aloud the threat of scandal written by Susan under pressure from Gettys. The camera has by now entered the apartment along with three of the four characters. Susan soon joins them, again trying to rationalize away her letter as Gettys' idea, not her own. Then, in an oddly tender moment, she turns to Emily, introduces herself, and discretely assures Mrs. Kane that her relationship with Charles is not sexual. But Emily is not interested in a heart-to-heart exchange. She is interested only in the meaning of Susan's threatening letter. This is an exercise in power, not an opportunity to get acquainted.

Gettys, having retreated to the background, now speaks up, answering Emily's question and adding his own crushing blow to Susan's appeal for understanding. Kane joins Gettys at the back of the room. Bright, almost incandescent backlighting, provided by a lamp, highlights their dark figures. The camera shifts a little to the right, eliminating Susan from the frame as Kane and Gettys joust with words, trying to justify their actions to Emily, who occupies the foreground. Rejecting Kane's mock description of him as a "gentleman," Gettys moves forward to join Emily, explaining why her husband is even less deserving of that title. The struggle between Kane and Gettys acquires an oddly moral dimension, at least in *their* minds. Kane retaliates weakly with a flurry of insults, until silenced by Gettys shouting, "We're talking now about what *you* are!" Susan suddenly bursts into the camera frame, selfishly appealing to Kane to cooperate with Gettys, who contemptuously interrupts her with an offer to bargain with Kane. "More of a chance than he'd give me" is another attempt at ethical upsmanship. Unless Kane withdraws from the election, he threatens, every newspaper except the *Inquirer* will carry the story of Kane's illicit affair with Susan. Moving towards Gettys, Susan protests that no such affair took place. But she is again rudely overruled. She turns to make her case to Emily, but is again silenced by Gettys. Poor Susan is literally surrounded by three powerful characters who largely ignore her.

Conceding the advantage to Gettys, Emily tells Kane the decision of whether or not to accept terms of conditional surrender has already been made for him. Now the smallest figure in the camera frame, Kane feebly objects, calling upon the good will of the voting public to bolster his cause. The other three characters, occupying the foreground, look at him. For a moment they form an alliance of disparate but complementary self-interests. Each for a different reason wants Kane to yield. From a reverse angle, with Kane now in the foreground and the other characters in the background and facing the camera, the fragility of that alliance is obvious. Emily's argument in favor of her husband withdrawing from the election centers around their son's welfare. Susan, for different reasons, lends support to Emily's argument yet is contemptuously cut off by Emily, who behaves much more civilly towards Gettys.

Refusing to leave with Emily, Kane declares his determination to stay and fight on alone. In a frontal shot he moves forward, now matching Susan and Gettys in size. Defying one character off screen and two on his flanks, he issues what amounts to a personal manifesto, perhaps formulated on the day Thatcher and his parents conspired to exile him from home. "There's only one person in the world to decide what I'm going to do, and that's *me*." Once powerless to remain with his beloved mother, he now refuses to let anyone to deprive him of the electorate's love. Emily responds, rather mysteriously, "You decided what you were going to do, Charles, some time ago." Does she refer to Kane's original decision to get involved with Susan? Or to something even further back? Maybe she cynically implies that her marriage to Kane was built around Kane's desire for social advancement and political self-promotion from the start. It is the film's first and only hint that even the cool and rather snobbish Emily Kane has experienced disappointment and heartache in her materially privileged life.

Though visually smaller than Kane, Gettys quietly taunts him before leaving. The effectiveness of that taunt is evident from Kane's bombastic reaction. How different from the protagonist's encounters with Thatcher and Carter. He practically froths at the mouth as he pursues the departing Gettys from a safe distance, like a dog pursuing a formidable enemy. Kane screams insults and threats. Cutting to ever more distant perspectives as it follows Gettys down the stairs, the camera renders Kane's tirade progressively less potent. Eventually it is nothing more than a distant, off screen shout of "Sing-Sing!" (the infamous prison to which Kane threatens to send Gettys) as we, Gettys, and Emily part company outside the apartment building. Gettys shuts the door and Kane's feeble threat is displaced by the innocuous sound of a distant automobile horn. Just empty noise.

In the context of what just occurred upstairs, Gettys and Emily say goodbye in a remarkably civil manner. He doffs his hat and offers her a ride. She politely declines, thanking him. However flawed Kane again proves himself to be in this scene, the hypocritical civility of his wife and political foe somehow seems less admirable than his naked display of partisan passion.

The scene's final image of the door to Susan's apartment building slowly transforms into a photograph. The camera pulls back to reveal the photo as part of a front page story in the *Chronicle*, rival to Kane's *Inquirer*. This is the same headline and picture we saw in

"News on the March." But this time its dramatic impact is much greater, because we have just witnessed the dramatic *personal* story behind the headline and photo.

The off screen voice of a street vendor hawking copies of the *Chronicle* forms an aural bridge between scenes. The new scene begins with a big close-up of Jed Leland, looking disgruntled as the vendor tries to sell him a paper. This is a reversal of an earlier scene in which an *Inquirer* vendor tried to sell a copy to the equally disgruntled Herbert Carter. Both Leland and Kane receive their comeuppance after years of practicing irresponsible journalism. Carter would be pleased, if he were still alive. Leland retreats to a nearby saloon to drown his disappointment. Mr. Bernstein, on the other hand, is more a man of action, and blindly loyal to Kane. In the next brief scene, at the *Inquirer* office, he selects "Fraud at Polls!" over "Kane Elected!" as the headline for the next issue of Kane's newspaper. The fact that both versions of the headline were prepared ahead of time is proof that the *Inquirer* is more or less a propaganda vehicle for its owner.

A new scene begins with a shot of a discarded copy of the "Fraud at Polls!" *Inquirer* headline, then broadens its scope to show us a drunk Jed Leland approaching Kane's campaign headquarters in the *Inquirer* building. He staggers through a mess of campaign confetti being cleaned up by one of Kane's beloved working class laborers. Kane's campaign song plays softly and wistfully on accordion—a painful, ghostly reminder of what might have been. In different ways it speaks for the broken dreams of both Leland and Kane. Still a gentleman, and still loyal to the working class, in spite of his anger at Kane, Leland tosses his cigar into the street cleaner's cart rather than on the ground.

Inside campaign headquarters the party hacks silently depart—rats deserting a sinking ship. Kane emerges from his office, rubbing his aching back and looking weary. Faithful Bernstein lingers to offer consolation, but is sent home. Kane will face defeat alone. Light shining through the Venetian blinds on his office windows throws dark stripes across a campaign poster on the far wall—ironic echoes of the convict stripes in which Kane threatened to dress Jim Gettys. Thanks to his public scandal with Susan, they seem more applicable to Kane's situation.

As Kane walks across the room he looks old, ungainly, almost feeble. The prominent ceiling looms oppressively over his head. Leland enters the room and belligerently approaches his boss. This is his first direct challenge to Kane, who circles around him warily, searching for an angle of rebuttal. "I've set back the cause of reform, is that it?" he asks, verbalizing the charge against him for Leland but adding his own dose of sarcasm to undermine it. "It's obvious the people prefer Jim Gettys to me" is an attempt to shift all blame for the election results onto the voters. They betrayed him instead of the other way around.

When Leland first confronts Kane they both stand under the skylight in the ceiling. When Kane walks away to distance himself from the friend he knows is about to scold him, Leland remains under the skylight, aesthetically benefitting from the power of its illumination as he criticizes Kane for treating the voters as personal property, dispensing liberty to them like a prince to vassals. The camera shoots this little speech from a distance. Leland appears smaller than Kane's legs in the extreme foreground, yet the skylight compensates for the mismatch in size.

By criticizing the protagonist for a fault Kane has exhibited as long as he can remember, Leland slightly undercuts his own moral credibility. He had to get drunk in order to vent the disapproval he's felt for a long time. Continuing his verbal barrage, he takes two steps towards Kane and seems a little bigger in the process. Kane too steps forward. His legs appear colossal, but his feet shuffle wearily, belying any impression of strength. And he is stopped in his tracks by more cutting words from Jed. Then he tries to distract Leland by offering to get drunk with him. He refers to Leland by his full first name, Jedediah, as though formally beseeching his old friend. But Leland will not be distracted from his purpose, and even incorporates Kane's offer into his assault by accusing Kane of being incapable of getting drunk. In other words, of being, unlike normal people, unable to occasionally give up his desperate need to control everything.

Kane shuffles forward to re-join Leland under the skylight. Annoyed, he tells his adversary to go home. Leland refuses, stubbornly finishing his point about organized labor being a threat to Kane's selfishly motivated philanthropy. Advising Kane to move to a desert island and "lord it over the monkeys," Leland savagely if unwittingly anticipates the protagonist's eventual retreat to Xanadu, where among the few inhabitants under his rule will indeed be several monkeys kept in a cage. Kane manages to turn this insult back on its point of origin, suggesting that, like Leland, one of those monkeys will no doubt let him know when he does something wrong. But Leland does not back down. "You're not very drunk" is Kane's reluctant admission that Leland's arguments are coherent enough to pack a punch.

Leland's attack continues. Booze has made him relentless. "You don't care about anything except you" is blunt, cruel, and accurate. "You just want to persuade people that you love them so much that they ought to love you back. Only you want love on your own terms" sends Kane retreating to the comfort of a pitcher of alcohol on a nearby table. What was intended for celebrating a political victory now serves as consolation for something worse than a political defeat. Kane towers over the camera, which looks up at the action from floor level. But again he looks like a teetering rather than powerful giant. Then a new camera angle offers a mirror image of an earlier shot, with Leland in the background looking very small vis-a-vis Kane's huge legs in the foreground. But Leland closes that gap, lessening the visual discrepancy and amplifying his verbal attack. By requesting a transfer to their Chicago newspaper he signals an end to their long friendship. There is real panic in Kane's startled reply. With the exception of his mother, Kane has never faced the loss of someone so important to him. Leland's garbled next line and confession of drunkenness gives Kane a tactical opening, provoking a smile and a chuckle of relief from the beleaguered tycoon. But Leland sharply reiterates his request for transfer, so Kane tries to overrule him with brute authority disguised as a compliment. "You're too valuable here" refers more to Leland's value to Kane than to the newspaper. Leland counters that maneuver by resigning. But before he finishes that resignation Kane backs down, agrees to the Chicago transfer, and joins his old friend in the solace of a drink. Better a distant friend than no friend at all.

Never one to accept defeat graciously, Kane employs a new tactic to dissuade Leland from going to Chicago, trying to *kid* his friend out of leaving by pointing out the Windy City's poor climate and lack of culture. Neither amused nor moved, Leland specifies a timetable for his departure. Viewed from a low camera angle, the two men look like boxers facing off at center ring. Kane concedes the bout to Leland. But by getting in the last verbal punch, he aims to salvage a philosophical victory. Appropriating an earlier criticism that Leland leveled against him, Kane proposes,"a toast, Jedediah, to love on my terms. Those are the only terms anybody ever knows. His own." "Anybody" presumably includes Jed Leland. And from what we see of all the major characters in *Citizen Kane*, the protagonist may be right. Kane's flaws are an inflated (by wealth, fame, and power) version of flaws exhibited by the people around him. There is a fundamental self-centeredness about each of the supporting characters. Even the actions of Mary Kane seem dictated by her desperate need to protect Charles from his father. She has no idea how sending the boy away with Thatcher might adversely affect his outlook and life. Leland too demands love on his own terms. And when he doesn't get it, he bails out. Only Bernstein stays with Kane through thick and thin. But *his* love is more like unconditional worship.

The newspaper headline "Kane Marries 'Singer'" is accompanied by celebratory music. The headline slowly dissolves into a shot of Kane and Susan Alexander, just married, descending the steps of a courthouse and heading for their car. They are surrounded by a mob of reporters and photographers. Striking one of the latter on the head with his cane, Kane treats them all as intruders on his privacy. But when another of the photographers announces that he is from the *Inquirer*, Kane abruptly changes his attitude. Assured of favorable rather than hostile publicity, the great yellow journalist now welcomes the attention. Inside the car Susan reacts giddily to that same attention — not at all like the young woman who was terrified at the prospect of public scandal earlier. The reason for her and Kane's quick recovery from that scandal is revealed in Kane's answer to a reporter's question. "We're going to be a great opera star." In other words, Kane has already embarked on a new crusade to win the hearts and minds of the American public. The word "we're" offers a clear indication that Kane intends to achieve popular acceptance vicariously through his new bride. When a reporter asks Susan if she will be singing with the Metropolitan Opera, Kane replies *for* her, in the affirmative. He is already her Svengali.

Terribly naive, Susan is caught up in the excitement of her new marriage and budding career. She is emotionally swept up by the power of Kane's audacity, vision, and wealth, much as the more worldly and intelligent Jed Leland was at the start of the *Inquirer* enterprise and political crusade. Susan is particularly impressed by Kane's promise to build her an opera house if she is not invited to sing at the Met. She doesn't yet know what public rejection and ridicule feel like. Kane, on the other hand, knows all too well, but is too needy for public acceptance to acknowledge the possibility of another rejection. Building a new opera house "won't be necessary," he insists. An echo of his confident assertion in "News on the March" that there will be no war in Europe. He is wrong on both counts.

Kane's optimism is immediately undercut by another seemingly triumphant *Inquirer* headline. "Kane Builds Opera House" segues into a big close-up of Susan, in full operatic make-up and costume, singing. A look of panic on her face. Is she in character for her performance, or is her panic real? The vocal and then visual intrusion of her singing coach screaming "No! No! No!" at her *before* a performance tells us it is real. Susan turns to face him. Show from an oblique angle, she looks extremely vulnerable — a far cry from the jubilant young woman we saw in Kane's car. In rapid succession the aural and visual assault on Susan Alexander multiplies. Her coach's criticism is compounded by other, competing demands on her attention. An off screen orchestra plays an overture, signaling the start of the opera. The camera pulls back a little to show us another man adjusting Susan's costume and placing a ridiculously grandiose hat on her head. Above her a light blinks, prompting everyone but the performers to exit the stage.

As the camera pulls back further, retaining Susan as its central figure, many people fuss at and around her. A painted backdrop falls into place. Susan speaks, but we hear nothing of what she says amid the commotion of last second preparations. Finally the stage hands depart. From a camera perspective almost equivalent to that of the audience, we watch Susan's opera debut. Yet our overall perspective exceeds that of the audience because we got a glimpse of Susan's private terror backstage. Withdrawing still further from Susan's experience of the event, the camera now floats upward into the opera house rafters, where two stage hands standing on a catwalk offer the first public review of her work. Susan's already inadequate voice sounds even weaker from this height. One of the men looks at his companion and pinches his nose. Susan's performance stinks. At this point in the scene we are inclined to find his gesture both accurate and amusing. From compassionate close-up to cruel, off screen detachment, the camera and soundtrack beautifully capture the emotional diversity of Susan's opera debut in a single, brief scene.

The next scene opens with Kane, fresh from attending Susan's opera debut, silently slipping into the City Room of the *Chicago Daily Inquirer*. He looks disappointed, beaten. Across the room Mr. Bernstein orchestrates the favorable reviews that will appear in the newspaper's next issue. He gets complete cooperation from the reviewers. Kane interjects himself into this strategy session. Looking like an enormous bear in his full-length fur coat, he *encourages* his employees' obsequious behavior and confirms front page coverage for Susan. He is becoming more accustomed to the role of tyrant, commanding rather than seducing cooperation as he once did. The only sour note in this little sycophantic symphony is provided by the absent Jed Leland, who is in his private office off screen, writing a review of Susan's acting. Ignoring Bernstein's attempts to restrain him, Kane strides purposefully across the floor and into Leland's office. Camera angle, set design (pillars and light fixtures in particular), and lighting exaggerate the distance he traverses. For our benefit and that of the reviewers standing next to him, Bernstein sadly explains that metaphorical gap in other terms, revealing that Kane and Leland haven't spoken to each other in years. Then he hurries off in pursuit of his boss, hoping to mediate between the two estranged friends.

The first shot inside Leland's office focuses on Jed, in the foreground, slumped unconscious over his typewriter, a half empty bottle of liquor nearby. If Kane had appeared in this first office shot, his dominating presence would have distracted us from Leland, whose condition is a clue to his state of mind. Obviously things have not gone well for him since his split with Kane.

Bernstein enters the office and tries unsuccessfully to rouse Leland. Kane instructs him to close the door, isolating their interaction from the prying eyes and ears of the other reporters. Bernstein, the diplomat, explains that Leland is not in the habit of getting drunk, but that sounds more like an effort to save Leland from getting fired than to report the facts accurately. If Bernstein is lying, then Leland apparently never recovered from his disillusionment with Kane. Which suggests that Leland is still emotionally dependent on his former friend. If Bernstein is telling the truth, then it is specifically the task of reviewing Susan's performance, and of therefore betraying Kane, that drove Leland to get drunk. Whichever the case, Bernstein misreads the nature of Kane's concern in the matter. Kane is more interested in what Leland wrote about Susan than in his ex-friend's weakness for booze. At Kane's insistence, Bernstein reads aloud Leland's incomplete and unfavorable review.

Kane angrily rips Leland's unfinished notice out of the typewriter, then with a laugh verbally adds to it in the same critical spirit. Bernstein is slow to comprehend what Kane is doing. He doesn't understand Kane's need to restore his own moral integrity in the eyes of Jed Leland, who years earlier broke off their friendship because of Kane's lack of same. For the moment the need to prove himself to Jed, and to himself, overrides Kane's desire to win public acceptance through Susan's operatic career. "I'm gonna finish Mr. Leland's notice" is spoken, however, with a tinge of vengeful triumph rather than reconciliation.

An extreme close-up of typewriter keys banging out the word "weak" on paper says it all. In fact it says more than the typist intends. The idea of "weak" is reinforced visually by the fuzzy edges of the typed letters themselves. But the weakness on display here is not confined to Susan's performance. Kane's flawed pride and Leland's inability to free himself entirely of Kane are also forms of weakness.

With Kane's aggressive typing heard in the distance, Leland awakens to discover the review missing from his typewriter. Bernstein updates him on the situation. Leland's first reaction to news of Kane's arrival is one of surprise, even happiness. He has missed his old friend. But then cynicism sets in as he concludes that Kane is rewriting his review to make it more positive. Bernstein challenges that conclusion, grimly and rather naively defending his boss's integrity by explaining Kane's intention to finish the review in the manner Leland started it. "I guess that'll show you." Bernstein accepts without reservation or scrutiny that Kane's behavior in the matter is more honorable than Leland's. He does not anticipate the contradictory nature of Kane's reaction to Leland's supposed betrayal.

A tight shot of Kane seated at a typewriter in the outer office at foreground left, completing Leland's review, includes Jed approaching from the far background at screen right. A row of pillars, a railing, ceiling beams, and multiple patches of light and shadow heighten our visual sense of the great emotional gulf between the two men. Leland stops at middle distance. Bernstein's tiny silhouette is visible in the lighted doorway of Leland's office, far away. Each of the three characters occupies a separate visual plane in this deep focus portrait. The three old friends have never been further apart, emotionally.

A flicker of Kane's eye to the right (his left) indicates his awareness of Leland's presence. Without looking at his former friend, he offers a polite greeting, only to undermine any possibility of reconciliation with his next line. "You're fired" is accompanied by the harsh sound of the typewriter carriage returning to its starting position as Kane begins a new line of the review. Like a door slamming shut in Leland's face, that sound is Kane's deliberate punctuation mark ending *all* relations, personal and business, between Leland and himself. "You're fired" and the typewriter sound are aesthetically complementary but morally contradictory. Kane takes petty revenge on Leland while simultaneously proving, at least to his own satisfaction, his journalistic integrity by completing Leland's review as originally intended. A close-up of Leland registers his shock and anger at Kane's actions. Without a word of reply, he departs.

A line separating shadow from light across the City Room door becomes a transition device to the next scene, which returns to the hospital sun deck where Leland is being interviewed by Thompson. For a lingering moment images from past and present occupy the screen simultaneously, divided by that line. To the left of what had been a shadowy image of the younger Leland leaving the newspaper office we now see the lighter image of old Leland on the hospital sun deck. The age contrast is striking. To the right of the line we now see a shadowy image of Kane completing Leland's review. This transition image lingers before the Kane side fades into shadow. While it lasts the dual image yields a powerful impression of the emotional impact being fired by Kane still has on old Leland, who seems lost in the recollection of it until Thompson's voice intrudes from off screen, breaking the mood of Leland's painful reverie.

Thompson is clearly more interested in Kane's side of the story than in Leland's. Asking why Kane completed Leland's bad notice, Thompson still does not appreciate the contradictory nature of his subject. Leland, growing impatient, interrupts the reporter with an explanation. Kane was always trying to prove something to other people. Building an opera house for Susan was one example. By expressing these opinions in a rather forced casual manner, Leland tries to deflate Kane's aura of mystery and importance as a public figure. Perhaps he gets a measure of revenge on his old boss by getting in the final word. He downgrades the fabled Xanadu to "Sloppy Joe's." But Leland too is an emotionally divided man. He strikes a proud, defiant pose while boasting of not answering a letter Kane sent to him from Xanadu a few years ago. But in the next breath he expresses regret at doing nothing to relieve his old friend's loneliness. Then his bitterness returns and he describes Xanadu as Kane's "absolute monarchy," built in reaction to Kane's disappointment with the world at large.

Leland's loud call for a nurse indirectly signals the end of Thompson's access to his storehouse of memories about Kane. The old man is tired, or impatient, or perhaps too sad to continue reminiscing about past conflicts and present regrets. Two nurses arrive in response to his call. For a moment they remain anonymous bodies without faces—cold figures of institutional authority, dressed in white. Which is in part how Leland perceives them. He reacts to their arrival with annoyance, as though they had summoned him instead of the other way around. When he stands up to leave with them the camera tilts up and we see their faces. They do not look like heartless, cruel tyrants. Nevertheless, Leland makes a snide remark to Thompson about their lack of physical beauty clashing with the general perception of nurses. Maybe it is impossible *not* to resent people on whom you are so dependent due to your own frailties. Leland's attitude towards his nurses is similar to Bernstein's towards the assistants who withhold information from him about Leland's health and whereabouts because it might upset him, and Susan's resentment of a domineering husband who makes all of her important decisions and treats her like a child. But unlike Leland or Bernstein, Susan is young and strong enough to rebel.

The loneliness and unhappiness of Jed Leland in old age are particularly evident at the end of this scene. He jokes with Thompson that the cigars he requested must be smuggled into the hospital in disguise, because his young doctor wants to keep him alive. An idea that Leland finds amusing. The implication is that he no longer finds life worth living. Propped up by the nurses, he shuffles off into the background. No other patients now occupy the sun deck with him. Like the dear friends and bitter enemies from his past, they too have disappeared. Background music echoes his unenviable situation. We observe his departure from over Thompson's right shoulder. Perhaps the reporter is beginning to comprehend the emotional depth and complexity of the life he is investigating, as well as the lives of the people he has interviewed.

The next scene begins with a close-up of Susan Alexander's publicity portrait outside the El Rancho nightclub in Atlantic City. The camera repeats its cautious approach to the real Susan, up over the roof and down through a skylight. But the rain, lightning, and thunder from the earlier scene have yielded to calm. And so too has Susan's mood. Still drinking but no longer drunk, she allows Thompson to ask questions. Bernard Herrmann's somber musical introduction to this scene is displaced by soft piano blues originating inside the nightclub. Another variation of the song "It Can't Be Love," heard earlier and later in the film as first a foreshadowing and then an echo of a broken marriage. This local music quietly reinforces our impression that Susan, in the aftermath of her bad marriage to Kane, is emotionally damaged yet wiser than she was as a young woman. Her voice too has a rougher quality than it did when she first met Kane. Under Welles's direction Dorothy Commingore gives a remarkable performance, arousing irritation and sympathy at the same time.

"You wouldn't wanna know a lot about what comes to my mind about myself and Mr. Charlie Kane" sets the hostile tone of Susan's memories, putting her on a par with Jed Leland and Thatcher, and at odds with Bernstein. The camera closes in on her almost imperceptibly as she vents her bitterness at all the singing she had to do for Kane. She disputes Thompson's suggestion that Kane did her an honor by marrying her, pointing out that marriage was never mentioned until after their relationship became public knowledge and Emily Norton divorced him.

Like the transition from the City Room of the *Chicago Daily Inquirer* to Leland's hospital sun deck, the transition from interview at El Rancho to Susan taking music lessons at Kane's residence is very gradual, for a reason. The background scenery at the nightclub darkens and is displaced by a setting from the past as Susan's memories of Kane come to life and draw from her one terrifically concise expression of resentment and revenge. Her face now the only brightly lit object in the shot, she grins in bitter triumph and tells Thompson, who is nearly lost in shadow and all but irrelevant to both Susan and us, "Everything was his idea, except my leaving him." This is the angry flip side of the grieving Susan we saw during Thompson's first attempt to interview her. Musically too the transition between scenes is subtle. "It Can't Be Love," played on piano at the nightclub, segues effortlessly to an aria from *The Barber of Seville*, which is linked in Susan's mind with the painful experience of singing lessons and a disastrous opera career.

The camera slowly dollies in on the humiliating start of that career. An accompanist and Susan's singing coach, Matisti, are seated at a piano while Susan stands nearby, trying her best to follow instructions. Far in the background Kane silently enters the room and stands in the doorway, observing while unobserved, as he did at the start of the *Chicago Daily Inquirer* City Room scene. Frustrated with his student's lack of talent, a frazzled Matisti stands and critiques her in a melodramatic manner itself worthy of the opera stage. Full of grand gestures and volume, he reminds one of Kane's performance at the political rally. Susan's thin voice, slim figure, and timid personality are overwhelmed by Matisti's barrage. Clearly he is a better singer than is she. But Susan is singing for *two*, and the rebuttal to Matisti's cruel verdict that she is incapable of singing opera comes from her bolder half. Even from across the room Kane's voice booms as loudly as Matisti's. Approaching and confronting the teacher face to face, Kane narrowly defines Matisti's job as to train Susan's voice, not give his opinion of it. Reinforcing the point, Kane hints at the sinister possibility of retaliation, via the resources of his newspaper empire, should Matisti exceed the boundaries set for him. Nor is Kane moved by Matisti's timid plea on behalf of his reputation within the musical world. Adding to our impression of Kane's mastery of the situation, he doesn't even deign to look at the music teacher while rejecting the man's plea. Just as he refused to look at Leland while firing him. Instead, Kane smiles reassuringly at Susan.

Protest over, the music lesson resumes. But it is soon interrupted by another obstacle to Kane's larger goal of gaining public acceptance through opera: Susan's acute embarrassment. She stops singing. Kane quietly but firmly orders her to continue. She reluctantly obeys. And with her inadequate voice as a backdrop, Kane grins triumphantly at the seated, humbled Matisti and comments, "I thought you'd see it my way." During his confrontations with Leland, Kane at least maintained a pretense of fairness and respect. No longer. Poor Susan must deal with the protagonist at his worst, despite the much more promising start to their relationship on a deserted New York street corner.

Susan's opera debut, as presumably told from her point of view, begins the same way we saw it earlier, when it was told from Leland's. Of course in both cases the camera and soundtrack give us more detailed information than the interviewees could. After a repeat of the first shot from the earlier opera scene, the camera shifts perspectives, this time looking from the back of the stage to the front instead of the reverse. It now subjectively overlaps Susan's point of view on stage rather than Leland's in the audience. After the stage hands, coaches, costume and make-up people leave the stage, Susan stands nearly alone, facing a rising curtain, bright lights, and an unseen, unsympathetic audience seated in the darkness beyond. Susan's fellow performers, standing near the wings of the stage, are barely visible and of little comfort to her. By filming the action in extreme long shot and from behind Susan, Welles both approximates her vantage point and evokes the vulnerability of her small figure against an overwhelming background. From this position we see a different show than the one Leland saw. The passionate, melodramatic music of the opera now speaks for *Susan's* terror rather than for the fictional predicament of her character.

Breaking away from Susan's point of view, unless we are seeing things from the vantage point of her imagination, the camera surveys the reactions of several members of the audience, beginning with a godlike close-up of Kane presiding over the event from a private box high up in the concert hall. His rigid smile expresses more determination than pleasure. Light from the stage illuminates his face. The heads of companions in the background remain in shadow. Susan's performance is Kane's ticket to public acceptance. A reverse angle shot shows the back of Kane's head in the foreground while the tiny figure of Susan Alexander struggles on stage far below him. Jed Leland, meanwhile, slouches in one of the cheaper seats on the main floor. He is more intrigued by his copy of the official program than by Susan's poor performance. And it *is* poor. During a pause in the singing the camera shoots her legs slinking across the stage in an unintentional parody of seductiveness. Those legs pass by the prompter's box, where Matisti squints his eyes in disgust. Next we see Bernstein and some of Kane's other cronies dutifully attending to the performance of their boss's wife. But the task proves too much for Bernstein, whose attention is soon distracted elsewhere. Opera is not his cup of tea. As this shot slowly dissolves into one of Susan on stage, images of Susan and Bernstein overlap, and he appears to look directly *away* from her. She senses his and the whole audience's rejection of her.

A lap dissolve transports us further along in Susan's performance. Matisti struggles with his mediocre student. Bernstein struggles to stay awake. Leland struggles against disgust and boredom by methodically shredding his program. Whether or not Susan notices these reactions from her audience, she certainly *feels* them. Kane, on the other hand, remains passionately riveted on his wife's performance, and is distracted only for a moment by the insulting comments made by someone nearby. Susan, both in vivid close-up and extreme long shot, the latter juxtaposing her small figure with Kane's large head, seems to beg her husband for mercy through her performance. We get two dramas for the price of one. But the audience seated in the opera house is not aware of Susan's subtext. Her private appeal to Kane, coming appropriately during a climax in the music, is very real and very powerful, but mixes with and is counterpointed by two comic reactions to her *public* performance. Leland completes his shredding job, which speaks eloquently of his disapproval. Matisti accidentally bangs his hand on the roof of the prompter's box in a vain effort to help Susan reach a difficult high note. These comic bits add plaintiveness to rather than detract from our appreciation of Susan's ordeal as she reaches up towards Kane while struggling to sustain a high note at the conclusion of the opera.

Accompanied by an orchestral flourish, Susan's character collapses and dies. The house lights come up. Leland does not applaud. The hands of spectators behind him offer only subdued, polite applause. Bernstein and Kane's other sycophants clap enthusiastically. Kane, in close-up, remains fixated on the stage and for a moment oblivious of the audience around him. The camera pulls back to show the tepid applause of his companions. Only when that applause fades, during the awkward presentation of a huge bouquet of flowers to the thin and frail-looking Susan, does he become aware of his surroundings. He stands and applauds with fierce determination, trying to impose his false enthusiasm on the rest of the audience. He fails. His clapping continues after everyone else's stops. Finally Kane too stops, suddenly self-conscious and embarrassed. *Citizen Kane* is a critical portrait of wealth, power, and arrogance carried to extremes. But it is also, especially at moments like this, a profoundly sympathetic portrait of human fallibility in general. Fallibility that in the cases of Charles Foster Kane and Susan Alexander is inflated by their celebrity.

Orson Welles thrived on sharp contrast, whether within a scene (pathos and comedy during Susan's performance) or between two scenes. A close-up of Jed Leland's *Inquirer* review of Susan's performance is accompanied by Susan's off screen voice screaming complaints at Kane, who by completing that review tried to impress Leland and ended up betraying Susan, whom he manipulated into an opera career in the first place. Satisfying one's personal needs all the time is a complicated business. As for Susan, the hapless figure of the previous scene is now fiercely aggressive, ripping into her husband for allowing Leland to spoil her debut. She has no idea that Kane completed Leland's review. For the moment she is the prototypical, egomaniacal artiste, expecting the world to fall at her feet, and her manager to see that it does. She has become another Kane, if less sophisticated and therefore less charming.

Kane, wearing a robe, smoking a pipe, sitting in a chair, trying to read his morning newspaper, looks like a henpecked husband, dominated by his shrieking wife. He winces under her verbal assault, and is relieved to be distracted by a knock at the door. But he is *not* relieved by the letter handed to him by the messenger who knocked. Quick and startling shots of Susan intrude on Kane as he reads the letter, which was sent by Leland. The former friend has returned the shredded remains of a $25,000 check that Kane sent to him. In retrospect, we realize that Kane's cruel firing of Leland back in the City Room of the *Chicago Daily Inquirer* was followed by a kind of apology in the form of a bribe. Note that Leland did not speak of that little detail during his interview with Thompson, thereby leaving both us and the reporter with a completely negative impression of Kane's behavior toward him. Nor did Leland reveal that along with the torn up check he included Kane's original Declaration of Principles, which he admired so long ago. Not telling Thompson about returning the Declaration to Kane was perhaps as much an attempt to assuage his own guilt as sending Leland a check for $25,000 was for Kane. The fact that both objects occupy the same envelope is another example of Welles's predilection for portraying the contradictions within his characters. *We* know, from his interview with Thompson, that Leland felt some regret at having rejected Kane so completely. But the rejected Kane will never know it.

Susan knows little about the circumstances of Kane and Leland's split. She is consumed by her own predicament. "You're awfully funny, aren't you!" is her unsympathetic response to Kane's rueful comment about the "antique" Declaration. She prattles on about her own problems while Kane, tearing up the Declaration as though emotionally turning his back on Jed Leland forever (we know, from Leland's interview, that Kane tries to renew their friendship after Susan divorces him), insists that she carry on with her singing. After all, what else does *he* have left? Leland's rejection reinvigorates Kane's determination to bury the past and pursue acceptance in the present, through Susan's career. "I don't propose to have myself made ridiculous" is how he characterizes his decision that she continue. She is a victim of forces she doesn't understand. Both characters are at this moment totally insensitive to the other's suffering. But Kane remains dominant, for the time being. As Susan's verbal protest rises to a crescendo, "Why don't you leave me alone!," Kane yells in rebuttal, "My reasons satisfy me, Susan!" Offering no explanation of those reasons, he just bullies her into compliance. Closing the physical gap between them, he literally overshadows her as he repeats his command that she continue to perform.

In contrast to our impression of her at the start of the scene, Susan again appears helpless, as she did at the end of the previous scene. She backs halfway out of Kane's imposing shadow. But that action is less a signal of her defiance than a means of allowing us to see the expression on her face, which is now more one of hopeless resignation than of desperate appeal for mercy, as it was during her performance on stage.

The agony of Susan's post-debut opera career is distilled into a brief but powerful montage of images and sounds. Front page stories from Kane newspapers spanning the country herald Susan's appearances. Accompanying those articles are publicity photos of the diva looking confident and seductive. These impressions overlap and are counterpointed by action shots of her performing on stage, looking inadequate and uncomfortable. Audiences from across the country sit in stony silence. Backstage lights repeatedly flicker off and on, signaling the start of many performances. Matisti repeatedly harangues Susan from the prompter's box. Kane repeatedly gazes down at her from his high perch in the audience. Susan's desperately inadequate voice, doubled and trebled as one performance overlaps another, gradually rises to an hysterical crescendo, chased by relentlessly pounding music that grows louder and louder. The aesthetic effect is cumulative. So too is the emotional effect on Susan.

The whole cacophonous montage crashes to a halt in a startling combination of visual and aural metaphors. The flickering backstage light breaks a filament and goes black while Susan's voice suddenly fades and grinds to a halt, like a record player switched off. The mechanical nature of these metaphors emphasizes the involuntary nature of Susan's emotional collapse. Kane reduced her to a performing machine and she breaks down like one. This astonishing, moving, yet abstract portrait of human frailty is followed by an equally moving but more realistic portrait of the consequences of Susan's breakdown. Peter Conrad, in *Orson Welles: The Stories of His Life*, claims that Welles brooded about James Whale's 1935 film *The Bride of Frankenstein* while making *Citizen Kane* (Conrad, pp.167–168). Whether that's true or not, Susan's opera montage breakdown finds a thematic and stylistic parallel in the emotional breakdown of the Female Creature in *Bride*. Both reluctant opera star and synthetic woman are in a sense manufactured by dynamic male characters who manipulate them to achieves goals the men are compulsively driven to pursue.

In Susan's darkened bedroom we see a tight shot of her shadowy, blurred face as she lies unconscious in bed. Her head, with its frazzled hair, is propped at an awkward angle. Her breathing is erratic and labored. Between her and the camera are a drinking glass with a spoon in it and an open medicine bottle. Susan has overdosed in an attempt to commit suicide.

Far in the background is the bedroom door. Sounds of knocking, the knob turning, pounding, and finally of a body heaving itself against the other side of that door follow in quick succession. But we, through the stationary camera on the side of the bed furthest from the door, remain as detached as Susan. The action at the door seems remote, until Kane and a servant burst through and Kane approaches the bed. Stunned, he examines Susan's face and orders his servant to fetch a doctor. He appears genuinely concerned, not selfishly annoyed, as he softly calls out Susan's name. Alfred Bazin (Bazin, p.82) describes this scene as a "sequence shot," or a static shot containing all the information necessary for interpretation. In most films prior to *Citizen Kane*, Bazin contends, that information would have been presented in a series of shots instead of just one. I would add that by anchoring the camera at Susan's bedside Welles keeps us more attuned to her suffering than to Kane's anxiety. And by doing so, Welles deepens our understanding of Kane's selfishness.

The camera angle remains unchanged as we advance to the next scene. A doctor's black bag replaces the glass, spoon, and medicine bottle in the extreme foreground. The gloomy shadows surrounding Susan's suicide attempt yield to brighter lighting as the doctor's bag is pulled away from in front of the camera. But while Susan sleeps fitfully under the bedcovers, Kane maneuvers to conceal the truth of the matter from the public. His suggestion that she accidentally drank the wrong substance, as a result of excitement and confusion, rather than deliberately, out of humiliation and terror at the thought of performing in another opera, is really a command to the doctor that the incident be officially interpreted as such. The concern Kane exhibited in the previous scene has quickly yielded to a more selfish priority. Kane has reverted to habit. The doctor, intimidated by Kane, is quick to concur, at the cost of his own professional ethics.

Kane's silent vigil at Susan's bedside returns us to his compassionate side. Several lap dissolves inform us that he watches over her throughout the night, until she awakens at dawn. In a tight shot we see her hair and face wet from her ordeal. Lit by sunlight from the window, she turns her head and sees Kane, a dark and vague figure leaning into the camera frame from the opposite side. She wearily explains to him her reason for trying to kill herself. "You don't know what it means to know that a whole audience just doesn't want you." But he does. It's just that their reactions to public rejection differ. "That's when you've got to fight them" insists the darker figure. A hint of panic spreads across Susan's face. But in a reverse angle shot the dark figure of Kane looks human again, and sounds merciful, promising Susan that she won't have to sing in public anymore. By adding, "It's their loss," Kane perpetuates the fantasy with which he launched Susan's career in the first place. After failing to win public acceptance in politics, he desperately tried to do so in the arts. By insisting that the end of Susan's career is the public's loss, he indirectly blames *her* inability to persevere for his second failure to win public approval. Nevertheless, Susan is greatly relieved when Kane relents. As she slowly recovers we can just barely hear, in the background, a gentle, bittersweet version of the aria Susan practiced before her opera debut, to the dissatisfaction of her singing coach. It is reminiscent of the soft version of Kane's campaign song heard as a drunken Leland approached the *Inquirer* building after Kane's defeat. Both pieces of music offer stark, melancholy counterpoint to their original renditions.

A shortened, two shot version of the camera's first approach to Xanadu recaptures a little of the opening scene's funereal atmosphere. Inside the castle the marriage of Kane and Susan has ground to a halt. Always searching out dramatic contrasts, Welles gives us a portrait of Susan Alexander as different from the pathetic suicide case as the suicide case was from the angry diva berating her husband for the bad review she got in his newspaper. An over the shoulder close-up of Susan working on a jigsaw puzzle pulls back a little to reveal a portrait of both wealth (the diamond tiara in her hair) and boredom.

Kane arrives during the next shot. The cavernous Xanadu magnifies certain qualities of the two characters and their relationship. Viewed initially from a great distance, Kane looks tiny and his voice sounds thin. The camera pans with him as he crosses over to a huge fireplace where Susan sits working on her puzzle. His walk is slow and arthritic. He is thicker around the middle than when we last saw him. Herrmann's background music matches the desultory, static mood of Kane's world. There is a fire in the mammoth hearth, but not much in Kane himself. Susan, on the other hand, has found new life since we last saw her. She still looks young. She fantasizes aloud about the night life in New York and complains about her inactive existence at Xanadu. Her complaint is whiny, irritating, and unsophisticated. But understandable. Harlan Lebo points out that the statue of a woman next to the fireplace and behind Susan is a larger duplicate of the one appearing on a table beside Kane's chair in an earlier scene where Susan sings for him in the parlor of the apartment he rented for her (Lebo, p.65). Metaphorically Susan is Kane's pretty statue—someone to have around for display. In the present scene the shadowy figure of a hideous gargoyle seems to menace the female statue. Whatever her character flaws, Susan does not deserve to be a prisoner of Kane's needs.

Still possessing his verbal wit, even if he is physically diminished, Kane offers a smart rebuttal for each of his wife's complaints. But when she in turn complains about his habit of making a joke out of everything, she strikes a nerve. His smile fades and he walks away from her. Joking is one of his defense mechanisms, and he doesn't like to be reminded of it. Fleeing from his wife's increasingly whiny pleas, Kane retreats to the fireplace. He turns his back to it as though to warm his arthritic joints. But from a distance the fireplace looks vaguely like a giant mouth about to swallow its owner. He is a prisoner of his own impulses. Kane rejects Susan's pleas with quiet firmness. Xanadu is his home now and he doesn't intend to leave it. In a way, Xanadu is the prior equivalent to the paperweight snow scene into which Kane imaginatively retreats at the end of his life, after Susan leaves him and Xanadu is no longer a sanctuary for him. But for now the castle remains his private fortress. As Leland told Thompson, "He was disappointed in the world so he built one of his own. An absolute monarchy." Xanadu is the expensive product of Kane's emotional withdrawal from all human relationships save one. And that one is compelled to share his prison cell with him. Kane is as determined now to barricade himself and Susan inside Xanadu as he once was to foist himself, through her, upon the inhospitable world of grand opera.

A quick montage of six shots, accompanied by the musical equivalent of a ticking clock, show Susan's hands working on various puzzles. Each shot is taken from an angle different from its neighbors, and shows different jewels on Susan's wrist and fingers. As the old song says, she's only a bird in a gilded cage. Each puzzle depicts an exotic, far-off locale — wishful dreams of escape.

Later, Kane descends an enormous staircase, starkly lit by high contrast lighting that highlights every detail of Xanadu's interior, giving it tremendous texture. We can *feel* this overwhelming environment in all its hollow splendor. Splendor consisting of, according to Robert Carringer (Carringer, *Kane*, p.61), a hodgepodge of architectural and artistic styles. Kane's appetite for collecting is omnivorous. The background music is again bleak and static — the musical equivalent of a mausoleum. As the camera pans to the right with Kane, Susan is brought into the frame, reclining on the floor near the fireplace, working on yet another puzzle. She seems miles distant from her husband, and emotionally is. Kane asks, "What are you doing?," which is the same line he spoke in the first puzzle scene. It is as if neither character had any contact with the other between those two scenes. A low angle shot of Susan pictures her surrounded by visually prominent inanimate objects, including a large bellows and two statues. She is more than ever, from Kane's point of view, just part of the decor. One piece out of *Kane's* private, enormous jigsaw puzzle. Placing her next to the bellows, which is essentially a windbag, may be Welles's sly comment on Susan's inclination to nag. But her ability to occasionally, sometimes fiercely stand up for herself, regardless of her sometimes irritating manner, earns her both respect and sympathy, and certainly puts demands on Dorothy Commingore as an actor. Her Susan Alexander is *Citizen Kane*'s equivalent of Vivien Leigh's Blanche DuBois in *A Streetcar Named Desire*, and the polar opposite of Desdemona in Welles's screen adaptation of *Othello*.

Kane sits in a chair so far from the fireplace that he and Susan have to yell at each other to be heard. The camera alternates between nearly subjective shots from the perspectives of both characters. Another pointless debate commences. Kane inquires how Susan can be certain she hasn't done the same puzzle more than once. His implied criticism of the pointlessness of her hobby is hypocritical for two reasons. First, by isolating her at Xanadu he compels her to find her own, solitary amusement. Second, we see no evidence of variety in *his* activities at Xanadu either. Susan effectively retaliates by debunking Kane's hobby of collecting statues, and he concedes the point, describing it as a habit. At least Susan *enjoys* her puzzles. Kane seems more interested in accumulating than appreciating his art collection. And the same goes for his collection of people.

Kane's proposal of a picnic with some friends is a small concession to Susan's desire for excitement. It is less a concession than a tip for services rendered, as Leland once described Kane's brand of generosity. Susan has every right to be bitter about her marriage, and yet her harsh rejection of Kane's offer seems cruel, partly because of his advancing age and feebleness. Complaining about the inconvenience of camping out in a tent and giving up the comforts of home, Susan too proves a hypocrite. In spite of her lack of freedom, she is accustomed to the life of luxury Kane provides. But when she describes her husband's offer to friends to join them on a picnic as a command rather than an invitation, she hits the nail on the head. And her criticism is validated by the final shot of the scene. Shooting from behind Kane, whose huge chair is a veritable throne, the camera depicts Susan as barely discernable amidst the clutter of Kane's possessions. Ignoring her complaint, Kane falls back on his power to compel. Above his head, on his side of the fireplace, is a large male statue. The female statue stands on the other side. Widely separated, the statues also face in opposite directions, reflecting the lack of communication between Kane and Susan, who face and speak to each other but with little in the way of understanding or sympathy. They are not much different than Kane and Emily at the end of the breakfast montage.

A frontal medium shot of Susan and Kane seated in the back of their chauffeured limousine, on their way to the picnic, is a grotesquely comic portrait of their disintegrating marriage. Both characters are fashionably dressed in expensive clothes and similar hats. Both stare blankly ahead. But there the resemblance ends. "You never give me anything I really care about," Susan whines. Kane glances at her but does not respond, perhaps unable to come up with an effective rebuttal. Of course, there is some irony in Susan's expression of discontent while wearing the fancy clothes Kane bought for her. I wonder if Stanley Kubrick had this scene in mind when he filmed Redmond Barry and Lady Lyndon in a carriage, returning home after their wedding, in *Barry Lyndon*.

The loud, brassy music in this scene mocks both Kane's tyrannical, elephantine notion of a picnic as well as Susan's hypocrisy. It is particularly effective in the second shot. A heavy, safari-like rhythm in the low notes accompanies a long line of black automobiles trailing behind Kane's along a Florida beach. Obligated to participate in Kane's desperate, ponderous effort to hang on to his young wife by keeping her amused, the couple's friends, or parasitic entourage as the case may be, tag along behind. Their parade of automobiles looks more like a funeral procession than a picnic.

A close-up of a black man singing a blues number opens the picnic scene. "It can't be love, for there is no true love," etc., is an appropriately pessimistic theme song for Kane's failed and failing excursions into romance. The singer turns away from the camera and saunters back to his all black band. Carefree white couples dance nearby or sit gathered around the band, enjoying the music. The camera then tracks left with Kane's butler, Raymond, as he scrutinizes the festivities, passing a formal dining table, complete with candelabra. A roasting pig turns on a spit over an open fire. The Florida Everglades forms an exotic backdrop to this exhibition of material splendor and shallow cynicism. Shallow, that is, for the guests, but not necessarily for the band, who play their blues with conviction.

Slowly the camera dollies past the anachronism of patrician elegance, plebeian music, and raw nature, zeroing in on one of the tents in the far background. Animated birds glide between and around the tents, looking like prehistoric pterodactyls from another great RKO movie, *King Kong* (1933). An appropriate prelude to the domestic battle about to take place inside the protagonist's tent. A worn out Kane slumps in his chair, listening to his

Citizen Kane. **Kane (Orson Welles) and Susan (Dorothy Comingore) try to communicate within the vast expanse of Xanadu. The male and female statues visually linked to them, and facing away from each other, symbolize their failure.**

still young and feisty wife harangue him about the state of their marriage. Susan, closer to the camera, appears larger than her husband. Her complaint is the usual one, simply phrased but deadly accurate: "Oh, sure, you give me things. But that don't mean anything to you!" Kane, in a weary voice, does not challenge her. He merely asks her not to be so loud. She ignores him, continuing in the same vein and at the same volume. He tells her to stop. She doesn't. Summoning what remains of his old, domineering self, Kane rises from his chair and shouts back. Meanwhile, outside, the unsentimental song about love reaches a pounding climax. The young guests gathered around the band clap to the music. They enjoy the rhythm, but comprehend little of the sentiment expressed earlier in the lyrics. They resemble Kane, Leland, and Bernstein at the start of the *Inquirer* enterprise more than they do the quarreling couple in the tent.

Back inside that tent, Kane stands over a kneeling Susan, once again visually dominating her. Behind him are the ornate patterns of the tent fabric and a decorative lamp. With his bald head and almond shaped eyes, Kane looks like an oriental potentate of old—the absolute ruler of his empire. But looks are deceiving. A close-up of Susan pictures a *defiant* subject, her eyes unblinking and her jaw set. Kane's half-whisper conveys little strength as he tries to pacify her. "Whatever I do, I do because I love you." Susan rejects that claim in almost the same words Jed Leland used against him after the political campaign debacle years earlier. Kane doesn't love her, she insists. He simply tries to buy *her* love. The camera remains in close-up on her as she receives Kane's reply — a sharp slap across the face. Susan's remark cut to the bone, and he reacts accordingly. The truth hurts both of them, in different ways. Susan, however, recovers composure quickly, which she failed to do in the scene where Kane verbally browbeat her into continuing her opera career after her disastrous debut. She refuses to accept an apology from him. He tells her he has none to give. Neither backs down or attempts to reconcile this time. They have reached a stalemate.

While Kane and Susan spar, "It Can't Be Love" plays in the background. The two characters are a sad confirmation of the song's lyrical message. After Kane slaps his wife, the song ends and is displaced by the faint, off screen sound of a woman screaming, apparently with glee. Perhaps the result of happy guests enjoying themselves. But when isolated from its visual source and heard in the context of Kane slapping Susan, the scream becomes Susan's surrogate protest of her husband's abuse. And in a broader context, the hysterical laughter of a young woman having fun, perhaps with her lover, carries us back to the first scene in Susan Alexander's apartment, where a dashing and much younger Charlie Kane chased away the pain of Susan's toothache by making *her* laugh. Sound and image in the present scene combine in a magical way to evoke past and present simultaneously. The dissolution of Kane and Susan's relationship into bitter recrimination and violence is rendered more tragic by a subtle, indirect reminder of its happy beginnings.

Susan gets her revenge at Xanadu. On his way to inform his boss that Susan wants to see him in her bedroom, Raymond walks past a large, stained glass window. One of the images depicted on that window is an eye. Raymond is one of many eyes through which we catch glimpses of the life of Charles Foster Kane. Collectively those glimpses resemble the whole window — a jagged mosaic of contradictions.

The camera pans right with Raymond as he walks down a hallway from foreground to background, encountering and then following Kane from background to foreground. By staging the movement of characters in depth within a single shot, Welles reinforces our impression of Xanadu's great size. Adding to that impression is the slight echo effect when Raymond speaks.

Statues from various historical periods and in various artistic styles are visible at various distances from the camera. Some are in shadow and some are brightly lit, again emphasizing the visual depth of field. The statues are also inanimate stand-ins for the many *real* people who have come and gone in Kane's life. Xanadu is a metaphorical portrait of the protagonist's long life. On a more immediate level, statues are for Kane easier to deal with than people. They do not disappoint, but neither do they offer much comfort. One of the living props that Kane chooses to ignore is Raymond, until the butler mentions Susan's summons. Kane winces, anticipating her intention. Informed that Susan's maid has been packing her things since morning, Kane departs without a word. The butler watches him go.

At the start of the next scene, Kane, heavily shadowed in extreme foreground, opens the door to Susan's room, which by contrast is brightly lit. Note that this time, unlike the scene involving Susan's suicide attempt, we perceive the entrance from Kane's point of view rather than Susan's. And what a difference in Susan herself between those scenes. She and her maid are comparatively small figures in the background as Kane enters. But counterpointing his visual prominence, Susan boldly declares her intention to leave Xanadu immediately. After the maid exits, Kane reacts angrily to his wife's impropriety, slamming the door in our face as he notes that their guests will know what she's done. At this stage in his life, Kane sounds rather like Emily Kane worrying about the propriety of staying up and attending parties all night. Unlike the maid, Raymond, and the unseen guests at Xanadu, and thanks to Susan's recollection of what happens next, we get to eavesdrop on the final break-up of a marriage. The camera takes us inside Susan's bedroom.

Standing in front of Susan's open suitcase lying on the bed, Kane seems dwarfed by the instrument of her departure as he protests her action. Judging by his words he seems less afraid of losing Susan's companionship than of appearing to the public as too old, impotent, and foolish to hang onto her. In a side view of their confrontation Susan is uncharacteristically calm, resolute, and sophisticated. In the foreground, on Susan's side of the screen, is a porcelain doll lying on the bed. Susan has seemed childlike ever since Kane met her, and he has treated her accordingly. But she certainly seems grown-up now. Ironically, her cool demeanor matches the doll's face, yet the doll is one of the possessions she leaves behind at Xanadu.

Kane tries to prevent his wife's departure by embracing her. It is the first and only time we witness an overtly romantic gesture between them. And it fails, pathetically. Susan pulls away. From the camera's low angle perspective we see animal figures painted on the ceiling crossbeams—another visual suggestion that this is the room of a child rather than an adult. But the child has grown up and learned to defy her parent.

A shot of Susan pausing near the door, the back of her head visible in the foreground, while Kane humbly begs her to stay from the background, reverses their positions from the beginning of the scene. But Kane cannot help being Kane. He moves closer to Susan, visually dominating her again. A moment later he modifies, or clarifies, his plea. "You can't do this to me" undercuts his previous humility by dumping all blame for her departure on Susan. In reaction shots Susan appears genuinely touched by her husband's appeal, until that little qualification proves to her that nothing about his attitude has changed, or ever will.

With a quiet touch of cruelty, of which she was incapable until now, Susan opens the door and walks out of Kane's life. He watches her recede into the far background, framed by the ornate archways of Xanadu, within which he tried unsuccessfully to imprison her. The scene began with Kane as a large figure in the foreground berating a smaller Susan in the background. The scenes ends with the same visual disproportion, but a tactical and emotional reversal. Susan triumphs by steadfastly walking away from Kane, and from the camera that is for the moment subjectively tied to his wounded ego. By showing us her departure from Kane's point of view, Welles encourages us to feel his pain at yet another, if well-deserved, abandonment. From a dramatic standpoint it would have been foolishly constrictive for Welles to limit his camera to the point of view of the character reminiscing about Kane. Besides, as we soon discover, Susan is very capable, in retrospect, of feeling sorry for the man who treated her so badly.

The image of Susan's departure loses focus like a dissolving dream as the camera returns to her interview with Thompson at the El Rancho. Susan lights up a cigarette as though, in classic cinema terms at least, she had just enjoyed a satisfying sexual experience. Recollecting her liberation from Kane may be even better than sex. It is also the first time we've seen Susan smoke. She's come a long way since the naive and sweet girl she was when she first met Kane.

Susan snuffs out her cigarette and picks up her glass of booze. Celebration of one particular, satisfying memory is displaced by a desire to forget the past in broader terms. That Susan consented to be interviewed by Thompson contradicts her initial reaction to his request. Now she not only answers his questions, she points him in the direction of Kane's butler, who "knows where all the bodies are buried." Behind Susan we see chairs piled on top of tables, which was not the case when the interview began. It is a purely visual indication that the interview has lasted a long time.

Another of Susan's contradictions is her attitude towards wealth. During much of her marriage to Kane, even when they argued, Susan seemed to relish the material comforts he provided for her. In the present scene, however, she dismisses the loss of her sizable divorce settlement as trivial. Ten years of economic depression are to her nothing compared to decades of emotional tyranny by Kane. Yet when Thompson expresses pity for the man who oppressed her, Susan reveals her final contradiction. "Don't you think I do?" she says quietly, looking Thompson straight in the eye. Her own eyes are heavily ringed with the burden of more than just age. She follows her comment with a stiff drink. Like Leland, she feels guilt as well as resentment, anger, disappointment, and nostalgia when she thinks about Charles Foster Kane.

Tilting her head up to take a drink, Susan notices sunshine peeking through the skylight off screen. "It's morning already," she remarks in a voice full of false cheer. Contradicting that verbal cheer, she pulls her coat tighter around her body. It's a big, cold, cruel world out there, as it was outside Leland's hospital sun deck and Bernstein's corporate office. The camera pulls up and away from Susan, withdrawing from her life along the same route it approached. She half-jokingly suggests that Thompson return someday and tell her the story of *his* life. Despite her initial hostility, she has drawn a measure of comfort from the interview, just as Bernstein and Leland did from theirs. Thompson's mercenary mission has been therapeutic for them. For a short while their lives have re-acquired some vitality and value, if only in relation to their acquaintances with Kane.

The camera's elaborate withdrawal from Susan Alexander is a measure of the deep privacy of the thoughts and feelings which we glimpsed. It is neither simple nor easy to know someone intimately. Herrmann's background music reminds us of the fragility of that intimacy as we part company with Susan. Dorothy Commingore's astonishingly convincing performance in this scene conveys all the nuances of her complex character.

The black outline of the neon sign on the roof of Susan's nightclub sanctuary stands out sharply against the bright morning sky, matching the black outline of the giant "K" atop the main gate at Xanadu, Kane's last refuge, which opens the next scene. The difference between the two images is that Susan's name on the El Rancho sign is now obscured by darkness, reflecting her return to obscurity from the points of view of Thompson, of us, and of the public at large. Kane's giant "K," by contrast, is still prominent, as echoed by Herrmann's big, brassy re-statement of the protagonist's power motif.

Inside Xanadu, Thompson questions Raymond about Rosebud. The butler's face is at first concealed by shadow, except when fitfully lit by the flicker of a match as he lights a cigarette. Unlike the other interviewees, Raymond reveals nothing about his private life. His disclosures are as mercenary in their purpose as was Rawlston's motive for sending Thompson off in search of Rosebud. "How much is it worth to you?" he asks, getting right to the point. One can imagine old Charlie Kane, after Susan's departure, spending his last years being spied upon and perhaps even manipulated by this crafty butler, who makes even Walter P. Thatcher look warm by comparison.

Peddling information for a thousand dollars, Raymond steps into the light and glances back at Thompson, enticing the reporter with the prospect of enlightenment about Rosebud. Thompson consents and reluctantly follows Raymond down a large staircase towards the great hall where earlier we watched Kane and Susan's estrangement play out. The butler brags of being in charge of Xanadu, puffing up his importance in anticipation of a big payoff. Insolently stubbing out his cigarette on a marble column, he further boasts that he knew how to "handle" the "old man" when Kane "acted kind of funny." "Kind of funny" is about the extent of Raymond's insight into Kane's character. As usual, Welles's camera and soundtrack give us more than does his storyteller. In Raymond's case, *much* more.

Welles once stated (Welles/Bogdanovich, p.72) that the screaming cockatoo in the extreme foreground of the shot where Susan, observed by Raymond, walks across a veranda overlooking the ocean and out of Kane's life had no other meaning than to wake up his audience at this late stage of the movie. Maybe. But the screeching bird also metaphorically echoes the emotional shock to Kane inflicted by Susan's departure. A member of Kane's animal menagerie speaks for its master, just as a burned out back stage light spoke for Susan's distress at the conclusion of the opera montage. Susan's desertion is a blow from which Kane will never recover.

As viewed by Raymond, the figure of Kane standing in the doorway of Susan's bedroom is minuscule. The camera, carrying us beyond the butler's point of view, cuts to a much closer shot of Kane as he unsteadily returns inside the room and packs the last of Susan's suitcases. A low camera angle accentuates the stiffness of his movements, the oppressiveness of the cheerfully painted ceiling, and then the fury of Kane's subsequent rage. His fumbling agitation slips into fury as Kane hurls piece after piece of Susan's luggage out the open door. He *will* have the last word in their dispute, by rejecting his wife more spectacularly than she did him. This scene is equivalent to Kane firing Leland and before that Kane telling Emily that he intends to stay with Susan. Bug-eyed with anger, Kane looks both powerful and pathetic as he destroys everything in the room that reminds him of Susan. Among those items is a bottle of booze hidden behind books on a shelf. Kane scarcely gives it a glance before throwing it across the room. *We*, however, perceive the bottle as one of Susan's methods of escape from the pain Kane, however unintentionally, inflicted on her. Perhaps the books too, and there are many of them, were another means of escape.

Kane's rampage sweeps back and forth and up and down through the room until it stops, abruptly, in the extreme foreground of the camera frame. His hand and arm are all we see of him as he pauses, then picks up the glass paperweight we saw twice earlier in the film: once in Susan's first apartment and once in Kane's hand at the moment of his death. By restricting our present view of Kane to his hand and arm, Welles focuses our attention on the character's change of heart, and the trigger for that change. Kane's hand and the glass ball say all we need to know. Grasping the paperweight, Kane walks away from the camera until his face and body too are entirely visible. He stops to look at the object in his hand.

In a tight frontal shot that again excludes his face, Kane's definition of and emotional attachment to the paperweight is conveyed by his softly spoken "Rosebud" and by the firm manner in which he grasps the object. He turns the glass ball over in his hand. It's fake snow springs to life. The shiny metal "K" hanging from Kane's vest has flipped upside down during his rampage, symbolizing the toppling of his imperial reign in the present as a result of Susan's rebellion. The paperweight snow scene, and what it represents to Kane, triggers Kane's subsequent retreat into the past, although we don't recognize that fact until later. And in keeping with Welles's love of dramatic contradiction, Kane finds the inspiration for his consolation among the belongings of his now despised and soon to be former wife.

The camera slowly tilts up to show Kane's face. His mouth opens. His eyes are wet with tears. He has never looked older. In a reverse angle shot Raymond leads a concerned or perhaps merely curious crowd of servants gathered outside the bedroom door. The camera returns to a close-up of Kane. When he returned to the *New York Inquirer* offices after his European vacation, and again when he emerged from an auditorium after delivering a rousing campaign speech, the camera backtracked with Kane, conveying to us the force of his personality and will. Now, to the hushed accompaniment of the Rosebud motif, the camera retreats in the face of Kane's trance-like exit from Susan's bedroom. Oblivious of the people gathered around him, and slipping the glass paperweight into his pocket, he withdraws completely into himself. He shuffles forward through a vaulted corridor, past ornately framed mirrors on opposing walls. The camera angle shows us Kane reflected again and again, to infinity, in those mirrors. His footsteps sound hollow on the cold, hard floor. Kane is utterly alone, with a thousand contradictory variations of himself. Variations supplied by his former friends and lovers, by himself, and by the relentless march of time that subtly alters and in the end extinguishes memory. The camera lingers on the mirrors after Kane passes out of the frame, leaving nothing but multiplied images of emptiness. Anticipating Kane's death, this chilling impression also evokes a world depopulated of family, friends, and lovers. But if this is *our* perception of Kane, Kane himself has found consolation in another image. At a terrible cost, he has found peace. Like anyone who cannot bear the situation in which he finds himself, Kane manufactures a better one. The opera house was a retreat from politics. Xanadu was a retreat from the opera. Rosebud is a retreat from Xanadu.

We return to Thompson's interview with Raymond. In an unsympathetic, matter-of-fact voice, the butler recounts a second time he heard Kane say "Rosebud," shortly before dying. Adding that Kane said "all kinds of things that didn't mean anything," the butler reduces Rosebud to insignificance and betrays his own colossal insensitivity to and ignorance of Kane's private life. Bernstein, Leland, and Susan did not know precisely what Rosebud meant to Kane, but they all possessed some insight into the protagonist's character, and therefore prepared *us* to better understand Kane's emotional attachment to Rosebud when its literal meaning is revealed. Thompson mocks the butler's attitude by sarcastically describing it as sentimental. That Thompson bothers to note Raymond's callousness is a measure of his own increased sensitivity since the start of his investigation. The reporter has discovered both more and less than the object of his quest.

Thompson punishes Raymond's mercenary efforts by refusing to pay for the butler's inadequate information about Rosebud. He walks away. Raymond tags along, still angling for a payoff. As the camera pulls back into a high angle extreme long shot, their conversation gets absorbed into the larger tableau of Xanadu's Great Hall, littered with Kane's belongings and crawling with reporters and photographers, each looking for a scoop about the castle's deceased owner. They look like ants scrambling over spilled sugar. Overlapping dialog among the reporters reveals many different and largely trivial concerns. No one person is capable of emotionally or intellectually filling this huge, cavernous space. From a camera perspective close to Thompson's, we look up at two men on a second story walkway above the Great Hall—far, far away. They carry on a brief and notably banal conversation with some of their colleagues on the floor below.

Standing beside each other, Raymond is brightly lit while Thompson stands in shadow—a visual contrast marking the difference in their emotional perspectives as the butler asks the reporter what he thinks Kane's property is worth. "Millions, if anybody wants it," replies Thompson, implying that by a criterion other than purely financial Kane's property is nearly valueless to anyone but its dead, former owner. The camera tracks the two men as they stroll through some of those possessions, including many statues. Raymond, still currying favor with Thompson, puts what he thinks is a less mercenary spin on his own point of view, remarking that at least Kane brought all this art to America. But that observation ignores Kane's selfish motive for doing so. And a passing comment by one of the other reporters about one of Kane's Venus statues ("Twenty-five thousand bucks. That's a lot of money to pay for a dame without a head.") undercuts Raymond's claim to cultural enrichment for the nation.

Our camera tour of Kane's possessions continues, adding *Inquirer* office gifts and family relics to the eclectic collection. Kane's "Welcome Home" trophy shares space with a two dollar pot-bellied stove from Mary Kane's Boarding House. The latter was probably one of the items Kane was going to look at in a New York warehouse when he was sidetracked by his first encounter with Susan. Description of those items by the reporters inventorying Kane's property conveys nothing of the emotional significance they once had for Kane — significance *we* now appreciate because of Thompson's interviews. To one reporter the trophy and the stove are "junk" mixed in with valuable "art." But in a dramatic context, the former are much more valuable than the latter. Thompson and Raymonds' trek through the relics of Kane's life acquires an entourage as other reporters gather round and ask for an assessment of Kane's passion for collecting things. Raymond, typically shallow, compares his former employer to a crow. Thompson, nearest the camera, facing the other reporters but with his face still largely concealed from view by shadows and by his hat (he now too, like the film's major characters, has acquired the depth of mystery), speculates more compassionately that all of Kane's possessions add up to Charles Foster Kane. One of his compatriots jokes, "Or Rosebud? How 'bout it, Jerry?" That draws a collective chuckle from the assembled reporters. But Thompson's demeanor remains sober, more respectful of the subject of his investigation.

The camera slowly pulls away from the group as the scene draws to a conclusion, just as it withdrew from Susan at the end of her interview. At the same time, Thompson takes a box of jigsaw puzzle pieces from the hands of a colleague and slowly separates *himself* from the group. The puzzle pieces probably belonged to Susan, and for a moment Thompson handles them like sacred relics. One of the other reporters comments optimistically, like Rawlston in the projection room scene, that solving the mystery of Rosebud would explain *everything* about Kane.

Thompson disagrees. He speculates that Rosebud might have been "something he couldn't get or something he lost," but insists that discovering what it was could not fully explain Charles Foster Kane. "I don't think any word can explain a man's life" refers to *all* men, not just the protagonist. Manufacturing a metaphor out of one of Susan's precious possessions, he compares Rosebud to a missing piece in a jigsaw puzzle. This proves an insightful metaphor, even after Rosebud's identity is revealed. There is a touch of melancholy in Thompson's voice as he offers his metaphor to the other reporters. Visually he is surrounded by countless, scattered pieces of the Kane puzzle.

The camera withdraws further and further from the reporters. Thompson puts on his coat and leads them out of Xanadu. "We'll miss the train" marks the official end of his quest, and of his emotional link to Kane. The reporters, like Kane and each of his former acquaintances who shared their memories of him, part company and go their separate ways, emphasizing again the fragility of the ties that bind.

Thompson and his colleagues wend their way through and out of Kane's maze of "junk" and "art." The camera and the background music linger behind, taking us further *into* that private puzzle. The camera dissolves to a high angle shot of Kane's vast collection, now occupying every square inch of the frame. That image in turn dissolves smoothly into the next shot, picturing the same collection but from a closer range. Reinforced by the awestruck music, the camera glides over the accumulated relics of Kane's life as it might over the ruins of an extinct civilization. The reporters and Raymond are gone. There is no one but us left to appreciate the haunting majesty of it all. A lifetime of memories and associations, now jumbled together with little rhyme or reason, stretches out before us.

Inching closer and closer to Kane's possessions as it glides above them, the camera zeroes in on an old wooden sled deposited next to a pair of family photographs: one of Kane as a child standing next to his mother, the other of Kane as a young adult with a deceptively happy smile on his face. Two very different slices of one life, side by side. Suddenly a pair of anonymous hands enters the frame, grabs the sled, and hauls it away. The camera now *cuts* to the next shot, deliberately breaking the magical mood of its predecessors. It and we anxiously pursue the man with the sled. He remains faceless and anonymous as he tosses the sled into Xanadu's fiery furnace. "Throw that junk" orders Raymond, supervising the disposal activity from nearby. The sled joins other remnants of Kane's past being tossed into the furnace by other indifferent hands. What a wonderful moment of poetic justice. The one interviewee who wanted to profit from Thompson's search for Rosebud has no idea that he just ordered its destruction.

Ignoring the ignorant butler and indifferent laborers, the camera travels to the mouth of the furnace and shows us the word "Rosebud" printed on the top of the sled. With the Rosebud motif screaming out of the soundtrack, protesting the destruction of so emotionally potent if financially worthless a relic, the camera cuts to an extreme close-up, and then dollies even closer. The death of the object of Kane's dying thoughts is slow and agonizing, as though in death Kane himself were fighting extinction. Layer after layer of paint on the sled bubbles and evaporates in the heat, until the word "Rosebud" disappears forever.

The camera cuts to a shot outside Xanadu. From an extremely low angle we look up at black smoke emanating from the furnace, spewing out the castle's chimney and dispersing in the air. Kane's power motif, played by full orchestra, trumpets the tragic end of not just a great, and greatly flawed, public figure, but the common end of each one of us. It is extraordinary that the most potent symbol of that end is the casual disposal of a simple, inexpensive, overlooked toy. A piece of "junk" that for us alone adds one more piece to the Charles Foster Kane puzzle. Thompson was right. Rosebud does not explain the entirety of Kane's life. But it does explain the final, private thoughts and perhaps the last few desolate years of that life. In the wake of Susan's desertion, Kane's yearning for the love and security of a lost childhood may well be a sentimental fantasy. Maybe being raised by Mary and Jim Kane would have been worse, not better, than a childhood with Thatcher and Company. It is impossible to judge from the sketchy evidence provided by the boarding house scene in Colorado. Joseph McBride isn't even certain that Mary Kane sent her son away in order to shield him from Jim (McBride, p.42). The important fact here is that Kane *believed* he had lost out on a happier life as a result of being sent away from home. And that belief profoundly affected his relations with other people and with the world at large.

Reversing its tilt from up to down, and dissolving from the smoke of Kane's burning possessions to the chain link fence surrounding Xanadu, the camera returns to its point of origin, back where the movie began, to a close-up of the "No Trespassing" sign. Just as we withdrew from Susan's life in the same manner we intruded upon it, so we do now from Kane's. Despite its forbidding black letters, we ignored the sign's warning and, through the magic of great acting, powerful music, and various film techniques, attained the illusion of intimacy with the person who erected that sign. "No Trespassing" is our jumping off point into and out of that magical illusion.

A final shot of the gigantic "K" atop the gate to Kane's estate, with Xanadu still emitting black smoke far in the distance, reminds us that Rosebud is now a *permanent* mystery. Egyptian hieroglyphics without a Rosetta Stone. Kane's life as a whole will become less and less a knowable thing and more and more a public commodity and myth as time goes by and his old acquaintances die off.

Bernard Herrmann's music wraps things up with a big chord in a major key, aesthetically removing us from the previous mood of mystery, intimacy, and tragedy. Ringing down the curtain still further on his magic act, Welles gives us a formal introduction to the cast members who so memorably brought their characters to life in *Citizen Kane*. Performing lines of their original dialog, but in a slightly different manner, the actors seem a bit off—less convincing than they were within the framework of the story. And the rousing exit music supplied by Herrmann reinforces that impression. Welles accomplishes two different goals at the same time: providing his Mercury players with some well-deserved publicity, and sending his audience out of the theater with a reminder of how powerfully moving and fragile the filmed illusion of reality can be.

In his 1972 movie *F for Fake* Welles remarks that "Almost any story is some kind of lie." In the first scene of that film, Welles, dressed in a magician's cape, performs a trick for a young boy at a train station. He changes a key into a coin, then changes the coin back into a key. In *Citizen Kane* he does something similar, transforming a tin-plated, superficial, newsreel portrait of Charles Foster Kane into a rich, multidimensional, keenly intimate collage of the same subject. Then, at the end of the story, he reminds us that this brilliant illusion was all done with a bag of tricks. Which doesn't diminish the reality or profundity of the magic. But it does encourage us to be aware of art's potential for deception, which is what *F for Fake* is all about. "I must believe that art itself is real," says Welles late in the film, quoting a dying art forger, who in the end turns out to be nothing but a forgery himself. And therefore so is the quote. Or is it? Just because the quote is falsely attributed to a phony character doesn't mean its content has no validity, any more than a novel or short story has no roots in reality because it is fictional.

Late in *F for Fake* Welles walks between two enormous glass lenses, which from the camera's perspective distort his figure. I am reminded of a similar occurrence near the beginning of *Citizen Kane*, when we first see Kane's private nurse as a distorted reflection in a fragment of the broken glass paperweight Kane dropped from his hand when he died. Kane's attempt to *direct* his entire adult life—to stage manage, costume, light, and even score the characters and events in his private production—is not far different from what Welles did in his movies. Except that Kane seldom if ever acknowledged or perhaps even recognized the tricks and deceptions behind his colossal efforts. In the end he gazed into a crystal ball and believed everything he saw there.

2

The Magnificent Ambersons:
A House Divided

The Magnificent Ambersons (1942) is one of the most difficult of Orson Welles's films to assess, *as* a Welles film, because of the extensive revisions made to it during post-production. In *The Magnificent Ambersons: A Reconstruction* Robert L. Carringer provided a text to work from, based on the March 12th, 1942 cutting continuity derived from a version of the film that existed when Welles left work on the project to go to South America on assignment for the United States government. There is disagreement about who was more responsible for instigating that trip, the government or Welles himself, and about what delayed Welles's return to Hollywood to defend his besieged masterpiece. Whatever the case may be, the movie eventually released to the public runs approximately eighty-eight minutes. The longer, March 12th version ran just under 132 minutes. Between the two many scenes were cut, rearranged, and added without authorization by Welles. Also added was some new music neither composed nor supervised by Bernard Herrmann. But if Welles had retained control of *Ambersons*, what final form would the film have taken? The director insisted it would have been a better movie than *Citizen Kane*, "if they'd just left it as it was" (Welles/Bogdanovich, p.95). But would Welles himself have "just left it as it was?" Carringer claims that due to the uncomfortably autobiographical material in the film Welles intended to make severe cuts which would have seriously damaged it. But why choose to film such uncomfortable material in the first place? Nevertheless, Carringer's reconstruction of a longer version of *The Magnificent Ambersons* is an invaluable tool for evaluating the existing version.

Ambersons begins in the same manner as *Citizen Kane*, with two title cards featuring white letters on a black background, and no music. But if we are led to expect a repeat of *Kane*'s first scene, Welles surprises us. Instead of gothic imagery, brooding music, and no dialog, *Ambersons* begins with narration by Welles, then adds sentimental music (a variation on a waltz by Emil Waldteufel) and cheerful imagery. By leading off with narration over a black screen, Welles briefly carries us back to a pre-movie era of storytelling, evoking a nostalgia for the good old days. But not everything about *Amberson*'s opening contradicts *Kane*'s. The earlier film begins at the tragic end of its protagonist's life. *Ambersons* contains a small kernel of gloom within its nostalgic introductory portrait of the past. "All the years that saw their midland town spread and darken into a city" foreshadows the demise of a way of life instead of the death of one individual.

The first scene in *The Magnificent Ambersons* is a picture postcard come to life. In extreme long shot from a flat frontal angle we watch a mule-drawn streetcar pull up in front of a large house in a small, midwestern American town. No deep focus photography here. The image is deliberately two-dimensional and rather artificial, adding to our sense of detachment from the world it depicts. The people in it are shown too far away to be recognizable as individuals. Leisurely background music and Welles's very literal description of what happens on screen, as though *Ambersons* were going to be more an illustrated novel than a movie, generates a warm feeling of nostalgia. And nostalgia requires distance, emotional as well as physical and temporal, in order to sustain believability. In a way, Welles is taking us on a journey *into* Charlie Kane's crystal ball.

The social order sketched in the first scene is notable for its tranquil pace, genteel chivalry, and spirit of cooperation. While patiently waiting for a woman who called out from the house, the streetcar's driver and male passengers exit the vehicle in order to push it back onto the track from which the mule dislodged it. And they do so in a manner suggesting that such cooperative effort was commonplace at the time. For a moment Welles convinces us that we've traveled back to those *good* old days. And by commenting that "the faster we're carried, the less time we have to spare" (a direct quote from Booth Tarkington's novel), he challenges the notion that technological and social progress are synonymous.

In the longer version of the film the streetcar scene is followed immediately by three more brief scenes involving the same house in the background, as viewed through the course of two seasonal changes. The last of these scenes introduces us to Eugene Morgan and Isabel Amberson, two of the movie's major character. The short version of *Ambersons* cuts away from the house and streetcar for a brief montage about changing fashions in clothes. There are several dramatic advantages to the arrangement of scenes in the longer version. By showing us the anonymous house and anonymous people on the street in front of it over the course of several seasons, via deceptively slow lap dissolves with no change in camera angle, Welles mimics the mind's effortless and often deceptive blending of separate, distant memories, whether personal (private recollections) or collective (public myths). Streetcar passengers magically change into pedestrians in winter coats and children throwing snowballs and sliding on ice. Snow gilds the roof and windows of the house, rendering it even more picturesque than it was already. Day eases into night. Then the snow disappears, replaced by a string of bright lanterns hung across the front of the house. The pedestrians are back in their warm weather attire. Much has changed, and yet because the camera has not moved, our overall impression is of something singular and constant.

In a fourth shot from the same camera angle and distance, this time at night, the house appears dark and obscure. Nameless pedestrians are replaced by Eugene Morgan and a group of male friends carrying musical instruments. Viewed initially in extreme long shot, and therefore anonymously, like the streetcar passengers and pedestrians in the earlier shots, they serve merely to illustrate a social custom of the period, as described by the narrator. The custom of a gentleman serenading a pretty girl on a summer evening. But by crossing the street and approaching the camera, Eugene breaks through his anonymity to become an identifiable character on a personal mission. He accidentally stumbles and falls onto his fiddle, shattering it. He looks up in consternation at the girl he was trying to impress. That girl, Isabel Amberson, observes him disapprovingly from an upper story window in her family's mansion. They exchange meaningful glances in a pair of close-ups. But we don't yet know their names. Nor do we hear them speak. There is no local sound in this scene. The action remains subordinate to the narrator's description of a quaint old custom. Eugene's blunder, as viewed through a generalized haze of nostalgic reminiscence, is comic, charming, and trivial. Only with hindsight do we recognize it as a pivotal, tragic event in the lives of Eugene and Isabel. Like *Citizen Kane*, *The Magnificent Ambersons* both fondly embraces and coolly scrutinizes its subject. Some later scenes, or elements within them, reinforce the nostalgia evoked at the beginning. Others undercut that nostalgia, not so much by falsifying it as by adding human detail to what starts out as an abstraction. In its own way *The Magnificent Ambersons* is as much an exploration of contrary perspectives as is *Citizen Kane*, with its multiple portraits of one character.

A visual montage about changing fashions in the 1870's occurs after the house montage in the longer version of the film. This seems appropriate because our first close-up view of Eugene Morgan should occur when he crosses the street to serenade Isabel and thereby transforms himself from an anonymous figure incidental to the narration into an identifiable character with a life of his own, including private motives and real consequences to his actions.

The fashion montage begins with a shot of men in a saloon, all wearing the customary stovepipe hat of the period. The saloon's swinging doors conceal their faces and most of their bodies, maintaining their visual anonymity. All local sound is displaced by narration, further distancing us from the men we don't quite see. In the next two shots we *clearly* see three of the film's major characters: Wilbur Minafer, Isabel Amberson, and Major Amberson, all bending to the whims of fashion. But still no local sound. Within those portraits of social conformity, however, we also glimpse a few character traits which, with the benefit of hindsight, we recognize as having significant impact on future events. Wilbur, his head bearing a stovepipe hat, stiffly rows his sweetheart, Isabel, in a boat on a lake. Another quaint custom of the period. But more to the point, Wilbur has apparently displaced Eugene in Isabel's affections. In the next shot we see Major Amberson, Isabel's father. *His* stovepipe hat gets knocked off his head by a snowball. He turns to scold the person who threw it, but when he sees who it is his face breaks into a broad smile. Could the snowball assailant be Isabel, whom he spoils as much as she will in turn spoil her child in later years? And does his general overindulgence of her influence her unwillingness to forgive Eugene for his social blunder, and choose the extremely conventional Wilbur Minafer to replace him? But these are dark undercurrents to what is on the surface a sunny portrait of an American past.

Eugene Morgan joins the fashion parade, appearing first as a reflection in an ornate, oval-framed mirror — another quaint pictorial device contributing to our feeling of nostalgia. Eugene's snooty expression as he changes hat styles gently mocks his slavery to passing fads, while the tone of Welles's narration does the same from outside the visual frame. Herrmann's accompanying set of jaunty variations adds a slightly mechanical tempo to this portrait of habitual behavior. Shots of Eugene's feet tell a tale of shifting trends in men's shoes, each as frivolous as the one before it. The camera travels up to his fashionably uncreased, tight trousers. We next see our hero in his long underwear, struggling to maintain balance and dignity while keeping up with changing styles. Then come the overcoats: short and tan yielding to long and dark. Twice we see Eugene approach a full-length mirror, admire his appearance in it, then turn and walk away. The visual effect suggests something akin to being trapped in a revolving door, going round and round but getting nowhere.

Eugene's segment of the fashion montage culminates in a portrait of him standing outside the front door of his home, wearing clothes entirely different from anything he tried on earlier. The fickleness of fashion echoes the fickleness of the human heart, as Eugene soon discovers

Much of Eugene's trek from his home to the Amberson mansion is missing from the short version of the movie. Judging from Carringer's reconstruction of that footage, it reinforces our earlier impression of public civility. Eugene tips his hat in greeting to almost everyone he encounters, as a matter of habit. Missing too is Welles's narration about the extreme thriftiness of the people of that era, who in spite of their general prosperity are still tied to the values of their ancestors—pioneers who often lacked money to spend on anything but basic necessities. Again the emphasis is on the dominating influence of tradition, even when it clashes with changing circumstances. Removing this little lecture on thrift renders what's left of the narration less meaningful. "Against so homespun a background, the magnificence of the Ambersons was as conspicuous as a brass band at a funeral." *What* homespun background? Without the remarks about pioneer thrift, there is no historical context. Bit *with* those remarks, we perceive the conspicuous consumption of the Ambersons as a significant *break* with tradition. As the standard bearers of a *new* lifestyle, the Ambersons, especially George Minafer Amberson, will in time become the standard bearers of an old and outmoded lifestyle. Not that conspicuous consumption soon goes out of style. But the sources of income that underpin it will. By reminding us of the pioneer past preceding the social order depicted at the start of the movie, Welles illustrates the unrelenting, often merciless process of social change.

Occasional remarks by small groups of the town's citizens are a gauge of contemporary perceptions and values. Serving as a sort of Greek Chorus, these busybodies gossip about the town's most prominent family. Their admiration for the material magnificence of the Amberson mansion reflects a recent shift in public values from thriftiness to conspicuous consumption. Edited out of their first commentary is one mildly indignant comment about the "Almighty Dollar" as a new measure of social prominence. The transition from old values to new ones is a fitful, contentious affair. The magnificence of the Ambersons is admired by some people, disapproved of by others.

Two shots, widely separated by a black screen, show Eugene twice calling for Isabel at the front door of the Amberson mansion. Both times he is turned away by the family's butler, despite Eugene's observance of the courtship customs of the period. His clothes are fashionable. He brings candy and then flowers for his sweetheart. But his earlier social blunder, the botched serenade, destroyed his romantic credibility with Isabel, even though it seemed trivial to *us* at the time. The butler's second rebuff of Eugene on behalf of Isabel is slightly more blunt than the first, indicative of Isabel's hardening attitude.

Another group of town gossips ponders Eugene's romantic folly from a distance. Fanny Minafer, soon to be an in-law of the Ambersons, is among them. She gives no hint that she has romantic feelings herself for Eugene. That is a passion too private to be shared with casual acquaintances. Her participation in this scene reminds us, in hindsight, that *everyone* leads a complex private life that remains mostly hidden from public view. At present the depth of Fanny's affection for Eugene is no more evident to us that the depth of Eugene's disappointment over Isabel is to Fanny and her companions.

The presence of Eugene's rickety, experimental, steam-powered automobile in the scene of his rejection by Isabel is dramatically appropriate on two levels. First, in spite of its fragile, almost comic appearance, it is a harbinger of great change to come, and of the Amberson family's consequent fall from grace. Eugene will not succeed in wooing Isabel, but he will eventually eclipse Isabel and her family in terms of social status, wealth, and influence on the future. Unintentionally the automobile becomes his instrument of revenge against the woman who rejected him, and against her son by another man. From long distance we observe Eugene and his contraption pull away from the Amberson mansion, which looks so much larger, more solid, and permanent by comparison. That impression is an illusion.

Among the town gossips is a middle-aged man named Roger Bronson, who wistfully describes Isabel Amberson as a "delightful looking young lady." Does Bronson harbor secret feelings for her, as Fanny Minafer does for Eugene? Or Jed Leland for Emily Norton and Mr. Bernstein for his mysterious woman in white in *Citizen Kane*? By constructing his story the way he does, with later revelations about people and events we mistakenly thought we understood at first glance, Welles encourages us to think about the truth that lies beneath surface appearances.

Eugene's encounter with Isabel and Wilbur outside an ice cream parlor is on its surface another lighthearted affair. Despite frowns between them, the male rivals tip their hats to each other in greeting. Isabel, however, turns up her nose at Eugene and walks away, half leading and half dragged by the fashionably large dog she holds on a leash. The cute little whistle emitted by Eugene's automobile, the stylish clothes worn by all three characters, and Herrmann's background music do nothing to darken the mood of this scene. Besides, how could anything tragic happen outside an *ice cream* parlor? The nostalgia of the film's opening scenes continues to prevail, though Welles is slowly shifting dramatic gears from the generalized to the specific, and from the nostalgic to the tragic. Gradually it dawns on Eugene that he and Isabel are not destined to be together. We are so informed by a series of brief vignettes featuring the gossip of their fellow citizens, who appear in the midst of everyday, mundane activities and locations that render Welles's re-creation of the past so convincing.

Jack Amberson swings around in a barber chair where he is getting a shave. Facing the camera and a group of companions, he defends his sister's selection of Wilbur Minafer over Eugene Morgan. Years later, after Wilbur's death, he will facilitate Eugene and Isabels' desire to be with each other. But for now he foresees none of the heartache caused by her petulant preference for Wilbur. A relatively young man from a wealthy family, Jack in this scene has more respect for Wilbur as a "steady" businessman than for Eugene as a romantic dreamer. And judging by the number of men listening to him, visible as reflections in a mirror behind Jack, his opinion matters. But in a dress shop down the street, several of the town's women are divided over the same topic.

Two of the women imply that Isabel's preference for Wilbur over Eugene is absurd. A third defends it as sensible, especially for a "showy" girl like Isabel. The old pioneer notion that conspicuous consumption is sinful rears its head once more. A fourth gossip, Mrs. Foster, consolidates those contradictory views by first explaining how Eugene's bungled serenade gave Isabel the impression that he didn't really care about her, then qualifies that statement by remarking that Isabel probably misinterpreted the blunder. She pays tribute to the power of tradition by insisting that it's too late for Isabel to change her mind now that her engagement to Wilbur has been announced. Becoming the center of her companions' collective attention, Mrs. Foster expounds on both the likely extravagance of an Amberson/Minafer wedding (arranged by the bride's family) and the likely thriftiness of the honeymoon to follow (Wilbur's part of the bargain). She even prognosticates on the outcome of their merger: "the worst spoiled lot of children this town will ever see." She's wrong about the number of children Isabel and Wilbur will have, but not about character of the child. However, the casual manner of Mrs. Foster's speculation, like Jack's casual manner of approving Isabel's choice of Wilbur over Eugene, betrays her incomprehension of the serious emotional consequences of what she otherwise so accurately predicts. The Ambersons, Minafers, and Morgans are mere entertainment to her, rather like the "News on the March" version of the life and death of Charles Foster Kane.

For the time being, snappy narration, music, and imagery validate Mrs. Foster's glib predictions. Young George Minafer is shown charging recklessly through town in his pony cart, oblivious of the people he nearly runs down. Welles magnifies our impression of his speed by showing the boy's cart rushing headlong towards and then rapidly past the camera, in contrast to earlier, more static images portraying a more leisurely pace of life.

Observing the ruckus caused by George, Roger Bronson remarks to a companion that he looks forward to seeing the boy get his "comeuppance" some day. Pride goeth before a fall, and so forth. Bronson's wish is expressed as casually as was Mrs. Foster's prediction. It is unlikely that he has in mind the terrible comeuppance that eventually befalls George Amberson Minafer. In fact, *our* recollection of Bronson's wish, thanks to the narrator's use of the word comeuppance later in the story, will outlast the wish itself.

The incident that makes George's comeuppance a more personal and passionate concern for Bronson is a fight between young Minafer and Bronson's son, Elijah. The confrontation is initiated by Elijah, who while standing in his own yard makes fun of George's girlish curls as the latter rides by in his cart. Elijah appears to be as much a spoiled brat as is George. Dressed in a ribboned hat, tie, and fancy clothes, he is only slightly less effeminate in appearance than the target of his insult. Perhaps *both* boys are the objects of excessive attention from their mothers. Both are also reminiscent, to a degree, of young Charlie Kane in the Colorado boarding house scene in *Citizen Kane*. Except that Kane loses the affection, protection, and indulgence of his mother at an early age. George will not.

Accepting a dare, George jumps over a fence and attacks his foe on Elijah's home turf. Soon Elijah is on the ground, taking a beating, and hollering for (who else?) his mother. Instead, Roger Bronson comes to the rescue, pulling George off his son. Disrespecting any authority save his own, George punches the elder Bronson in the stomach, just as young Kane, with a bit more justification, struck Walter Thatcher with a sled. Bronson, who a few years earlier (in real time, but only a few moments ago in *reel* time, and therefore more noticeable to us than to him) expressed a fondness for Isabel Amberson, now describes George as a "disgrace to your mother." This provokes a furious reaction from George, who is passionately attached to Isabel. He strikes the man who insulted her. As for Bronson, he has apparently long forgotten his attraction to Isabel. Unaware that Elijah instigated the fight, he cannot see the ironic parallel between his own domestic situation and that of the Minafers. Although we never meet Mrs. Bronson, it isn't too farfetched to speculate that her marriage to Mr. Bronson, like that of Isabel to Wilbur, is less than passionate. Her spoiled brat of a son called out to *her* rather than to his father — probably because she, like Isabel, lavishes her otherwise unfulfilled affection on her child. But all of this is subtext. On its surface this scene, like its predecessors, plays as lighthearted period comedy. Only later in the film do we begin to understand the grim personal dimensions of this still largely collective trip down memory lane.

George Minafer takes center stage at his own trial, following his attack on the Bronsons. Standing center screen on the sprawling lawn outside the Amberson mansion, he is surrounded by his parents and grandfather. But because he stands while they are seated, he is visually dominant. All four characters are elegantly dressed in the fashion of their time, place, and class. But George is absurdly resplendent, looking like a Scottish lord in a kilt and cap, leaning regally on his walking stick. He is the focus of everyone else's attention and indulgence as he lies and evades his way out of trouble. The mansion in the background looks like a palace. Welles shoots this scene in a single shot and from a stationary, flat frontal perspective, creating the equivalent of a formal portrait such as might hang in the manor house of a European aristocrat. George's self-defense is, not surprisingly, based on the notion of his superior social rank. Bronson's letter of complaint to his parents is not to be taken seriously because Bronson is an inferior sort of person.

The reactions of the three adults to George's insolence vary in degree, but are equally ineffective as discipline. Major Amberson mildly objects to George's characterization of Bronson, whom we later discover is a good friend of the family, as a liar. But a moment later he undercuts himself by laughing out loud at the boy's outrageous snobbery, which he finds charming. Wilbur openly disapproves of the Major's laughter, but is too timid to criticize George directly. He yields parental authority to Isabel, who makes a half-hearted attempt to chastise her son, then undermines herself by shifting her disapproval to Bronson, criticizing his letter about George as tactless (George's punch to Bronson's stomach *wasn't* tactless?). And when she extracts a promise from George never to use bad words again (the boy told Bronson to go to hell), he hedges on his commitment by adding a qualifier, "unless I get mad at somebody." As he quietly says this he eases his way out of the fixed camera frame and away from adult admonishment. It is such an obvious maneuver that his judge and jury cannot help but find it delightfully disarming. And so does Herrmann's music.

Roger Bronson returns in another brief communal commentary. Following his painful confrontation with George, he now eagerly anticipates a comeuppance when George goes away to school. But as a prognosticator he falls short of Mrs. Foster. In a virtual replay of an earlier scene, George Minafer, now grown to a young man of college age, again rampages through his hometown streets in a horse-drawn buggy, treating everyone he encounters as insolently as he did ten years earlier. Camera angles and background music are similar to what they were in the earlier street rampage scene. But beneath the surface some things have changed, and will change even more.

The film's longer version contains a scene involving George visiting a boys' club he started before leaving town for school. The Friends of the Ace is an organization devoted to the usual stuff of youthful male bonding: alcohol, gambling, and secrecy, held together by a smattering of parliamentary ritual. George returns to club headquarters to find his place as President usurped by a rival named Fred Kinney. But George founded the organization. Rent for the meeting room is paid for by George's grandfather. Even the gavel Fred wields belongs to the Amberson family. Proffering a proverbial stick in one hand (the threat of closing down the meeting room) and a carrot in the other (the promise of liquor), George reclaims his high office. Fred resigns and departs. This scene is straight out of Tarkington's novel. But without the missing footage from the movie it is impossible to evaluate the nuances Welles might have given it. In broad terms the scene shows us George's cavalier treatment of his peers, some of whom show up at the subsequent Amberson Christmas ball. George lies, bullies, and exploits his family's status in order to get his way. Making a mockery of the democratic process, he gives us a glimpse of how Charlie Kane might have performed as Governor of New York, if he had won that election.

From roughly the same distance and camera angle as we last saw Eugene Morgan depart after being turned away by Isabel, we now see a stream of carriages arrive at the Amberson mansion and drop off guests invited to a grand ball given in honor of George's return from college for the Christmas holidays. Every window in the house glows bright, warm, and inviting on this frosty winter night. Ironically, we cross the mansion's threshold with the man who was refused entry twenty years earlier. This time Eugene Morgan is accompanied by his teenage daughter, Lucy. The sound of a cold wind and the fluttering of Lucy's coat outside the mansion hint at the fragility of the fairy tale realm within. From a partly subjective, low angle camera perspective, we follow the Morgans through the doorway. We see the interior of Isabel's home as they see it, in vibrant detail. Tinkling chandelier, beamed ceilings, and carved wood. For Eugene, a lost, lamented past magically returns to life, as it does for Charlie Kane when he sees Rosebud in a glass paperweight. But for Eugene it is not entirely a fantasy. The past is not quite dead, and old mistakes might be correctable. Counterpointing this revival of hope for Eugene is the narrator's opening comment that this Amberson ball will be "the last of the great, long-remembered dances that everybody talked about." In other words, if this scene is a new beginning for Eugene, it is in other respects the beginning of the end for the Amberson family.

While Lucy and Eugene go their separate ways inside the mansion, the camera takes us on a brief walking tour of the festivities. The opulence of the mansion's furnishings and decor is complemented by the conviviality of the guests and the warmth of the sentimental music played by hired musicians — all of which holds at bay the winter chill outside. But soon we encounter the hint of a different kind of chill *inside* the mansion. Only a small one, registered in the brief encounter between Major Amberson and John Minafer, brother to Wilbur and great uncle to George. From out of the collective din of pleasant conversation comes, as we slowly approach the official reception line, the more specific sound of John Minafer tactlessly joking about where inside the great mansion Major Amberson's corpse should lie in state "when the time comes." Before moving up the reception line to embarrass George, John relishes the look of disapproval he puts on the Major's face. We and the camera are too far away at first to see that expression, but we catch a glimpse of it as the Major passes out of the camera frame at foreground right. This is the first hint of disunity within the extended Amberson family. And although trivial and comic, on its surface, it foreshadows larger cracks to come.

The camera closes to a tight shot of George, Isabel, John, and Eugene — the first of many examples of Welles following multiple threads of interaction in a single shot, portraying human relations as layered, fragmented, and often contradictory at the same time. Each character has little or no idea what transpires just a few feet away — a fact emphasizing his or her isolation from the others. John Minafer annoys George with an embarrassing remark while in the same image Eugene hesitantly, reverently approaches Isabel, who in turn watches her son's predicament with amusement. Even the departing Major is, for a moment, a player in this orchestra of human actions and reactions. And by approaching these characters as they come and go, the camera encourages us to feel that we too are participating in this fluid social mix.

Cutting to a tighter shot of Eugene and Isabel alone, the camera reduces the dramatic equation to two. For a moment they are alone in the world, seeing each other for the first time in twenty years. The moment ends when Eugene invites George back into the picture with a warm greeting. George responds to that warmth with his standard, formal, phony greeting,"Remember you very well indeed." The two have never met before. This is not the last time George will demonstrate a preference for form over substance in social matters. Eugene inclines to the opposite, but not always. In another shot of he and Isabel alone, he tells her he hopes to see her again now that he has moved back into town. Then, masking the romantic passion underlying that hope, he politely inquires where he might find Isabel's husband, Wilbur. Another shot change brings George back into the equation. He glares at the impudent stranger over Isabel's shoulder. Pictured alone again with his former sweetheart, Eugene tells Isabel he will return later to claim a dance. In and of itself it is an innocent remark, but in the context of Isabel's prior comment about Wilbur not caring for parties it seems like a tactical maneuver — contrasting his own sociability with his rival's lack thereof.

The dance of shifting emotions continues as the camera cuts to a broader view. George still glares disapprovingly at Eugene, who in turn greets the returning Major Amberson, who obviously prefers Eugene's company to John Minafer's. Eugene and the Major depart while George and Isabel continue to greet newly arrived guests. George employs his stock salutation. But that empty formality acquires new meaning when Lucy Morgan approaches him. He is struck by her beauty. And while their new relationship commences on the left side of the screen, an old friendship is renewed on the right. Jack Amberson warmly calls out to Eugene as he passes in and out of our view. Two separate but significant encounters between the Ambersons and the Morgans occur within a few feet of each other, yet are mutually oblivious. George doesn't even realize he is talking to Eugene's daughter.

With a trace of possessive regret, Isabel sends George off to dance with Lucy. Tracked by the camera, the young couple pass by Jack and Eugene walking in the opposite direction. We catch a snippet of conversation between the latter gentlemen before they pass out of hearing range. Welles uses sound to reinforce our appreciation of variety and change — of multiple centers of action isolated from yet occasionally intersecting and even interacting with one another. A seemingly trivial misunderstanding between George and Lucy dramatizes the point further. When she inquires, "Who's that?", referring to Jack, George mistakenly thinks she is referring to Eugene. Having already forgotten the unimportant stranger's name from Isabel's introduction, George dismisses Eugene as that "the queer-looking duck." Then he refers to the other man a Uncle Jack, unwittingly informing Lucy that he is unaware of the connection between Eugene and herself. By not immediately enlightening George on the matter, she cleverly lets him reveal more about his character than he would perhaps want to. And as they ascend a grand staircase to the mansion's second story she slyly remarks on the arrogance she has already sensed in him. But her subtle sarcasm passes over his head.

George and Lucy stroll leisurely up the staircase. But the camera is now stationary, fixed halfway up the stairs. We observe them approach from the right, pivot with them as they pass by, then watch them recede off to the left, George's voice fading as they go. They merge back into the melange of conversations and interactions that make up the ball as a whole. That impression of multiplicity and shifting is emphasized by several other couples making the same trek up the stairs. Complementing the sound and camera work, high contrast lighting brings out every surface detail of the mansion's decor. The variety of shapes and textures in that decor matches the variety of human encounters.

Sizable cuts in the ball sequence include John Minafer embarrassing his family again, Fanny Minafer's introduction to Lucy, and Wilbur's brief appearance to spirit John away. Who knows what dynamic interplay of camera, setting, characters, and soundtrack we miss because someone other that Welles thought it slowed the film's pacing too much and diverted attention from the budding romance between George and Lucy. The larger point of the ball sequence is that nothing, not even a romance between two major characters, occurs in a vacuum. Particularly in a house and a social circle as large as the Ambersons.

We rejoin George and Lucy as she is greeted in passing by several admiring young men. Highly territorial, George is annoyed by the competition. Acknowledging that some of the young men belonged to a club he once led, he claims to be no longer interested in them and wonders why his mother bothered to invite them to the ball. Not long ago he was *very* possessive of that club. His dismissive attitude now seems fickle and shallow. And he reinforces that impression by adding that his mother needn't worry about offending the parents of former friends he no longer needs or wants. Lucy pretends to be impressed by George's self-importance, thereby drawing him out further on the subject. But Lucy is more impressed than she admits to herself. Is it possible that she is attracted to George because he is so unlike her beloved father? And that George feels the same away about her because, unlike his mother, Lucy does not indulge him?

A moment after exchanging polite greetings with a passing guest, in accordance with the rules of propriety, George informs Lucy, "Anybody that really is anybody ought to be able to do about as they like in their own town, I should think." That is George's contradiction in a nutshell. He is part petty conformist and part arrogant snob. Lucy unwittingly reinforces that contradiction when she refers to him alternately as "Mr. Amberson" and "Mr. Minafer." Tempermentally he is a cross between the once willful and snobbish Isabel and the sober, conformist Wilbur.

The petty conformist comes out in George when he takes offence to being waved at from a distance by Eugene, who is barely an acquaintance. Lucy corrects his mistaken perception, pointing out that Eugene was waving at her, not him. But that revelation triggers the young man's jealousy, so he still resents Eugene. Either way, George comes off looking petty.

As she and George resume their stroll arm in arm, Lucy marvels at the sheer splendor of the mansion and the ball. She may be playing mind games with her host, but she is also entranced by the privileged world he comes from and represents. For the remainder of the movie she is both drawn to and repelled by him, much as Welles is drawn to and repelled by the world he re-creates in this film.

Lucy sits on a step part way up the grand staircase, overlooking the dance floor below. George sits beside her. The location suits Lucy, who remains partly detached from but keenly interested in everything she sees and hears at the ball. George, however, is not capable of such a balanced perspective. Tactlessly, he insults her by denigrating her father's new invention — the horseless carriage, which after all represents a rude intrusion of something revolutionary into George's perfect, privileged, stable world. Lucy slyly retaliates by commenting that her father has known the Amberson family for a long time but does not "boast" of it. George catches the implication and is, as Lucy desired, slightly offended. So *he* then retaliates by declaring that most girls are "pretty fresh," meaning insolent, and could be cured by attending a *man's* college for a year or so. Yet we see no evidence that attending such a college cured George. Behaving insolently himself, he demands to know from whom Lucy received the bouquet of flowers she has carried since he met her and over which she now fusses.

Perhaps Lucy fusses over her flowers out of embarrassment, because George was right, if hypocritical, about her being fresh. By not telling him that Eugene is her father, she is even fresher than George realizes. From the dance floor below, Eugene calls up to Lucy for a dance. Deliberately provoking George's jealousy, Lucy tells him that Eugene gave her the flowers. But George is relieved rather than jealous. How could some "old widower" compete with a young Amberson? Then Lucy drops the bombshell she's concealed ever since George referred to her father as a "queer-looking duck." Eugene is her father, and also a widower. George's brief triumph turns to shame.

Eugene climbs the staircase to join Lucy. His former dancing partner, Fanny Minafer, departs. Then Isabel joins him on the stairs. Noticing that Lucy is still with George, Eugene diplomatically does not insist on the dance she promised him earlier. Always a gentleman, he in many ways exemplifies the best qualities of his era. Yet his invention will accelerate the destruction of that era. George, on the other hand, embodies some of the worst traits of his era, yet will fight the hardest to preserve it. He hustles Lucy off to the dance floor, leaving her father behind.

Edited out of this scene is a gathering of Isabel, Eugene, Jack, and Fanny at the bottom of the staircase after George and Lucy depart. Strolling from room to room, this collection of middle-aged men and women converse lightheartedly about the naivete of youth and the ravages of age, work, and wrinkles. Jack plays the cynic of the group, remarking on the inevitability of hardship in every life, regardless of the strength and confidence of youth. Isabel speaks of shielding George from such hardships by taking some of them upon herself. She naively speculates about a future time when there will be no hardships for anyone, and consequently no wrinkles. Eugene's philosophy lies somewhere between Jack's cynicism and Isabel's utopian fancy. He knows what causes wrinkles: age, trouble, and work. But he sees none of those wrinkles on Isabel's face, attributing her serenity to her "faith" in "everything." What he perhaps really means, but cannot say openly, is her faith in their eventual union. Jack playfully mocks the romantic naivete of *both* Isabel and Eugene by pretending to concede the debate. Fanny, meanwhile, contributes little to the discussion about wrinkles, parents, children, and hardship. All of those topics cut too close to the bone for her to joke about.

As the film now exists, immediately after George and Lucys' departure for the dance floor we cut to Isabel, Eugene, Jack, and Fanny approaching a punch bowl at the *conclusion* of their conversational stroll. Major Amberson presides over the bowl. Wilbur joins the group from another direction. The whole ball is like a whirling square dance of interaction, with new partnerships constantly forming, dissolving, and re-forming. Eugene declines the Major's offer of eggnog. Amused, the Major indelicately observes that Eugene has kept his promise never to drink again after the serenade fiasco. But a pledge kept for twenty years is not a trivial thing. It suggests that Eugene's deep regret at losing Isabel during one drunken escapade has not diminished in all that time. Behaving boorishly, like John Minafer did to *him* earlier, the Major points out that if Eugene had not fallen on his bass fiddle Isabel would not have accepted Wilbur's proposal of marriage. He even solicits Wilbur's opinion on the matter, then teases Isabel for blushing in embarrassment. Wilbur cheerfully seconds the Major's theory, and expresses gratitude for Eugene's blunder. For Wilbur and the Major, it's all water under the bridge. For Eugene, Isabel, and Fanny, it is not. But polite smiles all around successfully mask private heartache.

The characters realign themselves. Fanny adds her two cents worth to the conversation, re-emphasizing what is to her the most important fact of the matter — that Wilbur got and kept Isabel. Though perhaps intended only to divert Eugene's romantic attention away from Isabel and towards herself, Fanny's comment unintentionally exacerbates his pain. Eugene looks away from *all* his Amberson and Minafer companions, and towards a happy distraction off screen. Lucy passes by with George. *She* is the object that compensates Eugene for losing Isabel, just as George is Isabel's compensation for losing Eugene. And he describes Lucy's impact on his life with the same word, "important," that Fanny used to describe Wilbur's impact on Isabel's. Lucy, in turn, reacts to the sound of her name as if a lover had spoken it. Clearly she and her father are very dear to each other.

The camera pans left as a group consisting of Eugene, the Major, and Jack catch up with and pass by Lucy and George on the left while a separate group made up of Isabel, Wilbur, and Fanny pass by on the right. The Major and Eugene trade their former, emotionally charged topic of conversation for something trivial and safe — smoking. Jack, however, cannot help stirring the pot a bit more, turning back to Lucy in passing and commenting, "Do your ears burn, young lady?", referring to Eugene's affectionate comment about her. Lucy laughs, unaware that the conversation to which Jack refers involved her father's painful loss of Isabel.

Our attention returns to George and Lucy as they stop at the buffet table, after an invitation politely extended by George and just as politely accepted by Lucy. Their facade of civility masks budding passions which manifest themselves in indirect ways. Thinking they are alone again, George makes sport of Lucy's family name, calling it "funny." She retaliates by making fun of his consistently self-centered point of view. "Everyone *else's* name always is." Eugene, eavesdropping from a few feet away, approaches them from George's blind side. When George switches targets to Lucy's first name, Eugene interjects, "Lucy," then departs again. Is he defending his daughter against rudeness? Or merely assisting the mutual flirtation between his daughter and Isabel's son? In either case, George is miffed by the interference, which contributes one more building block to George's growing resentment of Eugene. Over time those blocks will form an impenetrable wall.

By way of apologizing for his rudeness, George pays Lucy a sincere compliment. But their romantic moment is spoiled by the rapid approach of three anonymous guests in search of a particular delicacy at the buffet table. So George and Lucy depart.

Missing from the short version of the movie is most of what Robert Carringer describes as a "four-minute, single-take, horseshoe-shaped tracking shot" (Carringer, *Ambersons*, p.97n) featuring a conversation between Eugene and Jack as they stroll from the refreshment area to the ballroom. Jack, blunt as usual, criticizes both George and George's doting mother. Eugene concedes that George is foolish, prideful, and superficial, but cannot help siding with Isabel, as he did in their earlier debate about youth, hardship, and old age. Eugene's indulgence of George is a byproduct of his love for Isabel. Though not denying the bad in young Minafer, he chooses to accentuate the boy's potential for good. Jack's assessment, by contrast, is not blinded by romantic love. His vague warning that the better one knows George the less there is to admire proves prophetic. And he perceptively links the smugness and selfishness of George to the same qualities in Isabel when, as a young woman, she foolishly rejected Eugene.

Briefly distracted from the dialog between Jack and Eugene, the camera pursues the conclusion of a search for olives by the anonymous guests we saw at the buffet table in the previous scene. After criticizing olives as at best an acquired taste, which only slaves to fashion would trouble themselves to acquire, one of the group proceeds to exhibit that slavish behavior. Along the way she bumps into Eugene, allowing the camera to rejoin the debate between Eugene and Jack. Trivial and comic on its surface, the olive hunt unobtrusively illustrates the often denied yet clearly evident power of social rank to establish collective values. A power that George Minafer Amberson will insist on retaining.

In the film as we now have it, the camera joins Jack and Eugene at the end of their private discussion, just as Isabel and Wilbur cross their path. Eugene abandons his cynical friend for a dance with Isabel, but not before engaging in a final, good-natured debate. Jack remarks on the return of old times, gently kidding Eugene and Isabel about their lingering passion for one another. Eugene insists that old times are dead. There are only *new* times. Contradicting Jack is only for fun. The enthusiasm with which Eugene speaks of "new times" stems from his revived, if unspoken, hope for reversing the terrible disappointment he experienced in the "old times." He and Jack merely clothe the same thought in different terminology. Meanwhile, Wilbur, unaware of the subtext of Jack and Eugenes' brief debate, smiles graciously as he recedes into the background with Jack while we follow Eugene and

Isabel out onto the dance floor. The orchestra strikes up a lively tune, which grows louder as the former lovers begin to dance. We *feel* their mutual joy in the music and in the grace of their movements together.

Almost immediately that joy is counterpointed by George's entry into the camera frame, with Lucy on his arm. He says nothing to Lucy about his mother and Eugene. But his eyes are momentarily riveted on them, and his smile is forced. The camera allows Isabel and Eugene to pass by, switching attention to their children. Lucy casually inquires about George's college studies. Still distracted by the sight of his mother so obviously enjoying herself with Eugene, he asks Lucy to repeat the question. But like the camera, if somewhat tardily, he is soon absorbed in another dispute with his pretty companion. She insists people ought to study something "useful" in college. He cannot imagine training for a profession. "What do they ever get out of life? " What do they know about *real* things?" he challenges, glancing around at the many professional men on the dance floor. Maybe he is defending such "real," underappreciated pursuits as the arts, or philosophy. No. Responding to Lucy's question about what he wants to become, George matter-of-factly answers, "a yachtsman." So much for lofty goals. We share in Lucy's astonishment as George whisks her off to dance, to the same vibrant music that accompanied Eugene and Isabel. The young couple disappears into the anonymous whirl of dancing couples, and is displaced in the foreground by the return of their parents, who seem much more of like mind.

A lap dissolve transports us forward in time to a nearly empty, darkened ballroom. The party is over. But the passion lingers. Absorbed in each other, Isabel and Eugene are still dancing, alone in the far background — two small figures dwarfed by the massive elegance of the Amberson mansion. Chiaroscuro lighting highlights that contrast by supplying a gilt edge to surface details. Musicians in the foreground serenade the distant couple. Seen in silhouette, with *no* surface detail, the musicians are abstract, almost magical figures, whose sole function is to perpetuate the romantic mood of the dancers. A Christmas tree in the nearer foreground of this shot adds to the dreamlike quality of the image. But it also hints that Eugene and Isabels' reverie is, like the holidays, a fleeting thing. Even the music, a variation on the waltz heard at the beginning of the movie, harkens back to the "dead" old times Eugene referred to earlier.

The camera cuts closer to Eugene and Isabel, whose graceful movement together is unspoiled by dialog. *That* intrusion arrives from the grand staircase in the background. Lucy and George clamber down the steps like noisy children at play. Their mood is flirtatious, but their dialog is argumentative. Lucy defends her father's invention against George's insults. What they are *really* arguing about is Eugene Morgan, not his invention. Eugene as a father, as an admirer of George's mother, and as a man pursuing a "useful" profession. In other words, Eugene as an example of manhood against whom George is measured by Lucy.

Seeing her father and Isabel dancing, Lucy sits down on the steps and watches them from a respectful distance. She imagines what Eugene must be feeling at this moment. George sits beside her, but possessing no such powers of empathy continues to argue his case against automobiles. And just as he was distracted from Lucy's question about college studies in the previous scene, she now barely acknowledges one of *his* comments. They are at this moment a portrait of disharmony, in contrast to their parents.

The camera slowly closes in on Lucy and George, leaving Eugene and Isabel behind. George, glancing at the dancers off screen, indirectly attacks his rival for Isabel's attention by advising that Eugene get out of the horseless carriage business. Lucy is hurt by that insensitive remark, spoken at a moment when she feels great sympathy for her long-suffering father. She masks that hurt with sarcasm, expressing mock gratitude for the business advice of someone so unqualified as George to give it. But matters are soon smoothed over with laughter and polite words. Lucy is intrigued by the very qualities in George that make him so different from her father. Just as, twenty years earlier, Eugene was attracted to a selfish and snobbish Isabel. Much is left unsaid between Lucy and George. Most of what they do say to each other is just verbal sparring—clever and stimulating, but not very direct. For a moment Lucy seems on the verge of breaking that pattern and speaking honestly to her companion. Then *he* gets distracted by the dancers off screen, as she was earlier. The moment passes. Lucy suppresses her urge and follows the direction of George's gaze. An opportunity for genuine communication is lost.

Eugene and Isabel keep dancing, oblivious of their audience. We return to George and Lucy in a tight shot. Finally, perhaps because both are distracted from each other by the sight of their parents, they agree on something. Namely, the beauty and grace of Isabel Amberson Minafer. Lucy sees Isabel through her father's eyes. George, incapable of seeing things from anyone else's point of view, sees her through his own. The agreement is coincidental, and short-lived. George quickly exploits Lucy's generous words about his mother to disparage younger girls in general, and by implication Lucy in particular. Another flirtatious insult. Then, politely helping Lucy up and resuming his stroll with her, he brashly declares his intention instead of requesting her permission to call for her at her house the next day, to take her for a sleigh ride. Lucy balks, claiming a conflicting commitment, which sparks another argument between them. Is her other commitment real, or just her way of chastising George's rudeness?

The camera pulls back to show Isabel and Eugene in the foreground while their children now occupy the background. Two romantic couples—a study in contrast. One has the opportunity for romance, but are too proud to make a smooth ride of it. The other has the inclination, but lacks opportunity. Eugene and Isabel are awakened from their private reverie by the end of the serenade, by Jack Amberson's loud voice complimenting their performance from off screen, and by Lucy softly calling to her father from the background. From several directions the outside world intrudes on the enchanted couple, diminishing but not quite breaking the magic spell they've woven.

The camera returns to Lucy and George as their argument resumes. He tries to verbally bully her into cooperation. She merely smiles and walks away. George is left alone and frustrated. Jack, Fanny, and Isabel enter the camera frame and pass by him, all of them more concerned with the Morgans than with his romantic problems. Irritated, George summons Jack back to the foreground to question him about Eugene. Perhaps retaliating against Lucy for rejecting him, he directs his anger at her father, complaining about Eugene's overly familiar manner with Isabel and Fanny. Yet visible far in the background, it is Fanny and Isabel who make a fuss over the Morgans—especially Eugene.

Jack likes to stir up a little mischief with everyone. His vain and overly sensitive nephew is an easy target. Jack informs him of Eugene's popularity as a young man, and of Fanny's long held romantic interest in Eugene. Then he teases George about his obvious interest in Lucy. Annoyed, George walks away and joins the others near the entryway.

Dialog, imagery, and relationships overlap in passing. While George renews his demand of Lucy, Jack inquires about Eugene's automobile, Isabel expresses concern about Fanny keeping warm in the cold night air, and Eugene and Isabel bid each other goodnight. Particularly striking is a medium close-up of Isabel, looking anxiously off screen left after the departed Eugene. Her emotions are unspoken yet unmistakable. Visible behind and on either side of her, Lucy and George continue to argue about their sleigh outing. *Their* feelings, by contrast, are bluntly expressed. George demands that she be ready for him to call on her the following afternoon. She refuses. He insists. She casually relents, as though on a whim rather than from intimidation. Meanwhile, the very different concerns of Jack and Fanny are expressed by their distant, off screen voices as they admire Eugene's invention. James Naremore, though using a different scene to illustrate his point, remarks on Welles's "multiplication of artistic stimuli, so that he not only expresses psychology through the settings but gives us the feeling of many actions, visual and aural, occurring simultaneously" (Naremore, p.128). That layered sensibility sustains our awareness of the multiple points of view in play—paralleling, intersecting, clashing with and/or altering each other over the course of time.

Overlapping dramas at the door are aesthetically sharpened by the fact that three of the characters' heads appear nearly in silhouette, highlighted by the bright white of Lucy's coat, by an ice-encrusted window, by a picture frame in the background, and by Isabel's sparkly dress. The illuminated window allows us to see Isabel's facial profile, so still and focused as she watches Eugene depart. Lucy's face too is starkly outlined as she spars with what might be the man of *her* dreams. George's profile, by contrast, is obscured by shadows, and vaguely sinister for it. After Lucy departs, he starts to close the door. Isabel seems inclined to stand in the doorway a bit longer, gazing out after her beloved Eugene. By closing the door and blocking her view, George foreshadows the role he will eventually play in spoiling the renewed romance between his mother and Eugene.

Outside, Fanny and Jack say goodnight to Eugene and Lucy, who depart in their horseless carriage. Welles hides that machine from our view by filming it from a great distance and from behind a fence. During the Morgans' ride home the bulk of it remains below the camera frame. Eugene's automobile plays such an important role in the *next* day's action that Welles wisely did not spoil the surprise of its design in *this* one.

The camera slowly closes in on father and daughter as Lucy offers her frank opinion of George Amberson Minafer ("arrogant and domineering") while discreetly seeking Eugene's advice on the prospect of romance. Hopelessly biased by George's connection to Isabel, Eugene minimizes the young man's flaws and emphasizes the "fine stuff in him." Smiling indulgently, Lucy recognizes the source of her father's bias. Nevertheless, his favorable opinion probably influences her decision to pursue a relationship with George, in spite of her own better judgement. Removed from the end of this scene in the short version of the movie is a brief dialog about Isabel and why she married Wilbur Minafer. Eugene makes light of it as though it were not important, shielding both Lucy and himself from pain.

Back at the mansion, the other half of this romantic quartet have a private conversation of their own. Concealed by shadows in a second floor corridor, Isabel tells George of her concern for Wilbur's health, which she believes has been adversely affected by some bad investments he made. True to form, George is too self-centered to have noticed his father's problem. When Isabel brings it to his attention, George predictably interprets Wilbur's illness according to his own concerns, jumping to the erroneous conclusion that Eugene Morgan, whom he already resents, had something to do with Wilbur's bad investments. This brief conversation in the shadows of the Amberson mansion reveals dark, if unconscious, motivations in both mother and son. Perhaps Isabel's comment about Wilbur's declining health is as much a furtive wish as it is a sympathetic concern. Especially in the wake of her enchanting reunion with Eugene.

Suddenly the dialog between mother and son is illuminated by a flood of light coming from Wilbur's room as he opens the door and steps out. He looks tired and worried, as Isabel described. A second disruption comes from the opposite direction as Fanny and

Jack return from bidding goodnight to the Morgans. Isabel tactfully changes the subject of her conversation with George, inquiring if "dear" Wilbur had trouble sleeping. George is not as tactful. He bluntly interrogates Wilbur about whether or not Eugene tried to get the Major to invest money in his "sewing machine," as he contemptuously refers to the automobile. Viewed from over Wilbur's right shoulder, with his face now brightly lit, George is a portrait of aggression, determined to undermine Eugene's credibility with the family.

Challenging George from far away off screen but in a loud voice, Fanny defends Eugene and describes her nephew as "silly." In a reverse angle shot we see her in the background. Isabel is physically positioned and emotionally trapped between their competing viewpoints. She challenges her son's hostility towards Eugene, but in a much gentler manner than did Fanny.

The camera returns to a tight shot of father and son. George persists with his grudge against Eugene. Surprisingly, Wilbur employs George's accusation to challenge his son's spendthrift ways, comparing George to the reckless Eugene Morgan of twenty years ago. "Only he [Eugene] didn't have a mother to get money out of a grandfather for him" is an amazingly blunt, even savage attack. Or would be if George had any respect for his father's opinion, or capacity for self-examination. Like Isabel, George, and Fanny, Wilbur too harbors deep-seated desires and grudges he does not openly acknowledge. A reaction shot of Isabel and Fanny captures their astonishment at Wilbur's critique of George. But it is astonishment masked by a habitually genteel facade. Isabel blinks and opens her mouth slightly. Fanny lowers one arm. That's all. Wilbur turns and walks away from this potential moment of truth with his son. Returning to his room, he refers back to George's original question, insisting that Eugene needs no financial backers for his invention. While doing so, Wilbur wears a trace of a smile, as though pleased to have stood up to his son and his wife for perhaps the first time in his timid life.

George, in a big frontal close-up, looks and sounds like a petulant child as he whines about Eugene bringing his invention to town. Unable to convict Eugene on the bad investment charge, he resorts to a less rational, more vague complaint. Wilbur, from off screen, curtly suggests that George address his concerns directly to Eugene. Isabel positions herself between George and Wilbur, as a buffer to their confrontation. Following Wilbur into their room, she promises to say goodnight to George in *his* room before retiring. Then she closes the door and shuts out the light that moments earlier illuminated *her* secret and perhaps disingenuous concern about Wilbur's health.

Deserted by his parents, George is not yet ready to give up the fight, so he calls out in a loud whisper to Fanny. His illuminated, belligerent face stands out against a black background. Fanny accepts his challenge as he joins her. The two of them appear as small, distant figures as they leave one corridor, and again in the next shot as they approach the camera up an adjoining corridor. The sheer size and ornate complexity of the Amberson mansion echoes the emotional complexity and history of the family that occupies it. Lurking behind the present confrontation are a thousand others rooted in the past. George and Fanny argue about Eugene and Wilbur as though incapable of comprehending each other's point of view. George reads his own dislike of Morgan into Wilbur's decision not to accept Eugene's invitation to ride in the horseless carriage the following day. Fanny, predisposed to favor Eugene at this point in the story, attaches other motives to her brother's decision. Meanwhile, far in the background, a servant extinguishes some lights. He is beneath the notice of his employers, despite being close enough to eavesdrop on their conversation if he were so inclined.

Jack emerges from his own bedroom to say goodnight. But his voice merely adds to the cacophony of clashing perspectives. George replies goodnight. So does Fanny, but in a peeved tone of voice carried over from her anger at George, who resumes his verbal attack on Eugene. Disgusted with this latest in what is obviously a long history of spats between George and Fanny, Jack tells them both to shut up and returns to his room. Even though Fanny is defending Jack's friend, Eugene, against George's unfair criticism, she and Jack are not allies in this scene. Jack's disgust with the long history of enmity between Fanny and George cancels out any potential alliance, which in turn exacerbates Fanny's feelings of persecution. She seems to believe that everyone is against her.

Standing outside the door to her room, Fanny changes her tone from outrage to innocence as she informs George that she's advised Isabel to give a little dinner party. Trying to mask her real motive for making that recommendation, she answers George's inquiry," For who?", indirectly. Addressing George's grammar rather than his question, she replies, "For *whom*, Georgie." Annoyed, George mocks her by repeating her words in a high, sarcastic tone of voice. One gets the impression this is not the first time Fanny has corrected his grammar. Every dialog between these two characters carries the weight of their long and acrimonious past. Did Fanny try to play the parental disciplinarian to George that Isabel and Wilbur failed to play when he was growing up?

Irritated by George's mockery of her, Fanny informs him that the party is for the Morgans. What she was embarrassed to reveal only a moment earlier now serves her as a means of retaliation. George predictably objects. Fanny, enjoying his alarm, mocks his protest in the same, high tone of voice with which he mocked her. But when he explains his objection, "It wouldn't look well," she misinterprets his words, gets flustered, and like an angry parent tries to "march" the young brat off to his room. Failing in that, she retreats to the shelter of her own. George has no clue what he did to trigger her outburst. And in his ignorance he exacerbates the situation, drawing Fanny back into the hallway to defend herself against what she wrongly assumes is George's sly accusation that she is using Isabel to lure Eugene to the mansion for her own benefit. But George simply isn't that perceptive. Meanwhile, Jack complains loudly from off screen, reminding us that the argument between George and Fanny does not occur in a vacuum.

George's moral objection to inviting the Morgans for dinner was not directed at Fanny's secret motive for suggesting the idea to Isabel. But his discovery of that secret motive suddenly gives him the upper hand in their dispute. Fanny tries to mock him as she did earlier. But that tactic no longer works. Temporarily vanquished, she returns to her room and slams the door shut, feebly ordering George to mind his own business. Ignoring her, George smiles to himself as he departs. He is greatly relieved that his silly old aunt rather than his beloved mother is interested in Eugene.

Jack emerges again from his bedroom to protest the continuing ruckus. George exults in his double victory, over Fanny and over Eugene, by exclaiming, "I will be shot," referring metaphorically to his astonishment at learning the truth behind the dinner invitation. Turning back to face Fanny's closed door, he repeats the phrase loudly enough for her to hear it. A cruel twisting of the knife in her heart. She reacts from off screen with audible dismay. Jack echoes her, but in a different tone of voice and from a different emotion. He understands nothing of what transpired between George and Fanny. He is merely disgusted with both of them for disturbing his peace. He returns to his room and closes the door. George blithely walks away from the camera and down the hallway, laughing out loud to himself. The three characters could not be more out of touch with each other than at the end of this scene.

While and Ambersons and Minafers discuss the Morgans, the Morgans continue to discuss the Minafers and Ambersons, in a brief scene missing from the short version of the movie. Lucy and her father talk about the good and bad in George as they park their automobile in a stable. Modes of transportation are in an awkward transitional phase. What will eventually become a garage is still a shelter for horses, who are not happy to share their space with Eugene's noisy contraption.

Discussing George with much more sympathy than George displayed about him, Eugene attributes both the good and bad in the young man to three factors: "He's Isabel's child. He's an Amberson. He's a boy." A clever way of acknowledging the contradictions inherent in human nature and nurture. Because of his abiding love for Isabel, Eugene is blind to the extent of the bad in George, and its potential to ruin his own, Isabel's, and Lucy's future happiness.

The reflection of a passing horse-drawn sleigh in a misty stream surrounded by snow, accompanied by music like tinkling sleigh bells, generates a picturesque impression of winter recreation from long ago. Like some of the film's opening shots, that impression is rather abstract — a glittering generality, which is then counterpointed by a shot of Eugene Morgan vigorously cranking the stalled engine of his horseless carriage. His companions stand by helplessly, hopping from foot to foot in the snow to keep warm. And the music has stopped, only to resume with the next shot, which returns to the sleigh as it approaches the camera along a winding country road, moving smoothly and soundlessly. The relative anonymity of this impression is maintained by tree branches and lighting that obscure the identity of the sleigh's occupants, preserving for a bit longer the nostalgic generality of an old mode of transportation versus the more specific and less appealing new.

Two shots of the undercarriage of the automobile inform us of Eugene's continuing frustration. The sleigh, meanwhile, continues on its merry way, background music and all. The smoothness of its forward movement contrasts with the up and down bounce of the stalled automobile, now viewed from above as Eugene cranks harder and harder. And again the counterpoint is repeated, until finally the horseless carriage sputters to life. Eugene scrambles in behind the wheel to steer while urging his former passengers to give the vehicle a push. Jack Amberson trips and falls in the effort. But in spite of setbacks, everyone laughs and has a good time. Welles's critique of new technology plays out, for the moment, in a genteel manner. Eugene's automobile, while revolutionary in its day, appears to *us* as old-fashioned and non-threatening. Another example of the illusion of perspective.

The sleigh loses anonymity as it catches up to and races past its revolutionary competitor. George is the sleigh's driver, and Lucy his passenger. And since we have already glimpsed the dark side of George's attachment to old ways, the sleigh is now a bit less charming than it was a moment earlier. "Get a horse!" he yells derisively at the automobile's inventor and passengers. But friendly greetings are exchanged as the sleigh passes by. Riding a wave of overconfidence, as he has often done riding through the streets in town, George gets careless and takes a curve in the road too fast. The sleigh overturns. He and Lucy are dumped out and tumble down a steep embankment that is, fortunately, cushioned by a thick blanket of snow. But if the potential hazards of riding in a one-horse open sleigh diminish its quaint charm, the manner in which George gallantly breaks Lucy's fall with his own body reinforces our appreciation for the old ways. Potential tragedy turns into romantic triumph. Lying in each others arms at the bottom of the embankment, George and Lucy share their first kiss. Concerned passengers from the automobile rush to the scene to help. But behind the good intentions, good cheer, and Bernard Herrmann's warm music, are gentle reminders of lurking emotional conflicts. George and Lucy's romantic moment is interrupted by their parents, just as *they* disrupted Eugene and Isabels' private dance the night before. Eugene helps Lucy and then Isabel climb back up the embankment to the road. Fanny focuses her concern on Lucy, perhaps because of her affection for Eugene and a lingering anger at George. Isabel fusses over her son, to his embarrassment. Shared laughter and relief that no one got hurt in the accident mask but don't eliminate these tensions.

George mildly curses the fleeing horse that only a moment earlier was the champion of his cause. *The Magnificent Ambersons* is a perpetual balancing act of nostalgia and scrutiny. If the old ways take it on the chin as a result of the sleigh accident, the scales of criticism tip in the opposite direction when Eugene's automobile stalls again just as its passengers are about to climb aboard. George is offended by his mother's incessant overprotection, and by Eugene's expectation that he push the automobile while Eugene attempts to re-start it. In other words, George both resents being and expects to be treated as someone special. But if George's attitude is contradictory, so is Eugene's. He fondly describes Isabel as "divinely ridiculous" for fussing over her son. She gently calls him to task, suggesting that his two words cancel out each other, rendering her "nothing in particular." The loud sound of the automobile starting conveniently interrupts this little debate before Eugene has to explain his meaning. In her own sweet way, Isabel pinpoints for us the contrary nature of Eugene's affection for her. Clearly he both adores and disagrees with Isabel for her excessive devotion to George. The quality in her character with which he finds fault is the same quality that intensifies his love for her. Which begs the question, how would the two of them have gotten along as a married couple? Perhaps a twenty year absence made Eugene's heart grow fonder, just as an even longer gap helped Welles look back fondly on the lifestyle of mid-America in the late 19th Century. Of course, if Isabel had married Eugene she might not have needed to divert so much of her love and devotion away from her husband and towards her child, who in turn might not have become such a spoiled brat.

Urged on facetiously by Jack, Lucy, and Fanny in the back seat, all three for different reasons critical of his egotism, George reluctantly pushes Eugene's contraption while it spews gasoline fumes in his face. Success, then failure. The engine dies again. Gentleman Jack gets out to help push, but from the side instead of the rear. George continues to breathe in the vehicle's filthy exhaust. Repeated shots of him doing so are Welles's sly comment on the price of pollution that we continue to pay for technological progress. And yet it is pleasurable to see that price imposed on someone who is so arrogant about the superiority of the past, and of his own privileged status within it. George *deserves* a slap in the face by the modern age.

In conversation with Lucy, Fanny flatters Eugene and happily recollects her own version of old times, when she had hopes of getting together with him. Jack strikes up a jolly song to cheer on efforts to re-start the automobile. Fanny's giddiness and Jack's good cheer reinforce each other. The horseless carriage finally starts to move. Other passengers join in the singing. One big happy family. Except for George, hanging on to the back of the vehicle, looking like an outsider and straining to be included in the festivities. Lucy brings him inside, emotionally speaking, by thanking him for breaking her fall when the sleigh tipped. George tries to take advantage of her gratitude. "How about that kiss," he brags. Not yet willing to openly confess her attraction to him, and thereby make herself vulnerable, Lucy takes refuge in the communal song. So George follows suit, obnoxiously intruding his loud and discordant voice on others more harmoniously blended. A pair of big close-ups tell us more about the affection between George and Lucy than they are willing to tell each other. In an effort to be more a part of the group, George sticks his head between Jack's and Fanny's while continuing to blurt out the song's lyrics. Neither of them are impressed with his boorish behavior. He, in turn, is not pleased with *their* reactions. Nevertheless, the communal song continues uninterrupted—each singer with his or her own reasons for participating. And when the camera cuts to a shot of Isabel and Eugene sitting contentedly beside each other in the front seat, all trace of discord disappears.

Welles gives us a long shot of the automobile resuming its journey through snow-covered woods. Visible in the distance, through tree branches, are telephone poles and wires—tokens of technological progress marring an otherwise pristine natural landscape. But in the scene's final shot those wires and poles are gone. In extreme long shot the horseless carriage, now seemingly as much a part of the nostalgic past as the wintery rural landscape, chugs up over an embankment by a wooden fence. The rickety machine is dwarfed by Nature, especially by a snow-covered tree dominating the center of the screen. Visible far in the distance at left is the still small community the passengers call home, its most prominent feature a church steeple. As the automobile recedes into the distance, the happy song of its passengers fades too. The song itself is a nostalgic relic of the past. But its lyrics, celebrating wealth, social status, and the romantic advantages that accompany both, are not all that dated.

Welles closes the scene with an iris-out shot. A black circle envelopes and eventually engulfs the imagery. A quaint nod to the silent movie era, this device also formally, abstractly concludes Part One of *The Magnificent Ambersons*. After this scene the personal conflicts among and within the characters dispels much of the nostalgic glow through which until now we have largely viewed the past. Excised from the end of this scene is a self-conscious discussion among the automobile's passengers about technological change and the distortion of nostalgic reflection. Without this dialog the final shot leaves us with a haunting impression of optimistic, unsuspecting characters moving unsteadily towards future change and calamity. Like Charlie Kane playing happily in the snow outside his mother's boarding house, while inside his future *un*happiness is being planned for him. What we lose with the excised dialog is a reminder and further elaboration of various conflicts dividing the characters, including Jack's cynicism versus Eugene's nostalgia and George's snobbery versus Lucy's critical and amused detachment.

Hammering home the fact that old times are gone, along with the sentimental fondness with which we bade them farewell, a new scene opens with a close-up of the front door of the Amberson mansion. A black funeral ribbon hangs from it, signaling a death in the family. Grim background music emphasizes the point. Then Eugene Morgan's shadow appears on the door, rather ominously, despite the fact that the shadowed figure removes his hat out of respect for the family of the deceased. We view the shadow partly with George's point of view in mind, as a threat to the rigid order of the Amberson family. Sam, the butler, opens the door and admits Eugene and Lucy, as he has done or refused to do in earlier scenes, under very different circumstances.

Inside the house the traditional ritual of public mourning is underway. From what would be the corpse's perspective, if he still had one, we watch mourners file by in a mute show of respect. A low camera angle emphasizes the heavily decorated walls and ceiling in the background—physical metaphors of the elaborate social customs which govern this and so many other activities. Jack and the Major stand at their appointed stations, greeting mourners as they arrive. Even Herrmann's music pauses, as though afraid to overstep propriety.

Eugene and Lucy appear shocked by Wilbur's death. Although we do not yet know, except by process of elimination, that it is Wilbur who died, with hindsight we can judge Eugene's grim facial expression as either a sincere token of grief or a discrete suppression of his revived hope for a second chance to be with Isabel.

The camera pans left with the Morgans as they join members of Wilbur's family. They wordlessly split into three separate units as they form a procession. Eugene, taking the dead man's place, walks with Isabel at the head of the group. George and Lucy bring up the rear. In the middle walks Fanny, alone. She gazes hungrily at Eugene as he passes by on his way to comfort Isabel. Having just lost her brother, Fanny must cope with her grief by herself. So intense is her feeling of desolation that it cannot be masked by the customary stoicism displayed by the other characters. In her wretchedness, Fanny earns a special close-up at the end of the scene. And Herrmann's music returns, ignoring public propriety and plugging subjectively into Fanny's private emotions.

A brief scene at the cemetery, showing us Wilbur's tombstone, was replaced in the shorter version of the movie with an equally brief Greek Chorus scene, which also identifies the dead man. Roger Bronson comments to his fellow citizens, "Town'll hardly know he's gone." An accurate if cruel observation, casually offered, in stark contrast to Fanny's intense sorrow in the previous scene.

Also missing from the short version is an insert shot of George's college diploma, accompanied by a boisterous college song. Life goes on. Bronson was right, for the most part. Wilbur's death does not weigh heavily on the minds of the people who knew him, except for his sister. A low angle shot of the Amberson mansion at night, fitfully lit by flashes of lightning, presents an image straight out of a gothic horror film, and dramatically prefigures the private tensions and family conflicts about to burst forth within the mansion from this point in the story forward. The aesthetics of gothic horror, as defined by Hollywood in the 1930's and 40's, were incorporated by Welles in many of his films. *Citizen Kane*'s Xanadu and *Macbeth*'s Dunsinane (in fact, almost every image in *Macbeth*) are prime examples.

George and Fanny occupy the Amberson kitchen. As in the first El Rancho and Bernstein office scenes in *Citizen Kane*, rain and thunder accentuate the isolation of the characters involved. So does the sheer size of the kitchen. With the camera positioned near a table where George sits stuffing his mouth with food, Fanny approaches from far across the room. Their conversation is so casual that sometimes it seems disconnected, as if each was hardly aware of the other. They are two people with a long history between them, talking at one another as much from habit as from a desire to communicate. They are like perpetually feuding siblings captured in a rare, quiet, almost unconscious moment of civility. According to Welles (Welles/Bogdanovich, p.127), the dialog in this scene was largely improvised by the actors, after lengthy rehearsals to establish rhythm and a working intimacy between them. They speak in a kind of shorthand typical of people who have known each other for many years.

George's ravenous appetite is reminiscent of Charlie Kane's, except that George bolts his food in a more childish manner. Both characters have a great appetite for life, and are similar in their bullying methods of getting what they want. And both are comparatively wealthy. But their early childhoods, presumably one source of their enormous appetites, are very different. One lacks a mother's love and attention. The other gets too much of it.

George and Fannys' conversation occurs amidst the everyday clutter of the Amberson kitchen, and by implication echoes innumerable late night snacks and conversations of the past. Between his casual comments about strawberry shortcake and her mild rebukes of his eating habits (again she plays the role of disciplinarian that Isabel would not), the topic of the Morgans gradually becomes the focus of their meandering dialog. Neither character picks a fight with the other. They *blunder* into it. Fanny, who suffers the most during this encounter, interrupts George's rare compliment about her baking to pursue the matter of

Eugene Morgan's developing relationship with Isabel. Describing it as "odd" that Isabel did not mention to her than Eugene accompanied George and his mother on the train back to town after attending George's college graduation, Fanny really means "suspicious." Oblivious of his Aunt's real concern, George tells her that Jack encouraged Eugene to make the trip with them. *We* can surmise that Jack is playing cupid for Eugene and Isabel in the wake of Wilbur's death. And yet that thought doesn't occur to insensitive George, even when he remarks that Eugene seemed distracted during the trip home and is also dressing better these days. George, Fanny, and Jack are, at this point in the story, largely ignorant of each other's perspectives of Eugene and Isabel. They are like three trains on separate sets of tracks, approaching a point of collision.

Jack saunters into the kitchen. Overhearing George's comment about Eugene's recently improved taste in clothes, and perhaps trying to conceal from George his own role as cupid between Isabel and Eugene, Jack teases Fanny about failing to encourage a "prize bachelor" who dresses up for her. He knows very well that Eugene is dressing up for Isabel, not Fanny. George picks up on Jack's diversionary tactic and runs with it, because he *likes* the idea of Eugene pursuing his aunt rather than his mother. In typically boorish fashion he speculates that Eugene might soon pay an official call on him in order to ask his permission to marry Fanny. The unintended victim of George and Jacks' separately motivated yet similar jibes, poor Fanny bursts out crying and flees the room, slamming the door behind her. No other actress portrays repressed emotions quite like Agnes Moorhead. In Fanny those emotions occasionally boil to the surface, causing her great humiliation and pain. In Mary Kane they remain under stern control, yet vividly expressed by the manner in which Moorhead portrays that self-control. One wonders what the actress could have done with Lady Macbeth in Welles 1948 film adaptation of *Macbeth*.

George and Jack react differently to Fanny's outburst. Initially, both men face in the direction of her departure. Then George turns to face Jack and complains stupidly that Fanny's moodiness has not abated in spite of the money she inherited from Wilbur's insurance. As though money were her primary concern. Jack then turns away from George, sits down at the table where George sat earlier, and sympathetically ponders aloud the emptiness of Fanny's life. He regrets his and Georges' callous disregard for her feelings. George walks to the sink in the background. His silence and slowness of movement suggest that he shares Jack's remorse and compassion. But appearances are deceptive. He and Jack now occupy positions in the kitchen that Fanny and George occupied at the start of the scene. And they are equally far apart in emotional terms. In the short version of the movie the scene ends at this point, giving us the impression that George feels bad about teasing Fanny. The longer version undercuts any such impression.

Glancing out the window, George cries out in alarm and runs outside into the pouring rain. Jack follows him. The cause of George's dismay is not Fanny's distress, but the foundations of some apartment buildings the Major is allowing to be constructed on Amberson property. Jack says the Major needs the money he'll get from renting those apartments. George is appalled at so naked and public a display of financial neediness. Jack recognizes and yields to new economic trends. George refuses to do so if it in any way diminishes his social status, which is of much more concern to him than Aunt Fanny's loneliness and shame.

Counterpointing the gloom of the kitchen/construction site scene, its successor opens with a bang, sparks, and much good cheer as Eugene and Lucy escort Isabel, Fanny, and George on a tour of Eugene's new automobile factory. The socioeconomic fortunes of the Morgans and the Ambersons are moving in opposite directions. The camera opens with a shot of workers hammering and welding automobile parts in the foreground, while in the background the upper class visitors admire their noisy efforts. Tracking left with Eugene and his companions, the camera tells two separate stories simultaneously. In the foreground is a small, crude forerunner of Henry Ford's assembly line. It is loud, dirty, and no doubt a little dangerous for the workers. In the background are the elegantly dressed proprietors (Eugene and Lucy) of this new process, and the elegantly dressed soon-to-be victims of same.

Independently of the workers, the Morgans, Minafers, and Ambersons act out their own story. They are thrilled by the dynamic sights and sounds of the new factory. Joining his mother and Eugene, George exuberantly remarks on her improved spirits and recommends that she return to the factory every time she gets the blues. He has never sounded so generous. Eugene gallantly drops back to escort Fanny, who contradicts George by declaring that Isabel never gets the blues, and wishing out loud that she could be more like her sister-in-law. Fanny says this while gazing hopefully at Eugene, as if he might defend *her* fine qualities. She wears a mourning dress almost identical to Isabel's, which may be another attempt to displace Isabel in Eugene's affections. But before he can respond to Fanny's remarks, Isabel intrudes, commenting on the pleasure she gets from seeing Eugene's success. Disappointed, Fanny discretely steps back and out of their way. Meanwhile, George and Lucy, visible in the background, are getting along just fine on their own.

Eugene points to his original horseless carriage, the steam-powered Morgan Invincible, now on display as a museum piece in the factory. Isabel wistfully acknowledges, "I remember." Perhaps the machine brings back bittersweet memories of when Eugene courted her in such a contraption, and she rejected him. Fanny tries to re-insert herself into the conversation by remarking, "How quaint," which betrays her ignorance of what the Morgan Invincible means to Isabel and Eugene (as Rosebud did to Kane) and also fails to get her noticed. Pronouncing the new Morgan automobile "beautiful," Fanny could just as well be describing Eugene himself. Note that the newer model is titled simply the "Morgan." No longer "Invincible." Nor is the spirit of its inventor. Eugene may be more sophisticated now than he was twenty years ago, but he is more vulnerable too.

While Eugene and Isabel examine one side of the new Morgan automobile, Lucy comments to George and Fanny on the other side that her father and Isabel look wonderful together. Neither George nor Fanny endorse Lucy's enthusiasm, though for different reasons. Fanny is jealous of Isabel's happiness, while George is just too insensitive to recognize the cause of that happiness, and its threat to his own. Lucy recognizes the cause of her father's joy and rejoices in it.

As the two groups reunite, Lucy and George promptly break off again to be by themselves. Fanny is invited to join hands with Isabel and Eugene as Isabel commemorates the occasion by calling on Eugene's three oldest friends (herself, Fanny, and the absent Jack) to congratulate him on his great business success. Eugene's passionately romantic response is equally masked in terms of friendship. Fanny, recognizing her emotional exile in spite of her physical link to the other two, looks away from them.

Removed from the short version of the movie is a brief scene outside the factory. Lucy and George comment on their parents' sentimentality, which seems a little ironic as they ride away from the automobile factory in an old-fashioned horse-drawn buggy. Following them are the sentimental old fools riding in a newfangled automobile. According to Carringer, some radical changes occur in the short version of the film at this point.

Eugene's automobile catches up to and zips by George's buggy (as George's sleigh once zipped by Eugene's stalled automobile), making lots of noise and kicking up clouds of dust and exhaust fumes, and making us sympathetic to George's stated preference for a horse. Ironically, Eugene's disruptive drive through the streets of town, done to impress Isabel, is reminiscent of George's youthful rampages through the same streets in a horse-drawn cart. Roles have reversed, to a degree.

After the automobile passes them by, George is free to take Lucy and us on a leisurely excursion through his town. The camera shoots from a slightly low, oblique angle, giving us glimpses of pedestrians, houses, trees, storefronts, and the roof of a passing buggy — quaint, tranquil sights occasionally marred by ugly telegraph wires. But if our buggy ride evokes a slower and in some respects more appealing lifestyle, dialog provides counterbalance. Lucy refuses to consent to their engagement, primarily because George hasn't chosen a profession. He prefers to remain a gentleman of honor (meaning leisure) who occasionally involves himself in charities and movements which he cannot even define. In plainer terms, he prefers to continue living off the income provided by his grandfather instead of earning a living on his own.

George quickly surmises that Lucy's objections to his "ideals," which is a mighty fancy word to describe his life of leisure, are rooted in her *father's* objections. Eugene and Lucy recognize Isabel and George as "divinely ridiculous," yet neither can overcome their affection for that absurd combination. Eugene cannot pull his heart out of the past he shared with Isabel, and Lucy cannot resist the lure of a more generalized, elegant past which in her eyes George embodies. But at least she tries. When George brings up the topic of marriage, she urges their horse to go faster in order to avoid talking about it. George stops that maneuver, slowing the horse to a more conversational pace again. But when his subsequent conversation with Lucy turns argumentative again, *George* spurs the horse on in order to end it. Another example of a dramatic reversal.

Another carriage ride features a conversation between Jack and the Major, who are as hesitant and evasive about discussing the family's dwindling finances as Lucy and George were about discussing marriage and opposing ideals. Instead of addressing the matter directly, the Major *jokes* about George's profligate ways. Like Isabel, the Major has long spoiled the young man. Jack, the supposed cynic, doesn't want to see his father confront the painful realities of life. When the Major asks a rhetorical question about George, "Wonder what he thinks I'm made of?", Jack transforms that rueful inquiry into a compliment, describing his father's *heart* rather than his pocket book as golden. But the Major in turn transforms Jack's compliment into yet another lament, about the noisy disruption of his life caused by the necessary construction of rental units on his property. So Jack urges his father to simply avoid thinking about such matters. But the Major twists even that well-meaning remark into something disturbing. Anticipating his own mortality, he half embraces death as the ultimate escape from life's unpleasant realities.

The brooding quality of this conversation is enhanced by both sight and sound. The scene takes place at night. Jack and the Major are intermittently and harshly lit by the glare of street lamps, exaggerating the age lines on their faces. And the carriage squeaks as it bounces along the street, reminding us that it is an aging, dying mode of transportation — like the Major, whose slurred drawl sounds very tired.

Stripped from the short version of the film is another night scene, set on the porch of the Amberson mansion. Fanny and Isabel sit in chairs, George on the steps. Surviving photographs of the scene suggest a relaxed, subdued atmosphere. The characters are far enough apart from one another to be somewhat lost in their own thoughts. As I imagine it, dialog plays out similar to the way it did between Fanny and George in the kitchen scene. Seemingly casual and disconnected.

If Jack tried to ease his father's troubled mind in the previous scene, Fanny does the opposite to her nephew in this scene. Currying favor with George, who ignores her, she questions the commercial future of automobiles, indirectly insulting Eugene. Unable to steal Eugene's affection away from Isabel by direct means, she solicits George as an ally to help break them apart. Isabel, typically, does not detect the malice in Fanny's words.

Trying to get George's attention, Fanny deliberately mistakes Isabel's whistling for his. The ploy doesn't work. Isabel, meanwhile, points out a nosy neighbor, Mrs. Johnson, spying on them from across the street. She also comments on the approaching death of summer. Then she withdraws inside the house to read a book, leaving George and Fanny alone. Fanny wastes no time using Isabel's own words against her, insinuating to George that talking about death so soon after Wilbur's passing is rather insensitive. She reminds George of the traditional period of mourning a widow should observe. Clearly she wants George to act as a barrier between Isabel and Eugene for as long as possible.

Indifferent to Fanny's needs and preoccupied with his own romantic troubles, George daydreams that Lucy comes to him renouncing her father and begging for forgiveness. Pure wish fulfillment, and pure nonsense. Playing God in his own fantasy, George magnanimously pardons his penitent lover. But even in their fantasies Welles's characters are full of contradictions. Moments after pardoning Lucy, George imagines her flirting with other young men. His arrogance battles his jealousy, and loses. He leaves the porch and returns inside the house, muttering "Riffraff!" and slamming the door behind him. George may not yet pay any heed to the tactical maneuvers of Aunt Fanny, but his romantic frustration renders him ripe for an alliance with her.

In the short version of *The Magnificent Ambersons* a brief romantic interlude between Isabel and Eugene occurs immediately after the factory scene, prematurely anticipating their new relationship. In the longer version this interlude occurs after the various conversations described above. As a result of these intervening scenes we are more aware of the stormy family circumstances Eugene and Isabel must consider before informing George of their mutual love. Fittingly, Welles sets their interlude on the same, picturesque lawn where we earlier witnessed Isabel's indulgence of young George after his bad behavior towards Mr. Bronson. The location reminds us of George's unseen but emotionally lurking presence. As does Isabel's attempt to delay informing George of her love for Eugene. From its initial, distant overview, the camera twice cuts closer to Eugene and Isabel to capture their fragile intimacy. In close-up they seem isolated and safe from outside forces hostile to their love. But Isabel's worried plea to postpone telling George implies that she anticipates trouble.

Supper in the Amberson's spacious dining room brings all of the principle characters except Lucy together in the same place at the same time. Conversation around the table is convivial, at first. But the unlit chandelier hanging over everyone's heads foreshadows a gloomy outcome, and when contrasted with the vibrantly lit chandelier in the reception hall during the Christmas ball scene reflects the declining financial and social fortunes of the Ambersons.

Major Amberson starts things off brightly enough by affectionately referring to the absent Lucy as "my best girl." He makes the Morgans seem already members of the family. Isabel explains Lucy's absence, while the camera shows Fanny and George watching her from the opposite side of the screen. Emotionally, aunt and nephew parallel one another. George is uncomfortable at the mention of Lucy because of their recent argument. And Fanny resents all of Isabel's dealings with the Morgans. Leaning forward in her chair and turning to face her nephew, Fanny breaks the visual and emotional parallel by confronting

The Magnificent Ambersons. Eugene Morgan (Joseph Cotten) and Isabel Amberson (Dolores Costello) enjoy a romantic moment together. But the Amberson mansion looming in the background reminds us of the familial forces driving them apart.

George about Lucy's absence. With a touch of sarcasm she provokes his ill feelings towards the Morgans, which in turn serves her larger purpose of keeping Isabel and Eugene apart. The Major unwittingly furthers Fanny's agenda by teasing George about his spat with Lucy. Smiling, Fanny glances back and forth between George and the Major, keenly scrutinizing their interaction.

    Sensing a dangerous turn in the conversation, Jack changes the subject, inquiring about Eugene's new competition in the automobile business. The Major follows suit, teasing Eugene that he might be driven out of business by that competition, or that the success of both competitors might drive everyone else off the streets. Visually bracketed between Jack and the Major, Eugene defends himself by noting that automobiles will help the community grow. But Jack undermines that defense by pointing out that such expansion will erode property values in the older, Amberson part of town. The Major soberly echoes that concern, and Eugene admits that progress cannot be stopped, whatever its consequences. Thus a discussion originally intended by Jack to deflect attention from a more divisive topic suddenly *turns* divisive, and ironically supplies George with an opening to attack the man Jack was trying to protect. Reversals abound in this scene as everyone pursues his or her own agenda.

Interrupting Eugene in mid-sentence, George declares automobiles a "useless nuisance." Isabel and Jack are embarrassed. The Major again unwittingly aggravates the situation by requesting clarification. George obliges. Embarrassed, Eugene looks down at his plate and fidgets. Jack again rushes to his defense, describing George's remarks as offensive. George's subsequent silence suggests that Jack's reproach was effective. But in the longer version of the film George talks back.

Pictured alone, thereby adding weight to what he says and how he says it, Eugene surprisingly defends his critic by refining George's crude argument. He speculates on the potentially harmful effects of automobiles on the lives and souls of people. He hints at social changes both monumental and subtle, in peace and war. From an 1890's perspective he vaguely anticipates the mechanized horrors of World Wars One and Two. "It may be that George is right," he admits, glancing at his accuser. Now it is George's turn to look down in embarrassment, the way Eugene did earlier. This dinner scene involving conflicting concerns and differing perspectives masked by a patina of civility is echoed in another dinner scene, in Welles's 1946 movie *The Stranger*. In that film ex-Nazi Franz Kindler, posing as American college professor Charles Rankin, tries to hide his true loyalties by proclaiming extreme anti-Nazi views during a dinner conversation with an undercover FBI agent. But he betrays himself by the savagery of those phony views, advocating the extermination of all Germans. In *Ambersons* George's attack on Eugene's invention is so intense it becomes obvious he is really targeting the inventor.

An exchange of close-ups between Eugene and George makes them seem of closer minds than they have ever been, especially after Eugene's concession to George's criticism of the automobile. But that visual impression is an illusion. George hasn't the imagination to see the future possibilities of technology, good or bad. He attacked the automobile as a convenient means of attacking Eugene for a crime (prejudicing Lucy's mind against George) having nothing to do with the impact of the internal combustion engine on civilization at large. Therefore George cannot reciprocate Eugene's magnanimous gesture. Instead of apologizing for his rudeness, George says nothing. So Eugene politely excuses himself and departs. Fanny, Jack, and the Major, each for his or her own reasons, accompany him, leaving George and Isabel alone. George moves closer to his mother.

Isabel timidly chastises George for hurting Eugene's feelings. Typically, George refuses to acknowledge Eugene's pain or his own rudeness. Jack returns, changing the mood of the scene yet again. Instead of returning to the dining table to confront his nephew at close range, Jack fires sarcastic volleys at him from across the room while pacifying his own anger with a cigar. But at least he *tries* to restrain himself. George too maintains emotional distance by not turning around to face his uncle or to acknowledge the sting of Jack's remarks. Responding to George's non-response, Jack turns *his* back on the young man. But by verbally targeting George's rocky romance with Lucy in order to punish George for insulting Eugene, Jack finds the chink in his nephew's armor. Wounded, George throws down his napkin and storms out of the room without a word. Isabel stands up in alarm, but is powerless to do anything. She is caught between two loves that cannot be reconciled to each other and neither of which she can give up.

Outside the dining room, in the shadowy silence of the huge reception hall, Fanny joins her angry nephew, half whispering encouragement to him. In her desperation to separate Eugene from Isabel she again tries to ally herself with George's most selfish impulses. And to that ignoble end she calls on the newly sainted memory of her brother, George's late father, Wilbur Minafer. But the long history of antagonism between Fanny and George complicates her attempt to form common cause. George is rightly suspicious of her motives, if not her sanity. And Fanny is quick to fall back on her favorite self-defense against George's cruel insults—martyrdom. She complains that he has picked on her ever since he was a child. Her feelings of persecution work against her efforts to manipulate him.

Bickering, the two characters walk up the grand staircase towards their respective rooms. Fanny takes the lead. George drops back, distancing himself from her unseemly display. Large, stained glass windows in the background illuminate him, while Fanny's off screen voice prattles on. But Fanny is clever. By referring to *public* gossip about Isabel and Eugenes' romance, she eliminates herself as the primary source of that revelation and gives it greater credibility in the mind of her nephew, who generally disregards *her* opinions. Shocked, George pursues Fanny up the staircase. She turns and, resuming her climb, walks away from him, feigning innocence while deliberately misinterpreting George's rude behavior towards Eugene as a product of his concern for Isabel's reputation. In fact, George's rudeness was triggered by his quarrel with Lucy. But it is Fanny's selfish intention to replace Lucy with Isabel as a bone of contention between the two men.

Emotional seduction alternates with bitter confrontation as Fanny and George repeatedly pause to face each other, then resume their climb, with Fanny now tactically in the lead. At one point the camera looks up as though spying on them from below. The absence of music so far in this scene adds to our impression of the vastness and architectural complexity of the mansion. Its many nooks and crannies correspond to the multiple, overlapping nuances of relations among its occupants. A long history of past events impinges on and shapes current developments, complicating Fanny's attempt to manipulate her nephew.

George scoffs at Fanny's allegation of public gossip about Isabel and Eugene. Invoking Jack's name to back him up, George claims that any such gossip would be about *Fanny's* rather than Isabel's attempts to romance Eugene. And he adds that Fanny herself said earlier that Isabel's only reason for spending time with Eugene was to encourage his interest in Fanny. Exasperated, Fanny is torn between maneuvering George into an alliance and venting her pent-up anger over ill treatment by him. She degrades herself by exploiting her own painful sense of insignificance to lend credibility to the notion that public gossip must be about Isabel rather than herself, because no one would believe a romantic attachment between Fanny and Eugene. George cannot argue with that, because he too has a low opinion of Fanny.

Casting aside all moral restraint, Fanny reveals that Isabel was once engaged to Eugene and that it is public knowledge that she never loved another man. What an insult to George's newfound respect for Wilbur. To avoid being exposed as a liar for saying in an earlier scene that there was no gossip about Isabel and Eugene, Fanny takes shelter in a loophole. "It would never have amounted to anything if Wilbur had lived." George expands on that new idea. "You mean Morgan might have married you?" That is not the point Fanny was trying to make. But George's remark exposes a raw nerve, throwing her back on the defensive. Gathering up her fragile pride, she unconvincingly speculates that she might have refused such a proposal even if it had been offered. Which is a complete self-deception. George, however, wastes his new tactical advantage. He asks Fanny if Eugene's recent attentions to the widowed Isabel have validated the public's false (in George's mind) perception that Isabel was in love with Eugene before Wilbur died. Fanny, placing a phony hand of sympathy on George, happily confirms his suspicion, pretending to be surprised that he hadn't realized it before now.

The fury Aunt Fanny deliberately provokes in George proves greater than her ability to control it. Grabbing her firmly by the arms, George extorts from her an admission that one of her best friends, the notoriously nosy Mrs. Johnson, about whom Isabel spoke during the missing front porch scene, is involved in spreading the vicious gossip. Again the past burdens the present. Isabel's casual observation from an earlier scene now inadvertently helps Fanny sabotage her relationship with Eugene.

George abruptly leaves Fanny and heads downstairs. The camera remains on Fanny, who watches him go with a look of panic on her face. She asks him what he intends to do. The sound of the mansion's front door slamming shut is all the reply she gets. Fanny has become a genteel version of Lady Macbeth, inciting someone else to violence, then losing control over that violence and unable to cope with its consequences, resulting in her own emotional breakdown.

The sound of one door slamming shut is displaced by the sight of another door opening. Mrs. Johnson greets George, and us via a briefly subjective camera, in the traditionally if superficially polite manner of the era. Like Lucy Morgan at the ball, she mistakenly identifies George as an Amberson, then corrects her mistake. And it is as an outraged *Minafer* that George calls on her. Before his father's death he would have been flattered to be called an Amberson.

With George we enter Mrs. Johnson's comfortable though not lavish home. Could envy of the Amberson wealth be one motive for her gossip about Isabel? When George steps in front of the camera, displaying his stiffly tense back to us, the camera is no longer subjective. George struggles to control his anger. Uncomfortable at broaching an uncivil topic, he confronts, then turns away from, then again confronts his host, finally blurting out the point of his visit. Likewise, Mrs. Johnson alternately turns her back on and confronts her guest. She refuses to answer his questions, pointing out that they are not in a court of law. Closing the physical distance between them, George appropriates her defense and turns it against her, loudly insisting that she might soon find herself in a court of law. But as he raves on about forcing his way into every house in town to discover the source of gossip about his mother, Mrs. Johnson turns again to face him, interrupts his tirade, and tactically trumps him. Turning his words against him, as he did hers, she shouts," You'll know something pretty quick! You'll know you're out on the street!" Then she orders him to leave her house. As one of the town's leading gossips, she may know more about Major Amberson's financial troubles than does George. If so, that knowledge gives her some satisfaction while under attack by the most arrogant of the Ambersons.

A direct cut to the next scene comments sarcastically on the confrontation between George and Mrs. Johnson. A close-up of a groaning faucet dispensing hot water into a bathtub occupied by Jack Amberson echoes his subsequent expression of disgust at George's misguided defense of Isabel's public reputation. The defective plumbing is also another indication of the creeping decay taking root in the once new and magnificent Amberson mansion. Decay the family no longer has the money to repair, as Mrs. Johnson implied.

The scene's third shot shows George in the foreground, arguing with while facing away from Jack, visible in the background. George seems to concede a tactical advantage to Jack by not facing him. But the image on screen is an illusion. When George's head moves out of the camera frame we suddenly realize that we were looking at Jack's reflection in a mirror. George *was* facing Jack, and concedes nothing to his uncle's argument that by confronting and denying gossip he unintentionally validates it.

To the continued sounds of faulty plumbing, Jack and George shout at each other. At last they are having a frank discussion about Isabel and Eugene. Missing from the short version of the movie is Jack's warning to George not to confront Isabel about the scandal because of her ill health (Carringer, *Ambersons*, pp.189–191). This is the first we or George learn about her medical problems. And because this revelation has been omitted from the existing film, we lack an understanding of one reason why George does not confront his mother directly and immediately about the gossip.

In the next scene Eugene arrives at the mansion by automobile. Visible in the background is the home of Mrs. Johnson, where gossip has already helped to doom Eugene's mission to failure. How differently that same house appeared to us at the start of the film, when it served as a generic representation of gracious living and communal generosity. Bernard Herrmann's music picks up on the foreshadowing imagery. Its grim tone adds to the subsequent encounter between Eugene and George a feeling of inevitability, rooted in George's stubborn inability to rise above his own selfish impulses, which were in turn nurtured by many years of maternal indulgence. George observes Eugene's arrival from an upper story window. From a low camera angle he appears haughty and stern. And when the camera adopts George's point of view, Eugene appears small, vulnerable, and naively confident.

Viewed in close-up from outside as Eugene rings the doorbell off screen, the inner set of the mansion's double doors, with their ornate knobs and window decorations, is equivalent to the fortified entrance to a castle. Viewed through the frosted glass in those doors, George appears remote and cold. Dismissing the maid, he contemptuously refers to the off screen visitor as a mere peddler. With unblinking eyes and a rigidly set jaw, George opens the inner door, then the outer door, and confronts Eugene, refusing him admittance. By employing a double set of doors, Welles aesthetically magnifies George's rejection of Eugene.

There is an eerie symmetry between George's refusal to admit Eugene into the Amberson mansion in this scene and the butler's refusal, at Isabel's instruction, to do so decades earlier. The spoiled, selfish, petulant young woman is displaced by her spoiled, selfish, petulant son. But the victim remains the same. After George slams the door in his face, it is now *Eugene's* figure that is rendered obscure by the frosted glass. But that obscurity contributes to our understanding of his reaction. Because we cannot see his facial expression, we notice more his body's delayed withdrawal from the door, as a result of the shock of being exiled from Isabel. But he is still too much of a gentleman to protest. Background music that faded out during the confrontation between George and Eugene now returns, its heavy sense of gloom echoing the broader significance of George's action. Significance that George himself does not yet comprehend. Unless he changes his mind soon, he has doomed his mother and Eugene to unhappiness, possibly shortened Isabel's life, severely damaged his own relationship with Lucy, and all but guaranteed the comeuppance prophesied for him so long ago by Roger Bronson.

The door George slams shut as he returns inside the mansion lap dissolves to a shot of Isabel, dressed for her outing with Eugene, anxiously gazing out a window in anticipation of his arrival. As the door/Isabel image implies, George's rejection of Eugene is also a rejection of any consideration for Isabel's happiness. Viewed by a camera looking in from outside the window, Isabel is framed by a narrow opening in dark, diaphanous curtains resembling a mourning veil, indicative of the traditional mourning period within which George wants to entrap and ensure his mother's love — ostensibly for Wilbur, but in fact for himself. Visible to the far right of Isabel is a framed portrait of Wilbur that George placed there in a scene preceding Eugene's arrival at the mansion but cut from the shortened version of the movie. The portrait is intended to remind Isabel of her marital duty. But Isabel ignores the portrait. Her love, as public gossip speculates, has always belonged to Eugene.

Gone from the short version of the film is an encounter between George and Isabel soon after Eugene's attempt to call on her. Heeding Jack's earlier warning about his mother's delicate health, George says little to her, lying about whom he turned away at the door.

Isabel, still expecting Eugene to come for her, expresses concern about George getting enough to eat. As always, her loyalties are hopelessly divided between son and lover. She has no clue that her son just condemned her to a life of loneliness. And even if she did it would not diminish her blind devotion to him.

Isabel finally notices the portrait of Wilbur that George intended her to see, but is not sufficiently moved by it to forsake her steadfast love for Eugene, as George hoped she would. Disappointed, George leaves the room. Isabel resumes her vigil for the lover who will never come.

George's idealization of his late father allows him to righteously battle Eugene for Isabel's love. This action has at least two echoes in Welles's film adaptation of *Macbeth*. While contemplating the murder of Duncan, Macbeth exaggerates the King's virtues in order to counteract his own violent ambition. Oddly enough, the murderous Macbeth employs this self-delusion to a morally superior purpose than does George. Later in *Macbeth*, the young son of Macduff questions his father's courage, then moments later reverses himself and furiously defends Macduff's character against charges of treason by Macbeth.

Responding to the sound of someone's arrival at the mansion's front door, Isabel encounters Jack instead of Eugene in the reception hall. Observed by the camera from a high angle and at a great distance, the two characters are almost lost in the decorative patterns of the enormous mansion. A portion of the first floor ceiling looms heavily over their heads. The entire emotional weight of the Amberson family, past and present, weighs down on them.

Returning from a visit with Eugene, Jack takes Isabel into an adjoining room to tell her the bad news about what happened between Eugene and George. Instead of following them, the camera drifts upward, spying George leaning over a second floor railing, from where he was eavesdropping on his mother and uncle. An off screen whisper draws the camera's attention up to a third floor railing, from where Fanny was eavesdropping on Isabel, Jack, *and* George. From the camera's low angle vantage point, George and Fanny appear far away from us and from each other. And the mansion itself seems more than ever a sinister, towering, multi-leveled structure reflecting its resident family, which has splintered into separate and often hostile points of view.

Ominous music reinforces an atmosphere of conspiracy as Fanny scurries down the staircase to join George. Avoiding her, George descends halfway to the first floor. When Fanny gets his attention they are still far apart, physically and emotionally. Fanny knows what Jack and Isabel are discussing behind closed doors. She also knows that George intends to interrupt them. Frantic and forceful, she races down the staircase to stop him. Large shadows and heavy wood decor add greatly to our impression of dark passions at work here.

Pushing George back up the stairs, berating him, clamping her hand over his mouth to silence him, Fanny again plays the part of parental disciplinarian that his parents never did. Curiously, George lets her get away with it. Like many spoiled brats, he is alternately unruly and submissive. Stopping near the camera, aunt and nephew argue about Isabel and Eugene. Exploding in whispered anger and pent-up guilt, Fanny scolds George the way he should have been scolded a long time ago. Then she turns that critical eye on herself. Facing the painful truth about everyone and everything all at once, she verges on a nervous breakdown. A lifetime of frustration and regret comes into focus in Agnes Moorhead's performance as Fanny reluctantly *forces* the terrible words out of her mouth — out of her *gut*.

Understanding little of what Fanny tells him, George is irritated that she has suddenly turned against him and his crusade to separate Isabel and Eugene. At the sound of Jack's departure downstairs, George turns away from his aunt and starts down the steps. But

The Magnificent Ambersons. Levels and shadows divide Fanny Minafer (Agnes Moorehead) from George Minafer (Tim Holt) as she spies on him while he eavesdrops on his unseen mother and her brother. No two members of the Amberson family see eye to eye at this point in the story.

again he yields to Fanny's command not to disturb Isabel. "Let her alone!" she repeats in a desperate whisper. It is Fanny's finest hour, morally speaking, as she makes a passionate plea on behalf of her rival for Eugene. "Let her alone!" is more than a plea for George not to disturb Isabel at this particular moment. It is a demand that George stop interfering in Isabel's love life altogether. Returning up the stairs, George obeys the *first* meaning of Fanny's command. But he will ignore the second.

Eugene's letter of appeal to Isabel is handled differently in the film's two versions. In the short version we start with a shot of Eugene seated at his desk at home, writing and then in voiceover reading his letter to us. During that voice over the camera segues to a long shot of the reception hall at the Amberson mansion, then dissolves to a shot of Isabel alone, reading Eugene's letter. The longer version of the movie concentrates exclusively on Isabel, who reads the letter while Eugene's voiceover reveals its content. The room Isabel occupies is dimly lit. When she sits down to read Eugene's letter black circles appear under her eyes—evidence of sleeplessness and worry. But when she looks up from the letter, just as Eugene's voiceover urges her to be strong and to fight for their future together, her eyes glow with determination. She stands and walks forward, tracked by the camera. But then she stops, indecision in her movements and in her eyes.

Roy Webb's background music replaces Bernard Herrmann's in this scene. Webb's composition, particularly a brief violin solo, sweetly sentimentalizes what Eugene's letter describes more ironically as Isabel's "selfless and perfect motherhood." Musically we lose touch with the destructive forces lurking just beneath the surface of this scene. It is too late in the story for such pure, superficial sentiment. In part because Isabel's "selfless and perfect motherhood" is to a large extent responsible for the emotional battle in which Isabel, Eugene, and George are now embroiled.

Isabel gives Eugene's letter to George to read. Missing from the short version of the film is his immediate reaction to it, in the privacy of his bedroom. At first he is inclined to toss the letter into the fireplace. Instead he keeps it in his hand. Emerging from his room, he shuts the door firmly behind him and strides purposefully towards Isabel's room, through a long hallway that evokes the great emotional distance between them. Responding off screen to her son's knock, Isabel sounds hopeful. Entering her room, George destroys that hope, but in different ways depending on which version of the film we're dealing with. In Welles's now lost version (Carringer, *Ambersons*, pp.205–207) George dominates the conversation, denigrating Eugene and the letter. He no longer heeds Jack's earlier advice not to upset his mother because of her delicate health. And his cruelty is consistent with the determined and angry manner in which George approached Isabel's room. Isabel is unable to fight back, as Eugene's letter urged her to do. George casts himself as the offended party. How else would we expect so immature a young man to react to Eugene's insightful critique of his character? Under Welles's direction this must have been a pivotal scene in the film, partly because we witness George browbeating his mother for the first time. Previously his objections to her relationship with Eugene were expressed only to other people.

Robert Wise, the film's editor, directed the existing version of the bedroom scene. The end result is the same, but the route to that result is quite different. Wise softens George's entrance into the room and his subsequent confrontation with Isabel. The young man is less cruel and domineering in his selfishness. He is reluctant to discuss Eugene's letter. Ashamed of himself, he avoids eye contact with his mother and walks away from her. There may be a hint of Oedipal fixation in him when he stands beside her bed, but any hint of aggression fades when he sits down on that bed in a confused daze. Isabel presses her son's head to her body, soothing away his childish fears and promising to delay matters with Eugene and go away on a trip with George instead. Backed by Roy Webb's saccharine music, the action translates into pure, self-sacrificial maternal love rather than dysfunctional family drama. As though Wise took literally Eugene's description of Isabel's devotion as "selfless and perfect." Whereas the points of Welles's version is that Isabel's devotion is *neither* selfless nor perfect. Stemming in the first place from her lack of passion for Wilbur, her blind loyalty to and indulgence of George cripples him, encouraging his worst impulses and perpetuating his childish outlook. Gone too from the short version of *The Magnificent Ambersons* is a brief scene in George's bedroom. Isabel slips a letter under his door. George reads her pathetic surrender to his wishes. She explains that she also wrote to Eugene, ending their relationship. Trapped between contradictory loves, she can no more disappoint Eugene face to face than she can risk upsetting George by crying in his presence. Aside from its self-effacing tone, Isabel's letter addresses George like a lover from whom she begs forgiveness. George reads the letter while lying on his bed. It is difficult to assess the missing scene merely by a written description of it. But one can almost sense a callow contentment in George when, midway through the letter, he rolls over on his stomach, like a child lolling in his crib, secure in the exclusive love of his mother. But what of the script description, "George to foreground — Frowning," after he finishes reading the letter (Carringer, *Ambersons*, p.209)? Does that frown signify a glimmer of guilt over destroying his mother's happiness?

Sometime later, George encounters Lucy on a downtown street. It is an awkward meeting for both. Predictably, Lucy breaks the ice first, with a civil greeting. George had already walked passed without acknowledging her. Removing his hat, he approaches her meekly. But he cannot broach the issue that divides them, so he merely asks permission to walk with her.

Lucy too masks her true feelings, a mixture of anger and lingering affection, behind a casual smile. But some of that anger speaks through her request that George talk about something pleasant because her father has been too glum lately to talk with her. George is still too selfishly obtuse to detect the subtext of her remark. He even has the gall to complain about *her* lack of consideration for going away on a trip, following their previous argument, without telling him in advance. She retaliates by blithely comparing their previous romance to a children's game that got out of hand and had to stop.

Accompanying Lucy and George on their stroll, we see passing glimpses of storefronts that remind us of domestic routines they might have experienced together if things had turned out differently for them as a couple. A bank, an interior decorations shop, a haberdashery, a drapery shop, a movie theater, and a pharmacy. Meanwhile, other pedestrians pass by behind and in front (visible as reflections on storefront windows) of the young pair, ignorant of and detached from their problems.

Lucy maintains her cheerful demeanor when George tells her he is leaving with Isabel on an extended vacation. George is flabbergasted at her outward lack of reaction. Of course he's a hypocrite for being so, since he displayed far less consideration for the feelings of Isabel and Eugene. George bids Lucy a sad farewell and walks away. The camera remains on Lucy. Her smile fades when George can no longer see her, then brightens again when he looks back in her direction and reminds her that they might never see each other again. Mortified that she will not acknowledge their love, he storms off without looking at her again. By telling George to convey her love to Isabel, Lucy fires a parting if well-disguised verbal shot by reminding him of the breech *he* created between their two families. Lucy could not have executed a better revenge on George if she had yelled at him. But, of course, her feelings for George are contradictory. And by giving us a big, gooey close-up of her sad face after George departs, the short version of the movie unfortunately makes obvious what should be subtle.

Before leaving, George melodramatically threatened to step into the nearby pharmacy for something to stop him from dying of shock as a result of Lucy's cool reaction to his vacation news. Obviously he imparted that news in order to elicit from her a declaration of love. In the wake of George's departure, the woman he accused of callousness steps into the pharmacy to request medical aid, which George only *threatened* to do. Her feelings of love are much deeper than his. So much so that she faints while waiting for the druggist to fetch her medicine.

Gone too from the existing movie is an important scene involving Fanny and the Major, sitting and talking at night on the front porch of the mansion while automobiles pass by in the background. That busy traffic is perhaps the key to the business decision they make in this scene. With property values down, the failure of rental property to bring in sufficient income, and Jack's encouragement from abroad, Fanny and the Major decide to invest in a new automobile headlight company. They belatedly hop on the economic bandwagon Eugene Morgan helped set in motion. The Major speculates optimistically (or is it sarcastically?) that he and Fanny might become millionaires. But as Eugene pondered a few scenes ago at the Amberson dining table, the automobile creates as much hardship as it does benefit. Unintentionally, Eugene gets revenge on the entire Amberson family for Isabel's double rejection of him.

The Major mentions to Fanny Isabel's desire, expressed in letters from Europe, to return home. Fanny diverts conversation back to the topic of investments, perhaps because of the guilt she feels about Isabel leaving home with George. But as events turn out, investment is *not* a safe topic for Fanny Minafer.

Jack's return from abroad is handled differently in the two versions of the movie. In the long version Jack draws an ironic parallel between the Ambersons and the Morgans as he and Lucy emerge from a chauffeur driven automobile and approach the Morgans' new mansion. In his typically sardonic way Jack speculates that the Morgans and their magnificent new residence will inevitably suffer the same fate as the once prosperous Ambersons. Taking no offense at his remark, Lucy affectionately takes Jack by the arm. These two characters share a similar outlook. Though not true cynics, both are able to view people and events, including themselves at times, with minimal sentiment. Eugene is capable of viewing his invention in the same manner, but cannot do so with Isabel.

The short version of this already brief scene eliminates Jack's ironic prediction about the Morgans' future, replacing it with innocuous small talk. The ensuing conversation inside the parlor of the Morgan mansion is, however, preserved largely intact. From the camera's fixed point of view, Jack sits between Lucy and Eugene. The immobility of the camera and the absence of background music reinforces the intimacy of their conversation.

In contrast to his flippant manner with Lucy outside the house, Jack is now uncomfortable and awkward, because he brings bad news for Eugene. Taking a cigar from the table in front of him, he pacifies his nerves by fiddling with it as he reluctantly informs the Morgans that Isabel is very ill. He intimates that she wants to return home. And that while George is not physically preventing her from doing so, he uses emotional manipulation to keep her abroad. Eugene seconds that opinion — twice, for emphasis. His view of George has hardened since he first spoke about the young man with Lucy, after the ball, and even since he wrote his letter of appeal to Isabel.

Eventually Isabel does return home. George carries her from the train station to a, predictably, horse-drawn carriage. By shooting from a low angle and limiting most of the action to the lower half of the screen, Welles emphasizes the ornate, antiquated architecture of the station's roof and places a lot of empty sky above Isabel, making her seem even more frail. Inside the claustrophobic, dark interior of the carriage, fitfully brightened by light and scenery visible through a window, Isabel leans on her son's shoulder. In emotional as well as visual terms, George selfishly keeps her in the dark, all to himself.

Eugene's attempt to call on Isabel at the Amberson mansion is handled differently in the film's two versions. In the Welles version George cruelly exploits a distraught Aunt Fanny to keep Eugene away from his mother, after allowing Major Amberson to enter Isabel's room. There is no direct confrontation between George and Eugene. And Jack does not participate in the action at all. In the revised version of this scene, shot by someone other than Welles, George confronts Eugene face to face in the reception hall. Unlike the previous time he called for Isabel, to take her out for a drive, this time Eugene ignores George's objections and starts up the stairs to Isabel's room. Until Fanny and Jack of their own volition intervene, reinforcing and legitimizing George's objection. And leaving us with the false impression that perhaps George really is motivated by concern for his mother's welfare rather than by jealous resentment of Eugene.

Retained in the non-Welles version of the scene are two very Wellesian shots of George watching Eugene's departure from an upstairs window, similar to an earlier shot of George watching Eugene approach the house to take Isabel out for a ride. These images strengthen our perception of George as a petty, possessive young man, even on the brink of his mother's death. We see it especially in a close-up of his glaring face, reflected off the window pane, blended with an extreme long shot of Eugene's small figure retreating into the distance. Heavy shadows between the two figures further distance them from each other, while Bernard Herrmann's music quietly conveys the to us the full moral horror of George's action, which George himself does not yet comprehend.

A nurse's voice diverts George's attention from the window and Eugene. A huge close-up of George's head captures the emotional impact on him as his attention shifts from vanquished foe to dying mother. Getting rid of his rival is a brief, hollow victory. In shock, he now walks slowly through the shrouded hallway between his own and Isabel's room. He is much less bold and arrogant this time than when he approached Isabel's room after reading Eugene's letter.

George kneels at his mother's bedside. Her face looks haggard, recalling the face of Susan Alexander after her suicide attempt and while she conversed with the man who drove her to that desperate act. George is here equivalent to Charlie Kane. But Isabel is no Susan, who openly pleaded for release from the hell to which Kane consigned her. Isabel, true to form, is even while lying on her deathbed more concerned with her son's welfare than with her own. Her overprotectiveness resembles that of Mary Kane. Is George what Charlie Kane might have become if he had been raised to adulthood by his mother? It might seem ludicrous that in her hour of desperation Isabel could still exhibit so much blind devotion to her selfish son. But remember that her extreme attachment to George is partly a product of her repressed passion for Eugene. When George prevented it from fulfilling itself after Wilbur's death, Isabel's starved desire redoubled itself back on George. Because of George, George is all she's got. So she gives him everything *she's* got.

Isabel is surrounded by spidery shadows formed by light filtering into the room through lace curtained windows. Figuratively speaking, Isabel is trapped in a web made up of George's selfish manipulation and by her own physical and emotional weakness. She inquires about the Morgans. Jealous, George lets go of her hand. To his meager credit, however, he tells her about Eugene's attempt to visit her, which he did *not* do when Eugene called on her earlier to take her out for a ride. Expressing her wish to have seen Eugene one more time, Isabel unintentionally guarantees that George will eventually feel the full guilt of having denied his mother's last wish.

Concerned about Isabel's weakening condition, the nurse sends George away, as George previously did Eugene. She pulls the curtains over the window, deepening the web-like shadows over Isabel's face, yet paradoxically heightening the patient's sparkling eyes as she looks anxiously after her departing son. Those eyes and that devotion will haunt George to the end of his days.

Removed from the short version of the movie is a scene in George's room, where George desperately tries to generate hope and reduce his own shame by telling Jack that a New York doctor informed him earlier that Isabel might recover. Jack walks away without comment, refusing to play George's game. The removal of this scene reduces our sense of acrimony within the family.

The subsequent scene is thankfully left intact, yielding a powerful impression of the devastating impact Isabel's death has on the surviving family members. It begins with a close-up of the Major lying on George's bed. He awakens from a fitful sleep, echoed by Herrmann's restless music. Then he reacts with alarm to something he sees off screen. As he gets out of bed, the camera retreats just far enough to reveal George as the source of the Major's alarm. A Harvard University pennant hanging on the wall above George's bed is a bitter visual reminder of happier, carefree times. The camera pans right with the Major as he walks past his nephew and out of the room, presumably heading for Isabel's. Then we see the source of *George's* alarm, which in turn alarmed the Major. It is Fanny, who arrived from Isabel's bedside moments earlier and now hugs her nephew with great compassion, reassuring George that his mother loved him. By staggering our exposure to the reactions of the Major, George, and Fanny in this scene, Welles both intensifies their dramatic potency and gives them individuality. The continuation of Herrmann's restless dream music after the Major awakens informs us that nightmare has become reality. The odd visual timing in this scene makes us feel a bit unsure, unhinged, even unreal, which is often the way it feels in the immediate aftermath of losing a loved one.

The Ambersons are a house divided against itself, in spite of or perhaps even because of their grief over Isabel's death. That isolation is immediately evident in the next scene, beginning with a frontal close-up of the Major sitting in a throne-like chair, his ancient face illuminated by flickering light from a fireplace. The narrator speaks for him, disclosing doubts and fears too private and intense for him to share. As a result of Isabel's death, the Major fears his own impending extinction, and suddenly doubts the value of everything he achieved and acquired in his long life. Missing from this scene are narrative references to the Major's Civil War combat experience and his thoughts about Isabel. War was the Major's first brush with death, and now seems more relevant to his life than all the intervening years of business triumph and failure. Isabel, who preceded her father in death and is therefore, he hopes, in a position to be his guide in the afterlife, offers some consolation to the Major, soothing his fear of the unknown. Removing the Isabel reference from this scene has the effect, intended or not, of *deepening* our impression of the Major's fear.

Also edited out of the scene is an off screen dialog between Fanny and Jack concerning a missing deed to the mansion and their disastrous investment in the automobile headlight business. Those pragmatic concerns counterpoint the Major's private thoughts about mortality and cosmic meaning. Welles again emphasizes the emotional disparity within the Amberson family following Isabel's death.

In the existing version of the scene all that remains of Jack and Fannys' contribution is Jack questioning his father, from off screen, about the deed to the house. Jack's voice sounds remote, as does that of George, who joins in. The Major, preoccupied with other matters, cannot recall when he gave the deed to Isabel. Then his focus returns inward. George dismisses the importance Jack attaches to the deed. He still has little appreciation for the financial realities that underpin his privileged lifestyle. Or else he doesn't want to upset his grandfather about it. Removed from the end of this scene is George's off screen voice asking his grandfather if he would like a glass of water. Not much comfort for an old man wrestling with larger questions about his life.

Following the Major's death, Jack leaves Midland in search of employment. His farewell scene with George at the train station is cut in half in the short version of the movie. Gone is his explanation that as an ex-Congressman he is traveling to Washington DC to apply for an overseas consulship. Gone too is George's display of generosity as he tries to give Jack more money than Jack requests. As for *emotional* support, George has less to offer. He is unable to comprehend Jack's parting, pessimistic, sardonic comments about the meaninglessness of his future profession as a foreign consul, the painful prospect of never seeing his family again, and the inevitability of his own obscure death, marked only by a few "dusty curios" (Carringer, *Ambersons*, p.239) passed on to surviving family members. It is a melancholy portrait of loneliness, enhanced by the train station's high ceiling arching heavily over the characters in a low angle shot.

What survives of this scene is Jack's reminiscence about an incident long ago when, in the same spot where he and George now stand, he said goodbye to a girl he loved. At the time he didn't think he would survive the pain of their parting. With bittersweet hindsight he notes otherwise. He has no idea where the girl is now, if she is still alive, or if she ever thinks of him. If she does, he speculates, her thoughts are probably rooted in outdated impressions of him. Expanding on that point, Jack remarks that his parting from the girl took place in the *old* station, before the current one was built, and that it was formerly known as the "depot." Passions fade. Places and names change. Even memories become distorted. So bachelor Jack too had a woman in white (Bernstein) and an Emily Norton (Leland).

In his book-length interview with Welles, Peter Bogdanovich recalled an occasion at his home when he and a group of friends watched *The Magnificent Ambersons* on television. Welles too was present, but found the experience painful and left the room. Bogdanovich assumed that Welles's discomfort was caused by seeing the changes made to his movie by the studio, against his wishes. Much later Welles explained, "That just made me angry. Don't you see? It was because it's the past — it's over" (Welles/Bogdanovich, p.132). Much of Welles's work in film evokes an acute awareness of the ravages of time on the individual. A keen sense of loss brought on by age: loss of friends; of experiences, whether good or bad, that help anchor one's existence; of memory itself, both our own and other people's memories of us. Jack, as he says goodbye to George and his hometown for possibly the last time, ponders that inevitable loss in this scene. His personal sense of loss is linked, in *The Magnificent Ambersons* and again in Welles's *Chimes at Midnight*, to a broader, cultural sense of mutability. Jack, Fanny, the Major, and eventually George all experience the sorrow and disorientation of losing both a patrician way of life and the people, objects, settings, activities, and good health that were such intimate parts of their lives in earlier days. Charlie Kane's nostalgic fixation on a childhood represented by Rosebud is a desperate attempt to recapture what was but is no longer, or maybe what never was but *should* have been, or what in his faulty recollection *seems* to have been. We all play that game. But it is extraordinary that Orson Welles was at so young an age so interested in and skilled at dramatizing that sense of loss and its potential effects, both beneficial and corrosive, on human outlook and behavior. Part of the balancing act in *The Magnificent Ambersons* is that George Minafer benefits emotionally from his losses while Fanny and Isabel are destroyed by them.

The point of Jack's lengthy speech, like that of Bernstein's story about the woman in white in *Citizen Kane*, is that life is ever-changing, memory is fleeting and often faulty, and that the ties that bind people together are fragile at best. In his roundabout, hard boiled way, Jack tries to tell George that he loves and will miss him. That expression of love comes out as a mixture of affection and censure — the latter for the terrible thing George did to Isabel and Eugene. But affection comes out on top. And by telling George that somebody else in town might feel the same way about him, Jack does his bit to patch things up between George and Lucy. A remarkable act of kindness, in view of George's crimes. And in return George says nothing. Gives nothing.

Just as it appears Jack is about to give George some serious advice about Lucy, he is interrupted by the sound of his train about to pull out of the station and an off screen announcement summoning passengers. Another untimely interruption, validating the view of life Jack expressed moments earlier. He grabs his bags and runs for the train after bidding George a quick farewell. Receding from George and from us, he fades into a hazy mass of light streaming into the station through windows in the background. In its own way this final parting is as moving and memorable as Susan Alexander's parting from Charlie Kane. But Susan's departure is an act of self-preservation and revenge. Jack's is a painful economic necessity and maybe even a self-sacrifice. He doesn't want to be a financial burden on George. Of course, it was Jack's bad investment advice that cost Fanny and the Major their nest egg.

The comeuppance of George Minafer Amberson commences with his solitary walk back to the mansion he can no longer call his home. Shooting from a low angle, the subjective camera glides slowly through the streets of his hometown as the narrator describes George's inner turmoil. Buildings loom large and ugly, totally lacking in the grace we associate with the Amberson mansion. Electrical and telegraph wires and poles proliferate everywhere. Houses are crammed together, leaving no space in between for broad lawns or elegant gardens. Many of them aren't even houses. They're apartment buildings. A series of lap dissolves pile these visual eyesores one on top of another. No people are visible to give the structures a lived-in feel. In George's eyes the buildings are more like alien creatures than human dwellings. His once familiar world has been invaded by the equivalent of Martians.

Tragically stripped from the film's shortened version is much of the middle section of this scene, as Welles shot it. In subjective alignment with George we see locations linked to specific childhood memories described by the narrator. Thus a broad sense of social change and loss blends with and is intensified by loss of a more private nature. Bernard Herrmann's eerie yet melancholy music could just as easily be a portrait of the Moon. George has become a stranger in a strange land.

The last structure we were intended to see during George's final journey home is, logically, the Amberson mansion. His sanctuary. His Xanadu. Unfortunately that image is forever stripped from *our* experience of the movie, as the mansion itself soon will be from George. According to Carringer (Carringer, *Ambersons*, p.245) much footage was shot, again from George's vantage point, inside the deserted mansion, which seems like a perfect counterpoint to our earlier exploration of the mansion during the Christmas ball. One can only imagine a dramatic effect similar to that of the traveling shot at Kane's Xanadu where we glide over the accumulated relics of a life that exists no more. The private equivalent of walking through the ruins of a dead civilization. Except this time we would have toured those ruins in the company of a character who feels their loss personally.

Carringer speculates that Welles was not satisfied with the results of the now missing footage, which was shot at his instruction but not under his immediate supervision. Or maybe Welles never intended to use the footage. But from a dramatic standpoint, a second tour of the mansion, under vastly different circumstances from our first tour, seems a brilliant way to impress upon an audience the shattering changes in George's life. The stillness and silence. The absence of all those varied activities that once filled the house: flirtations, arguments, confidences, conspiracies, romantic interludes, gossip, grief, dancing, and music, among others. It is also fitting to conclude a montage portrait of a rapidly changing community with a somber visit to the house that was once but is no longer its cultural center.

The short version of *Ambersons* skips over George's tour of boyhood haunts and most of his stroll through the mansion, joining his sad journey in Isabel's bedroom. For a son just waking up to the fact that he destroyed his mother's last chance at happiness and possibly hastened her death, that room is now a private heart of darkness. From a black screen the camera pulls back, seemingly out of George's head, to show George in silhouette, kneeling at the side of Isabel's bed. Hands folded in prayer, he quietly begs her forgiveness. Visually the camera detaches us from our previously subjective link to George in order to let us witness his first expression of remorse from a distance. Bathed in a mixture of shadow and light, Isabel's bed is stripped of its coverings, magnifying our awareness of her absence. By the end of the camera's reverse dolly George is a small figure in a very large room. The spaciousness of privilege has become an unenviable emptiness. George's appeal for forgiveness is shifted, in the short version of the movie, from the end of the scene to the beginning. And his desperate clutching at a sheet on his mother's bed is eliminated. Welles's narration of the scene too is pruned. Gone are his remarks about impending changes to Isabel's room: the construction of new walls to facilitate conversion of the mansion into a boarding house. Still, the butchered scene generates a powerful impression of regret, loss, and irony. By speaking of George's comeuppance, the narrator reminds us of Roger Bronson's prophecy from years earlier, then intensifies our sense of George's isolation by informing us that citizens who so wished for that event no longer remember doing so. Some of them aren't even alive anymore. Another grim confirmation of Jack Amberson's view of life as a thing akin to "loose quicksilver in a nest of cracks."

Missing from the end of George's bitter homecoming are exterior shots of the mansion revealing broken windows and scrawled graffiti, adding public insult to private injury.

In the long version of the film, George's journey home is followed by a scene involving George and Fanny trying to cope with financial ruin. Carringer says the first four shots of the scene were done by someone other than Welles, whose original footage resumes with the fifth shot (Carringer, *Ambersons*, p.242). The director's intention was to shoot the entire scene in one shot lasting several minutes. At least we're compensated for the loss by Agnes Moorhead's riveting performance as Fanny reluctantly confesses to George that she is unable to pay any of their expenses because she lost all her money in the automobile headlight fiasco.

Neither character is particularly admirable as the scene begins. Fanny, whining about being "left in the lurch" by her nephew, slumps to the floor, her back resting against the now disconnected and cold water heater. George mercilessly berates her. Playing at the opposite end of the emotional scale from her Mary Kane, Moorhead lets all of Fanny's fears and weaknesses cascade out of her in a convincing breakdown. The genteel emotional restraint that governs most of the characters most of the time in *Ambersons* no longer operates in her. And the result is shocking.

Welles's less conventional and more dynamic visual approach is very evident with the fifth shot in this scene, showing Fanny on the floor reacting to the black, looming figure of George in the near foreground. The lighting contrast is more severe now than in the previous four shots. So distraught is Fanny that her breathing is out of sync with her words, strangling some of them. She loses control of her faculties. Pathos, confusion, and rage mix together. Wishing that the water heater were still hot enough to scald her, as punishment for her sins, Fanny is on the verge of suicidal panic.

George pulls Fanny up off the floor. She laughs wildly as he, yelling at her to stop, drags her out of the room. The camera tracks with them, capturing her hysteria but also serving the second dramatic function of showing us what has happened to the mansion. We travel from room to room, each one lit only by harsh sunlight through windows. Furniture is draped with sheets, in a state of disuse between owners. The camera distances us from George and Fanny, rendering them small figures in the mansion's gloomy, cavernous interior. In counterpoint to that visual gloom, George's finer qualities at last begin to shine through in his words and behavior. Holding Fanny by the hand, he soothes her with ideas on how they might economize to get by. But then, turning away from his aunt, he ponders the disparity between their minimum needs and his woefully inadequate, projected salary at a job he hasn't even begun yet. George has of necessity become one of the money-grubbers he found so distasteful earlier in the film.

George's visit to Roger Bronson's office, seeking a job that pays immediately so he can install Fanny in the boarding house of her choice, is filmed in a single shot, within which the two characters move around quite a bit. At first Bronson sits comfortably at his desk to hear George's request. But when he learns that George and Fannys' financial troubles stem partly from Fanny's bad investment in the headlight business, Bronson paces uncomfortably while admitting some responsibility for that investment. The surprising thing here is that Bronson tries to do the right thing by the grandson of his old friend, Major Amberson. Long forgotten is the eagerness with which he anticipated George Minafer's comeuppance, after the young George punched him in the stomach.

Instead of relishing George's current predicament, Bronson reluctantly agrees to help the young man get a quick paying but dangerous job handling dynamite in a factory. And through the windows of Bronson's office we hear reminders (traffic bells and whistles) of the busy new world that now compels George to be practical.

Though occurring earlier in the short version of *Ambersons*, a scene involving Eugene and Lucy strolling through *their* elegant garden was originally placed after the scene in Bronson's office. The Morgans too, in spite of their newly acquired wealth, must cope with the aftermath of tragic events at the Amberson mansion. Backed by pensive organ music, Lucy tells her father in allegorical code about her mixed feelings for George. She employs a story about an Indian tribe that evicted its evil chief but could not find a suitable replacement. Obviously George is the evil chief in her life. And now, after the "unpleasant excitement" he brought her, she claims to desire only peace, quiet, and the company of her adored father. She is turning into another Isabel, with Eugene as her surrogate George instead of George as her surrogate Eugene. Her father gently pokes fun at her allegory. Avoiding any mention of George's name, perhaps because he still resents the young man's interference in his and Isabels' happiness, he expresses hope that someday she will be able to forget the chief's name and presumably get on with her life. Oddly enough, Welles's original placement of this scene yields a dramatic advantage for George, whose moral improvement in the three previous scenes somewhat undercuts Lucy's unflattering portrait of him in her allegory.

George Minafer Amberson is not the victim of a dynamite explosion, as might be expected. He is struck down by an automobile — an invention of the man *he* grievously injured in a different way. We join the scene as he is being carried unconscious to an ambulance. A fire truck bell, a crowd of curious onlookers, and engine exhaust smoke contribute a modern sense of chaos to the event, in marked contrast to the film's opening portrait of slow-paced life in a small town.

The dapper young driver of the automobile that struck George behaves much like his victim once did. In a loud, belligerent voice he denies responsibility for the accident, blaming it all on George. In reel time it isn't long ago that young Minafer raced *his* buggy through these same streets, recklessly disregarding the safety of pedestrians. Compounding that irony, though removed from the short version of the movie, a policeman at the site of the accident contemptuously describes the victim as lower class "riffraff," the same term George once employed to dismiss annoying people who were socially inferior to himself.

In close-up a newspaper headline spells out, "Auto Casualties Mount," accompanied by a satirical cartoon of a skeleton driving an automobile over a row of bodies. According to Carringer the headline originally read, "Automobile Butchery!", which is more suited to a newspaper that is part of Charles Foster Kane's *Inquirer* empire (Carringer, *Ambersons*, p.259). Jed Leland's "Stage Reviews" column is visible at the far left side of the page. Kane's crusading but irresponsible brand of journalism would likely have sensationalized a story like George's accident.

A reverse angle shot shows us a glum Eugene Morgan reading that newspaper article. In the short version of the film he does so at home, with Lucy standing beside him. To the saccharine strains of Roy Webb's soaring strings, Lucy declares her intention to go to George at the hospital. Eugene does not offer to accompany her, so she walks away from him and past the camera, with loving determination written on her face. Hearing the front door close, Eugene follows her in the same manner. One can almost hear Welles groan from his grave at this reworking of his scene.

In the lost Welles version of the same scene, Eugene sits alone in the shadows of his office at the automobile factory as he reads about George's accident. He resolves to visit George in the hospital without prodding from Lucy. And she anticipates that he will do just that, as we learn from Eugene's chauffeur. This puts Eugene in a more favorable light than does the revised version of the scene. His compassion conquers his resentment without outside encouragement. But that happy development was originally intended by Welles to be dramatically counterpointed by a follow-up scene removed from the short version of the movie and replaced with an ending that does the opposite.

In the final scene of *Ambersons* as it now exists, Eugene and Fanny emerge from George's hospital room and walk up a hallway towards the camera. He tells her about his reconciliation with George and of George's mystical feeling that Isabel somehow arranged it. Fanny appears completely recovered from her emotional breakdown at the mansion. The camera backtracks with the characters. And when Eugene speculates rapturously that Isabel must have used him to rescue her son, presumably from his depression at having caused her and Eugene so much pain, the camera closes in to a tight shot of Fanny's face. She has tears in her eyes. Is she still heartbroken over her unrequited love for Eugene, and the ghost-like return of her rival, Isabel? The camera swings to a close-up of Eugene, rhapsodizing about his "one true love." Webb's swelling music does not question his faith.

The camera pulls back just enough to show both characters at the same time. Fanny's beatific smile banishes any thought that she is still consumed by disappointment. All past conflicts are miraculously resolved. All lingering wounds, self-inflicted and otherwise, are miraculously healed. Not even the scars remain. In the same manner that Lucy and then Eugene walked out of the camera frame on their way to visit George at the hospital in the previous scene, Eugene and Fanny now walk past the camera wearing expressions of sublime contentment. Joseph McBride finds this revised scene so confusing it leaves the impression that Eugene has discovered his "true love" for *Fanny* rather than Isabel (McBride, p.82).

In Welles's original ending, Eugene's mood following his visit to George in the hospital is equally euphoric, and is expressed in many of the same words he uses in the revised ending. But that euphoria occurs in a very different setting and context. Instead of the hospital he is in the boarding house where Fanny Minafer resides. And the Fanny with whom he shares his newfound contentment is, unlike her counterpart at the hospital, still a badly damaged person, judging by her actions and her minimal responses to Eugene. The boarding house surrounds her with nosy neighbors. Privacy is scarce, and territory jealously guarded. When Eugene and Fanny retire to the parlor to converse alone, she bluntly asks its prior occupant to leave. And the occupant is not shy about showing his displeasure at the disruption of *his* privacy, tossing down the book he was reading as he departs. How claustrophobic this residence must feel to someone who once resided at the spacious Amberson mansion.

Fanny's replies to Eugene never contradict him. But neither do they offer support. They seem perfunctory, detached, as though her overly strained emotions were no longer capable of sympathy or empathy. The cutting continuity's frequent references to the creaking of her chair as she rocks back and forth suggests that Fanny takes comfort in mindless repetition. The creaking itself is an appropriate metaphor for her fragile state of mind. Still photos from the scene (Carringer, *Ambersons*, pp.264, 266, and 268) show a vacant expression in Fanny's eyes as Eugene talks about what he believes to be Isabel's mystical intervention to reconcile him with George. "She stares off tensely" doesn't sound much like the rapturous expression we see on her face in the revised, hospital scene. And several references to Eugene's shadow passing over Fanny's face recall images of Charlie Kane's shadow hovering oppressively over Susan in *Citizen Kane*. Eugene certainly intends no harm to Fanny. Nevertheless, his presence and his words seem to cause her great distress in the Welles version of the film's ending.

The farewell between Fanny and Eugene is appropriately anticlimactic. She cannot say what she feels, assuming she still *can* feel anything. And he either cannot comprehend her shattered state of mind or is too much of a gentleman to mention it. The unspoken truth between them is that *his* emotional salvation confirms *her* tragedy. Isabel will always be a barrier between them. So they simply part company: Fanny returning to the dubious companionship of her fellow boarders, and Eugene returning to his automobile, which soon disappears into a stream of traffic. In tracing a family history as diverse and dramatic as that of the Ambersons, Minafers, and Morgans, Welles leaves no character behind, in the sense that he accounts for the entangled emotional fates of them all rather than suppressing one in order to validate another. Eugene's consolation is inseparable from Fanny's loneliness. George's reformation is inseparable from Isabel's suffering and death.

Formal, glamorous portraits of the actors appear during the movie's end credits, which are spoken by Welles rather than printed on screen. We see the performers out of character, reminding us of the illusory nature of what we previously saw and heard. A picture of Booth Tarkington's original novel further removes the story from our sense of immediate reality. Finally we see a shot of a microphone pulling away from a movie camera and disappearing into a haze of light and shadow in the distance. Like Jack Amberson disappearing into the distance at the end of his farewell scene with George in the train station, this shot reminds us that even our experience and subsequent recollections of *The Magnificent Ambersons* are fleeting.

3

The Lady from Shanghai:
Lethal Habits

The Lady from Shanghai, like *The Magnificent Ambersons*, did not turn out the way Orson Welles intended. Harry Cohn, head of Columbia Studios at the time, did not grant Welles the right of final cut, as the director enjoyed with *Citizen Kane*. Nor did he allow Welles to work with a composer of his choice. And yet somehow the film works, sometimes beautifully and sometimes in spite of itself. Adapted from the Sherwood King novel *If I Die Before I Wake*, *The Lady from Shanghai* is a classic film noir blend of romance and betrayal, passion and cold calculation. A mix well suited to Welles's flair for dramatizing the contradictions in human nature.

Citizen Kane's "News on the March" mimics and mocks the newsreel style of its time in order to tell the story of Charles Foster Kane from one, narrow perspective. Scratchy film stock, jarring juxtapositions, and crude, melodramatic background music contribute to the illusion that we are watching a genuine newsreel, with all of that format's faults and assets. In *The Lady from Shanghai* Welles plays off and often mocks the conventions of the film noir genre in order to tell the story of a poor romantic sailor who gets involved with some wealthy, manipulative cynics. Like "News on the March," *Shanghai* contains many inconsistencies. Unlike "News on the March," not all of *Shanghai*'s inconsistencies are orchestrated by Welles. But somehow even the unintended ones add to our impression of mounting confusion in the life of protagonist Michael O'Hara.

Among the presumably deliberate stylistic inconsistencies in *The Lady from Shanghai*, typically Wellesian deep focus images intermingle with conventional, shallow focus shots more characteristic of 1940's Hollywood genre films. And sharp focus alternates with soft focus. Less a matter of choice are a number of backscreened process shots that clash with location footage filmed mostly in Mexico. Welles was forced to bring his crew back to Hollywood before completing location shooting. Yet he admitted that he rather liked the process shots because they give part of the movie a "dreamlike" quality (Welles/Bogdanovich, p.191). The director was less enamored of Heinz Roemheld's background score, over which he had no influence. Roemheld's melodramatic music is conventional film noir stuff, and clashes with some of the local music used in the Mexico and Chinatown scenes. Considering the terrific results Welles obtained from working with a variety of composers in films both before and after *Shanghai*, it's a pity he didn't get a chance to do so in this film as well. But even Roemheld's heavy-handed music helps keep an audience off balance as it jumps from romantic overkill to sudden, surprising outbursts of shock to sinister diminuendos. Nothing is quite what it seems in a story that runs the gamut from love to betrayal to courtroom farce, and from the open sea to a Mexican resort to a Chinese theater to an American amusement park.

Shangai's opening credits are conventional in appearance, in stark contrast to those for *Citizen Kane* and *The Magnificent Ambersons*. Big, traditional font letters printed over restless ocean waves. Welles put together a temporary music track for his film, including a George Antheil piece for the opening. Roemheld substitutes a splashy version of "Please Don't Love Me," an obligatory torch song sung by Rita Hayworth later in the movie. Not at all what the director wanted. And yet Roemheld's music is evocative of Michael O'Hara's naively passionate view of love in general and his view of Rita Hayworth's character in particular. If O'Hara rather than Welles had directed *Shanghai*, Roemheld's music would have perfectly suited his artistic vision. A soaring romantic theme plays over Hayworth's lead credit and over all subsequent credits save one — that of Orson Welles. During the few seconds his name appears on screen the music turns sinister. Yet Welles does not play a villain in the movie. Rita does. Perhaps the rules of Hollywood stardom dictated that Hayworth be given the romantic theme music. It's more fun to think that Harry Cohn ordered the sinister music linked to Orson's credit, as revenge for Welles's marriage to and tampering with the screen goddess image of Harry's favorite, most bankable star.

Following the credits the music diminishes to a whisper and shifts from romantic to mildly foreboding. Combined with two panoramic images of New York City's skyline and the low bellow of a passing tugboat, the music evokes a classic film noir feeling of dark, private passions lurking beneath a civilized public facade. Passions such as those on display in the next scene, set in Central Park. Speaking in voiceover narration, and with the benefit of hindsight, Michael O'Hara confesses to being an incorrigible fool. Hindsight is usually sharper than foresight, unless distorted by emotional need, as was the case with Charlie Kane's recollections of childhood.

"Please Don't Love Me" returns, with some dramatic justification, when Michael first encounters what quickly becomes the woman of his dreams. The camera closes in on Elsa Bannister as Michael elaborates on his loss of good judgement. Brilliantly lit, she is a bright vision of beauty in her mostly white dress and platinum blond hair, set off by the blackness of the carriage in which she rides, the horse pulling that carriage, the uniform of the carriage driver, and the night in general. But the closer we get to Elsa the more bored and distracted she looks. The camera begins to withdraw from her, then cuts to a tight shot of Michael O'Hara approaching the carriage on foot. In Central Park we approach Elsa Bannister at a moment of discontent in her life, then draw back to watch the approach of a potential remedy for that discontent.

Juxtaposed medium close-ups of Elsa and Michael emphasize their different appearances. She looks elegant and fresh. He looks a little ragged around the edges. Not exactly Cary Grant, but not a tramp either. Michael's initial romantic maneuver elicits from Elsa an expression more predatory than flirtatious. With the advantage of hindsight the narrator notes a hint of danger in that expression. But his counterpart, locked in the present, cannot see it.

Like the early scenes in *The Magnificent Ambersons*, the Central Park scene begins without local sound. Distancing us from the encounter between Michael and Elsa, narration and imagery carry the load of exposition. With his own years of hindsight, Welles wished he had eliminated much of the characters' subsequent dialog in this scene, which would have further distanced us from them (Welles/Bogdanovich, p.195). But the dialog *does* exist. And Roemheld's repetition of the film's love theme immerses us in Michael's instant infatuation with Elsa. Nothing in the music undercuts or modifies our impression of the protagonist's gushing sincerity, which is at odds with the sexual subtext of their flirtation. Michael offers Elsa a cigarette — a major currency of emotional exchange in film noir. After a brief, teasing show of reluctance, she accepts the cigarette, wraps it in her white hanky, and puts it in her sparkly black purse. Their exchange of glances says it all. Bargain proposed and accepted. In spite of Michael's sentimental narration and Roemheld's sentimental music, the characters are negotiating a sexual deal rather than a romantic commitment. "And from that moment on, I did not use my head very much." No, Michael let another part of his anatomy do his thinking. "Except to be thinking of her" puts a sweet face on his sexual fixation.

Some time after his brief encounter with Elsa, Michael finds her purse lying on the ground, the cigarette he gave her and the white hanky in which she wrapped it conveniently left visible. The promise of sex is still on his mind when he hears Elsa cry out for help as she is dragged into the woods by three young thugs. Like the placement of her purse, her cries for help sound more calculated than spontaneous. And if she stages the assault for the purpose of getting Michael more involved with her, he quickly takes the bait, charging to Elsa's rescue.

The battle of Central Park is not entirely convincing. Welles accentuates its violence by increasing the film speed, or by removing a few frames when punches are thrown and bodies go flying. The effect is not helped by Roemheld's music, which mimics the physical action too closely in an attempt to reinforce it. Welles expressed disapproval of this technique (Welles/Bogdanovich, p.195). But he compensates for the bad by keeping the fight brief and by explaining, through narration, that the three men Michael battles are not professional criminals, making his quick victory less farfetched.

Most conveniently the carriage driver lets Michael, who is a stranger to him, borrow his vehicle to take Elsa home. Or maybe Elsa secretly arranged for the loan. Standing in the driver's perch above and behind Elsa, Michael appears to be in control of the situation. He drives the carriage and leads the conversation. The camera tilts up and down to show Michael and Elsa separately as they talk, visually making the point that they come from different worlds. Neither really understands the other, in spite of the superficial conviviality of their dialog. Re-creating Elsa in his own preferred image of womanhood, Michael calls her Rosalie, the Princess of Central Park.

He discovers, to his surprise, that her roots are more worldly. Her parents were White Russian and were driven out of Russia during the 1917 Bolshevik Revolution. Dispossession, danger, and struggle are her heritage. When asked if she likes to gamble, Elsa replies soberly that she does it for a living, implying that for her *life* itself is a gamble. But if she is not the fairy princess Michael initially envisioned, neither is he quite as inexperienced as she assumes. She bets him a dollar he's never heard of the city where she was born. He has, noting its location on the coast of China and pronouncing it the "second wickedest city in the world." Elsa pays off her gambling debt to him.

After surprising each other about their worldly experience, Michael and Elsa continue their discussion for a time as equals, comparing notes on Macao, the wickedest city in the world, and on Shanghai. Elsa worked in both places. "As a gambler?" Michael asks. Elsa's evasive reply hints at a different profession, although one that might be considered a form of gambling. "You need more than luck in Shanghai," Elsa remarks in the same somber tone of voice as her earlier comment about gambling. If life itself is a gamble, you have to cultivate an advantage, even cheat, in order to survive.

From a slightly low camera angle we see Michael talking to Elsa through an opening in the carriage canopy. Their separate worlds have found a common theme, although during Elsa's remark about needing more than luck to survive in Shanghai the camera tilts down to show her alone. She keeps some aspects of her past closely guarded. Still the initial barriers between these two characters is breached. And Michael now further reduces them, abandoning his driver's perch to join Elsa in the passenger compartment, while insisting that he can maintain control of the carriage from that more intimate position. Not quite true. A taxi approaches from what is now Michael's blind side and nearly collides with the carriage. Michael can no more safely drive the carriage from the passenger compartment than he can objectively scrutinize Elsa after becoming infatuated with her. But that is a lesson he does not learn from the near-accident in this scene.

Michael too has a dark past which he prefers to keep to himself. Elsa notices his aversion to the police. When they abandon the carriage after their encounter with a taxi, she asks him about it. He sidesteps the question by answering it indirectly, commenting on the variable hospitality of jails around the world. Australia has the nicest, and Spain the worst. Elsa draws the logical conclusion that Michael has spent time inside those jails. What law did he break in Spain, she inquires. Adopting the same, sober tone of voice Elsa did while discussing Shanghai and gambling, Michael admits to killing a man there. Elsa is surprised. One can almost see the wheels in her mind begin to turn, assessing Michael's potential for violence and how it might serve her secret scheme to get rid of her husband. Revealing nothing of that scheme to Michael or to us, she lightens the mood by transforming Michael's grim admission into a joke: "Just now you almost killed a girl," she laughs, referring to their near-accident. Her maneuver to increase their intimacy works. Michael jokes back, prompting Elsa to comment on *American* jails, as though from experience. That, in turn, draws a sardonic comment from Michael about the questionable fairness of the American judicial system. He describes a recent case in which a man was found innocent of murder after shooting his wife five times in the head and claiming in court that he thought she was an intruder. His exoneration came about through the efforts of his defense attorney, whom Michael describes as the "world's greatest criminal lawyer, if not the world's greatest criminal." Like George Minafer unknowingly insulting Eugene Morgan in front of Morgan's daughter, in the Christmas ball scene from *The Magnificent Ambersons*, Michael unknowingly insults criminal lawyer Arthur Bannister in front of his wife, Elsa. But it turns out that Elsa's dislike of Arthur far exceeds Michael's. And Michael's contempt neatly serves her hidden agenda.

As they walk from the abandoned carriage to a parking garage where her car is located, Elsa offers Michael a job on her husband's yacht, shipping out the next day for the west coast by way of the Panama Canal. She is genuinely surprised at his moral objection to getting involved with a married woman. Obviously *she* has no such qualms. The lightness of her dress and hair counterpoint the darkness of Michael's clothing and the shadowy garage. But if that lightness is traditionally a symbol of goodness, it is ironic here. Elsa hands Michael a calling card retrieved from the same purse into which she carefully tucked his cigarette earlier. He tears it up and throws it away. She searches her purse again for a replacement. And Michael surprises her again, handing her the pistol he found in that purse after she tossed it away in Central Park. Lighting a cigarette, often a gesture of worldly wisdom in the film noir genre, he suspiciously questions why she would discard such a weapon while being attacked. The implication is that she did it on purpose and that the attack was staged. Elsa plays innocent, claiming she didn't know how to fire the weapon and therefore wanted Michael to find it. Not likely for a working girl who survived Macao and Shanghai. Michael doesn't buy her story. Frustrated and angry, Elsa drives away without another word.

As Michael and Elsa walked into the parking garage they passed a man standing near the entryway. It is George Grisby, law partner to Elsa's husband. He and Elsa exchanged surreptitious glances in passing. With hindsight we recognize this encounter as more than coincidental. George was waiting for Elsa at the garage. Have the two of them already hatched a plot against Arthur, and is Michael an unsuspecting pawn in that plot? Is George as much of a romantic slave to Elsa as Michael will eventually become? George's formal clothing suggests that he was trying to impress her. Perhaps Elsa's encounter with Michael was an unscheduled but useful diversion on her way to an illicit rendezvous with Grisby.

As Michael walks to the garage exit to watch Elsa's car depart, he is trailed by another mysterious stranger, Sidney Broom, whom we later discover to be Arthur Bannister's hired detective. Broom emerges from behind a pillar which previously concealed him from view. "Some dame, ain't she," he comments, his voice dripping with sarcasm. A parking attendant echoes that sentiment, without the sarcasm. Obviously Broom knows more about Elsa than does the attendant. Before leaving Broom bids goodnight to Grisby. George is not happy to see him, and exits in the opposite direction. The parking attendant, speaking to Michael, elaborates on his admiration for Elsa by pointing out that her husband, Arthur Bannister, brought her fancy car all the way from San Francisco to New York. This is the first time Michael makes a connection between Elsa and "the world's greatest criminal lawyer, or the world's greatest criminal." As the scene ends we watch him gazing intently in the direction of Elsa's departure. His face registers both interest and wariness—a contradictory perspective echoing both Broom's cynical contempt for Elsa and the parking attendant's uncritical admiration for her.

The parking garage scene is an example of Welles's layering of action, like the post-campaign speech confrontation in Susan Alexander's apartment in *Citizen Kane* and the post-ball departure scene in the entryway of the Amberson mansion in *The Magnificent Ambersons*. Each of the five characters involved has a unique, limited perspective of what is happening. And each has his or her own agenda.

Arthur Bannister makes his first appearance the next day, at the Sailors' Hiring Hall. It begins with a shot of his legs, each supplemented by a handheld cane, stiffly moving forward among other, less encumbered legs and accompanied by Roemheld's sinister descending chords. We're almost in horror film territory here, until the camera tilts up to reveal Arthur's face. The music softens and so does our impression of this monster. He is middle-aged, plain-looking, and wearing a straw hat. The narrator remarks that New York is not as big a city as it pretends to be. Compared, presumably, to the "wicked" Macao and the dangerous Shanghai. Arthur too is less intimidating than he pretends to be. As cynical, manipulative, and ruthless as he, Elsa, and George will later seem to be, all of them are recognizably human villains with human weaknesses and emotional vulnerabilities.

Communication between characters is always complicated in a Welles movie. Unable to lure Michael aboard Arthur's yacht with her charms, Elsa sends Arthur to do it with money. That her husband is willing to perform such a humiliating task should set off warning bells in Michael's brain, but doesn't. In retrospect his narrator persona admits to have been a much bigger "boob" than he originally thought. As for Arthur, he must navigate through two intermediaries, Goldie and Bjornson, in order to reach Michael.

The business relationship between Arthur and Michael begins as a power struggle.

Arthur strives for an initial advantage by sternly interrogating his prospective new employee about his drinking habits. O'Hara responds by boasting of his affinity for alcohol. We learn from his sailor friends, Goldie and Bjornson, that Michael fought against the fascists in the Spanish Civil War, and knows how to hurt a guy. There is steel beneath his blarny. Besides, he doesn't need Bannister's job. So the resourceful lawyer changes tactics and invites Michael to share a drink at a nearby bar while they discuss the job offer. With hindsight we recognize that Arthur tolerates Michael's insolence only because of his own desperate need to win the affections of his wife, Elsa, whose only loyalty to him is a consequence of blackmail.

When Michael discovers the identity of his prospective boss, his tactical advantage doubles. Tying his necktie most casually, to impress Arthur with his indifference, Michael introduces Bannister to his acquaintances as the world's greatest lawyer. He puffs up Bannister's reputation in order to demonstrate his own superiority by subsequently toying with so prominent a man. He deliberately humiliates Arthur by telling Jake and Goldie that Bannister was sent by his own wife to fetch Michael. Then he rubs salt in that wound by inviting his friends to share in the drinks Arthur offered to buy, and by informing Arthur in advance that he intends to turn down the job offer. Then Michael rudely walks away. By the end of the scene Michael is as carelessly certain of his ability to manipulate Arthur as Arthur was incorrectly confident of his power over Michael at the beginning of the scene. At different times each man thinks of the other as equivalent to the pet monkey Goldie keeps on a leash.

Michael's advantage continues into the next scene, where he, Arthur, Goldie, and Jake converse in a bar booth. The camera closes in on them and then remains static for the rest of the scene, allowing the characters and their dialog to tell most of the story. Physically smaller and weaker than the three sea-faring men, Bannister is already drunk while they remain sober. Michael, seated opposite, pitilessly scrutinizes the lawyer, who explains to the others that Michael rescued his wife from an assault. His bitter tone of voice betrays his resentment of the "tough guy" that Michael is and that Arthur would like to be.

Jake philosophically undercuts the "tough guy" description by expounding on his contrary theory of an "edge," which is anything inherited or acquired that gives one person a tactical advantage over another. Physical size and strength are just two of many such factors. Singing talent, illustrated by a professional singer performing "Please Don't Love Me" on a nearby jukebox, is another. So is "a bankroll in your pocket," which describes Bannister's advantage over Michael. A large painting of an ocean liner hanging on the wall above the booth visually reminds us, in appropriately nautical terms, of a world of wealth, status, and privilege to which Arthur belongs and Michael does not. Amused, Michael casually endorses Jake's theory. But he doesn't take it to heart. And later he will pay dearly for his smug sense of superiority over the crippled man across the table. Arthur, on the other hand, takes comfort from Jake's theory. "Bear it in mind" he warns Michael as they glare at each other. But a moment later poor Arthur passes out, dead drunk, sabotaging his attempt to intimidate his rival for Elsa's affections. Goldie then asks a dumb question about Jake's theory, ending the discussion and the scene on a deceptively lighthearted note.

Michael escorts a drunken Bannister to the lawyer's yacht. The narrator, as always looking back on a scene from the future, notes the irony of which his on-screen self is unaware. It is Michael who is "unconscious" and "helpless," in the sense of being vulnerable to exploitation by other people, while the literally unconscious and helpless Arthur Bannister is as dangerous as a "rattlesnake."

Arthur thanks O'Hara for returning him to his yacht. But the Bannister's little dachshund barks at the stranger, echoing Arthur's *true* feelings about Michael. Arthur may yield to his wife's extramarital whims, but he hates doing so. She too, however, must obey the perverse rules of their strange marital arrangement. Dressed in high fashion nautical clothes supplied by her husband's fortune, she ignores Arthur as he is hauled aboard. But when Arthur twice summons her to follow him, calling her by the bitterly ironic name of "lover," she reluctantly obeys. Their enslavement is mutual.

Before following her husband down into the yacht's cabin, Elsa whispers a confidential plea to Michael to accept the job and remain on board. The camera shows their intimate moment in three close-ups, visually isolating them from other characters even as Arthur's irritating voice intrudes from off screen. Elsa's plea for help is deliberately vague, allowing Michael's and our imagination to speculate on the cause of her distress. Does Arthur beat her? Is she being kept against her will?

Following Elsa's departure her plea is reinforced by three other characters with three very different motives. Sidney Broom, pretending to be a sailor, appeals to Michael's sense of adventure to sign on as bosun for the voyage. But his demeanor is so smarmy that it's difficult to tell if he is being sincere or sarcastic. In that he echoes Arthur's contradictory feelings about hiring the protagonist. Michael recognizes Broom as one of the men he saw in the parking garage the previous night. Broom denies it, though doesn't sound concerned about it one way or the other. He is an arrogant man who eventually pays dearly for his overconfidence.

Bessie, the Bannister's black servant, makes an apparently heartfelt plea, on behalf of Elsa, for Michael to stay. "She needs you bad." But in whose interest does she really act — Elsa's or Arthur's? In a later scene we learn of her family's desperate financial dependence on Arthur. Maybe she acts as his agent of persuasion in this scene. And even if she is motivated more by sentiment than money, she might harbor false notions about Elsa's innocence and vulnerability. Is Bessie fooling Michael, or herself?

Goldie adds his two cents worth to the argument in favor of Michael accepting a job aboard the yacht. Needing work, he hopes to tag along. Welles visually emphasizes distinctions among the separate pleas made to Michael by Broom, Bessie, and Goldie. Their voices come at Michael from different directions, causing him to turn his head for each one. He looks confused. But his affirmative reply to their pleas occurs in a close-up of Michael alone. He has his own motive for taking the job. And the sly grin on his face as he does so suggests that he thinks *he* possesses the tactical edge in this situation.

A montage of images showing the yacht at sea and Michael shouting orders to other sailors gives us a condensed impression of the cooperation and coordination required to sail a boat. The spectacle of diversity and conflict among the characters on board is put on hold until the vessel drops anchor somewhere in the West Indies. The final shot in the montage is a stern view of the yacht, showing the vessel's name. "Circe" is a character out of Greek mythology. The goddess of a particularly degrading form of love, she poisoned her husband and cast evil spells turning her victims into animals. Only Odysseus, the hero of Homer's *The Odyssey*, evaded her enchantment. Presumably Michael O'Hara is the Odysseus of this voyage, although his survival is more a matter of luck than fate.

A long shot of Elsa diving off a rocky cliff and into the ocean below is actually a reflection in the lens of a telescope used by an admirer to get a close-up look at her. A glossy restatement of "Please Don't Love Me" echoes the observer's infatuation, in case we missed the point. But when the telescope is pulled away from the observer's face we see George Grisby instead of Michael O'Hara, whom we perhaps anticipated. Several conventionally exquisite portraits of Elsa follow, intermingled with reactions shots of George looking like a lovesick adolescent. He also looks sweaty, unattractive, and hopelessly out of his league.

Welles may have detested Roemheld's terribly blatant music in this scene, but it does convey Grisby's unambiguous and absurd adoration of Elsa.

The camera cuts to Michael on board the yacht. He too watches Mrs. Bannister with keen interest. But *his* face expresses fascination mixed with distrust, in contrast to the boyish, uncritical look on Grisby's face. Michael at least puts up a struggle. George has apparently given himself to Elsa body and soul.

Grisby's whiny, irritating voice interrupts Michael's observation of Elsa. Boarding the yacht, he suggests Michael go for a swim with Elsa. He even offers Michael the use of his swimsuit. Such generosity from a man who shares a passion for Elsa arouses our suspicion of Grisby's motive. And Elsa's as well. Perhaps Grisby is to Mrs. Bannister what the monkey on a leash was to Goldie. Certainly Elsa would have an emotional "edge" over him, if she chose to exercise it. Michael comments on having seen George in New York. But Grisby, like Sidney Broom before him, won't acknowledge the encounter and quickly changes the subject.

Grisby adopts a snide tone of voice in order to anger Michael as they discuss the man Michael reportedly killed in Spain. Who else could have told Grisby about that incident except Elsa, to whom Michael revealed it in New York? Upon learning that Michael's victim was a Franco spy, George tries to re-direct Michael's righteous anger towards himself by revealing his support for Franco's cause. Shown at close range, both Grisby and O'Hara sweat from the emotional intensity of their conversation, or is it from the tropical heat. Offering Michael a chance to kill him is a bizarre thing for George to do. But then, Grisby is a bizarre character, or *masquerades* as a bizarre character in order to disorient Michael and further his own, or a third party's, secret scheme.

Elsa calls out to Michael from the distant shore, re-directing the conversation back to her. Grisby again makes snide comments about Michael's relationship with her, goading O'Hara to retaliate. Michael threatens to punch him. Mission accomplished. As though on cue, George withdraws as Elsa climbs aboard. But his parting comment, "Wish she'd ask me to go swimming," seems more genuine than most of his dialog with Michael. Why wouldn't he stay to greet the woman he loves, unless leaving her alone with Michael is part of the plan he serves? Elsa, meanwhile, is surprised to see Michael follow George instead of attending to her. Before pushing off in a motorboat, Grisby tells Michael, "She'll ask *you* [to go swimming]. You wait and see," in a confidential voice. He seems almost to warn the protagonist about the romantic trap into which George himself has already fallen. Grisby's character is neatly balanced between deceiving Michael, probably on Elsa's behalf, and commenting critically, if cryptically, on his own and Michael's enslavement to the ruthless Mrs. Bannister.

Roemheld's background music underscores the ominous quality of George's sardonic warning, then repeats another overblown rendition of the love theme as Michael and Elsa rendezvous on the yacht. Elsa leaves her bathrobe half off, extending a silent invitation to Michael. Declining that invitation, he covers her shoulders with it, though moving closer to her in the process. She asks for a cigarette, in effect requesting Michael to repeat the sexual overture he made to her in Central Park. Adding that she also wants him to call her Rosalie, she signals her willingness to accept. But Michael hasn't yet overcome his wariness of a woman so willing to betray her husband. When she tries to kiss him, he slaps her. Elsa is genuinely shocked by his rejection. But only for a moment. In true film noir tradition, she employs a cigarette to reassert self-control.

Only a moment earlier she used the same object for a different purpose. Most versatile, those cigarettes. Regaining composure, Elsa changes her tactics against Michael's resistance.

With a quavering voice and appealing eyes, she claims to be no less afraid of romantic involvement than he is, and that her cold, calculating manner is just a facade she employs to control that fear.

Welles gives us lots of conventional Hollywood over-the-shoulder shots of the characters as their romantic fever, along with the overstated music, builds to a kiss. Elsa's climactic line, "Oh, Michael, what are we afraid of?" is delivered like a cliché. Very different from anything we heard in Citizen Kane or The Magnificent Ambersons. It is difficult to accept Elsa's emotional expressions at face value. And maybe that's the point of the story. With Mrs. Bannister and her cohorts, everything *is* feigned, for tactical reasons or because none of them is any longer capable of spontaneous feeling.

As though on cue again, Grisby shouts "So long, kiddies! Bye bye!" in a weirdly childish voice as he steers his motorboat away from the yacht. Judging from Elsa's dubious claim to be afraid of George finding out about her involvement with Michael, Grisby's disruption of the kiss may have been planned. First entice the protagonist, then erect an impediment to the fulfillment of his desires. An impediment Michael will in time want to overcome. But the strange quality of Grisby's voice might also be an indirect expression of his jealousy at seeing Elsa kiss Michael. A jealousy he strains to repress in order to effectively play his part in a larger plot that perhaps promises to fulfill *his* desire to be with her. Deception and *self*-deception are so deeply intertwined in this movie that it's difficult to get at the truth. "Now he knows about us!" Elsa tells Michael in alarm, or maybe *false* alarm. "I wish I did," replies O'Hara, voicing his confusion about his budding romance with her but also, on a broader level, about nearly everything and everyone he encounters in the story.

A night scene aboard the yacht is staged in a manner emphasizing the characters' isolation from each other. Arthur sits with his back against the mainmast, looking towards the stern. Elsa lies on top of the cabin roof, looking up at the evening sky. George sits with his back against the cabin wall, looking to port. None of these three characters look directly at anyone else, even when speaking to each other. Following two establishing shots showing all three of them, the camera cuts back and forth among individual shots of each as they exchange verbal jabs.

There is another kind of dramatic logic to the positioning of the three characters. Arthur, owner of the yacht and financially dominant, appropriately sits near the mainmast that powers the boat. George sits virtually at Elsa's feet, like a faithful dog. And Elsa's upward gaze suits her desire to escape from a loveless, passionless marriage to Arthur. Into this grim little gathering steps Michael, after having declared his intention to quit his job.

Elsa sings a bit of "Please Don't Love Me," her love/anti-love theme song. A haunting tune, it encapsulates her strange relationship with Michael, whom she intends to exploit and betray, but by whom she also wants to be loved and rescued. Arthur interrupts her song with dripping sarcasm, taunting her about Michael's impending departure. Grisby, meanwhile, picks up Elsa's song where she left off. "Don't take your love away" is his indirect plea to Elsa not to end their secret romance, or at least the promise of it. Hope springs eternal. But for Arthur, Grisby's serenade is an annoying distraction from his own effort to punish Elsa and her strong, young, healthy lover. So he tells George to shut up.

We learn from Arthur that Elsa told him Michael is planning to write a novel someday. Since we didn't hear Michael discuss that plan with Elsa, we can assume they've shared a few intimate moments since we last saw them. Discovering that Michael considers himself independent of the need for money, Arthur challenges his rival's naivete, employing a clever turn of phrase to insult him, and to transform his own lack of mobility into an advantage. But Michael trumps that insult with a clever line of his own. George sarcastically praises the efforts of both men. Since he resents both, he has no loyalty to either. Annoyed at this second interference by George, Arthur again tells him to shut up. Grisby laughs instead. Encouraging bad feelings between Michael and Arthur serves his own agenda, and perhaps Elsa's.

Bolstering his argument that money *can* buy health and happiness, Arthur tells the tale of how it got him out of a hospital bed and on his feet, and helped him triumph over an enemy who once kept him out of an exclusive social club because of Arthur's ethnic background. Bannister's yacht once belonged to the now bankrupt bigot he destroyed. An insert close-up of Grisby smirking when Arthur describes himself and his family as Manchester Greek suggests that George too is a bigot who looks down on his business partner. Maybe he really was a Franco sympathizer, as he told Michael.

Arthur concedes, "Each man has his own idea of happiness." Elsa hands her cigarette to George and asks him to light it. Complaining that he doesn't have a match, George nevertheless obeys, supplying a specific example of Arthur's general observation. It is George's masochistic notion of happiness to slavishly serve Elsa, which Michael observes. Arthur, meanwhile, insists that *everyone* needs money, and uses his servant, Bessie, to illustrate his case. While Bessie serves him coffee from a tray, Arthur describes her groveling gratitude to him for providing her with just enough income to pay for a three room house that accommodates two families. The former social outcast now lords it over *his* social inferiors. He even brags that Bessie was previously employed by the wealthy bigot he vanquished. In other words, Bessie's servitude is a trophy reminding Arthur of his sweet victory over a foe.

Michael lights Grisby's cigarette so that Grisby can in turn use his own cigarette to light Elsa's. Michael serves Elsa through Grisby. Calm and cool, Elsa ever so slightly adjusts her position for greater comfort. But if Michael and George are her slaves, Elsa too is enslaved, to Arthur. And he in turn is a slave to both his physical infirmities and his possessive love for her.

Sickened by what he witnesses on deck, Michael retreats to the cabin below, where the servants are gathered. He asks Bessie why she doesn't leave. She sternly reminds the idealistic "Mr. Poet" that she needs the money. Bannister was right about economic necessity. But then Bessie adds another reason for not quitting—her concern for "that poor little child," Elsa. Another Wellesian contradiction. Bessie the economic pragmatist is also a gullible sentimentalist. Her view of the most cynical, manipulative, and self-reliant person on board the yacht is extremely naive. She describes Elsa as a child while looking childlike herself due to her low position in the camera frame.

Under orders from her husband, Elsa resumes singing "Please Don't Love Me." Shooting from overhead, the infatuated camera closes obsessively on Elsa's beautiful face. In the cabin below, Michael looks up fitfully in the direction of her singing. His resolution to leave the yacht melts in the warmth of Elsa's musical plea. The most intriguing mystery in *The Lady from Shanghai* is to what extent Elsa Bannister feels the sentiments expressed in her theme song. Is she tempted to throw away her husband's fortune and run off with poor Michael, but in the end unable to overcome her need for the security of wealth? Or is she cynically committed to manipulation from beginning to end? "Please Don't Love Me" is overused in the film, but in this scene it serves a dramatic purpose. We are as tempted to pity and love Elsa from above as Michael O'Hara is from below.

One complaint Welles made in retrospect about this scene is its lack of "sound atmosphere" (Welles/Bogdanovich, p.195). A little wind and moving water to give us a richer sense of place—always a strong element in Welles's movies. On the other hand, the quiet stillness of the scene complements the intimacy of the characters' interaction. This is a tranquil, tropical moment of conversation, reflection, even philosophical debate among the four main characters. Michael is the only one to change location, leaving the cynicism of the deck inhabitants to join the servants below, then lured back up on deck by Elsa Bannister's siren song.

The sultry allure of Elsa's song is immediately counterpointed by a crude and unlyrical radio commercial as the next scene begins. Michael steers the yacht somewhere off a Carribean coastline. He also keeps an eye on Elsa, who is being pampered at the stern by Bessie. After Bessie departs Elsa approaches Michael to ask for help putting on a white jacket over her black bathing suit. This time Michael wears black, dissipating any symbolic carryover from the previous scene in which O'Hara and Grisby wore white while the Bannisters were dressed in black. Elsa switches off the radio because it interferes with her seduction of Michael, just as Grisby's singing interfered with Arthur's attempt to bait Elsa and Michael earlier. Yet Elsa's performance of "Please Don't Love Me" in the previous scene was as much an advertising pitch for Michael's devotion as the radio commercial is for the consumer's money, in spite of the aesthetic dissimilarity between the two songs. Reinforcing the point, another variation of Elsa's theme music arises on the soundtrack.

In the shot of Michael looking back at Elsa and Bessie from the boat's wheel, camera angle and lens emphasize the great length of the yacht's boom. This is a big vessel, befitting Arthur's professional success. But Nature is even bigger. In a subsequent shot of Michael and Elsa standing at the wheel we see a great expanse of water, a mountainous coastline, and cumulus clouds in the distance. The world through which Michael and Elsa navigate as individuals and as a couple is immense. That immensity adds exhilaration to their budding romance, but also renders them small and fragile by comparison.

Elsa silences the radio in order to resume her romantic assault on Michael. He, in turn, picks up on the last word *from* the radio commercial in order to resist that assault. He questions whether Elsa believes in "love" at all. Annoyed, she takes control of the yacht's wheel, which is her right as the owner's wife and Michael's boss. During their subsequent, brief debate about love and human nature, Michael repeatedly corrects Elsa's steering, and she repeatedly resists. It is a barely noticeable, perhaps even unconscious struggle, illustrating Elsa's inclination to follow old habits and Michael's determination to change her course for the better. Quoting a Chinese proverb, Elsa claims that love is fleeting and human nature unchanging. Michael pokes fun at her cynicism and postulates a larger, more hopeful definition of love. But he lacks the time to delineate his argument. Arthur steps into the camera frame and disrupts the romantic sparring. Referring sarcastically again to Elsa as "lover," he mocks her obvious *lack* of affection for him. She retaliates by claiming that Michael's decision to stay on board resulted from his change of heart about her. But Michael declares his independence from *both* Bannisters by insisting that he never makes up his mind about anything until it's over and done with. He is foolish to believe he cannot be manipulated by these people.

The narrator, Michael's less arrogant self from the future, explains to us that Arthur tried to give his wife the things she wanted, and admits that he, Michael O'Hara, tried to deny this fact while in the heat of infatuation with Mrs. Bannister. Arthur deserves some pity, and gets it. The less he speaks, the easier it is to feel sorry for him. At the start of the next scene Arthur and his companions climb a rocky Mexican shore towards a picnic he arranged for Elsa's entertainment. The camera pivots with him. He lurches from side to side on his crutches while Broom lends him a steadying hand. It is a slow, painful journey for the great lawyer. By contrast Elsa and Grisby stride easily past him and out of the camera frame. Carefree Latin music plays softly in the background, complementing Elsa and Grisbys' frame of mind but counterpointing Arthur's exertion and frustration.

The final insult to Arthur in this scene is supplied by Michael, who as narrator challenges both the lawyer's manhood and his efforts to gain Elsa's affection (even the narrator, with his detachment, cannot resist rooting for his on screen persona from time to time). Presumably one source of Elsa's discontent and boredom is her husband's inability to make love to her. Arthur's picnic excursion is as joyless and grotesque as was Charlie Kane's in the Florida Everglades. Both characters desperately seek to hold onto wives whom they have ruthlessly manipulated. Age diminishes Kane's ability to do so. Paralysis does the same for Arthur. On the way to the picnic Broom tries to warn Arthur about a plot against his life. Arthur claims to already know about it, and in a weary voice says he doesn't want to hear any more. "I want to enjoy myself." In other words, for a little while he wants to believe the illusion that Elsa is his devoted wife. Our sympathy for him is tempered by our recognition of how formidable an opponent he is for Elsa, Grisby, and Michael, or any combination of the three, depending on who is involved in the alleged plot.

A canoe ride through a swamp draws visual analogies between Elsa, the beauty of tropical birds, and the stealthy menace of snakes. Nature, human and otherwise, is both radiant and savage. Elsa is relaxed amidst Nature's spectacle of extreme contrasts. Having struggled for survival in some of the world's wickedest cities, she is fairly comfortable among the jungle's exotic predators. Michael, glancing from one creature to another, looks a bit bewildered. George, spotting the gaping jaws of a nearby alligator, nervously paddles his canoe a little faster.

A montage of shots depicts the principle characters separately pursuing their own amusement at a beach resort, surrounded by Mexicans playing music and preparing food. Children follow Goldie as he happily sips a native drink. Lighthearted, local music and bright sunshine reinforce the picnic's cheerful facade. Grisby spies on Arthur, Elsa, and Michael with a handheld telescope. *His* tactical edge. He smiles at what he sees, presumably because it furthers his and Elsa's scheme. At close range we observe Elsa telling Michael that Broom is not a sailor but a detective hired by Arthur to spy on her. The confidential tone of her voice is matched by the music, which is now more worldly and seductive than carefree. Elsa complains that Arthur wants to divorce her without giving her alimony. Michael insists that lack of money shouldn't bother her, and claims he knew all along that Broom was no sailor. He maintains his independence, or so he thinks, by demonstrating his moral superiority about money and his tactical savvy about Broom being a hostile agent. Pleased with himself, he walks away from Elsa, as though expecting her to follow him.

Evening. Same location. The background music, played by Arthur's hired musicians, turns mysterious and brooding. A torch-lit boat ride along the coast adds a touch of the exotic to the picnic. In one particularly striking shot the clouds above a distant mountaintop are brightly illuminated by the setting sun, contrasting the lower half of the screen where darkness envelops the boats and their passengers.

Relaxing on the beach after the day's festivities, George, Arthur, and Elsa can't help sniping at each other. Hammocks and a portable bar provide the basic comforts of home for these wealthy dabblers in Mexican culture. George and Arthur are nearly drunk. Elsa, as always, maintains self-control. Visible in the distance, behind them, the party atmosphere continues unabated. Only among the principles, as with Kane and Susan in their private tent at the Everglades picnic, does the mood turn nasty.

George pronounces Arthur's picnic a failure, yet simultaneously serves as Arthur's bartender. A lackey to the end, whether for Arthur or Elsa. Gazing at his wife, Arthur barely acknowledges George, who tries again to aggravate him by mentioning that Michael still intends to leave and that Arthur should stop him. Elsa feigns indifference about the matter.

Arthur, positioned between his companions, who may have rehearsed their dialog to achieve a particular goal, manages to irritate and divide them. By describing Michael as Elsa's bodyguard, he inflames George's jealousy while concealing his own. But when he elaborates by describing Michael as young and strong and Elsa as young and beautiful (in obvious contrast to his own age and physical condition), the indifference in his voice fades. Now he and George both gaze at Elsa. They look grim at the prospect of competing for her with the protagonist. They may hate each other, but for a moment they are of like mind.

Elsa stands up to leave, a trace of unhappiness in her eyes contrasting with the controlled smoothness of her movements. She is trapped in a loveless marriage because her desperate need for financial security, ingrained in her since childhood, prevents her from just leaving her husband. In a striking close-up of Elsa's face we see fire lit festivities occurring far in the background. They bear no relation to what she is feeling at this moment.

Arthur's tactical advantage over Elsa is implied in his quiet reply to her parting comment, "I don't have to listen to you talk like that." "Oh yes you do, lover" carries a load of hidden meaning. Blackmail is the foundation of their marriage. George makes a pathetic attempt to stop Arthur's bullying, but Arthur continues to snipe at Elsa by wondering aloud why Michael doesn't want to stay. Each of the three characters is shown in separate close-ups, isolated visually and emotionally from one another. Elsa seems distracted, sad, and sincere when she comments wearily, "Why should *anyone* want to be around us?" Self-loathing overtakes egotistical cynicism for a moment. But Arthur is not in a similarly reflective mood. He summons Broom to go fetch Michael so that he can further humiliate Elsa and George. But Broom isn't around, so Michael's friend Goldie answers the call. He scampers away to do Arthur's bidding like a trained monkey, taking a shortcut to Michael by splashing through the water.

Michael has chosen to spend his leisure time with the local people gathered around a bonfire. Reluctantly obeying Arthur's summons, he passes by and through various groups of Mexicans as he walks along the beach. Three of these transit images are obviously backscreened process shots, filmed at the studio after Welles was forced to halt location shooting in Mexico.

When Michael arrives, a drunken Arthur takes verbal aim at all three of his companions. He refers vaguely to George's loss of social status sometime in the past — another shadowy layer of the story, barely glimpsed but obviously helping to shape current events. Like Michael's participation in the Spanish Civil War, Elsa's childhood spent in exile in the Far East, and Arthur's struggles against discrimination and disability. Elsa's eyes remain riveted on Michael, but it is difficult to tell if she sees him as a means of escape from her own miserable cynicism or as merely a pawn to facilitate her lucrative escape from Arthur.

Witnessing the verbal cruelties of his pampered companions, Michael arrogantly threatens to retaliate in kind. Arthur, more amused than intimidated, insists that Michael's lack of knowledge about their pasts places him at a disadvantage. George, he points out, knows several incriminating things about him. And Arthur has something on Elsa, with which he evidently forced her into marriage. But in spite of this bravado, Arthur's inebriation betrays his underlying discontent, as it will Hank Quinlan's in *Touch of Evil*.

In one of Welles's classic storytelling scenes, Michael the would-be novelist scolds his cynical companions by telling them about a shark feeding frenzy he witnessed off the coast of Brazil. The frenzy became so violent and irrational that the sharks took to eating each other and finally themselves. As O'Hara tells this story we see behind him dark, ominous clouds hanging over the ocean far in the distance, highlighted by the fading glow of the setting sun. Nature in tune with *human* nature, for a moment. Michael's audience listens to his story in silence, looking uncomfortable at the allegorical mirror he holds up to them.

Having silenced the cynics, Michael departs. But his victory is illusory, and his moral lesson falls short of its mark. Arthur cleverly re-deploys Michael's shark metaphor to cruelly inflict yet another wound on George, who bitterly resents it. The feeding frenzy continues.

The yacht stops next in Acapulco. Stepping out of a rowboat and onto shore, Michael and George are shown through the webbing of a large fishing net. Both men are figuratively caught in someone else's web of intrigue without realizing it. Climbing up the rocky shore towards a cliff side resort, they are tracked by the camera as they weave their way through native Mexicans going about their daily business. The Mexican music is cheerful, as it was at the start of the picnic sequence. George brings up the subject of Elsa, probably by prearrangement with her. Describing Acapulco as one of her favorite places and claiming to know the best spots, George virtually extends Michael an invitation to escort Mrs. Bannister out on the town. At the mention of Acapulco's charms, Goldie wipes his hot, sweaty forehead, expresses a desire to get to San Francisco, and departs. One man's paradise is another man's hell hole. No two people see anything in exactly the same way.

George suddenly, surprisingly announces a proposition for Michael, who walks away from both George and the camera while looking back at them with a puzzled expression. He is both wary and intrigued. We rejoin the two characters later in their climb, with George now in the lead. With each scene change, the music changes. Its ethnic flavor and the subtlety of its dramatic shifts in relation to the characters and their conversation seems more likely a product of Welles than of Roemheld.

Building up to his strange proposal, George comments on the beauty of the scenery and tourists around them. Shadows from palm fronds cover his face, reflecting the tropical paradise he describes. Disinclined to trust Grisby, Michael contradicts him by noting the guilt and hunger within that paradise — the disparity between wealth and poverty in this "bright, guilty world."

In the next scene George and Michael continue their visually spectacular walk along the cliff top above Acapulco's beaches. The camera swoops down to join them, its movement emphasizing the progressive flow of their relationship and its brief intersection with passing tourists. Background music is now more overtly romantic and slightly mysterious, its dance rhythms complementary to tactical maneuvering. Before re-connecting with Michael and George, we skim past a conversation between a man and a woman walking in the opposite direction. "Darling, of course you pay me" he tells her, as though it should be obvious. We do not know specifically what they are talking about, but it seems likely that the woman was thinking romance while the man was thinking business arrangement. Ironically, the proposal George is about to make to Michael will seem like pure business but is more likely motivated by romance — the infatuation both men feel for Elsa Bannister.

George stops, causing Michael to stop and look back at him. "Think the world's going to end?" is a strange thing to say in the middle of what George previously described as paradise. He seems to have adopted Michael's slightly gloomy attitude about this "bright, guilty world." Michael concurs with George's apocalyptic remark, but in vague, romantic terms that seem less ominous. George resumes the lead in their trek as he explains his theory. Walking along the cliff top, he and Michaels' white-clothed figures stand out starkly against a dark background of ocean and hills. For a moment the world seems dark and the characters comparative bright.

Stopping and starting as they walk, George keeps his companion slightly off balance.

Dangling a carrot in front of a rabbit, he doles out bits and pieces of his vision of nuclear armageddon and his plan to survive it. He offers Michael five thousand dollars to help him. Removing his suit jacket, George looks more open and forthright in his shirt sleeves. His tactical dance of hesitant alliance with Michael resembles Joseph K's encounter with Hilda's prison guard husband in Welles's *The Trial*. They stop at the ruins of an old fortress overlooking the sea — an appropriate setting for a discussion about war and murder. In extreme close-up George reveals that he wants Michael to kill *him*. The camera immediately switches to a high angle shot showing both characters backed by a glittering ocean and sharp rocks far below them, creating a feeling of vertigo. Michael is shocked by George's request, and by George's sudden, grinning departure. "So long, fella!" Is George insane? The sultry Latin music has faded out, replaced now by a loud burst of strings and brass echoing Michael's emotional shock. Welles did not like this musical exclamation point by Roemheld (Welles/Bogdanovich, p.195). But it quickly subsides into something more quietly sinister. Like many of Roemheld's "Please Don't Love Me" variations, this outburst conveys a surface reality but no underlying contradictions. What appears to be Grisby's suicidal impulse in this scene later emerges as a plan for *survival*. And even *that* plan proves to be a mask concealing something else.

Michael and George's cliff top conversation is analogous to Othello and Iago discussing Desdemona's fidelity while walking along seaside battlements in Welles's 1952 film of *Othello*. In both scenes the character played by Welles is manipulated and deceived by his companion. But in *Othello* the victim of that manipulation and deception is a woman. In *The Lady from Shanghai* a woman is probably pulling the puppet strings controlling both O'Hara and Grisby.

In a lavish cliff top nightclub glimmering under starlight we witness the end of the latest Bannister marital spat. Elsa leaves her protesting husband seated at a table. Background music consists of Latin dance rhythms flavored with intrigue. In extreme long shot Elsa runs down a hillside towards Acapulco below. Her shimmering white dress matches the city's shimmering white buildings. At this moment she seems less a ruthless schemer than a profoundly unhappy woman seeking escape from marital hell. She is Susan Alexander fleeing Xanadu, but presented in more exotic, film noir terms. Her flight from patrician cliff top resort to plebian town below recalls Michael's flight from deck to cabin during the night scene aboard the yacht.

In Acapulco Elsa finds Michael. They stroll together through the streets, past people in cafes and past old, torn posters and graffiti on scarred, ancient walls—fading tokens of past events. Acapulco and Mexico have long histories, just as each of the main characters has a private history prior to his or her present entanglements. There are no emotionally unencumbered paradises or characters in this story. A solitary guitar speaks eloquently for the loneliness and yearning of Elsa and Michael. Elsa draws out Michael on the subject of Grisby's murder/suicide proposition. Then she expands on the theme of suicide, hinting at her own impulses to appropriate Arthur's pain pills to kill herself. Does she mean it? Or did she ask Michael about George so he would bring up the subject of suicide first, allowing her to describe to him the depth of her own desperation, then solicit his sympathy and involvement by asking him for moral guidance in the matter. She agrees with Michael that Grisby is mentally unstable, then places Arthur in the same category. She is soliciting an alliance with Michael against the two lawyers, and in the process overcoming Michael's distrust of her. But her manipulation of the protagonist is interrupted by Sidney Broom, emerging from the shadows where he was spying on them.

Broom tries to intimidate Michael with sarcasm. Michael retaliates with a savage punch to the head, in slightly fast motion to sharpen our impression of its violence. Michael then turns back to Elsa, but she has already fled the scene, running through the streets while tracked by the camera. We glimpse her fitfully through rounded archways. Visually she is as elusive as her motives are emotionally. Local music changes pace to match hers. Glancing back to see Michael following her, as she expected he would, Elsa darts into a café and then turns to face him in a very deliberate manner.

Michael dances with Elsa in the café. She cries and he melts, promising to carry her off to "one of the far places" to escape her troubles. She points out that they are already *in* one of the dark places. Running away is no answer. The pervasive evil of the world must be dealt with directly, and on its own terms. By questioning Michael's ability to take care of himself in such a world, Elsa also questions his ability to take care of *her*. The implication of her comments is that he must compromise his ethics in order to rescue and win her.

Elsa's seduction of Michael is again interrupted, this time by Goldie, who then does Michael a *second*, more deliberate favor by concealing from the police Michael's recent scuffle with Broom. In other words, Goldie supplies a tactical edge to Michael, but not necessarily to Elsa, whose recruitment of the protagonist into her private cause is once more sidetracked.

On the dock at Sausalito, California Michael waits for Elsa to arrive by motorboat. From a window in a dockside restaurant Grisby watches both of them. Elsa passes by Michael, discretely warning him to be careful. Michael *in*discretely follows her, as she no doubt anticipated he would. He insists that it's time for him to take her away with him. George is visible in the background, grinning at the would-be lovers. That smile makes no sense if he thought the romance brewing between Elsa and Michael were sincere on her part.

The romantic couple argue about the financial practicality of running away together until George calls out to them sarcastically, "Hello, kiddies." Elsa walks away from Michael, as though being seen with him by her husband's business partner were a risk. More likely her departure is a tactical ploy. Grisby's arrival reminds Michael of George's strange but potentially lucrative proposition at the precise moment the protagonist finds himself in need of money. Long forgotten is Michael's boast to Arthur, aboard the yacht, about not being a slave to money. Michael catches up to Elsa and suggests to her that five thousand dollars, the amount George offered him, could get them started in a life together. Elsa pauses to consider the idea, or to give Michael that impression, then walks away without replying. The fish is hooked, but the hook is not yet set. George reminds Michael of their scheduled business meeting. And perhaps to downplay his secret alliance with Elsa, George reminds her that Arthur is looking for her, and snidely promises not to tell his partner about her rendezvous with Michael. Elsa completes this facade of mutual hostility by walking past George without looking at or speaking to him. Then she walks past the camera with a cool, calculated look in her eyes. Michael follows her in hot pursuit, pleading for an answer to his romantic offer of rescue.

With a slight tug in her voice and a glimmer of fondness in her eyes, Elsa bids Michael farewell and leaves the building, making a show of reluctantly obeying her husband's summons. But before she's out of sight she turns to give Michael a final, yearning glance. Her every gesture and expression seems controlled. A reaction shot of Michael reveals a man watching him from the background while leaning against the outside wall of the restaurant. No Wellesian deep focus here. The man is out of focus and shown for only a moment. Is it Sidney Broom, Arthur Bannister's spy?

In the aftermath of Elsa's departure, George behaves rudely to Michael, even while negotiating their criminal partnership. Perhaps he resents Michael's involvement with Elsa and compensates himself by enjoying his tactical advantage over a rival so desperately in need of money. George's *stated* reasons for the phony murder pact are an unhappy marriage, a fear of impending nuclear war, and a desire to escape both. His quirky, childish mannerisms render his bizarre proposition more convincing, since the proposition itself sounds bizarre.

One scheme interrupts another. Or does it? Glancing in through the restaurant window from outside, Arthur interrupts negotiations between George and Michael to offer Michael a ride into town. This delays the conclusion of negotiations, thus keeping the protagonist in a state of confused anticipation. George invites Arthur inside for a drink, no doubt to dispel any notion that he and Michael are conspiring. Bannister ignores him. Who precisely is manipulating events here? Arthur's choice of words, "There's been a suggestion we drive you into town," implies that the idea was not his own. Was it Elsa's? Is she deliberately contributing to Michael confusion by delaying the completion of his business meeting with George? Or does the idea of inviting Michael to ride along originate with Arthur, acting on Broom's tip that Michael and George are conspiring against him? At times it seems like *everyone* is involved in a conspiracy against the protagonist.

George suggests another meeting with Michael at Grisby's law office later that night. Then he drops a bomb on the proceedings, telling Michael he wants him to sign a written confession of murder. A last gulp of beer, a loony grin, in extreme close-up to exaggerate the effect, and George has done his best to convince Michael of his instability. In terms of temperament, George behaves the opposite of Elsa, and therefore seems an unlikely partner for her. They have played their game of deception well.

While retrieving his gear from the trunk of Bannister's car, Michael is given a secret message from Elsa by Lee, the Bannister's oriental driver. Meet her at the aquarium at nine o'clock. A moment later Arthur sticks his head out the car window and in a cryptic tone of voice offers his legal services should Michael ever need them. The timing is weird, as though two separate plots against Michael were in fact one. But Arthur is not in cahoots with Elsa and George. He knows about their plot against him and relishes his tactical advantage. But does he falsely assume that Michael is their knowing partner in crime? Maybe it doesn't matter, since Arthur has another valid reason to resent the protagonist.

Dressed in a pinstripe suit and looking every bit the high-priced lawyer he did not during the sea voyage, George Grisby reads aloud the murder confession he drafted for Michael to sign. Books line the shelves of his law office. He must know what he is talking about when he discusses the legal ramification of his and Michael's plot. But also visible on the wall are ceremonial masks—tokens of George's expensive taste in art, and also a metaphor of his deceptiveness. Michael is seated far across the room, looking uncomfortable in a formal suit and sounding confused as he questions the credibility of so formal a confession allegedly written by someone as informal as himself.

The camera follows Grisby across the room to a wall safe concealed behind paneling. He is very confident, tapping Michael agreeably on the shoulder. What Welles himself described as corny Hawaiian music (Welles/Bogdanovich, p.195) plays on a radio, evoking the Pacific paradise George allegedly intends to hide out in after he and Michael execute their scheme. Sounding more rational now than earlier, which reassures his jittery partner, George explains the plan to fake his own murder in such a way as to allow him to collect his life insurance yet preclude the police from arresting Michael.

George's body language in this scene is relaxed and fluid. Michael, on the other hand, looks awkward and strained as he struggles to comprehend Grisby's dubious legal logic.

He twists and turns in his chair in order to follow George's movements around the room, which are perhaps *meant* to disorient the protagonist so he won't detect the flaw in George's plan that Arthur will point out later in the story. How can George collect his own life insurance when he is legally dead?

The shadowy elegance of Grisby's law office recalls that of Mr. Bernstein's corporate office in *Citizen Kane*. And there is a deeper parallel between the two characters. Bernstein yearns for a woman in white whom he encountered for only a moment during his youth. She is his persistent, unfulfilled romantic dream. Grisby perhaps believes he can achieve that romantic dream with Elsa Bannister. But what he sees in her is as much a fantasy as what Bernstein invests in *his* mystery woman. The corny Hawaiian music on the radio may be intended by Grisby to reinforce the phony plot he feeds to Michael, but it also mocks George's false perception of Elsa. Or so I assume, because Welles never openly shows Elsa conspiring with George. He never gives us a full peek behind *that* mask.

If the Hawaiian music echoes George's idealistic view of Elsa Bannister, the subsequent aquarium scene offers a more accurate analogy to her predatory motives and methods, although her beauty and romantic words counterpoint that visual analogy. Surrounded by glowing tanks full of ocean creatures, Michael and Elsa talk about love and escape while the soundtrack coos another variation of "Please Don't Love Me." For the first time Elsa seems caught up in Michael's romantic spirit, finally overcoming her financial dependence on Arthur. She and Michael kiss, until interrupted by a group of giggling schoolchildren and their guardians, spying on them from nearby. In a reaction shot over Michael's shoulder, Elsa looks detached and calculating again. She did *not* lose herself in the pleasure of Michael's kiss. The children are hustled away by their guardians. One of the latter, however, lingers to get another look at the lovers, until pushed away by her companion. It's a nice little Hitchcockian moment, touching on the insatiable curiosity of human nature. Elsa and Michael retreat to a more secluded section of the aquarium.

Referring to Michael's earlier claim to have access to five thousand dollars to finance their escape, Elsa voices concern that he has gotten involved in something foolish. Does she no longer care about money? Michael shows her the murder confession Grisby prepared for him to sign. She holds the document up to the light coming from a tank containing a moray eel. As she reads the confession she unwittingly and briefly moves in tandem with a shark swimming in another tank. The visual parallel between Elsa and predators of the sea tells a story in opposition to what Elsa has said and done thus far in the scene. In a close-up after she finishes reading the confession out loud, her eyes are nearly as expressionless as the shark's. Morally, if not emotionally, dead. Yet on a verbal level she argues *against* Michael's participation in George's crazy scheme, claiming that it is a set-up orchestrated by her husband. Welles often counterpoints imagery with sound or dialog.

Illuminated by aquarium tanks, Elsa and Michael walk through a setting of half light and half shadow. Motives too, especially Elsa's, are partly concealed. She claims to suspect a trap, yet advises Michael to cooperate with George so long as nobody gets hurt. But why get involved with Grisby at all if it's a trap set by Arthur? Obscuring the specious logic of her advice, Elsa returns quickly to the topic of romance, calling out to Michael as "my beloved, my beloved." In close-up silhouette they kiss, in the quivering light of the aquarium. Visually, if only for a moment, they are pure representations of passionate love. But their romantic dialog is less convincing than their silhouette, which is quickly displaced by a shot of Grisby's black automobile at the start of the next scene.

George is all business when he and Michael pull up in front of the Bannister residence. He dismisses Michael off to the kitchen to make coffee, as he would a servant. And Michael does as he is told. George has the tactical edge now because Michael needs money, because Elsa told Michael to play along with George's scheme, and because George knows more about what's really supposed to happen than does Michael.

From a distance we watch Grisby approach a man in the near foreground, in the Bannister's garden. We cannot see the stranger's face. But from the manner in which he tosses aside his cigarette and puts his hand in the pocket of his white suit jacket when he spots George, he appears confident that *he* has the edge in this encounter. The stranger is revealed to be Sidney Broom. Both he and George appear visually dominant in alternate shots. Then Broom makes a fatal mistake by informing George that he is the only person who knows about George's love for Elsa and of their plot to frame Michael for a murder George will commit. He also refuses George's request to delay a blackmail payoff until the following day, concerned that Grisby might flee the country. George has no option but to shoot Broom now, with the gun originally intended for use on someone else.

Three quick reaction shots reveal three very different perspectives of the shooting. Startled, Michael hears the shot from inside the Bannister kitchen. Cut to a topsy-turvy, extreme close-up of Broom's face, expressing shock and pain at his sudden reversal of fortune. Then the camera tilts up to show George standing over Broom's body. He too looks disconcerted, if to a lesser extent. But he quickly regains composure and walks away from his victim to attend to Michael, whom he knows will be curious about the gunfire. Sure enough, Michael heads for the kitchen door to go outside and investigate. But to *our* surprise, that action is intercut with a shot of Elsa, in an upstairs room in the same house, rushing to a window to see what's happening outside. At the start of the scene George told Michael that she was away at the movies. Either George lied to Michael, or Elsa lied to George.

George returns to the car and deposits his gun in the glove compartment before Michael shows up. He explains away the gunshots as "target practice," then tells Michael to use the same excuse for firing off a few rounds down by the boat landing, within hearing range of restaurant patrons who will then testify to it later. In other words, George uses the same lie to conceal Broom's murder from Michael that Michael is supposed to use to conceal their phony murder from the public and police.

Welles crosscuts among different sites of action. No one character is in a position to comprehend or control everything. From her upstairs room Elsa rings the intercom for Broom, whom she believes is downstairs. Dragging his mortally wounded body into the kitchen, Broom is startled by her ring. Simultaneously, a mile or so down the road, the car driven by Michael smashes into the back of a truck stopped at an intersection. Michael was distracted by George's increasingly bizarre behavior, which was perhaps intended by Grisby to keep Michael emotionally off balance and easier to manipulate, but on this occasion resulted in an accident Grisby did *not* intend. George even tries to steer the car clear of the truck at the last moment, but fails. The truck driver rushes back to the car to see if anyone got injured. Astutely, George incorporates this unforeseen accident into his overall plan. He gives the truck driver his business card, allegedly for insurance purposes but in fact so that the truck driver can later testify he saw George and Michael together. As Michael drives away, shadows from cracks in the car's windshield appear across Michael's face. O'Hara is the unwitting fly caught in the spider web of Grisby's deception. But George's face too is shadowed by that metaphorical web. Both characters are about to be betrayed by a third.

Back at the Bannister kitchen, Elsa offers to summon a doctor for the dying Sidney Broom. Her manner is not sadistic, but is certainly detached. Her capacity for sympathy has long been eroded by bitter experience. When Broom tells her that a real murder instead of a fake one is about to be committed, and that her husband is in danger, the camera closes in on Elsa's reaction. Her eyes widen. Is she concerned for Arthur's welfare? Or is she worried that her scheme with Grisby, if indeed one exists, has gone wrong? In either case, her eyes are emotionally vacant and her movements almost mechanically smooth as she turns her head. She is the human equivalent of the automated oil derricks in *Touch of Evil*.

At one point in the kitchen scene Broom explains to Elsa, "I got some lead in me — where it hurts." Such stylized film noir language distances us emotionally from his death, in a way we are not distanced from the deaths of Charlie Kane, Isabel Amberson Minafer, Hank Quinlan, Pete Menzies, Joseph K, and Falstaff. *The Lady from Shanghai* is a labyrinth — a game in which emotions are more feigned and manipulated than deeply felt, just as actions are often prearranged rather than spontaneous. Sidney Broom is not faking his death in this scene. But we see and hear his death through the distorted lens of film noir sensibilities, as though Welles's camera and soundtrack were infected with the cynicism of the characters themselves, who in trying to express genuine emotions can only badly feign them. The aesthetic effect is similar to Elsa and Arthur Bannister searching for reality amidst fun house mirror *reflections* of reality in the movie's last scene.

Arriving at dockside, George wipes blood from his injured hand on both the automobile's carpet and on Michael's clothing, taking advantage of the unplanned traffic accident that nearly destroyed his elaborate scheme. He instructs Michael to take the gun from the glove compartment — the same weapon George used to shoot Broom. Michael is now to be the victim of a *double* frame up.

The camera follows Michael and George up, down, and all around the dock as George gives his patsy final marching orders. Brief images of the two characters through the dock's wooden support slats foreshadow the more extreme visual disorientation of Joseph K's visit to and flight from Titorelli's apartment in *The Trial*, while camera movement prefigures the more elaborate bridge/covert surveillance scene at the end of *Touch of Evil*. We share in Michael's confusion. He is always the follower in Grisby's scheme, never the leader. George swipes Michael's sailor cap as though stealing a token of command. So confident of his own mastery of the situation is George that he laughs at Michael while leaving him on the dock. Michael asks why. George replies, "You'll find out," not bothering to disguise the menace in his voice. But as Grisby jumps into a motorboat to leave, we watch him in extreme long shot, his tiny figure overwhelmed by the heavy, dark, weblike structure of the dock. If Michael is entangled in a phony alliance with Grisby, George is equally enmeshed in a dubious conspiracy with *his* senior partner, who is about to modify their scheme without George's knowledge.

Visible through windows in the restaurant high above and behind Michael as he watches George depart are unwitting patrons who are maneuvered to play a role in Grisby's scenario. Images of couples dancing to soft jazz are part of a world Michael can at this point only dream about sharing with Elsa. In order to achieve that dream, or so he has been seduced into believing, Michael must participate in Grisby's melodrama. Shown from an extreme low angle, he fires the gun George gave him. High above his head is a neon "Liquor" sign attached to the restaurant. A functional metaphor, it reminds us of Michael's intoxication with Elsa Bannister, which in turn lead to his cooperation with Grisby.

After firing his gun, a wide-eyed Michael moves awkwardly beneath and across the dock. The camera tracks with him, but at a sufficient distance to be somewhat objective. He looks like a rat running through a maze. Restaurant patrons approach him from along connecting boardwalks, hesitating at the sight of his gun. He dutifully and foolishly repeats the phrase George gave him about doing a little target practice. He even apes George's bizarre emphasis on the first syllable of "target." The general consensus among the witnesses to this staged event is that Michael is drunk. He is, but not on booze. He's drunk on Elsa Bannister and the prospect of rescuing her from a loveless marriage and perhaps even from suicide.

Welles claimed that the latter half of this scene, from the gunshot onwards, was damaged by poor dubbing and music (Welles/Bogdanovich, p.196). Originally, he says, "a careful pattern of voices had been built up" but was replaced, against his wishes, with a "vague hullaballoo" diminishing the audience's feeling that maybe they are going crazy along with the protagonist.

While George returns to shore with another gun and a new plan in which Michael is an *un*witting participant, Michael calls Elsa from a pay phone. Instead he gets Sidney Broom, surprisingly still clinging to life in the Bannister kitchen. Seeking revenge on the man who shot him (Grisby), Broom warns Michael about a frame-up for the impending murder of Arthur Bannister.

Like the foolish knight errant he is, Michael rushes off to save Arthur Bannister from George Grisby. And he does so with the pistol George used to kill Broom, with George's blood on his clothes, and with a signed confession to George's murder in his pocket. Policemen gathered in front of Bannister and Grisbys' law offices quickly discover all three pieces of incriminating evidence, and jump to the logical conclusion. Surprising both Michael and us, a very much alive Arthur Bannister suddenly appears, preceded a moment earlier by his unmistakable voice and followed a moment later by George's corpse passing by on a stretcher. Welles loves to stagger his dramatic revelations, allowing their aesthetic effect to accumulate.

All of the story's principle characters collide in the same place at the same time when Elsa arrives by car. Arthur happily informs her that George was found dead in the street, with Michael's cap in his hand. The cap George intended to plant beside *Arthur's* corpse. Walking into a close-up, Elsa appears stunned at the news. Arthur exacerbates her distress by remarking that Michael will need a good lawyer, obviously referring to himself. At this point in the story it seems logical to assume that Arthur found out about George's plot to kill him and frame Michael, preemptively murdered George instead, and is leaving Michael once again to take the blame. But in *The Lady from Shanghai* nearly all initial conclusions are flawed.

Describing himself for the second time as a "big boob," the narrator sums up the bizarre situation in which his on screen persona finds himself—on trial for a murder he didn't commit and defended in court by the man who appears to have framed him. We observe Elsa's car approach up a San Francisco hill, then recede down the other side. The street ahead of her rises again. Like recent events in Michael's life, it's a roller coaster ride. Elsa's face appears calm as she passes by the camera. Not performing for anyone at this moment, she seems untroubled by either Grisby's murder or Michael's arrest. The narrator succinctly concludes, "Either me or the rest of the world is absolutely insane."

Elsa joins her husband in the lobby of the courthouse where Michael's trial will be held. Shown initially from a low angle, the lobby appears huge and imposing, with its large black dome looming over everyone. Individual voices sound hollow and thin. But this impression of institutional dominance is deceiving. In a frontal medium shot of the Bannisters seated on a public bench, we see a prominent "No Smoking By Order of the Chief of Police" sign on the wall behind them. Ignoring its edict, Arthur smokes a cigarette. Some individuals play by their own rules. But if Arthur defies the No Smoking rule, he feels obliged to observe others, including the unwritten social rule of schmoozing one's superior.

He interrupts his conversation with Elsa to exchange pleasantries with a passing judge, who after all might sit in judgement on one of Arthur's court cases. He even greets his opponent, District Attorney Galloway. Despite a hint of sarcasm in their exchange, the two men behave like professionals, emotionally detached from their case. Behind that facade of detachment, however, Arthur is emotionally *very* involved in the outcome of Michael's case — just not in the way one would expect of a defense attorney.

Elsa declines Arthur's offer of an escort to Michael's jail cell, preferring instead to visit the prisoner alone, which she contrarily suggests was Arthur's idea in the first place. Lighting a cigarette for herself, she defies both her husband and the "No Smoking" sign behind her.

Arthur argues that he is the best person to defend Michael because he lost a partner to the killer and must therefore, in the public's view, truly believe his client innocent of the crime. But when he tries to parlay that argument into physical contact with his wife, placing his hand affectionately on hers, she pulls away. Reacting to her rejection, he paints a grim legal picture of Michael's chances in court. Arthur wants his client to plead "excusable homicide." Then, playing the role of District Attorney, he piece by piece invalidates Elsa's "proof" of Michael's innocence. Yet he denies her counter accusation that he wants Michael convicted, claiming that he would not wish to make Irishman a martyr in her eyes. Arthur hesitantly touches the collar of Elsa's coat, then quickly withdraws his hand, afraid of another rejection. "I've got to defend him. I haven't any choice," he admits, trying to appear noble in his wife's eyes. But he cannot help backing up that phony show of nobility with an implicit threat of blackmail, which has always been the foundation of their marriage. "And neither have you," he warns. Neither Bannister is capable of trusting or relying on sentiment.

During their intense discussion the camera almost imperceptibly closes in on the Bannisters until the initial medium shot becomes a close-up. The distractions of their surroundings disappear from view as Michael's upcoming trial becomes for them less an institutional matter and more an extension of their dysfunctional relationship. The "No Smoking" sign and all the legal rules and regulations it represents shrink to nothing in the context of a private struggle for survival between husband and wife.

Elsa's visit to Michael's jail cell begins with a shot of another institutional sign hanging on a wall, this one warning of dire consequences for throwing cigarettes on the floor. Elsa advises Michael to conform to another legal norm, placing his trust in the hands of his defense attorney. Either she bought Arthur's claim that he would defend Michael to the best of his ability in order to prevent the accused from becoming a martyr in her eyes, or she secretly prefers that Michael pay the penalty for Grisby's murder rather than have her own involvement exposed.

The iron bars of Michael's cell are augmented by a fine wire mesh that visually reinforces the separation between prisoner and visitor. In a big close-up of their whispered conversation, Michael's face is so shadowy and indistinct it is almost a silhouette, while Elsa's appears incandescent it is so brightly lit. In emotional terms too they differ greatly. Elsa asks Michael why he killed Sidney Broom. Knowing full well he didn't, she does so only to deepen his despair. Michael insists that Grisby killed Broom, then intended to murder Arthur as part of an elaborate plan to fake his own death and escape from his wife, who would not give him a divorce. Elsa deals a heavy blow to Michael's defense by revealing that George didn't have a wife. And she does so with the same vacant stare we've seen from her on previous occasions. Does she feel nothing at all? Is she still manipulating the protagonist, painting him into a legal corner so he will panic and do something desperate?

The Lady from Shanghai. Elsa Bannister (Rita Hayworth) and Michael O'Hara (Orson Welles) discuss Michael's court case, but they are divided by much more than iron bars and wire mesh.

Elsa Bannister arrives in the courtroom during Michael's trial. The camera follows her as she searches for an open seat. She is fashionably dressed, with a white fur piece across her arm and a veil that distances her from everyone else. She appears very conscious of her celebrity status, in spite of the sobriety of her facial expression. As proof of that status, one of the spectators rudely jockeys for position to get a look at the famous Mrs. Bannister. Elsa's movements are, as usual, like those of a well-oiled machine. She says nothing. Contrast her demeanor with that of Goldie, who offers her a seat next to him.

Meanwhile, Arthur does a little manipulating of his own, using humor to discredit the testimony of a prosecution witness. In long shot images of the action the District Attorney, witness, Judge, defense attorney, defendant, and jury are dwarfed by the high ceiling and walls of the courtroom. The institutional process, with its strict rules and regulations, seems dominant. But that impression is subsequently undercut: by the prosecutor's irrelevant attempt to bolster his witness's credibility by slyly informing the jury that he is a devoted family man, by one member of the jury who is half-asleep, and by Arthur's and then Michael's keen notice of Elsa's arrival. Private concerns and illegitimate methods permeate the official proceedings. The camera closes in to capture Michael's reaction to seeing the woman he loves. She discreetly smiles back in apparent encouragement. Arthur stands and aggressively defends his client, or so it appears, by objecting to Galloway's line of questioning and requesting a declaration of mistrial. Arthur's objection is sustained by the Judge, but the mistrial is not granted. And the Judge elicits a few laughs for himself from the crowd at the expense of the two egotistical lawyers. *Everyone* in the courtroom has a personal agenda.

Parading his physical disability in front of the jurors to arouse their sympathy, Arthur deftly counters his opponent's previous ploy by getting the witness to admit that he has no wife or children. Predictable laughter from jurors and spectators. Arthur asks no further questions of this witness. He cannot discredit the testimony, so he contents himself with discrediting the District Attorney's tactics and, by association, the witness. But the prosecutor has a few tricks up his sleeve as well. He calls Arthur Bannister to the stand as his next witness. Surprised but confident, Arthur agrees. As he takes the stand we get a series of quick reaction shots among spectators and jurors, displaying a variety of reactions ranging from admiration to amusement to contempt, expressed in more than one language. There is no unanimity of perception in this courtroom. Visually too the emphasis is on diversity. The people reacting to Galloway's surprise tactic include young and old; oriental, caucasion, and African American; a woman wearing glasses and her companion who does not; Chinese and American slang; Bessie wearing a black dress seated in front of Elsa dressed in white. Immediately following this brief montage we see Michael O'Hara, sitting alone and talking to no one. He seems isolated from everyone else. And this portrait of isolation is repeated later in the scene.

Arthur's testimony is briefly disrupted by coughing and sneezing from spectators, and by laughter from a juror who idiotically finds it amusing when Galloway asks Bannister if he is "a member of the bar." Booze and the law profession. Double meaning. We get it. And *this* juror is sitting in judgement on another man fighting for his life? Fortunately the frivolous juror is castigated by two of his fellow jurors. Welles shows us all of this seemingly but not really trivial action in a single long shot, emphasizing the sheer variety of disruptions to the orderly flow of the legal process. Moments earlier he employed *numerous* shots to convey the variety of age, sex, race, language, and dress among the spectators reacting to Arthur being called to the witness stand. Welles was seldom satisfied to show something in only one way. He knew there were potentially *many* ways to convey dramatic content — some more effective for specific situations than others.

Arthur Bannister on the witness stand behaves more like a lawyer than a witness, challenging the District Attorney's legal right to ask certain questions. But the Judge overrules him and so Arthur adopts a new tactic, demanding the right to cross-examine himself. Reaction shots among spectators and jurors attest to their keen interest in his theatrical maneuver. Arthur facetiously ridicules his opponent's portrayal of Michael as a man who made arrangements to flee before committing murder. The spectators are amused. The jurors are amused. The court reporter is amused. Even the Judge chuckles, until he catches himself in this injudicious act and represses it. Theatrically reinforcing the effectiveness of Arthur's performance are the two canes he holds conspicuously between his disabled legs as he answers his own questions. Everyone is impressed by the way he overcomes his disability.

But in what begins as a long shot of Arthur leaving the witness stand, with sympathetic help from a bailiff, Galloway's right shoulder prominently intrudes into the camera frame in the near foreground. The theatrical power of surprise and spectacle shifts back to him as he summons Elsa Bannister to the witness stand. Arthur, lurching towards his opponent until they appear together in close-up, suddenly looks vulnerable. The prosecutor, by contrast, appears smug. Murmuring and smiles from the spectators confirm Galloway's triumph, and the fickleness of their emotions. They are more interested in entertainment than in justice, as they will be again in Welles's *The Trial*.

Galloway strikes hard and fast, pointing out that the Bannisters have no children. Arthur sadly glances at the floor. Elsa spikes his pain a little by replying "I" rather than "we" have no children. As her testimony continues the camera cuts away briefly to a spectator surreptitiously sticking her chewed gum under her chair. Previously in this scene we observed the same spectator looking alternately sober and amused. The gum incident is trivial, yet symptomatic of the frequent disconnection between institutional justice and private concerns.

By pointing out, in an increasingly strident voice, that Sidney Broom was both a butler in the Bannister home and a detective hired by Arthur to investigate divorce cases, Galloway portrays Michael and Elsa as illicit lovers and Arthur as a suspicious husband. Spectators lean forward in eager anticipation of Elsa's response. Sex is always an attention getter. The Judge overrules Arthur's objection and, grinning with more than judicial curiosity, orders Elsa to respond. In extreme close-up she tries to maintain self-control, reducing Michael's alleged infatuation with her to mere "respect." But when pressed, she admits to kissing the defendant.

Arthur Bannister, looking defeated and humiliated, declines to cross examine his wife. Yet his revenge on Michael and Elsa is secured by the same inaction that outwardly signals his defeat. Michael, meanwhile, appears yet again in an isolated shot that looks like it was filmed at a different time and location. He is the odd man out, witnessing yet playing no active role in the drama of his own fate.

Diversity is again the keynote as panoramic images of San Francisco are linked first to Lee, the Bannisters' driver, and a gathering of his Chinese-American acquaintances listening to the latest radio report about Michael's trial and then discussing it among themselves in Chinese, then to the Judge playing chess with himself in his private chambers while awaiting the jury's return from deliberation. He and his chess pieces are shown as a reflection off a window overlooking San Francisco and the bay area. His reflection seems small, insulated, and barely significant, tucked into an upper left corner of the much larger image of the city. Humming "Pop Goes the Weasel" to himself, he has little emotional stake in the outcome of the trial. In that he resembles Lee from the previous shot, who seemed more entertained by than concerned about the fate of "Black Irish," as Michael is sensationally dubbed by the radio report. The low drone of a ship's foghorn (ships are visible in the bay) links the reactions of Lee and the Judge by informing us that they occur at the same time. The whole city is caught up in Michael's trial, each individual according to his own inclinations but none of them intimately involved.

For the Judge the trial is equivalent to his chess game or to the song he hums. His detached perspective is implied in the next shot: an overhead view of the courtroom, where Michael, Arthur, Elsa, and a bailiff await the jury's return. The bailiff opens the blinds over a window near Elsa, adding the San Francisco cityscape, and the variety of private reactions to the trial that it implies, to the more intimate reactions of Elsa, Arthur, and Michael. Another foghorn aurally links and counterpoints their reactions to those of the Judge and Lee. Its mournful sound evokes the same sense of isolation it did when reporter Thompson approached Huntington Hospital to interview Jed Leland in *Citizen Kane*.

Unlike the atmosphere of casual interest we witnessed outside the courtroom, the mood *inside* the courtroom is intense. Enigmatic as always, Elsa sits by herself, observing Michael and Arthur across the room as they discuss the trial. It is impossible to tell if she scrutinizes them coldly, from a purely selfish perspective, or is suppresses a genuine concern for the defendant. The bailiff, meanwhile, goes about his appointed routine. His demeanor brings the detachment of the outside world into juxtaposition with the deeply personal involvement of the other three characters.

Another bailiff enters the Judge's chambers to announce the jury's return to the courtroom. Jostled out of his private world, the Judge is momentarily startled, knocking over his chess pieces. He reacts to the interruption as though embarrassed to be caught doing something he, as a judge, shouldn't. Returning to his official duties, he slips into his judicial robe and sprays his throat with something from his medicine cabinet. He looks like an opera star preparing for a performance. Visually Welles brackets him with two pompous images of nobility: a statuette and a picture on the wall, the latter briefly visible as a reflection off the medicine cabinet mirror. No doubt the Judge sees himself on a par with those two icons.

The Judge's throat medicine, employed to enhance his performance and prestige at the trial, is juxtaposed in back-to-back shots with Arthur Bannister's pain medicine, necessary to make his day-to-day life bearable. But if we are encouraged to sympathize with Arthur at the Judge's expense, that sympathy quickly dissipates when he informs Michael that he will enjoy losing the case and watching his client suffer while awaiting execution. He even intends to prolong that suffering by requesting, as any good defense attorney would, a stay of execution. And this act of professional malfeasance occurs while Arthur stands to show respect for the Judge and jury, re-entering the courtroom in the background. Arthur hasn't the slightest appreciation for the ethical contradiction between what he says and what he does at this moment.

The camera closes in to an exchange of extreme close-ups between attorney and client as they thrust and parry in a private battle beneath their public show of solidarity. Arthur believes he possesses a tactical edge in their contest because he knows Michael will be convicted and executed. But Michael, looking more menacing than at any previous time in the story, counters with an edge of his own, claiming to know who really killed Grisby. Elsa calls to him from across the room, silently directing his attention to Arthur's open bottle of pain pills on the table in front of him. Michael grabs the bottle and swallows some of the pills before anyone can stop him. Chaos erupts. Michael has employed Arthur's own resource to deny Arthur his revenge. But the question arises, is Elsa facilitating Michael's escape from state custody, or is she encouraging him to commit suicide? If the latter, was her motive to uncomplicate her own life by getting rid of someone who has become a liability, or to compassionately spare Michael the suffering that Arthur wants to prolong?

The same old woman who earlier jostled her companion in order to get a better look at Elsa now stands and shouts with glee, "Poison pills!" For her Michael's act of desperation is grand spectacle. Ignoring courtroom protocol, spectators leap out of their seats and pursue the defendant as he is carried out of the room by bailiffs and the District Attorney, who obviously wants this case brought to a victorious conclusion and therefore needs Michael kept alive, for the time being. Shown from a high camera angle, the spectators look like an unruly mob.

Welles's camera parallels the movements of court officials as Michael is hauled into the Judge's chambers. From inside those chambers it looks back towards the open doorway and shows the Judge, trapped between frenzied spectators forcing their way out of the courtroom in the background, and Galloway, who summons reporters and practically shoves the Judge out of his own chambers. Fittingly, the Judge is portrayed by Erskine Sanford, who played the equally ineffectual Herbert Carter in *Citizen Kane* and Roger Bronson in *The Magnificent Ambersons*. The District Attorney is less interested in justice than in preparing a statement for the press in order to counteract bad publicity for his case. He too exits the room, leaving a seemingly groggy Michael in the custody of one bailiff, who at Galloway's instructions tries to keep the defendant awake and moving until medical help arrives.

A ringing telephone adds to the general confusion of the scene. Then, suddenly, Michael revives from his phony torpor and knocks out the bailiff with a savage punch. He sends his poor victim crashing into the Judge's chess board, scattering the game pieces and metaphorically reducing the Judge's private little kingdom to mayhem. But the Judge's unanswered telephone lures another bailiff into the room. Michael moves quickly to cut off his escape, then, as the camera closes in on the action, punches him twice. The second blow drives the bailiff's head through the glass front of a bookcase. Welles emphasizes rather than minimizes the brutality of his desperate hero. Meanwhile, across the hall, the Judge tries unsuccessfully to regain control of his courtroom. He is barely discernable in the crowd. Perhaps thinking of his own reputation, he orders newspaper photographers not to take any pictures of the chaos. Having agendas of their own, they ignore him.

Unlike the first bailiff, who quickly succumbed to Michael's attack, the second one puts up a fierce battle. The defendant tries to collapse the heavy bookcase onto his enemy, who barely avoids it. Clearly Michael would rather kill the man than face execution. After a titanic struggle he finally knocks out the bailiff. There is nothing graceful about their fight scene. It is awkward and brutal, without restraint. Unfortunately the vivid and unusual impression Welles creates visually and with sound effects is weakened by Roemheld's intrusively conventional music.

Michael escapes from the courthouse by using the legal system against itself. He joins a departing jury from a different trial. They are being escorted to lunch by another bailiff. And Michael is fortunate to possess another tactical edge in the form of Goldie, who recognizes his buddy's escape maneuver and diverts police attention in the opposite direction. Getting Goldie a job on Arthur Bannister's yacht has yielded unexpected benefits for the protagonist.

The Judge enters his chambers and is annoyed to see his orderly sanctuary reduced to rubble. The camera travels with him from in front, then pulls up and away from him to scrutinize him more critically, from above, as he makes a fool of himself. He is more concerned about his broken window and scattered chess pieces than his injured and unconscious bailiffs, from whom he absurdly demands a "full report" of the incident.

One of the jury members with whom Michael exits the courtroom violates court rules by discussing her case outside the deliberation room. She is sternly reprimanded by the accompanying bailiff. But from what she says before she is silenced, we doubt her ability to sit in judgment. She believes the female defendant in her case is too attractive to be a criminal. From judge to lawyers to jurors to spectators, the courthouse scenes offer a grim view of the legal system in action.

Michael sneaks away from the jury and escapes. We watch him recede into city traffic. Then we watch him recede again, this time from Elsa's vantage point, peering out through a courtroom window. She leaves the room without a word of explanation to Arthur, who protests. Three characters visually overlapping but emotionally at odds with each other.

Welles cuts back and forth among Michael fleeing the police, the police hunting for him, and Elsa following him. Each party is isolated from the others. Michael finds temporary refuge in San Francisco's Chinatown district, adding to our sense of diversity bordering on confusion. Welles visually surrounds his protagonist with foreign elements, in a manner reminiscent of Josef von Sternberg's *Shanghai Express*, *The Scarlet Empress*, and *Morocco*. Roemheld's agitated background score is more effective than his fight scene music in the Judge's chambers. It is briefly displaced by the local sound of American jazz coming from a Chinese American establishment. Another jarring contradiction in a world full of them. By contrast, Elsa's command of the Chinese language, as she searches for Michael among Chinatown's inhabitants, makes her seem more at home in this exotic setting. Helped by several passersby, she tracks Michael to a Chinese theater.

Like a sailor fleeing his own past by sailing to exotic foreign ports, Michael seeks sanctuary in a Chinese theater. Our first sight of the ritualized, heavily costumed and made-up performances on the stage of that theater is visually framed by dark ceiling beams and the audience. The stage show is a thing set apart from the "reality" of Michael's story. A notably *foreign* thing, with sights and sounds very different from what we have seen and heard so far, yet matching the movie's film noir trappings as a highly stylized form of storytelling. Sitting down among a group of Chinese American spectators, *Michael* now looks foreign and out of place, while *they* appear at ease with and knowledgeable about the performance on stage. Outside the theater, meanwhile, the jarring juxtaposition of American jazz and Chinatown images is repeated as Elsa follows the same route Michael took.

Roemheld's film noir music returns as Elsa approaches the theater, then yields back again to Chinese music as she enters. When Michael spots her, we see her against a backdrop of the play on stage. The actors' costumes are no more elaborate or stylized than her dark fur jacket, dark hat, necklace, sculpted hair, and facial make-up. The artificiality of film noir is highlighted and magnified by the artificiality of Chinese theater.

Instead of rushing into the arms of her lover, Elsa proceeds backstage to a phone. Shots of her are interspliced with shots of the stage performance. There is intrigue everywhere — on stage, in the audience, and backstage. Elsa speaks by phone to her servant, Lee, whom she previously trusted to discretely inform Michael of their rendezvous at the aquarium. Maybe they are old acquaintances from her Shanghai days. Reacting to her summons, Lee and two other men jump into a car and drive away.

Elsa's phone call was facilitated by young Chinese American switchboard operators. In contrast to their ethnic compatriots on stage, these women are dressed and behave like typical Americans—or what we tend to think of as typical Americans. There is diversity everywhere, even *within* an ethnic community.

The police close in on Michael as Elsa takes a seat beside him in the theater audience. Welles intersplices their faces with those of several patrons watching the play. Expressing or feigning concern, Elsa asks him why he swallowed Arthur's pills. Michael acknowledges that he saw her silent appeal to him to do so, but assures her that he did not take all of them. He assumes that knowing he hasn't committed suicide comforts her. Maybe it doesn't. What clearly does *not* comfort Elsa is Michael's declaration that he needs to find the gun that killed Grisby in order to prove his innocence.

The arrival of the police draws suspicious glances from both the theater audience and the performers on stage, who momentarily break character and become entangled in the intrigue *off* stage. Meanwhile, adding to the multiplying crosscurrents of drama, Lee and his companions arrive at the theater.

Whatever Elsa's intentions towards Michael become after learning of his search for the gun that killed George, she does not want him captured by the police. She fakes a romantic embrace with him in order to hide him from them. "Don't move," she prudently instructs him. During their embrace Michael finds a pistol in her purse. Now he tells *her* not to move, but in a very different context. He accuses her of killing George. An extreme close-up of her vacant, remorseless stare seems to confirm that accusation. But then Michael collapses to the floor. The pills he swallowed to facilitate his escape from state custody suddenly become a liability. Another reversal.

Backstage, Lee and his companions cut electrical power to the lights, plunging the theater into darkness so they can remove Michael without being seen. The narrator informs us that Elsa murdered Grisby and now intends to kill Michael. But was that her original intention when she tracked him to the theater and phoned Lee for help? Or did it *become* her intention after Michael found her gun and realized that she killed Grisby? Like the protagonist, we are never certain of Elsa's feelings or motives.

Michael is hustled down an alley behind the theater by Lee and companions. According to Welles (Welles/Bogdanovich, p.196), Harry Cohn removed much of his original footage from the Chinese theater and subsequent Crazy House scenes. What remains is still powerful. Michael regains consciousness inside the Crazy House of a closed amusement park. An overhead, inverted, obliquely angled close-up of his reawakening goes radically *out* of focus instead of coming *into* focus as his eyes open. The more conscious he becomes, the less rational seems the world around him. An experience analogous to Joseph K's awakening from sleep at the beginning of *The Trial*.

An extreme close-up of Michael's head from the same camera angle overlaps with moving, black, web-like patterns. Is this a subjective impression of what Michael imagines? No. The next shot shows him on his feet, wandering dazed through the Crazy House. The web-like patterns are projected on an obliquely angled wall behind him. Emotional confusion is reinforced by physical illusion that was originally intended to entertain rather than terrorize. We're in *Macbeth* and *The Trial* territory now. Michael passes by several bizarre, illuminated backdrops, including one imprinted with the words, "Stand Up or Give Up," which in the context of Michael's situation carries a metaphorical message very different from its original meaning. Michael chooses to "Stand Up," as confirmed by the narrator, who informs us that even during this confusing journey through the Crazy House he was clear of mind about the evil of Elsa Bannister, including why she killed George Grisby and now wants to kill Michael. Visually, however, things get more chaotic for the protagonist as he passes from one lunatic, Caligari-inspired room to another. Twisting camera movements combine with wildly expressionistic sets to disorient us.

On a literal rather than metaphorical level, accepting the challenge of another "Stand Up or Give Up" sign sends Michael hurtling down a winding slide, through a giant dragon's mouth, and into an even more bizarre world where perception is warped by a combination of fun house mirrors and an unstable, revolving floor painted in bold geometric patterns. Dumping Michael in the closed Crazy House may have been a simple matter of convenience for Elsa and her allies. But his experience in that artificial environment echoes his experience in the real, or reel (film noir being as stylized as an amusement park) world earlier in the story.

Michael stumbles out of an expressionistic nightmare and into a comparatively normal looking storage room that, ironically, contains a dragon far more menacing than the one he confronted moments earlier. Looking a little like mad scientist Rotwang shining a flashlight on Maria, his kidnap victim in Fritz Lang's *Metropolis* (1926), Elsa shines her spotlight on Michael. Most of her body is concealed by shadow, except for her cold eyes and platinum blond hair. She calmly ushers Michael into the Magic Mirror Maze.

Unlike the fun house mirrors that distort the shapes of what they reflect, those in the Maze confuse by repetition rather than distortion. By projecting so many false visual echoes that it is difficult if not impossible to distinguish reality from illusion. Elsa admits to killing Grisby. She accuses George of going "mad" after killing Broom, but her own demeanor, unblinking eyes and flat tone of voice suggest madness. She insists that after George was eliminated she and Michael could have gone off together. Her declaration, "I love you," is one of the least convincing in the history of movies. Not because her love isn't real, but because it is unable to overcome her older, deeper emotional need for financial and material security.

No longer the trusting fool he once was, Michael inquires if Elsa originally intended to run away with George. In other words, is her latest declaration of love just another illusion, like most of the images of her that we see in the Maze? He paraphrases Elsa's earlier quote from a Chinese proverb, about people who follow their nature keeping their original nature in the end. He turns her own words against her. But if Michael is bitterly disillusioned now, he retains a trace of wistful romanticism, asking Elsa if she's never heard of a more optimistic philosophy — one allowing for positive change in human behavior. She admits she hasn't.

Whatever tiny spark of reconciliation flickers between Michael and Elsa, it is extinguished by the squeak and clack of Arthur's Bannister's leg braces and double canes arriving in the Magic Mirror Maze. We see and hear the emblems of his disability before we see his face or hear his voice. They are contradictory tokens of both his weakness and the dramatic power of his surprise entrance. When all of him comes into view, we see him as multiple, identical images, adding to our dual impressions of his physical weakness and tactical power. We cannot distinguish the real Arthur Bannister from his many reflections. And soon Elsa's reflections too are indistinguishable from the real woman. The false images these two characters see of each other foreshadow an incident in Welles's *Othello*, where the title character lies on his back and stares up at the sky. In his imagination, troubled by the alleged infidelity of his wife, the cries of seagulls floating in that sky are transformed into the laughter of his countrymen staring down at him from the battlements of his castle. Othello, Arthur, and Elsa will all be driven to acts of violence by distorted images.

Multiple, mostly reflected images of Arthur and Elsa Bannister intermingle within the same shots as Arthur lurches around the room while explaining their current situation as *he* sees it. By telling Elsa that he would have been willing to keep on playing their little game her way if she hadn't followed Michael out of the courthouse, but that she wasn't aware of that fact, he assumes that she acted on a false assumption about *him*. But then he contrarily speculates that she *wanted* him to follow her so that she could kill him, put the blame on Michael, and acquire the Bannister fortune for herself. That scenario might well be Arthur's illusion about *Elsa's* intentions. Neither he, we, nor Michael can be certain why she followed Michael out of the courthouse, or what she intended to do with Michael before he found in her purse the gun that killed George. There is a remote possibility that she would have run away with Michael and forsaken Arthur's fortune. But too many other possible scenarios confuse the picture. No character can fully trust any other character in this story.

Assuming that Elsa intends to kill him, blame Michael, and take his money, Arthur discloses that he has taken prior countermeasures. He gave District Attorney Galloway (former enemy, now useful ally) a letter exposing a variety of Elsa's dirty secrets. Upon hearing of Arthur's death, Galloway is to open that envelope and take appropriate legal action. Arthur cynically speculates that the District Attorney is as eager to hear of Arthur's death, so that he can open the envelope, as Elsa is to cause it.

In the end illusion becomes purely a matter of tactical advantage and disadvantage. In one remarkable shot Arthur brings a single image of Elsa into a camera frame full of his own reflections by merely switching on a light in the Maze. She is aiming her gun at him. But as Arthur remarks, it's difficult to distinguish a real target from a false reflection. Then he pulls out a gun of his own. Doubled by mirrors and closer to the camera, it seems more potent than his wife's weapon. But in a dramatic frontal close-up Arthur himself undercuts that impression of superiority. Bracketed by two reflections of Elsa, including a close-up of her head that partly overlaps his, Arthur wearily admits that killing his wife is the same as killing himself. They are so much alike: bitter, cynical, and despairing. "I'm pretty tired of both of us," he confesses. He commits the ultimate vanity—committing suicide by killing someone else.

In an orgy of gunshots, mirrors shatter, reflections disintegrate, and illusions disappear one by one. At the end of it all both husband and wife lie mortally wounded on the floor. Roemheld's melodramatic music detracts from the overall effect, but not enough to spoil the scene. An injured hand switches on the light, illuminating the whole area and diminishing much of the mystery of the Magic Mirror Maze. Fittingly, that hand belongs to Michael. The dying Bannisters are surrounded by the jagged shards of their splintered illusions. Even the camera lens appears to be cracked (another optical illusion). Arthur, lying on the floor, cannot resist a final, cruel jab at Elsa, commenting that she shouldn't have killed him because she's going to need a good lawyer. It is the same snide remark he once made to Michael. Arthur follows his ruthless, unforgiving nature to the bitter end. Elsa, on the other hand, tries to escape the shattered world of illusions, lurching out of the Maze and into a comparatively normal room adjacent. But it's too late. She collapses to the floor, dying. We observe her up close, at floor level. Michael coolly scrutinizes her from a distance, needing to break free of her emotional hold on him.

Death speeches are a sometimes useful movie cliché. Elsa is more honest and believable now than at any previous time in the story. She is stunned by the reality of George's, Arthur's, and now her own impending death. Previously it was all just a game to her. She admits her past mistakes. Michael, maintaining his distance from her as he walks towards an exit, comments that by dealing with evil instead of fighting it Elsa eventually gave in to it. Allowed it to dictate her behavior. But Elsa's pessimism is deeply rooted. She still insists that no one can defeat evil. Michael, facing away from her, argues that even if a person cannot win such a battle, as long as he keeps up the struggle he cannot lose either. It is a modest form of optimism.

As Michael walks out of the room, through a turnstile that casts prison bar-like shadows on the wall, Elsa panics. We watch his departure from near her vantage point on the floor. She begs him to stay, screaming "I don't want to die!" Welles shows her desperate appeal in silhouette, enhancing the dramatic effect by metaphorically showing us the darkness that consumes her. Michael hesitates for a moment, then departs. He must save himself, even though it feels like a betrayal of Elsa.

Outside, in the bright sunshine, Michael walks away from the Crazy House. The camera pivots with him, watching him go. He passes by the less ominous "Play Land" sign. The amusement park, the world, and life in general consists of more than just madness and crime. Leaving the amusement park behind, Michael heads towards the ocean far in the background. The traditional consolation for a troubled sailor, like *Moby Dick*'s Ishmael. The narrator sums up Michael's future prospects in the colorful phrases of the storyteller Michael intends to become. But even in those terms there is no clearcut resolution, and certainly no conventional happy ending. Arthur's note to the District Attorney will prove Michael innocent in the eyes of the law. But the narrator offers "stupid" as a more fitting description of himself. "Everybody is somebody's fool" he adds. Michael resolves to stay out of trouble and concentrate on getting old. Translation: he intends to play it safe from now on.

If Roemheld's sugary reprise of "Please Don't Love Me" clashes with the narrator's resolution, it nevertheless reminds us, as does the narrator, that Elsa Bannister will not be

The Lady from Shanghai. Elsa Bannister (Rita Hayworth) and Michael O'Hara (Orson Welles) debate the matter of good versus evil one last time before he walks out on her and she dies.

easy for Michael O'Hara to forget. "Maybe I'll die trying" are the last words spoken in the movie, as Michael's ever smaller figure recedes into the vast world. Like Charlie Kane, Bernstein, George Amberson, Fanny Minafer, and Isabel Amberson before him, and Macbeth, Hank Quinlan, and Falstaff after him, Michael O'Hara will be haunted by the past for the remainder of his life.

4

Touch of Evil: No Man's Land

A simple close-up of an anonymous pair of hands setting the timer on a homemade bomb begins the most elaborate single shot, lyrical dance of disparate elements in any Welles movie. The extreme length and extensive camera movement in *Touch of Evil*'s opening shot highlight the complexity of the coincidental and not so coincidental encounters it shows.

The anonymity of the bomber is maintained by careful staging and camera angle as he plants his weapon in the trunk of an automobile, whose owner is equally anonymous. The bomber leaves the scene moments before the driver, an older man, and his passenger, a young woman, climb into the car and drive away. The car wends its way through the streets of Los Robles, a border town between Mexico and the United States. It is dusk. The camera tracks them without breaking stride for a cut. But by doing so from various angles and distances, and at one point allowing a building to get between itself and the car, the camera makes *us* part of the passing, seemingly random jumble of characters who cross the victims' path. In *The Magic World of Orson Welles* James Naremore remarks that the great variety among the types of people and occupations on display in this shot contributes to our impression of diversity (Naremore, p.157).

Music originating from the car's radio, the radios in other vehicles, and various commercial establishments along the street adds to our impression of constantly shifting elements. Songs fade out and are replaced by others, as people often do in each other's lives. The musical effect is the result of a change made to the movie after Welles's death, but in accordance with the wishes he expressed in a lengthy memo sent to Universal Studio executives after the project was removed from his control. As originally release by Universal the opening shot was accompanied by theme music composed by Henry Mancini and visually overlayed with opening credits. Dramatically potent though that theme music is, its singularity and unchanging volume counteracts the visual effect of multiple, brief encounters. And the printed credits are distracting. But by patching together bits and pieces from Mancini's entire score and then playing them at varying volumes, the revised version of this scene complements rather than diminishes the effect Welles seems to have had in mind. Of course we cannot know for certain if Welles would approve of this revised, re-edited version of his film, produced by Rick Schmidlin and released on DVD by Universal Studios in 2000. But the logic behind it is sound, and so are the aesthetic results.

A traffic cop stops the victims' car to allow other vehicles to pass by on a connecting street. They pass in and out of our view, briefly intersecting with but unaffected by the drama of the vehicle we're tracking. At the next intersection the car is stopped again, allowing two pedestrians to cross the street. The elevated camera descends to near ground level and follows these new characters. For a moment two apparently loving couples, one on foot and the other in an automobile carrying a bomb, appear side by side. But that is a somewhat false impression, because one of the couples is involved in a casual pick-up instead of a committed relationship. At any rate, the victims' car passes out of the camera frame and out of the consciousness of the couple we now track on foot along a sidewalk. Even we, the audience, momentarily lose track of and perhaps even interest in the bomb-laden automobile.

Newlyweds Miguel and Susan Vargas have had only a passing, inconsequential encounter with a murder plot. Further up the street, after passing by numerous other pedestrians, they catch up to the victims' car, now stopped for a small herd of goats blocking its way. The Vargases easily sidestep the herd and continue their leisurely stroll. The victims' car now catches up with *them* at the border crossing, passing through almost simultaneously and paralleling them a short distance to the United States Customs and Immigration checkpoint. The two couples have no evident connection to each other, except that the driver of the car seems annoyed at the delay caused by the customs officer's recognition of and conversation with Miguel Vargas, an important Mexican law enforcement official specializing in drug busts—notably a recent case against someone by the name of Grandi.

Ironically, the officers' flattering chat with Miguel delays the Vargas's passage through the checkpoint, keeping them in dangerous proximity to the unexploded bomb in the trunk of the victims' car. After the Vargases depart, the customs officials turn their attention to that car. The driver, a man named Rudy Linnekar, is treated with some respect. But his companion, a blond stripper whose name we later discover to be Zita, is ignored when she complains repeatedly of the sound of ticking in her head. *We* know that ticking comes from the bomb in the trunk. If the officers were as attentive to her as they were to Miguel Vargas, the murders about to occur might be avoided. On the other hand, the officers themselves might have been killed if they had delayed the vehicle's departure while they searched it. So many developments ride on pure chance in this opening shot. The Linnekar car proceeds through the checkpoint unimpeded, passing out of view again as the camera rejoins Miguel and Susan walking along a street. We close in on the affectionate newlyweds as they stop to kiss.

The camera's long, lyrical dance and the Vargases' kiss are both violently disrupted by the sound of an explosion off screen. Cutting for the first time since the movie began, the camera shows us Linnekar's car blowing up with such violence it lifts off the ground, less than a minute after Susan and Miguel stood beside it at the checkpoint. If Susan had been killed and Miguel survived, one wonders with benefit of hindsight, would Miguel have protested Hank Quinlan's corrupt efforts to frame Manolo Sanchez for the crime?

James Naremore notes that the car explosion, like the death of Wilbur Minafer in *The Magnificent Ambersons*, sets many other events in motion (Naremore, p.103). It brings together characters, along with their emotional baggage, who were previously unknown to each other. The camera returns to the Vargases, but in a different mode now. No longer smooth, serene, and detached in its movements, it backtracks with them in a jerky, hand-held manner that mimics their anxiety and that of other spectators who crisscross their path as everybody runs towards the scene of the explosion. A low camera angle emphasizes the chaotic movements of the crowd and the dark night sky hanging over them.

The explosion not only disrupts the Vargases' kiss, it physically separates them. Apologizing for the delay in their personal plans, Miguel leaves his wife's side to do what a conscientious law enforcement official should do, go to the aid of a victim, despite being outside his jurisdiction. Susan follows him, to his dismay. He is concerned about her safety. This small action establishes a pattern in their relationship that will have more serious consequences later: Miguel's preoccupation with his job and Susan's tendency to be naively drawn into his business.

The violence of the crime against Linnekar and Zita is effectively conveyed by the chaos of the crime scene. Burning, smoking, widely scattered fragments of the automobile speak for the condition of the bodies as well. The noisy arrival of fire trucks and the spray of water add to the confusion. Miguel complains to his wife, "This could be very bad for us." "For us?" she asks, confused. "For Mexico, I mean," he clarifies. Miguel thinks of "us" as Mexican. Earlier, at the checkpoint, Susan made a point of informing the customs officer that she is an *American* citizen. Events later in the movie exacerbate their differences in identity and outlook. And the bi-national, bi-cultural, bi-racial schisms of the Vargases mirror the far more strained relations between the divided border communities. Miguel and Susan are lovers and allies, but not at all times and not in all ways.

Susan leaves the crime scene as American law enforcement officials begin to arrive. Miguel reconnoiters with some of them. Deputy District Attorney Al Schwartz barely acknowledges the Mexican in passing. Time and circumstance eventually transform that initial indifference into a strong alliance. On the other hand, Vargas and an American official named Blaine stop to converse. They are previously acquainted and on friendly terms. But when Blaine remarks that the bomb in Linnekar's car came from the Mexican side of the border, Vargas defensively modifies that assessment to, "The *car* did." Like a lawyer defending his client, he concedes nothing even though he already told Susan how bad the bombing could be for Mexico.

Briefly visible behind the arriving fire trucks are the skeletal outlines of oil derricks dotting the landscape on both sides of the border. More prominent in later scenes, they are visually potent representatives of the wealth that often feeds political corruption, and more importantly of the too-often machine-like reactions of people, most notably the soon to arrive Hank Quinlan, whose behavior and perceptions are locked into destructive and self-destructive patterns.

Creating a sense of separate yet interrelated story lines, the camera cuts away from the crime scene to Susan Vargas returning, at her husband's urging, to their honeymoon hotel on the Mexican side of the border. Jumping back and forth between Susan's and Miguel's activities was the director's original intention, to keep both characters alive in the minds of the audience. Part of an artistic vision that Jean Collet, in "*Touch of Evil*, or Orson Welles and the Thirst for Transcendence" (reprinted in English in *Touch of Evil—Orson Welles, Director*, edited by Terry Comito), describes as "a gaze that wishes to be every gaze at once" (Comito, p.252). When the studio opted for longer, continuous scenes, Welles requested a restoration of his crosscutting, which was not done until Rick Schmidlin's recent re-editing of the film. At least one critic, Frank Brady in *Citizen Welles: A Biography of Orson Welles*, prefers the studio's version of these scenes, complaining that Welles's crosscutting results in a "dilution of suspense" (Brady, p.506). Not by my reckoning.

Susan weaves in and out of busy pedestrian and automobile traffic, passing a neon sign advertising a dance hall named The Paradise. In the same shot we see a young Mexican male in a black leather jacket watching her a bit too keenly, undercutting the paradise reference. But his predatory facial expression is in turn undercut when he saves Susan from stepping into the path of a passing truck. *That* act of compassion is perhaps undercut by the metaphorical implication of another neon sign, advertising an insurance agency, visible in the same shot. We soon discover that the young Mexican, referred to henceforth and incorrectly as Pancho, is on a mission for his uncle, Joe Grandi, to use Susan to pressure Miguel into backing off his prosecution of Joe's brother for possession of narcotics. Blackmail is a form of insurance.

Knowing nothing of Pancho's hidden agenda, Susan automatically suspects the worst about him, expressing little gratitude for his help in avoiding the truck. Walking away from him, she also resists the attempts of passersby to intercede on Pancho's behalf when he tries to hand her a written message. She assumes he wants to pick her up for sex. Visually his black jacket contrasts with the white sweater she carries, amplifying the racial tension of their encounter. The darkness of the night and the imposing facade of a row of buildings in the background, exaggerated by Welles's oblique camera angle, also add to the tension between them. Despite being married to a prominent Mexican government official, Susan Vargas feels like a stranger in a strange land.

Standing in the middle of the street, Susan is surrounded by Pancho and his two intermediaries. A Spanish language neon sign hangs on one of the buildings in the background. Susan responds to this encirclement by foreign elements by mentioning her husband's political clout. Pancho, who understands and speaks English very well but chooses not to let Susan know it, reacts by grinning and crowding her. So she ups the ante again, threatening that her husband is "ready and willing to knock out all those pretty front teeth." At least she noticed his "pretty" teeth. More than one film critic has noted the underlying sexual tension between these two characters. And Susan does agree to follow Pancho back across the border to the American side on the rather flimsy premise that Pancho will show her something of interest to her husband. Or maybe she feels nothing too bad can happen to her on her *own* side of the border.

"Lead on, Pancho," Susan tells her companion. Not knowing his real name, she calls him Pancho because to her it sounds suitably Mexican and male, and therefore an adequate form of address. She intends no insult, but her companion perceives it as such, judging by something he says later to his uncle. Susan's latent racism is minor compared to the virulent bigotry displayed by another American, Hank Quinlan. On the other hand, Quinlan at least has a twisted rationale for his prejudice. Susan, as far as we can tell, does not.

More law enforcement officials gather at the sight of the explosion. Little things like Police Chief Gould shouting over the noise of a fire hose and Pete Menzies crossing in front of Gould and shouting his own words over the Chief's contribute to the overall confusion of the scene. Confusion of a more emotional kind reveals itself a moment later when District Attorney Adair jokes about the noise of the explosion, then abruptly adopts a sober, respectful demeanor when he sees the wreckage. Not greatly moved by the deaths of the victims, he nevertheless feels compelled to make a proper show of it.

Adair is dressed in formal attire, having just come from a banquet also attended by and in honor of the late Rudy Linnekar, whose friendship with the District Attorney obviously didn't amount to much. Linnekar gets an even colder sendoff from the coroner, who after examining the deceased announces, "you can strain him through a sieve." We observe this sarcasm from what would be the dead man's point of view, if he still had one. Even Linnekar's daughter, Marcia, arriving to identify her father's body, doesn't exhibit much in the way of sorrow. She seems sad, but hardly grief-stricken. And even her sadness diminishes when she is asked by the police about her father's female companion.

Captain Quinlan's delayed arrival serves two distinct dramatic purposes: to build up our anticipation about the story's central character, and to highlight Quinlan's status as a loner and an outsider with respect to other American officials gathered at the scene. Images of towering oil derricks viewed from low camera angles coincide with his arrival, reflecting his rigid attitudes about law enforcement and other matters. But as representations of greed they appear in *ironic* conjunction with him. Perhaps in contrast to the likes of Adair, Gould, and Linnekar, Quinlan is immune from political corruption based on financial gain. Hank's characters flaws are of a different sort. Emerging from his car in a solo shot, he looks bloated and scruffy. With his rumpled trenchcoat, puffy eyes, big cigar, and scowl, he is an intimidating mess. He treats his assistant and best friend, Sergeant Pete Menzies, shabbily, as though the man were only a lackey. Hank may not be a crook, but he *is* an arrogant bully.

Contrasting Quinlan's initial appearance and behavior are Vargas's. Having come from the same banquet as Linnekar and Adair, he expresses a sincere desire to meet Quinlan, described by Adair as "our local police celebrity." The coroner, played by Joseph Cotten but voiced over in this scene by Orson Welles, sniggers, "That's what you think." He is obviously familiar with Quinlan's professional stinginess and social prejudices. Why Welles replaced Cotten's voice with his own I don't know. But it is oddly appropriate, since Quinlan's cynicism has clearly engulfed the coroner as well. It is as though Jed Leland had succumbed to instead of rebelled against the corruption of Charlie Kane.

On the brink of Vargas's first encounter with Quinlan, we cut away to Susan's strange journey with Pancho. Believing that journey will help her husband, she trails after the man she earlier avoided like a disease. Aware of his tactical advantage, and probably resenting her previous behavior towards him, Pancho walks rapidly, forcing Susan, encumbered by high heeled shoes, to struggle to keep up with him. A tracking camera highlights his speed and her difficulty matching it. This action occurs along a street on the American side of the border that looks no less seedy and sinister than its Mexican counterpart. In the background a bright neon sign reads, "Jesus Saves." Maybe not in this neighborhood. Saxophone driven rock and roll plays as local music, echoing an undertone of sexual tension between the characters.

An unknown ally of Pancho directs Susan's attention to a baby held by a woman. As Susan reflexively obeys, another confederate snaps a photograph of her standing next to Pancho, who as if by prior arrangement moves closer to Susan and smiles at the camera. The incident is over as quickly as it began. Susan is too confused to figure it out. But in retrospect it is clear that the Grandi family's plot to disgrace, weaken, perhaps even blackmail Miguel Vargas has already begun. Susan is a naive, nearly helpless pawn in their hands.

Inside a dumpy hotel incongruously named the Ritz, Susan encounters Uncle Joe Grandi, whose brother Vincent is being prosecuted by Miguel in Mexico City. A short, squat man who masks his baldness with a bad toupee, Grandi is a little tin dictator. Not without power, but too full of himself to be the master criminal he pretends to be. Nevertheless, he has Mrs. Vargas at a disadvantage, surrounded by Pancho and Uncle Joe inside the hotel and a third family member lurking just outside the lobby window. Grandi circles his prey like a shark. But their initial conversation contradicts that impression. Susan does not yet appreciate the danger she is in. At Pancho's urging, Grandi asks why Susan refers to his nephew as Pancho. "Just for laughs, I guess," she replies. It doesn't occur to her that such a presumption might be insulting. Which does not, of course, justify the Grandi family's treatment of her in this and later scenes. But it does establish a pattern of *mutual* and not entirely unjustified hostility.

Dismissing his flunky lingering outside the window, Grandi primps in front of a mirror while revealing his identity to Susan, who is suitably impressed. He retrieves his pistol from Pancho and casually brandishes it in front of her. At this point in the story Uncle Joe is a combination of comic vanity and not so comical power. On the humorous side of that ledger is the name he chose for his nightclub. Grandi's Rancho Grande sounds like at attempt by a little man to project a much bigger image of himself. Edward G. Robinson in *Little Caesar* or James Cagney in *Public Enemy*. The absurdly large cigar sticking out of his mouth suits his self-image as a crime boss.

Uncle Joe tells Susan that the name Grandi isn't Mexican, and that his family has lived on *both* sides of the border for a long time. He seems defensive if not ashamed of his mixed cultural identity. In emotional terms the Grandis occupy a nebulous, somewhat disreputable middle ground between Quinlan, Susan, Adair, and Gould on the one hand and Miguel, Sanchez, and possibly Tanya on the other. Uncle Joe does not exhibit a great deal of self-assurance by assuring the wife of a prominent Mexican law enforcement official that he's got a permit for the gun he carries.

A sarcastic remark by Susan regarding the Grandi family's narcotics business triggers a confrontation with Uncle Joe. The camera closes to a tight shot of them. Grandi's angry shouts are answered by Susan at equal volume. His attempt to intimidate her by jutting his big cigar in her face is countered by her finger waving in *his* face. But Susan's confidence is rooted in her husband's authority and reputation. Grandi may lose this little skirmish, but he has already taken steps (the photograph of Susan standing beside Pancho) to even the score.

Returning to the site of the explosion, we see Hank Quinlan treated deferentially by his American colleagues. Police Chief Gould smiles at Hank's little joke about the cause of Linnekar's death, and is both puzzled and impressed by Quinlan's tactical decision not to question the dead man's daughter yet. Sergeant Menzies behaves like an adoring sycophant around the man who only minutes earlier called him a jackass. Then Quinlan notes that most of his colleagues are wearing "monkey suits" for a banquet in honor of Rudy Linnekar. Think back to the campaign rally in *Citizen Kane*, where party hacks rallied around Charlie Kane's candidacy for Governor of New York. Perhaps Gould and Adair were allied to Linnekar, who from what we hear about him was not exactly an upstanding citizen. Maybe they even took payoffs from him for political favors. Whatever the case, Hank Quinlan was not part of Linnekar's inner circle. The gist of this scene is that Hank Quinlan is a man both feared and in a sense excluded by the elite of Los Robles.

Adair sheepishly apologizes to Quinlan about the banquet, downplaying its importance. Hank maintains a tactical advantage over the District Attorney by constantly interrupting him, the same way Kane interrupted Herbert Carter as they jousted for control of the *Inquirer* in *Citizen Kane*. Quinlan senses what was going on behind his back, including the fact that "some kind of a Mexican" was invited to the banquet. The implication is that Hank is even more of an outsider than Vargas. Quinlan's reference to the Mexican is vaguely racist in tone, undercutting his sympathetic status as uncorrupted loner.

A shot of Miguel approaching the gathering of American officials briefly pictures him against the backdrop of a public "Welcome Stranger" sign. How Welles did love to use various signs in his movies. That official greeting, and the sign's description of Los Robles as both "picturesque" and "the Paris of the border," do not match what we've seen of the town so far or with Vargas's reception by Quinlan. Marking his territory like a lion, the American makes it clear that he, not Vargas, has jurisdiction over the Linnekar case. The Mexican indirectly challenges that authority by questioning Quinlan's conclusion that dynamite was used in the crime. The two men are shown in separate shots during this brief exchange, emphasizing their mutual alienation. And their contrasting physical appearances reinforce the point. Vargas is lean, clean-shaven, and smartly dressed. Quinlan is obese, unshaven, and wears wrinkled clothing. Yet both men are shown from low camera angles, with emblems of power and money looming over their heads: an oil derrick over Vargas's and power poles and lines over Quinlan's. Their localized contest is visually placed in the context of larger economic forces surrounding them. Both men are sincere crusaders against crime, although one of them has adopted corrupt methods. And if Vargas is the more noble of the two, we still might wonder what he and Susan were doing at the Linnekar banquet.

According to Sergeant Menzies, the source of Hank Quinlan's intuition about the Linnekar case is a game leg, injured by a bullet years ago. In a big close-up Hank Quinlan grins with satisfaction at Pete's effusive compliment. He is a proud man, whatever else he may be. Al Schwartz inadvertently upstages Quinlan's intuition by repeating Vargas's theory that the bomb was planted in Linnekar's car on the Mexican side of the border. Aside from the fact that this was originally Blaine's idea, which Miguel reluctantly accepted, that theory implicitly challenges Hank's authority to pursue the case. Gould mollifies Vargas by assuring him of complete cooperation. Vargas, still pictured separately from the Americans, in turn tries to pacify Quinlan by describing himself as merely an observer. *Not* pacified, Quinlan responds with a vaguely racist comment about Miguel's lack of a Mexican accent. Vargas remains diplomatic, assuring the American that he won't cause any trouble. Quinlan, shown in another big close-up with glaring, upturned eyes, replies to that softly spoken assurance with an equally soft-spoken yet decidedly menacing warning. Whatever pre-existing emotional barriers divided the film's two lead characters, they are exacerbated by developments during their first encounter.

Meanwhile, at the Hotel Ritz, multinational relations are equally strained. Susan looms over Uncle Joe Grandi while threatening him with the power of her husband's authority. Juxtaposition of this scene with its predecessor counterpoints Susan's aggressive brandishing of Miguel's political power with Miguel's *downplaying* of that same power in an effort to get along with Quinlan. Pancho, standing in the background, lends support to his uncle, who translates for Susan the younger man's question about whether or not Miguel is a jealous sort of husband. This is an indirect reference to the photo taken earlier of Susan and Pancho together. Not understanding the implied threat, Susan recklessly insults Grandi's physical features and social status. In a reaction shot we see intense resentment on the faces of both uncle and nephew. Susan does not deserve the terrible things they do to her later in the story. But her comments in this scene are foolish and borderline bigoted. She and Quinlan have something in common.

Unconvincingly shrugging off Susan's insult with a loud guffaw, Uncle Joe retreats to the comfort of his mirror. He *is* preoccupied with his physical appearance. Susan's insult struck a nerve. Rather than acknowledge the wound, Grandi vents his personal anger indirectly, complaining that Susan's husband has disrupted the peace and quiet of Los Robles. Not true. Vargas disrupted the Grandi family's illegal drug trade, which was Pancho's original hook to get Susan to accompany him to the hotel.

Crushing and tossing aside his cigar the way he'd like to do with Vargas (a symbol of *his* power and virility becomes a symbol of his *enemy's* power and virility), Grandi demands that Miguel stop persecuting his brother Vincent. Susan's courage wilts in the face of Grandi's anger. She meekly requests permission to leave. Reversing tactics, and by the way sounding like the "Welcome Stranger" sign that greeted Miguel in the previous scene, Uncle Joe is all politeness now, insisting that their meeting was strictly voluntary. But the low camera angle from which he and Pancho are shown conveys the menace beneath that pleasant facade. Susan quietly departs.

Heading back to the relative safety of the *Mexican* side of the border, which is ironic since she will later return to the American side for the same reason (old habits die hard), she spots two more of Grandi's gang watching her. The self-assurance she sporadically exhibited earlier has evaporated, for the time being.

As Susan leaves the Ritz we see in the background the neon "Jesus Saves" sign visually framed within the archway over the hotel entrance. The Ritz and all it signifies of Grandi power and corruption is clearly the more dominant force in Los Robles.

While Susan flees the American side of Los Robles for the comparative safety of Mexico, Hank Quinlan makes the same trip, but for a very different reason. Ignoring diplomatic protocol, he leads several reluctant American colleagues on an expedition to identify the stripper who died with Rudy Linnekar. And he masks his mission by claiming to be a mere tourist, like thousands of other people who cross the border every day. In his cynical wisdom he knows that more than of few of those innocent-looking tourists are up to no good.

Counterpointing Quinlan's boldness are his limp, his cane, and his massive bulk. Physically and, we discover later, emotionally he is a wreck. How and why he got that way are yet to be revealed. For now his infirmities strangely add to his aura of intimidation. The man who *should* be leading any investigation on Mexican soil is absent, as the Americans finally notice. Miguel has left the group to meet his wife at their hotel, across the street from the cabaret to which Quinlan's group is headed. The camera cuts to Miguel and Susan inside the hotel lobby. As she explains to him her strange adventure with the Grandis she glances briefly out the window at the Americans standing in the street, waiting for Miguel. From her and our vantage point they seem distant, small, and insignificant, until we and the camera return to them. Quinlan, returning to the group from the far background, is surprised that Susan doesn't look Mexican. There is unspoken disapproval and snickering titillation in his voice. And an unpleasant hint of agreement in the silent expressions of his companions. They may disagree about pursuing the murder investigation into Mexico, but they find common ground in a sexual taboo.

Jazz seeps into the street from a nearby establishment, mixing with distant sounds of automobile traffic. By varying the volume and quality of those sounds Welles encourages in us acute awareness of the depth of the setting, and therefore of the distances between characters—as he did more elaborately in the film's opening shot. There is aural and visual activity in the background as well as the foreground. Even a neon sign flickering on and off outside the hotel adds to our sense of multi-layered activity.

The camera pans right with one of Grandi's nephews, Risto, as he creeps towards the hotel entrance after following Susan across the border. That same pan becomes a backtrack (another change in perspective) when the camera picks up on Vargas leaving the hotel. He doesn't see Risto following him across the street and into an alley. Soft xylophone music, reminiscent of music heard at the El Rancho nightclub in *Citizen Kane*, accompanies them, contributing an ethereal, bluesy melancholy that echoed Susan's mood in the wake of Kane's death but in the present scene adds an element of sadness of which the characters are unaware. It is more a musical comment *on* rather than an emotional extension *of* them.

Action occurs in three separate layers. Risto surreptitiously follows Vargas, who in turn follows Quinlan's group, who discuss the Linnekar case among themselves while approaching the cabaret's back entrance. According to his lengthy memo to Universal Studios, Welles wanted to restore to this scene some overdubbed banter between Quinlan and Menzies during the shot of Vargas crossing the street from the hotel, thereby keeping Hank, Pete, and their little group aurally alive in our minds as we watch Risto and Vargas. Again Welles stresses the importance of achieving a kind of transcendent awareness of many things happening at once. Things that may or may not affect each other, but that constitute a complex amalgam of reality. The studio, however, had different priorities.

Layers collide. Just as one of Quinlan's companions calls back to Vargas to let him know where they're going, Risto calls *ahead* to Vargas to lure him away from the others. Miguel approaches Risto. Amid the windblown trash and worn, painted signs and posters that give this obscure alley some character depth, like various posters that chronicle Acapulco's political past in *The Lady from Shanghai*, Risto attacks Vargas with a bottle of acid. Miguel grabs the boy's arm in time to divert the acid, which strikes a poster on a nearby wall. The poster is an advertisement depicting the woman killed in the car bombing. The smiling face and alluring body depicted on the poster are likewise destroyed. Think back to the deceptively happy and confident poster image of Susan Alexander outside the El Rancho. We come to know and appreciate something of the sad reality behind that commercial facade. Zita's private history remains hidden from us. But with this oblique visual reference to Susan Alexander, Welles gives life and sympathy to a woman who appeared on screen only briefly, and to little advantage, in the first scene.

Risto too acquires some dimension as a character. Before tossing it at Vargas, he looks at his bottle of acid and hesitates. Does he have moral doubts? He is a hoodlum, but not yet a hardened criminal. Like Uncle Joe, he is something less than he pretends to be. Miguel is bigger and stronger than his attacker, but Risto is younger and faster, evading Vargas's pursuit through a maze of debris littering the alley.

Sergeant Menzies lingers behind Quinlan to see if Vargas is okay. It is perhaps coincidental that he is closest to Miguel when the attack occurs. He is the only member of Hank's group to realize the attack occurred at all. Nevertheless, his mild display of concern for the Mexican distinguishes his attitude from Quinlan's.

The investigation is nearly over by the time we cut to the cabaret's interior. In the foreground a stripper tells Quinlan she hardly knew Linnekar. Hank is disappointed and skeptical. By chance the music ends, some of the nightclub's lights are switched off, and a waiter starts putting up chairs just as Quinlan walks away from the stripper and calls out to Adair to leave with him. The conjunction of all these mini-events counterpoints the *dis*junction among the activities and concerns of Quinlan, Adair, and Schwartz. The camera tracks with Hank as he moves towards an exit, briefly crossing paths with Adair, who has not yet concluded *his* business (more personal than professional) with a different stripper, and Schwartz, who tries to tell Adair the results of his own investigation but is ignored by the horny old District Attorney.

Quinlan pauses for a moment to question the cabaret's proprietor about the dead girl. She confirms to us that the victim was indeed Zita, but either cannot or will not say more. Frustrated, Quinlan walks off camera, complaining of wasted time and soothing his frustration by munching on a candy bar — his preferred method of coping with discontent, and probably the cause of his obesity.

Adair enters the camera frame as Quinlan leaves it. His good cheer sharply counterpoints the Captain's displeasure. Obviously he is enjoying his visit to the cabaret, unburdened by a professional sense of duty to solve a crime. Adair is a frivolous man committed to nothing outside his own security and short term pleasure. He is less dangerous than Quinlan because of the lightweight nature of his corruption. He is also less capable of doing good. Adair gallantly removes his hat while bidding the proprietor goodnight, in contrast to Quinlan's surly, rude departure. And why not? Adair's primary mission was to flirt with the strippers. And in that he's been successful.

On the street outside, the American "tourists" reassemble, minus Sergeant Menzies, then split up as *Quinlan* this time yields to a private diversion, triggered by the antiquated sound of pianola music coming from the other side of the street. He does this while Adair lingers in the cabaret's open doorway, still pursuing *his* personal agenda with the strippers. The camera closes in on Quinlan, capturing his wistful facial expression as he mutters the name of a woman from his distant past. Tanya is a prostitute. Yet she holds a much deeper meaning for Hank Quinlan than the anonymous cabaret strippers do for Adair.

His dalliance concluded, Adair calls out to Quinlan for the entire group to return to the American side of the border. But Hank's dalliance is just beginning, so he ignores the group and hobbles over to Tanya's establishment. Pictured between a heavy wooden railing on Tanya's porch and a house in the background, and accompanied by blowing trash in the street, Quinlan looks small and fragile, which emotionally he is. He approaches the camera situated on that porch and pauses, taking another bite of his candy bar. Old habits die hard. Tanya is an even older habit, which Hank cultivated after the death of his wife. A slightly askew insert shot of an untended pianola playing an old tune captures the haunting nature of his attraction. The tune, the instrument, and the instrument's unseen owner return to Quinlan out of a distant, nearly dead past. Like Charlie Kane's Rosebud triggered by the sight of a reasonable facsimile, or a television broadcast of *The Magnificent Ambersons* that brought back powerful recollections of old times and old friends in Welles himself during a visit to the home of Peter Bogdanovich.

Quinlan stands on Tanya's threshold. The ghostly outline of an oil derrick looms far behind and above him, beyond the curved archway over Tanya's porch. As a spectral image it complements his sentimental journey down memory lane. But as a symbol of greed and power it counterpoints his sentiment. A bit of trash from the street blows past Quinlan's head — possibly a visual metaphor of Tanya, who either slipped or was discarded from Hank's life many years ago, and reappears now because of the power of music to reawaken old memories. Contrasting and thereby highlighting the lure of the pianola is the desolate sound of wind blowing in the street. Think of Eugene Morgan transiting from cold winter night to the vibrant warmth and brightness of the Amberson mansion, which he hadn't visited in twenty years, in *The Magnificent Ambersons*. The pianola is for Hank a beacon of light in an otherwise bleak world.

Quinlan walks out of the camera frame and into Tanya's house. The camera lingers in place for a moment, allowing us to see his companions gathered in the street, silently and apparently respectfully observing their leader.

Accompanying Quinlan into Tanya's home, we see its interior as he sees it — a cluttered place full of personal possessions accumulated over the span of a lifetime. Reminiscent of Susan Alexander's apartment, or Kane's Xanadu at the end of *Citizen Kane*. Quinlan stands visually aligned with a stuffed bull's head mounted on a wall and surrounded by banderillas. The slings and arrows of outrageous fortune. Hank has felt their sting, though we do not yet realize to what extent. From a reverse camera angle we watch him enter. More bric-a-brac surrounds us, including poker chips on a table in the near foreground, metaphorically telling us, as Tanya no doubt would and Elsa Bannister did, that life is a gamble. As in Susan Alexander's apartment and again in the Amberson mansion, the combination of light, shadow, and deep focus photography highlights the layered complexity of the house and its contents. Everything catches our eye at once, as though Welles wanted us to feel the depth of Tanya's personal history, especially as it relates to her uninvited visitor. Visually we are overwhelmed by the sheer density of a life we cannot possibly comprehend as a whole in the brief time we get to know it.

On the street outside, Blaine and Adair discuss Quinlan's unscheduled side trip. Adair obviously knows more about the history between Hank and Tanya than does Blaine. But his smirking innuendo about their past sexual relationship betrays a very shallow understanding of Hank's attachment to and sudden impulse to visit Tanya. Unlike Adair's interest in the cabaret strippers, Hank's interest is not limited to sex.

Quinlan ventures deeper into the maze-like house of his former lover, with its many rooms and belongings. From near his vantage point we observe Tanya herself finally emerge from still deeper within that maze, which in its visual complexity reflects the depths to which she has emotionally hidden herself from the rest of the world. Everything in her private sanctuary seems old, and old-fashioned. The lamp shades. The painting on the wall. The furniture. Tanya's gypsy dress and jewelry. She's the budget version of Norma Desmond in *Sunset Boulevard*, but tougher, wiser, and less accessible. Emotionally, Tanya froze solid long ago, in a distant past memorialized by her possessions.

The two dinosaurs scrutinize each other in opposing close-ups. Quinlan's half leer affirms Adair's sexual innuendo. But Tanya's expression is cold, unreceptive. "We're closed," she announces matter-of-factly, reinforcing the point by taking a drag on her cigarette. She goes about the routine business of cleaning up the place until Hank identifies himself. Then, like the archetypal Marlene Dietrich character from an old von Sternberg movie, she masks her interest and emotional vulnerability with feigned indifference and caustic humor. "You should lay off those candy bars," she advises, succinctly summing up decades of self-abuse by Quinlan. He abets her insult by adding booze to his list of bad habits. "You're a mess, honey" may not be sympathetic, but it is at least an honest assessment of Hank's current state of mind and body. Honesty he would not get from the likes of Adair and Gould. However, Tanya cannot shine that same honesty on herself. When Quinlan mentions that her pianola brings back old memories for him, Tanya refuses to admit the same, explaining its value to her as merely a lure for her younger customers. "It's so old it's new" turns nostalgia into a commercial commodity. She would no more acknowledge her sentimental attachment to the pianola than Shanghai Lily would openly admit her regret about losing Captain Harvey as her lover in *Shanghai Express*.

Terri Comito claims that Welles incorporated the popular movie personas of the major stars in *Touch of Evil* into the roles they play (Comito, p.31). Each star carries mythical baggage from his or her past into every new situation he or she encounters. Orson Welles is the bloated "genius" past his prime and artistically (i.e., ethically) compromised. Marlene Dietrich is the exotic, ageless embodiment of passion and cynicism duking it out inside the same person. Had Welles wanted Tanya to be anonymous, he could have chosen an unknown actress to play the part. But because of the unique cinematic past Dietrich brings with her to the role, in addition to her innate acting ability and bits of wardrobe borrowed from her previous movies, her presence adds to rather than detracts from Tanya. With her immaculately smooth skin and bright eyes, in contrast to the obvious signs of aging in Quinlan, she seems almost to have sprung directly from Hank's memory of who she was. Except that her *attitude* displays all the wear and tear that time and experience have inflicted on her. Dismissing the pianola as a commercial gimmick, she tells Hank she also has a television with which to entertain her customers. Certainly not to entertain herself. That wouldn't be strictly business, which is how she wants to portray herself. Yet the extensive accumulation of old junk in her house belies her facade of indifference.

Predictably, Tanya is very defensive. Quinlan asks her what she knows about the car bombing, but she wants nothing to do with the investigation. The nostalgic sounds of her pianola have ceased. Avoiding complications is a priority in her life now. Hank proposes a return visit to sample her homemade chili. "Better be careful. It may be too hot for you," is her semi-polite way of telling him he's in no condition to resume their old romance. His subdued sigh of resignation acknowledges as much. Pete Menzies arrives with news about the acid attack on Vargas, interrupting the Captain's nostalgic side trip. Tanya stands in the shadows of her sanctuary, watching them go. Her posture and cigarette smoke advertise indifference. But her lingering gaze betrays a spark of concern for her old flame.

Quinlan and Menzies rejoin Adair, Schwartz, and now Vargas in the street. But disagreement and confusion about the recent assault on Miguel breaks them up again. Hank correctly intuits that one of the Grandi boys attacked Miguel. There is potential here for an alliance between the two main characters. But contrary perspectives keep them divided. Vargas is skeptical of Quinlan's famous intuition. Quinlan implicitly insults Miguel's police skills by referring to "Vargas and his Keystone Kops." Miguel responds by pointing out that the Grandis accosted Susan in a dive on the *American* side of the border. Personal enmity between the two men is expanding to include national and cultural distinctions. Like Charlie Kane, Quinlan tries to confuse and discredit his opponent by constantly interrupting him. He dislikes Vargas because of his race, his nationality, his professional prestige, his youth, his good looks, and his pretty wife — the last three of which Quinlan has lost. Behaving more like Grandi's defense lawyer than a cop, Hank twists Miguel's complaint to make it sound like Susan willingly got picked up by Pancho for illicit purposes.

Adair tries to mediate between the combatants but fails miserably. He explains away Quinlan's rudeness by describing the Captain as "a born lawyer." But that is perceived as an insult by Quinlan, who then argues with Vargas, who *is* an attorney, on the distinction between lawyers and cops. "All a lawyer cares about is the law," Hank complains. If only that were true. But the prominent lawyers in other Welles movies, including Arthur Bannister in *The Lady from Shanghai* and the Advocate in *The Trial*, exploit the law for blatantly selfish purposes. Vargas, on the other hand, admits that law enforcement is a "dirty job" but insists that policemen as well as lawyers are tasked with doing it. Quinlan retorts this *his* job is to catch a murderer, implying that fidelity to the finer points of the law is of secondary importance. Their mutual dislike has expanded into the realm of political philosophy.

Large ferns waving in the night breeze behind Quinlan's back look like bizarre angel wings. The same kind of wings he later accuses Pete Menzies of aspiring to when he disparages the Sergeant for being self-righteous near the end of the movie. In the present scene it is Hank who self-righteously sees his pragmatic approach to law enforcement as morally superior to Vargas's more abstract approach. Henry Mancini's rumbling background music, emerging on the soundtrack as the debate ends and the group breaks up, echoes the ill wind brewing in Quinlan. Like the automated oil derricks visible in the background, Quinlan's machine-like reactions of hostility dictated by old, deeply rooted resentments.

Quinlan leads Menzies "back to civilization," meaning the American side of the border. And yet the bigoted Captain once had a romance with the raven-haired Tanya. That's part of Quinlan's contradictory personality. On one level he is a Don Quixote tilting at windmills, or oil derricks. On another he is a despairing, cynical, manipulative tyrant like the elder Charles Foster Kane.

Menzies, the faithful servant, encourages his frail boss to go home and rest. Glancing back in the direction of Vargas, Hank replies that they have a busy day ahead. The implication is that ferreting out the car bomber is no longer his only priority. The shadows of Quinlan and Menzies are thrown up against the wall of an old shed. As the two men walk away the camera follows their sinister shadows moving in the opposite direction and in effect pursuing Vargas. By contrast, Vargas displayed admirable restraint in the face of Quinlan's indifference to the Grandi family's intimidation of Susan. Behind Vargas the dimly lit horizon is littered with oil derricks. Machines functioning blindly. Like Quinlan's hatred.

Vargas returns to his hotel through deserted pre-dawn streets, accompanied by subdued but ominous background music reminding us of the hostility of Quinlan and Menzies that pursues him. Susan, meanwhile, is menaced in a different manner and by a different enemy, who should also be Quinlan's enemy. In a single motion the camera that observes Miguel cranes up and pans left to peer through an upper story window in a building across from the hotel. We see a dark, unrecognizable figure switching on a flashlight. In the hotel room opposite, Susan is spotlighted by the beam from that flashlight as she undresses. We see her as her peeping tom assailant does. By observing all three characters initially from a great distance, the camera renders them distinct components of an ever-changing tableau.

Confident and feisty again in the relative safety of her hotel room, Susan puts her sweater back on, switches on the overhead light, and yells at her assailant. Unable to get a reaction from him, she unscrews the overhead lightbulb and hurls it out her window and into his now darkened room. Miguel's arrival in his own dimly lit room triggers tension between husband and wife. Her frustration at being spied on by an intruder she cannot punish is vented on Miguel, who has no idea what just happened to her. Nor does she bother to explain. Exasperated, she exits the room with luggage in hand. Bewildered, he follows her, but has the presence of mind to return and close the door. Their dispute is not sufficient to disrupt his routine sense of order. A sense of order he *will* lose under more stressful conditions later.

If there is disharmony between the Vargases in this scene, the same thing plagues their enemies. Pancho, the peeping tom, now points his hostile beam of light at Risto, standing on the street below. Low and high camera angles emphasize the physical and emotional distance between them. Pancho reveals that Uncle Joe is angry at Risto and looking for him. Risto flees down the street that suddenly looks oppressive and dangerous for *him* instead of for Vargas, whom he was following. This visual effect is achieved with a tilted camera, a camera position low to the ground, eerie pre-dawn lighting, and the emptiness of the setting.

Uncle Joe spots Risto from a nearby phone booth and solicits the help of Sal, who previously photographed Susan and Pancho together in front of the Ritz Hotel, to catch the young man. Former allies are now at odds. But they are not mortal enemies. Uncle Joe even takes a moment to switch off the light in the phone booth before joining in the pursuit, just as Miguel took the time to close the door to his and Susan's hotel room as they left it. Later, in a much more tense situation, Hank Quinlan will *forget* a similarly trivial detail, and it will cost him dearly.

Grandi catches up with Risto and slaps him a few times as punishment for the foolish acid attack on Vargas. There may be a family power struggle behind their dispute. Risto's father is the man Vargas is prosecuting in Mexico City. Risto wants revenge. Uncle Joe wants it too, because Risto's father is his brother. But he also wants it understood that *he*, not his imprisoned brother, is now head of the family. Risto shows him little respect, waving a hand in Grandi's face to protest Uncle Joe's presumption of leadership. Almost childishly Grandi flails away with both of his hands to knock Risto's away. In the process he knocks off his own toupee. To his great annoyance Risto calls attention to that toupee lying on the ground. Uncle Joe's vanity is easily bruised. He is a poor excuse for a crime boss, and will get in way over his head when he forms a criminal alliance with Hank Quinlan.

Back at the hotel the Vargases continue bickering. Susan walks down the stairs and into the lobby while ignoring her husband, who trails after her, arguing that border towns like Los Robles bring out the worst in people and are not representative of Mexico as a whole. He speculates woefully on the likely unfavorable reaction of Susan's mother to their honeymoon hotel. Did Susan's mother object to her precious daughter marrying a Mexican in the first place? Susan's voice contains a hint of contempt when she mutters the Spanish word for telephone after the desk clerk summons Miguel to answer a phone call. Half shouting from across the room, she mocks her husband's approval that she is leaving for Mexico City by airplane. Little resentments are accumulating between them.

In an alley across the street, Uncle Joe and Risto grudgingly reach an understanding about how to handle the Vargases. Obviously Risto is more concerned about his incarcerated father than is Joe. Walls and poles in the alley are plastered with old posters, one on top of another, and all of them tattered, like the layers of family history that simultaneously unite and divide Uncle Joe and Risto. But for now Joe's toupee is restored to order and along with it a measure of family solidarity as Sal calls their collective attention to Miguel and Susan, visible through a window in the hotel lobby. Viewed from the Grandis' point of view, the Vargases look exposed and vulnerable, like figures in a shooting gallery. A reverse angle shows Uncle Joe, Risto, and Sal huddled together, all looking in the same direction and all of like mind. Joe hands an envelope to Sal and tells him to give it to Mrs. Vargas.

When Sal taps on the window of the hotel lobby and holds up an envelope for Susan to see, she assumes he is a Mexican trying to peddle postcards. She reacts like an annoyed American tourist. Unable to understand Spanish, she walks outside and tells him in English that she isn't interested. Sal hands her the envelope and departs. It contains a brief romantic message from Pancho, and a copy of the photograph Sal took of them earlier. But instead of driving a wedge between the Vargases, as Uncle Joe intends, the photo and its message brings them back together. Without showing her husband the contents of the envelope, Susan impulsively decides to remain with him in Los Robles. She assumes she is being supportive. In fact she will become a major liability for Miguel.

If solidarity between husband and wife is restored, new cracks in their alliance quickly form. Miguel needs to meet with Quinlan about a new lead in the Linnekar case. That's what the phone call in the lobby was about. Getting into their car with him, Susan says he can drop her off at a motel on the American side of the border, for safety's sake. Unintentionally she insults Miguel's pride as a Mexican and as a man. She tries to make up for it by changing the reason for her preference to comfort instead of safety, which is only slightly less demeaning to her husband.

As they drive away Miguel switches the car radio from music to news. We learn from that broadcast that Rudy Linnekar was a "public contractor," which involves the expenditure of public funds. And maybe illegal kickbacks to corrupt public officials? Perhaps District Attorney Adair had personal reasons for lending support to Rudy Linnekar at the banquet. *Touch of Evil* is permeated with a sense of corruption at all levels of society, from institutional to private.

Uncle Joe scurries around like a bantam cock as he gleefully plots revenge on Miguel and Susan. Getting into his car, he adjusts his toupee in the rearview mirror before driving off in hot pursuit of the Vargases. Reversing Miguel's action, Joe switches his car radio from the news report about Linnekar to music. At this point in the story he is unaware of the potential value the Linnekar case has for his own crusade against Vargas. That too will change.

Welles's excellent use of a hood-mounted camera later in the film to shoot a scene in a moving automobile renders the backscreened images of Miguel and Susan's journey to a motel on the American side of the border stylistically out of place. Welles did not shoot this scene. His original footage was re-shot and replaced by the studio, presumably for the sake of clarity. Also removed from scene, but not replaced, was more footage of Grandi than the existing scene contains. According to Welles, his original scene featured elaborate sound play between different radio broadcasts. To what dramatic effect we can only guess.

Driving towards Susan's motel, Miguel sums up the facts of the Linnekar case for her benefit. But his explanation sounds suspiciously like an attempt to clarify things for the film's audience. At any rate, Miguel's recitation is cut short by Susan's affectionate embrace. He stops the car and they kiss. Far behind them, Grandi races to catch up in his car. His ludicrous toupee rides too high on his windblown head. He looks like a buffoon, and an unlikely threat to the Vargases.

While Miguel and Susan embrace, a police car approaches them from the background, with its siren blaring. Quinlan, identifiable only by his hat, remains inside while Schwartz and Menzies emerge to convey his message. Hank has new information about the Linnekar case and wants Vargas to accompany the investigation team. With the scene as it now exists, a mixture of Welles's original footage and studio re-shoots, it is unclear how Quinlan tracks down the Vargases in their car. At least the conversation in this part of the scene is typically Wellesian, with overlapping dialog subtly emphasizing a slight disharmony among various points of view.

Miguel answers the call of duty, putting on his sunglasses as though shifting from a private, romantic concern to one more professional and detached. Susan, however, is reluctant to let him go, venting a bit of frustration by telling him not to bother phoning her later. Menzies, meanwhile, is delighted by the prospect of driving the beautiful Mrs. Vargas to her motel. He even doffs his hat to her. But that enthusiasm conflicts with his devotion to Quinlan. In his eager attention to Susan he forgets to give Quinlan back his cane before the police car departs. Perhaps feeling guilty about his oversight, Pete talks incessantly about his friend and hero as he and Susan drive along a desert road. Among the things we learn about Hank is how he once took a bullet in the leg that was meant for Menzies, and how he overcame a serious drinking problem. Sleepy and uninterested, Susan quickly falls asleep. She's been up all night. Circumstances preclude any meaningful communication between her and Menzies in this scene.

That Menzies takes his job seriously is indicated by his reaction to spotting Grandi's car following him and Susan. Viewed from a distance, beginning with a descending crane shot that captures the immense emptiness of the desert landscape, he stops and orders Uncle Joe out of his car. The camera dissolves to a shot of Menzies gently waking up Susan. They've reached the Mirador Motel. Susan is disappointed at its shabby appearance, which is kept off screen for the moment. Pete explains that it's the only motel available on this side of the border. Susan has only herself to blame for insisting on American accommodations. The camera cranes up a little as she steps out of the car and, noticing Grandi nearby, again expresses disappointment. Grandi had remained out of sight until now. We now realize that Menzies forced Uncle Joe to accompany him and Susan in Vargas's vehicle. He was protecting Susan, as a good cop should, but doesn't realize that by showing Uncle Joe where Susan will be staying he has made her vulnerable to Grandi's scheme to discredit Miguel. Pete informs Susan that she is the motel's only guest, as though that fact enhances her safety. Grandi chuckles to himself, knowing otherwise.

As Menzies and Grandi drive away in Miguel's car, an exhausted Susan watches them leave from the only shady spot visible for miles, beneath the motel roof overhang. The camera cranes up over the roof to observe the car receding in the distance, leaving the landscape oppressively still and quiet. One can't help think of a scene filmed two years later in which the same actress (Janet Leigh) arrives at an equally remote motel (Bates), but under very different aesthetic conditions. Darkness and driving rain versus bright, hot sunshine and dead calm.

Susan enters a small, sparsely furnished room rendered slightly gothic in appearance by a low camera angle. Instead of Norman Bates peering through a hole in the wall, the Mirador's Night Man gapes at Susan through a window. She doesn't see him and he quickly disappears. Moments later the room is filled with loud country music. Susan pounds the big speaker on the wall to silence it. The Night Man reappears at the window, carrying clean sheets for the bed and informing Susan it was he who switched on the music.

Dennis Weaver's Night Man, like Anthony Perkins's Norman Bates, is sexually repressed, prurient, and extremely nervous. Unlike Norman, he is not very bright, and a bit of a religious zealot, but certainly no serial killer. Just as certainly he is not what Susan had in mind when she expressed a preference for an American over a Mexican motel. Though not a threat to Susan, the Night Man proves useless to her when she *is* menaced by others. Susan's unintentional game of hide and seek with him at the front of the room sums up our initial impression of the Night Man as a character out of sync with everyone else.

Seen up close the Night Man is a blinking, twitching bundle of nerves, alternately afraid of and titillated by his only guest. He refuses to help her make up the bed and avoids getting close to her by hugging the room's walls until he can escape through the front door. Think of Norman Bate's inability to say the word "bathroom" to Marion Crane in Alfred Hitchcock's *Psycho*. The Night Man concludes his dialog with Susan from outside the cabin, through an open window that allows him a safe measure of separation. Only at the end of their conversation do we realize that he mistakenly thought, after seeing them arrive together, that Susan was brought to the motel by Uncle Joe Grandi. Maybe he assumes Susan is a prostitute, which would explain both his fear of and fascination with her. His emotional reactions are even less controlled, almost spastic, when Susan informs him that Grandi is under arrest. Aroused and self-righteous at the same time, he giggles stupidly and flees from Susan.

Welles inserts a brief visual illusion as the Night Man departs. Looking in through the cabin window from outside, we see Susan directly and the Night Man as a reflection off the window pane. When Susan pulls down the window shade to ensure her privacy from the strange man, we see his image more clearly, but of course reversed. The white shade is like a movie screen, both clarifying and falsifying what we see.

A police car containing Quinlan, Vargas, Schwartz, and a uniformed driver pulls into a Linnekar Construction Company work site just as a controlled dynamite blast is about to take place. From inside the car we see flag men frantically waving at us to stop. But we do not stop until the vehicle passes by them. In a subtle way we get to feel Hank Quinlan's official power and the arbitrary manner in which he wields it. A company foreman and a workman/ex-convict named Eddie Farnham approach the car. Viewed through window frames, they appear subservient to the law enforcement power concentrated inside the vehicle. Farnham, especially, looks overmatched, visually surrounded by Vargas, Schwartz, Quinlan, and the driver, all of whom are seated at various distances from the camera, creating a tunnel effect with Farnham visible at the far end of it.

The foreman is deferential towards Hank, anticipating the Captain's questions and having answers ready in advance. He says a man named Sanchez was fired from the company for playing around with Linnekar's daughter. He also confirms a report that some dynamite was recently stolen from the construction site. Farnham is less deferential than the foreman, until he spots Quinlan, who sharply questions him about when he got out of prison and who arranged for his job. Still, Farnham has one tactical edge — the unseen presence of his lawyer, behind whom he takes shelter, and same way Susan drew confidence from the implied presence of Miguel during her confrontation with the Grandis.

The police car departs after word arrives over the police radio that Sanchez has been caught. Quinlan, who has already made fun of Farnham's big ears, now taunts the ex-convict with the thinly veiled accusation of murdering Rudy Linnekar with stolen dynamite from this construction site. The detective's famous intuition, we learn later, tells him Sanchez, not Farnham, committed the crime. He intimidates the ex-con in this scene for the sheer sadistic pleasure of doing so. Hank may not take financial advantage of his job, but he does exploit it in other ways. By contrast, Miguel Vargas remains professionally detached behind his dark glasses throughout this scene.

Farnham advances towards the camera, which in turn advances towards him, as he glares tight-lipped at Quinlan's departing car. The relative motions of camera and subject magnify our impression of the intensity of his hostility towards Hank.

A descending crane shot combined with the sound of squealing tires as the police car rapidly approaches the camera and Sanchez's apartment conveys Quinlan's passion for bringing a criminal to justice. But the movements of Hank's body as he emerges from the vehicle are slow and stiff. If we are tempted to sympathize with the hobbled sheriff, that sympathy is tempered by his rudeness towards Vargas, whom he doesn't even look at while answering a question put to him by the Mexican. A moment later, however, we discover something of the legal odds he is up against in his efforts to bring a murderer to justice. Recognizing a lawyer's car parked outside the residence of suspect Manolo Sanchez, Schwartz points out that Howard Frantz was Farnham's lawyer too. Hank adds that Frantz was also Rudy Linnekar's attorney. And in the previous scene Schwartz mentioned that Frantz is also Grandi's attorney. The defense lawyer seems to be a perpetual foe of Quinlan's. No wonder Hank has such a low opinion of him and of his kind — including attorney Vargas. Inside the apartment, Sanchez panics at the sight of Quinlan through a window. He has heard about the Captain's rough methods. Frantz, meanwhile, is interested only in protecting his wealthy client, Marcia Linnekar, who happens to be Sanchez's lover. He has no respect at all for Sanchez.

Quinlan says nothing to Marcia, Manolo, or Frantz as he walks past them and into the bedroom off screen. It is a deliberate tactic to intimidate them. Frantz advises Marcia to let him talk for her. In desperation to save himself, Sanchez turns for help to two strangers, Schwartz and Vargas. Miguel exchanges a few words with him in Spanish. Quinlan protests from off screen. Miguel crosses over to him. Extremely protective of his legal jurisdiction, Hank is not appeased when Miguel explains that he merely informed Sanchez that Quinlan is in charge of the investigation.

Leaving Vargas, Quinlan rejoins the other characters in the living room. Perhaps as a concession to Frantz's presence, he switches tactics from intimidation to chatty, self-deprecating charm. He sits on a couch between Sanchez and Marcia, who stand on either side of him, and complains of age and fatigue. Then he feigns sympathy to get Marcia to talk about herself and her father. But Frantz enters the camera frame to silence her for her own legal protection. Sanchez too protests, on behalf of himself, and the interrogation disintegrates into argumentative chaos. Frantz departs with his client, informing Hank that any subsequent questions for Marcia will be answered only with her lawyer present.

Sanchez tries to follow Marcia out the door, but is blocked by Quinlan's subordinates.

Marcia seems to want to be with her lover, but is whisked away by Franz. Cop and lawyer have all the power here. Quinlan contemptuously ignores Sanchez, who has no attorney to shield him. Even Quinlan's fellow policemen bow to his authority. As per his instructions, nothing was searched before he arrived. Which makes it easier for him to plant evidence against the suspect. Hank even sends one of his detectives on a trivial errand to fetch coffee for him.

Sanchez crosses over to Vargas, who again speaks with him in Spanish until Quinlan interrupts them. And again Miguel diplomatically sides with the Captain, dismissing the suspect as "unpleasant" while crossing over to Quinlan's side of the room. Tentative alliances form and dissipate quickly in this scene. Vargas walks towards the door leading outside the apartment. Misinterpreting that action, Quinlan tells him to stay put. Miguel was merely searching for a telephone. He asks Sanchez about a phone in Spanish. Incorrectly assuming that Vargas has resumed interrogating the suspect about the Linnekar case, Quinlan again protests, slapping Sanchez across the face for replying in Spanish to Vargas's question. Miguel explains in English what he and Sanchez were discussing, in order to correct Hank's false impression. But a telephone is *not* all the two Mexican's talked about. Before adjourning to the bedroom to use the phone there, Miguel adds that Sanchez believes he is in for "the third degree" at the hands of Quinlan. "I assured him he has nothing to worry about," Vargas adds, facetiously. Quinlan bridles at the implied accusation, but can only retaliate with a lame insult about Vargas not being able to use an American telephone. Score one for the Mexican attorney. But Sanchez may pay the price for his countryman's brief victory.

Quinlan sends one of his men, Casey, into the bedroom to keep an eye on Vargas. Casey carries with him a bundle of love letters Sanchez exchanged with Marcia Linnekar. Quinlan jokes, "Save the good stuff for me." Considering his lack of self-restraint in so many other activities, it is believable that he might violate his professional detachment in such a manner.

The camera follows Casey into the bedroom while Quinlan's brutal interrogation of Sanchez is *heard* off screen. Miguel, unbeknownst to Quinlan, steps into a bathroom adjacent to the bedroom and washes his face. Casey takes no notice of it because he knows nothing about Hank's intention to plant evidence there later. Reaching for a towel, Vargas knocks over an empty shoe box. A moment later Al Schwartz shows up in the bathroom doorway, too late to notice the empty shoe box, which Miguel has put back on the shelf, yet just in time to avoid witnessing Quinlan's abuse of Sanchez in the living room. He and Vargas can, of course, *hear* that abuse. Miguel can do nothing legally to stop it. Schwartz could, but is too timid to stand up to Quinlan.

Vargas and Schwartz discuss who other than Sanchez might be guilty of the Linnekar murder. Miguel speculates, incorrectly as it turns out, that it might be Eddie Farnham. Schwartz concurs. Vargas even lays claim to a bit of intuition himself, implicitly challenging Quinlan's more heralded reputation for that investigative gift. Professional jealousy works both ways.

Quinlan and Sanchez enter the bedroom as Vargas and Schwartz emerge from the bathroom. They become a group again. Hank infuriates Sanchez by pointing out that Marcia set him up in an apartment he could not otherwise afford, that Rudy Linnekar objected to his daughter getting romantically involved with a Mexican shoe clerk, and that Sanchez therefore had a clear motive for the murder. The frustrated suspect retreats to another part of the room after bitterly mocking Hank's assessment of the case. Quinlan turns to Vargas and remarks, "Just because he speaks a little guilty, that don't make him innocent." A clever turn of phrase reminiscent of Charlie Kane's "I'd make my promises now, if I weren't too busy arranging to keep them." But it masks more than it explains. And Vargas is not impressed, arguing that the Captain needs evidence as well as motive to secure a conviction. "We'll get it," Hank replies cryptically. Harsh, film noir lighting from below visually conveys the corruption that is not yet openly discussed in the dialog.

Quinlan turns away from Vargas to take a cup of coffee from the flunky he sent to get it. He asks why the man didn't bring doughnuts or sweet rolls too, as though they were more important to him than Vargas's opinions about Sanchez. It is also a reminder of Quinlan's ungoverned appetites, like Charlie Kane's and George Minafer's. Beverle Houston, in an article entitled "Power and Dis-Integration in the Films of Orson Welles," describes the "central figure of desire and contradiction" in Welles's films as the "Power Baby," an "eating, sucking, foetus-like creature" suffering from "truncated development" for a variety of reasons (Houston, pp.2 and 6). Quinlan, Kane, George, Macbeth, the Advocate, and Falstaff are included in that category. I'm not sure I would include all of those characters, but certainly Hank Quinlan has degenerated into a self-indulgent, power hungry beast of sorts.

Vargas re-enters the camera frame and challenges Quinlan to place Sanchez at the scene of the crime. Schwartz, taking courage from Miguel's example, echoes that point. Quinlan parries both challenges while ignoring his off screen errand boy, who complains that Hank didn't request doughnuts. Vargas heads for the exit in the background. Quinlan, who likes to maintain strict control over an investigation scene, asks where he is going. Miguel's initial reply sounds like good news for Hank. "This is not my case." But his follow-up remark is vaguely insulting to the hyper-sensitive Captain. "This is not my country" is a backhanded expression of contempt for Quinlan's law enforcement methods, if not for Quinlan's country. "I'm *not* convinced" makes clear Vargas's doubts about the case against Sanchez.

Miguel rudely walks out during Quinlan's rebuttal and heads for a shop across the street. Putting on his sunglasses, he places both emotional and physical distance between himself and Hank's unsavory methods. A tracking camera propels *us* away from Quinlan's corruption too. But in the same shot we see Menzies and Grandi approaching from the background in Vargas's car. Miguel may seek an ethically more sanitary location from which to phone his wife, but neither he nor Susan can escape the corruption infusing and surrounding the Linnekar case.

Vargas politely asks a blind shopkeeper if he can use her telephone. On the wall of the shopkeeper's business establishment is a printed sign facetiously inviting anyone who would take advantage of a blind person to help themselves. Miguel is the kind of person who would not do such a thing, under most circumstances.

While Miguel tries to phone his wife at the Mirador Motel we see through the window behind him Sergeant Menzies using Quinlan's cane to prod a reluctant Grandi towards the Sanchez apartment. Inside the apartment they find Sanchez and others sitting around passively in the living room while Quinlan, off screen, supposedly searches the bedroom for evidence. Menzies heads for the bedroom to return his boss's cane. Surprised, Hank emerges from the bathroom complaining about Pete barging in on him. Pete's act of devotion, we realize later, unintentionally endangers Quinlan's scheme to plant evidence against Sanchez.

His large bulk looking particularly imposing from a low camera angle, Quinlan is in a foul mood when he confronts Grandi. Hank's irritation at Pete's interruption of his dirty deed is vented on Grandi when he learns that Uncle Joe was tailing Vargas's car. He knows Grandi is a threat to Miguel and Susan. But priority dictates that he return to the bathroom to secure the Sanchez case before dealing with Grandi. As he walks out of the camera frame a simple "Sit down" puts Uncle Joe on hold, while "Shut up" dismisses Grandi's protest about America being a "free country." Not Quinlan's America. Sanchez, meanwhile, stands up and anxiously watches the Captain, who returns to the bathroom off screen and shuts the door. The suspect has good reason to worry.

The Sanchez and Grandi cases only coincidentally cross paths, like the Vargases and Rudy Linnekar's automobile during the movie's first shot. Only later does Uncle Joe see an opportunity to exploit the Sanchez case for his own gain, which ironically parallels Vargas getting involved in the Linnekar case out of a professional sense of duty.

At the not so fabulous Mirador Motel, Susan Vargas lies on a bed in sexy underclothes, drying her flowing blond hair after a shower. Rock and roll music blares from a speaker on the wall of her cabin. Miguel's phone call comes through. A conversation about developments in the Linnekar investigation segues into a romantic exchange. New, softer music coming from the wall speaker now complements rather than clashes with Susan's new mood, which is then unintentionally disrupted by her husband. Misinterpreting his wife's words to him, Miguel concludes she would rather get some sleep than continue their flirtation. He is wrong, but hangs up before Susan can tell him so. Meanwhile, the blind shopkeeper, visible in the foreground of a long shot of Vargas talking on the phone, eavesdrops on Miguel's private conversation, rendering ironic her printed sign chastising would-be thieves. Eavesdropping, after all, is a form of theft.

Susan's sleepy, casual demeanor as she phones the motel's front desk and requests not to be disturbed is sharply counterpointed when the camera cuts to the man behind that desk. He turns to face the camera. It is Pancho, replying to Susan's request in flawless English, which until now we had no idea he could speak. "Nobody's going to get through to you, unless I say so" has a chilling double meaning for us, but not for Susan, who doesn't recognize Pancho's voice.

Miguel returns to the Sanchez apartment, where Menzies has joined the other characters passively waiting for Quinlan to complete his off screen search. Sanchez pleads alternately with Vargas and Menzies for understanding, admitting that money was at the root of his relationship with Marcia Linnekar, but insisting that *she* pursued *him*. Vargas remains skeptical but is willing to listen to the suspect within the parameters of Quinlan's English-only stipulation. Menzies is less willing, but not as closed-minded as Hank, who finally emerges from the rear of the apartment. Sanchez angrily mocks Quinlan's taunting accusation of him. The suspect's frustration is understandable, considering the stress he's under. But in legal terms, as Vargas points out, he is digging his own grave by facetiously admitting to conspiring with Marcia to kill her father. Quinlan laughs as he enters the camera frame, supremely confident now of his tactical edge over Sanchez. But he still jealously guards his professional turf by ending Miguel's unauthorized legal advice to the suspect.

Sitting on the couch and pleading fatigue, as he did earlier, Quinlan sends Menzies off to complete a search of the apartment. Trying to make it sound random, he directs Menzies to search the bedroom and bathroom, claiming to have restricted his own search to the suspect's desk. Grandi, noticing Quinlan's improved mood, stands to plead his case for release. Quinlan too rises, and puts Grandi back in his place. Uncle Joe wisely backs down and resumes his seat. Ironically, if Grandi had gotten his wish and been permitted to leave at this juncture, he would not be around to witness and subsequently exploit the growing rift between Quinlan and Vargas. On the other hand, if he did leave the apartment right now he might avoid a disastrous alliance with Quinlan and survived to the end of the story.

Touch of Evil. Left to right: Hank Quinlan (Orson Welles), Manolo Sanchez (Victor Milian), Pete Menzies (Joseph Calleia) and Mike Vargas (Charlton Heston) debate the Linnekar murder investigation. Each character looks at someone other than the person speaking to him, as everyone talks at cross-purposes.

Hank introduces Grandi as a brother of the man Vargas arrested on a narcotics charge. Discovering that Vargas was not previously acquainted with Uncle Joe, Hank limits their exchange of information by ordering Grandi to shut up. By keeping everyone else divided, Quinlan can more easily conquer. Wandering out of and then back into the camera frame, Quinlan is impatient for results of Pete's search. He warns Grandi not to try to intimidate Vargas with violence, though that warning is delivered more as a matter of form than with real conviction. Hank's mind is preoccupied with other matters.

Pete's off screen cry of triumph draws the other characters one by one out of the living room and into the bedroom. With the exception of Miguel. The camera moves in to a close-up of Vargas, who looks puzzled by Pete's discovery of incriminating evidence in the bathroom where Miguel washed up a few minutes earlier. He smokes a cigarette as though to pacify his concern, or focus his concentration. But as Quinlan and Sanchez argue vehemently off screen, the suspect's unexpected revelation that he and Marcia were secretly married triggers new curiosity in Miguel, who slowly advances towards the bedroom, passing by Menzies returning from same. Quinlan's faithful disciple gushes about his boss solving another case, and shamelessly basks in Hank's praise for helping him do it. Morally speaking, this is Pete's lowest moment in the film. He is at his most slavish and least critical. But from Pete's own perspective, his low point comes much later, when he feels impelled to betray Quinlan.

Quinlan gleefully re-enters the camera frame and, facing Vargas, pronounces the case solved. Sanchez then re-enters the frame too, complaining of a frame-up. He is surrounded by law enforcement officials taller than himself. Hank's moral reprimand of Sanchez is particularly effective when he tells the brief story of a woman who found a shoe containing a severed foot on a street near the explosion the previous night. This is another example of a Welles character becoming a storyteller within the framework of the larger story. Like Harry Lime excusing his own corruption by illustrating the relative cultural benefits of democracy and dictatorship in *The Third Man*, or the Advocate trying to intimidate Joseph K by reciting the Parable of the Law in *The Trial*, or Mr. Arkadin's tale about the scorpion and the frog, Quinlan's anecdote is as self-serving as it is true. Perhaps more so.

After Sanchez, pleading for help, is hauled away under arrest, Vargas learns that the sticks of dynamite stolen from the Linnekar Construction Company, minus the eight used to blow up Linnekar's car, were found by Menzies in a shoe box in the bathroom. Miguel insists he saw that same box empty only a short time earlier. Quinlan, caught off guard, unwisely dismisses that claim as a misguided attempt by one Mexican to defend another. He tries to discredit Vargas's claim by casting doubt on Vargas's motivation for making it.

Previously banished Uncle Joe keenly observes this confrontation from far in the background. When Miguel walks towards the door to leave, Grandi generously opens it for him. He is already eager to strike a bargain with Quinlan in Miguel's absence. Together they will neutralize Vargas. But Hank, pursuing his own agenda, follows Vargas to the doorway, provoking another confrontation. Against Quinlan's hypocritical charge of racial bias, Miguel explains in convincing detail how he knows the dynamite found in the bathroom was planted. This face-off culminates in Vargas's shouted accusation, "You framed him!" and Quinlan brandishing his cane at Vargas in a threatening manner.

Tossing aside his pacifying cigarette, and along with it his earlier determination to stay out of the Linnekar case, Vargas storms out of the apartment. Quinlan, watching him go, looks as baffled as old Charlie Kane just after Susan Alexander leaves him. He is too dazed to deal with the Grandi matter, of which Menzies reminds him. He can no longer operate on multiple fronts simultaneously, as he did earlier, as Kane often did so effortlessly, and as Welles himself frequently did while directing plays, performing on the radio, and making movies.

Leaving Quinlan to join Miguel in the street, Deputy District Attorney Al Schwartz finally chooses sides, more on faith than on proof. He did not see the empty shoe box in the suspect's bathroom, but he believes Vargas. Pete Menzies, however, remains loyal to his boss. But in spite of his sycophantic behavior in the apartment, he is not a blind fool. He warns Hank of the danger posed by Vargas, and urges compromise instead of confrontation. Quinlan hints darkly at a different course of action, in which somebody's reputation is going to be ruined. At this critical moment Grandi creeps back into the camera frame and speaks to the Captain in conspiratorial fashion.

Dogging Quinlan into the street, Grandi proposes an alliance between them to fight Vargas. Menzies now re-enters the camera frame and disrupts Grandi's proposition. Hank sends his loyal friend off on a mission, to get rid of him. After Pete departs, Grandi edges closer to the Captain. We view them from a new angle that puts Uncle Joe at less of a visual disadvantage than how we saw him in the apartment, and reflects his tentative victory over Quinlan's habitual aversion to criminals. Uncle Joe suggests continued negotiations over drinks. Hank insists he doesn't drink, but the movement of his mouth as he says so betrays his craving for it. No doubt to ease the pressure of the threat posed to him by Vargas.

Through a window from inside the Sanchez apartment, we watch with Pete Menzies as Uncle Joe leads Quinlan across the street towards a bar. The camera reverses angle so we see both the reflected image of Grandi and Hank and the direct image of Menzies, looking worried. His boss, on the other hand, looks like a helpless old man being led away by someone in charge of him, like the aged Jed Leland escorted off the hospital sun deck by a nurse in *Citizen Kane*. Curiously, Hank Quinlan starts and ends this long scene, from his arrival at the Sanchez apartment until now, looking old and feeble.

The shot looking in through a window at Menzies dissolves to a shot looking *out* through the window of Susan's cabin at the Mirador Motel. We see a peaceful desert landscape. Then Susan raises the shade from that window and we realize that we are looking *in*, not out. Welles the magician reminds us periodically how susceptible we are to illusion, optical and otherwise. Susan and Miguel are both currently under the illusion that she is safe from the consequences of his work.

The tranquil desert scenery is counterpointed by rock and roll music blaring inside Susan's cabin. That music then *complements* the noisy arrival of some leather-jacketed gang members outside, in two jalopies. We observe their arrival from several camera angles, including a partly subjective shot from behind Susan as she watches them through a window in her cabin. The latter image is like watching a movie on a theater screen. The window frame provides an illusion of detachment and safety, reinforced by Susan's flimsy nightie, which is more appropriate for a honeymoon, or watching a suspense movie on TV, than for defending herself against a gang assault.

As the rock and roll music ends, the camera cuts to a close-up of a hand changing stations on a car radio, from a newscast about Hank Quinlan and the Linnekar case to some Mexican music. We assume the hand belongs to a gang member in one of the jalopies, until a follow-up shot reveals that we've switched scenes. The hand belongs to Miguel Vargas, who is driving Al Schwartz and himself along a narrow street in Los Robles as they discuss their investigation of Hank Quinlan. Miguel probably changed radio stations because he was tired of hearing Quinlan praised for cracking the murder case. The lighthearted music displacing the newscast complements the confident tone of Miguel's conversation with Schwartz. But visually undercutting that confidence is our impression of the car's reckless speed as we look back at the two men from a camera mounted on the hood. Camera lens and position exaggerate our sense of speed. Figuratively speaking, Schwartz and Vargas travel down a very dangerous path as they plot to expose Hank Quinlan's corruption. In a reverse, high angle tracking shot the car seems to accelerate and Miguel turns up the music's volume, magnifying our impression of his foolhardiness as the car heads towards a field of oil derricks on the outskirts of town. Don Quixote tilting at windmills? In that analogy Vargas and Quinlan have something in common.

The brief confusion between the traveling scene and its predecessor, as to which car we are in and whose hand turns the radio dial, contributes to a broader parallel between Vargas and the Grandi gang. Both are overconfident, driving too fast over dangerous ground. If Vargas underestimates the danger to Susan and himself from the resentful Grandis and a desperate Hank Quinlan, the Grandis are naively oblivious to the danger of enraging a man like Vargas and of dealing with a man like Quinlan.

The Grandi assault on Susan takes shape slowly and insidiously, beginning with her unsuccessful phone complaint to the front desk about the loud music. The gang members manning the front desk have brought illegal drugs and a hypodermic needle with them. At least one of them is already high.

The Night Man enters the motel office and is immediately surrounded by the people who have usurped his authority. Even the camera closes in on him like one of the gang. He is slow to comprehend his situation, and at one point mindlessly imitates the bobbing head of the gang member who is high on drugs. The effect is funny and pathetic at the same time. The Night Man is not even aware he is aping the enemy, who ruthlessly shove him aside when another phone call from Susan comes through.

Susan tries to call police headquarters but is stymied by Pancho at the office switchboard. After effectively isolating Susan at the Mirador, Pancho tells his companions to "relax and have a ball," which is reminiscent of Susan referring to him as Pancho "just for laughs," His calculated cruelty is much worse than her thoughtless bigotry. Nevertheless, the latter fuels the former. Pancho is not just defending a relative being persecuted by Vargas. Nor is he blindly obeying Uncle Joe's instruction. He is also pursuing a personal agenda of revenge against the American who insulted him.

A close-up of glasses being filled with booze conveys the depth of Hank Quinlan's vulnerability to the little man pouring those drinks. The camera pulls back to show a grinning Uncle Joe carrying those drinks from the bar to Quinlan's table. Judging from Grandi's opening remark in this scene, they've already discussed how to deal with Vargas. Hank struggles valiantly to resist a partnership with Grandi, insisting that he won't tolerate Vargas being killed, and bluffing that Vargas cannot hurt him anyway.

Grandi moves to the background to answer an untimely phone call, probably from Pancho regarding Susan's attempt to contact the police. Quinlan, alone in the foreground, talks tough about refusing to be Grandi's partner, yet takes a drink from the glass Grandi poured for him. A sentimental pianola tune, like the one heard earlier at Tanya's place, plays on the jukebox behind him. Whether Hank selected the tune or it plays at random, it is for him powerfully evocative of his tragic past, including an event we don't yet know about — the murder of his wife. The combination of recollected pain and inhibition-reducing liquor weakens his resistance to a lowlife like Grandi, whose criminal intentions he spotted the moment they met in the Sanchez apartment. At the top of the camera frame a decorative, gauzy fabric hangs down from the bar's otherwise high ceiling, in effect forming a lower ceiling that feeds our impression of Quinlan's world closing in on him and forcing him to seek escape.

Returning to the table, Grandi rests one hand on the juke box as he proposes a deal to Quinlan and offers another drink to seal it. The emotional pain aroused by the juke box is for the moment Uncle Joe's great ally against Quinlan's fading resistance to temptation. Hank rejects the bargain again by insisting he no longer drinks. The evidence in his hand proves otherwise. He sets the glass down and pulls his hand away from it, but the damage is already done. A change in camera angle, now looking down on Quinlan from over Grandi's right shoulder, visually echoes Uncle Joe's dominance as he tells an off screen waitress to make Hank's next drink a big one and then inserts another coin in the jukebox to reinforce the Captain's melancholy, vulnerable state of mind.

The bargain scene between Quinlan and Grandi is echoed in two other Welles movies. In *Macbeth*, Banquo slyly encourages a reluctant Macbeth to commit a murder that would, according to the prophecy of three witches, benefit them both. And in the end Banquo, like Grandi, pays for that encouragement with his life. In *Mr. Arkadin*, the title character pours a glass of liquor for Van Stratton while making him a proposition which, unknown to Van Stratton, could result in the latter's death. Quinlan and Macbeth are in a sense morally superior to Grandi and Banquo because at some point their consciences rebel against the crimes they perpetrate. And yet at the same time their crimes are much worse than their partners because their capacities for violence are greater. Even Arkadin has a bit of a conscience when it comes to his daughter.

At the Mirador Susan lies in bed, unable to sleep due to the loud music in her room, now exacerbated by a loud party in an adjoining cabin. Grandi's plot against Vargas is progressing. Meanwhile, on the Mexican side of Los Robles, Vargas's plot against Quinlan progresses too. Schwartz leads his skeptical, grumbling American colleagues, Adair and Gould, into Vargas's hotel in order to show them documentary evidence of Quinlan's corruption. A backtracking and panning camera captures his companions' annoyance. Adair charges ahead of Schwartz and Gould to confront Miguel in the hotel lobby. But it's largely a bluff. Vargas's quiet, courtly demeanor disarms him. Only when he finds himself alone again with Gould and Schwartz, in the elevator, does Adair resume badmouthing Vargas—and even then only after taking his lead from Gould. As soon as Miguel rejoins them upstairs, Adair loses his nerve, smiles, becomes effusively complimentary, and even removes his hat. The camera tracks the characters from behind as they walk towards Vargas's room. The less fickle Chief Gould trails behind the others. At least *his* hostility towards Vargas is consistent, if unwarranted. Like Quinlan's.

Inside his hotel room Miguel's attention is inefficiently divided between presenting his case against Quinlan and checking up on his absent wife via the telephone. Dialog and staging reflect his dilemma as Adair and Gould move away from him while challenging his evidence against Quinlan. Schwartz, meanwhile, tries to warn him that Grandi owns the motel at which Susan is staying. Miguel, distracted by the phone, either doesn't hear or fails to comprehend the significance of what Schwartz says. Nor does he get through to Susan. He doesn't recognize Pancho's interfering voice any more than did Susan. In short, Vargas fails on *three* tactical fronts in this scene: he does not convince Adair and Gould of the case against Quinlan; he does not absorb Schwartz's warning about Grandi; and he is not able to contact his wife.

Pancho's phony excuse for not putting through Miguel's call is that Susan left instructions not to be disturbed. Which is abruptly undercut by a shot of Susan, *very* disturbed, banging on the wall in an effort to quiet a loud party next door. It seems to work. The music stops, only to be replaced by something far more disturbing. The whispered voice of one of the unseen revelers. Surrounded by the shadows of approaching night and looking vulnerable in her nightie, Susan is told of an impending attempt to get into her room by doped up gang members. Cut to a shot inside the adjoining room, where one female gang member tells another with sinister vagueness, "The fun is only beginning." Welles allows our imaginations to match Susan's, anticipating the worst before explaining Grandi's master plan in a different way.

We peer over Quinlan's left shoulder, following his gaze looking at a reflection of himself in a large mirror behind a bar. Framing that reflection at its bottom edge are two rows of drinking glasses. A slow, bluesy tune plays on the jukebox. Menzies enters, drawing Hank's attention away from himself. Pete has been searching for his boss in bars all over town, which is one measure of his devotion to Hank. He knew when he saw Grandi leading Hank away from the Sanchez apartment that Quinlan would fall off the wagon. Ending up in a Mexican bar so as not to "drink on my own beat" is Hank's pathetic attempt to cling to some semblance of professional integrity.

Menzies tries to tell Hank about Vargas's meeting with Adair and Gould, but Quinlan is preoccupied with the past, not the present. He reminisces about the strangulation murder of his wife and his failure as a rookie cop to crack the case and bring the killer to justice. That killer, he is convinced, was a "half breed." And there we have it. A glimpse at the whys and wherefores of Quinlan's racial bigotry and his willingness to use illegal means to convict criminals he intuits are guilty. The melancholy, moribund mood of this bar scene is strongly reminiscent of the El Rancho scenes in *Citizen Kane*, where Susan Alexander too was heavily burdened by the past.

Quinlan gradually returns to the present, sobering up with black coffee while bending Pete's ear about his late wife. Though often taking his subordinate for granted, Hank relies on Menzies for many things, including remembering to pick up his cane when he leaves. Quinlan's absentmindedness in this scene foreshadows a disaster yet to come, when he tries to get along without his faithful squire. Pete even pays Hank's bar tab as they exit. But in his effort to rescue Quinlan from past tragedy, Menzies refocus Hank's attention on the present challenge posed by Vargas, and sobers him up enough to put him back in the game. Failing to recognize the depths of his boss's desperation and corruption, Pete laughs conspiratorially at Quinlan's vow to retaliate against Vargas's "dirty" tactics with some of his own.

In Vargas's hotel room, across the street from the bar where Menzies found Hank, Miguel argues his case against Quinlan while visually sandwiched between skeptics Gould and Adair. Quinlan's unexpected arrival squashes any remote chance he had of succeeding. Hank too is initially pictured between the pivotal figures of Gould and Adair. He hobbles into the room, deliberately taking emotional advantage of his physical disability. His remark about not being sure if he is welcome or not echoes back to an earlier scene, when he subtly pointed out that he was not invited to the Linnekar banquet that Gould, Adair, and Vargas attended. An egotist playing a martyr. His drab, wrinkled trench coat and polka dot tie counterpoint the more formal attire of the other men, highlighting his outsider status. But as Quinlan moves further into the room his intimidating bulk more than offsets his fashion disadvantage, particularly from the camera's low angle perspective.

Quinlan and Vargas debate the finer points of law enforcement in a close-up profile. The visual contrast between them reinforces the differences in their arguments. Age versus youth. Puffy eyes versus clear eyes. Rumpled old hat versus black hair. Grizzled whiskers versus neatly trimmed mustache and clean shaven chin. Vargas argues in favor of strict adherence to the letter of the law. Quinlan make no direct challenge to that view. Instead, he sighs in exasperation and glances at the camera as though sharing with *us* his contempt for Vargas's naivete. Then he quietly, indirectly undercuts his opponent's high-minded logic by casually asking about Susan. In retrospect we understand the relevance of that seemingly irrelevant inquiry. Quinlan is countering Vargas's philosophical challenge with an emotional challenge similar to the one Hank himself had to face in the past. A challenge that, at least for Quinlan, reduces to nonsense Miguel's strict fidelity to the law.

Downplaying his reference to Susan so as not to incriminate himself, Quinlan saunters away from Vargas as though giving up the contest. Secretly confident of ultimate victory, thanks to his prior arrangement with Grandi, he allows himself to be distracted by a pigeon egg he picks out of a nest on the window sill. For a moment he becomes gentle, almost childlike. Falstaff smiling at his own fingertips and babbling about green fields moments before his death in *Chimes at Midnight*. But that is an illusion. Quinlan quickly turns belligerent when Vargas refers to Hank's ranch and testimony by a hired hand regarding sticks of dynamite the Captain purchased. Distracted from his distraction, Quinlan reflexively crushes the egg, spattering its contents on his coat. It is a spasmodic, mechanical reaction, like the pumping oil derricks. Vargas, still a gentleman, offers his handkerchief to clean up the mess. Such courtesies, especially to an enemy, won't last.

Confronted by evidence that the dynamite found in the Sanchez apartment came from his own ranch, Quinlan moves quickly to offset his foe's new advantage. And again he mounts an *indirect* challenge to Vargas's logic. Pulling his sheriff's badge out of his pocket, he tosses it aside and storms out of the room in a show of outrage. Gould tries to pacify him, without understanding the real peril of Vargas's challenge. Besides, Hank values loyalty above fair play—emotions above philosophical abstractions. The mere fact that Gould and Adair allowed Vargas to question his authority as a cop is, in his opinion, an act of betrayal. Of course his display of moral outrage is also a convenient way of avoiding a direct answer to Vargas's implied accusation.

A fast, low angle, backtracking camera carries us along with Quinlan's fury as he charges out of Vargas's hotel room. He complains, with justification, about the lousy conditions under which he's devoted thirty years of his life to his "dirty" job. Not quite so justified is his complaint that a "foreigner" was allowed to question the way he did that job. Gould and Adair follow him contritely. Stopping in a lounge between rooms, the characters unwittingly position themselves in a tactical manner. Quinlan stands alone in the background, on the verge of walking out. Adair and Gould occupy the middle ground, disputing which of them is more to blame for betraying Hank. Gould sounds suspiciously like Jim Kane (both characters are played by actor Harry Shannon) hypocritically protesting his devotion to son Charlie in *Citizen Kane*. Besting an overmatched Adair, he joins Quinlan in the background. Adair, in turn, gets rid of the guilt Gould dumped on him by transferring it to Vargas, who enters the camera frame at foreground right. The District Attorney who behaved so deferentially to the prominent Mexican official earlier now loudly demands that Vargas "crawl" to Quinlan and beg for forgiveness. Miguel quietly exits screen left. Adair and Gould depart with Quinlan in a different direction.

Vargas joins Schwartz in a nearby stairwell. Still loyal to Miguel, though not as passionately as Menzies is to Quinlan, he agrees to show Vargas the public records of Quinlan's old cases. As they depart Miguel declares his intention to make it a *quick* trip, so he can return to his wife. It is a cursory remark, betraying the fact that at this point in the story he is more concerned with proving Hank Quinlan's corruption than in protecting Susan. His attitude contrasts with Quinlan's consistent, passionate, though not always articulated preoccupation with *his* late wife. Is it possible that Hank too, like Vargas, took his wife for granted before he lost her?

Inside the elevator that returns them to the hotel lobby, Quinlan accepts his badge back from Gould. Together with Adair, they are packed into a cramped space, visually matching their much too cozy professional relationship. Quinlan startles his companions by accusing Miguel and Susan of being drug addicts. The shock of that revelation is punctuated by Hank himself when he noisily opens the elevator door. And he compounds his lie by claiming to have found a hypodermic needle belonging to the Vargases.

In the lobby we see Vargas and Schwartz in the background, leaving to gather more evidence against Quinlan. In the foreground Hank bears false witness against Vargas and Susan. Gould, Adair, and the tracking camera follow Quinlan outside the hotel, hanging on every word of his phony story. The next shot pans with Vargas's car as it departs on its honorable mission, then stops on Adair's face as he reacts warily to Quinlan's dishonorable counterattack. Gould too is cautious. He and Adair are lackeys, but they are smart enough to recognize the political danger to themselves of being linked to a false accusation against a high-ranking official of a foreign government. Archways at the front of the hotel loom over their heads, metaphorically echoing that danger. But Quinlan's promise to be "careful" elicits a grin from Gould, who perhaps knows a thing or two about Hank's skill at manipulating evidence.

Vargas and Schwartz enter the steel-vaulted Hall of Records. The clang of its door opening attests to the security of the place. Wall-to-wall and floor-to-ceiling file cabinets attest to the bureaucratic thoroughness of government records keeping. The entire set is a testament to Vargas's abstract ideal of law enforcement. Its imposing if somewhat sterile orderliness complements the neatness and formality of his suit, and of his hotel room earlier, while contrasting the untidiness of Quinlan's rumpled appearance and the emotionally charged clutter of Tanya's place. Magnify the honorable Hall of Records to grotesque proportions and you get the nightmarish court building in Welles's *The Trial*, where protagonist Joseph K gets lost in a maze of murky legal records and procedures. K's advocate, a character even more corrupt than Quinlan, exploits that bloated bureaucracy for purely selfish gain. Thus the same resource can assist either good or evil, depending on circumstances. Another ironic parallel to the Hall of Records is the Thatcher Memorial Library vault containing Thatcher's private journals in *Citizen Kane*. Both sets feature heavy metal doors and echo-producing acoustics. But Thatcher's vault is guarded with far too much reverence for its publically overvalued contents.

Employing his camera with beautiful economy in this one shot scene, Welles pans with the characters from the doorway to the interior, then back to the door after they finish retrieving some old case files. Between arrival and departure the two men verbally define the parameters of their relationship. Schwartz expects to lose his job as a consequence of helping Vargas, who in turn tries to minimize his partner's risk by building the case against Quinlan by himself. Though naive about the danger he and Susan face, Vargas has guts. *Lacking* the guts to tackle Quinlan alone, Schwartz is nevertheless more realistic about the danger of doing so. He also respects Quinlan's intuition about the guilt of Manolo Sanchez, which turns out to be well founded. Courage and wisdom do not always travel together.

The closing of the door to the Hall of Records, as Vargas and Schwartz leave, is followed immediately by the unlocking of the door to Susan's cabin at the Mirador. The parallel is clear. Miguel's access to the Hall of Records gives him a tactical edge over Quinlan. The Grandi gang's access to Susan gives Uncle Joe and Quinlan a tactical edge over Vargas. Frightened, Susan retreats to the bathroom, hoping to escape through a window there. But just outside that window looms another gang member.

Susan returns to the bedroom, where the unlocked door begins to open. The sinister slowness of the gang's invasion is counterpointed and yet somehow exacerbated by the loud, fast rock and roll music blaring from the wall speaker. Both are unwelcome intrusions on Susan's privacy. She retreats to the bed, like a child fleeing a monster from the closet. The shadow of one of the intruders passes over her face. A black silhouette passes between Susan, still dressed in her flimsy white nightie, and the camera. Pancho enters, with a crooked smile on his face. Again, low and high camera angles visually reinforce the contrast between menace and fear. Pancho closes the door. Both the Hall of Records scene and this one begin with a door opening and end with a door closing. That stylistic similarity reinforces the tactical parallel and moral contrast between the two events.

Tanya sits alone in her parlor, which is filled with relics from her past. Only a small television, sitting atop the pianola, looks modern, counterpointing everything around it, including Tanya herself. She appears as desolate as Quinlan did when he sat alone in a bar, staring at his reflection in a mirror. But the sources of her desolation are mostly hidden from us. Heavy shadows mix with harsh light from several local sources to etch the details of her private world. She sits in a chair, smoking, facing the pianola across the room. It plays a tune, yet there are no paying customers in sight. We assume she's listening to music for sentimental reasons—perhaps reminiscing about the past the way Quinlan did when he heard similar music the night before. From the camera's position behind and to Tanya's left, we cannot see her face, emphasizing the inviolable privacy of her emotional life.

A telephone call from Menzies, inquiring about Hank, draws her to an adjoining room. During their brief conversation we hear an off screen male voice summon Tanya back to the parlor. We also notice his hat hanging nearby. Until this moment we didn't realize she had a patron in the house. Our initial impression of Tanya's sentimental reverie is overturned. She is, at this point in her life, a cynical pragmatist who no longer allows herself to feel regret, disappointment, or compassion. That will change a little by the end of the story. But not yet. Callously remarking to Menzies that Hank's addiction has switched from liquor to candy, Tanya hangs up the phone and returns indifferently to her customer. But Pete informs her that Quinlan is on the booze again, perhaps planting a tiny seed of concern in her otherwise dormant emotions.

Cut back to the Mirador. Sentimental piano music is displaced by loud and decidedly unsentimental rock and roll. Sitting alone in the main office, his mouth overstuffed with food, the Night Man lowers a window shade to block out the setting sun, just as he blocks out any concern he might have for the plight of his only guest. Meanwhile, in Susan's cabin the hostile invasion continues. Three female gang members join the young men gathered around Susan's bed. The slowness of their movements is part of their deliberate attempt to terrorize her.

In the main office, the Night Man smugly switches off the loud music that annoys him. Secure now in his cloistered little world, he is very bold when not being confronted. As for Susan, the sudden absence of music in her cabin has a chilling rather than comforting effect, because it is replaced by the menacing voices of her assailants. "I wanna watch," says one of the women. "Hold her legs," whispers Pancho in a terrifying, visually distorted, frontal close-up. The scene ends with a cabin door slamming shut, blocking our view of Pancho and his companions as they haul a screaming, struggling Susan off the bed.

Later we find out they did less to her than we now imagine. Maybe Welles had to tone down the assault to placate the censors. But in purely dramatic terms this *is* a rape scene, setting the stage for Miguel's violent reaction to it later. A reaction sufficient to draw a parallel between Vargas and Quinlan, who lost a wife to violent assault years earlier.

The slamming of the door to Susan's cabin matches Pete Menzies yanking open the door to the Hall of Records, starting the next scene. Both are violent actions. One is the product of the Grandi family's and Quinlan's revenge *on* Vargas. The other is a product of Menzies' angry defense of Hank against attack *by* Vargas. Inside the vault Pete confronts Miguel, who is seated at a table examining the records of Quinlan's old cases. A low angle magnifies the Sergeant's hostility as he approaches his enemy. At first he keeps his hands in his pockets, looking more passive than he sounds. Then he grabs some documents out of Miguel's hands and brandishes a closed fist as though willing to battle for possession of them. He withdraws to the background to examine those documents. Vargas approaches him with no indication of physical menace, but a clear *verbal* threat. A camera shot from over the Mexican's dark shoulder, looking down at Pete's well-lit face, conveys Miguel's tactical edge.

The camera returns to its prior position, near the table. Menzies retreats from his foe, moving into the foreground while Vargas remains in the background. The nature of their confrontation changes too. Menzies, who began the action with a racist remark and a brief threat of violence, now solicits pity for his broken-down boss. Joseph Calleia's performance is very effective as Menzies shifts from bigot to devoted friend. Legally he is wrong. The pain in his voice is partly an acknowledgement of that fact. But his affection for and loyalty to Quinlan almost renders Vargas's crusade an act of cruelty instead of justice. Miguel calmly retrieves his evidence from off the floor where Menzies dropped it. He approaches and contemptuously walks past Menzies. Pausing at foreground left, and pointedly looking away from Menzies, who now occupies the background again, Vargas coldly advises him to save his tears for the undeserving victims Quinlan sent to the death house. Both men wield powerful arguments: one irrational but passionate, the other rational but dispassionate. Rows of file cabinets and overhead lights stretching from foreground to background heighten our impression of the distance between the two characters. Vargas walks off camera without so much as a backward glance at Menzies, who now appears small and defeated, with his thumbs back in his pockets, as they were at the start of the scene.

The image of a defeated Sergeant Menzies dissolves to an image of the Mirador's Night Man, looking equally small and vulnerable as he sits alone inside the heavily shadowed motel office. Someone has switched off the electric power. An ineffectual character, the Night Man was unable to help Susan in her hour of need. Now he quietly sings an old time hymn to himself, pacifying any fears or guilt he might be feeling. He is a little man lost in his own little world, which is suddenly invaded by an intruder. Vargas arrives in search of his wife. The Night Man flinches at any hint of a demand from the stranger. He is almost as afraid of Vargas as he was of the Grandi gang. Judging from his reply to Miguel's question about why the motel lights are off, we can't be sure if the Night Man refuses to repair the fuses the gang members tampered with or is simply incapable of doing so.

Easily distracted and jittery, the Night Man hovers too close to Vargas one moment and fearfully flees from him the next. He cannot quite focus on the questions put to him. Vargas shows great patience as he solicits information about Susan. However odd the Night Man may be, he provides the film with more than comic relief. He is a portrait of human weakness different from yet paralleling the flaws we see in other characters. He is hypocritical and inconsistent, yet less dangerous than others who are bolder and more intelligent. Quinlan and Vargas, the most intelligent and forceful characters in the story, are far more of a menace when sufficiently aroused. The circumstances of the Night Man's encounter with Susan Vargas may foreshadow Norman Bates's encounter with Marion Crane in *Psycho*, but the outcome does not. The Night Man is much too timid to do what Norman does.

In spite of his quirks, the Night Man tries his best to help Miguel solve the mystery of Susan's disappearance. A briskly paced tracking shot of him leading the way to Susan's abandoned cabin effectively captures his determination to do the right thing. The lack of lights, the emptiness of the deserted motel, and the moan of a desert night breeze generate an exceptionally creepy mood in this scene, as similar ingredients do in the scenes surrounding Duncan's murder in Welles *Macbeth*. We get a powerful sense that something unspeakably horrible has occurred here.

Searching Susan's dark cabin and finding nothing is almost more disturbing than discovering her lifeless body would have been, because it leaves too much to Vargas's and our imaginations. The Night Man complains of a stink in the room, adding to that disturbing impression. The stink of what? Gang rape? Murder? No, it's merely the stink of a half-smoked marijuana joint. But even that meager discovery terrifies the prudish Night Man, sending him fleeing outside. Vargas pursues him, now loudly *demanding* to know what happened to Susan. His patience and courtesy are beginning to slip away.

Frightened of so many things, including now Vargas, the Night Man retreats further into the distance. He clings to a tree, like a child hugging a stuffed toy for security, or Quinlan drawing comfort from a candy bar and a shot of booze. And yet even in this pathetic condition the tongue-tied Night Man makes an effort to explain to Vargas about the Grandi family's connection to the motel (something Al Schwartz tried to tell him earlier) and about where Vargas might find them.

Our last impression of the Night Man is that of a frightened little man, clinging to his floppy hat and a spindly tree as he watches Vargas drive away in search of Susan. Welles and Dennis Weaver make of him both a comic and a sympathetic character. A thoroughly human grotesque. Certainly the Night Man elicits more sympathy than the likes of Gould and Adair, who make little or no attempt to overcome their shortcomings. In his memo to Universal Studios Welles refers to Weaver's character as a "queerly likeable and diverting sort of man." That he is.

Inside the Ritz Hotel, on the "safe," American side of Los Robles, the door to one of the guest rooms opens just enough for us to see Susan Vargas lying unconscious on the bed. She is partly covered by a bed sheet. Otherwise she appears to be naked. The narrowness of the opening through which we view her adds to our impression of her involuntary confinement. A reverse angle shot, with Susan now in the foreground, generates the same visual effect. A heavy, ornate, metal bedpost frames her head, like the bars of a cage. We don't even know yet if she's alive or dead as Uncle Joe enters from the background. Percussive jazz filters into the room from a nightclub across the street. Pulsing light from a neon sign outside the window alternately brightens and darkens the room. This may be the Hotel Ritz, but it is definitely not located in the ritzy part of town.

Grandi speaks to two female members of the gang that kidnapped Susan. We did not suspect they were in the room until now. Seeing them in either of the scene's first two shots would have diminished our image of Susan's imprisonment. Their conversation informs us that Susan is alive, that she was not drugged but made to seem like she used illegal drugs, that the girls themselves did not use drugs, and that "we put on a good show to scare her." Possibly this explanation of what did and did not happen at the Mirador Motel allowed Welles to sneak the film by the censors. However, the matter of rape is not specifically denied. At any rate, the "good show" Grandi's gang put on for Susan is another Wellesian example of an illusion employed for tactical gain. Grandi has only to create the *impression* that Susan is a dope addict in order to discredit her husband. Unfortunately for Uncle Joe, his secret partner in crime is bent on transforming illusion into reality, for the same purpose.

Grandi returns to the shadowy corridor outside the room to summon his partner. From a distance we first see Hank Quinlan only as a hand holding a drinking glass up to a mouth. It's as narrow an image as our first glimpse of Susan in this scene. Both characters are captives: Susan of Grandi and Hank; Hank of the booze he resisted for years, until tonight. He limps towards Susan's room, his eyes glazed. Inside the room he stands over the unconscious victim. Is there a trace of pity in his face? A recognition of his own wife's plight in Susan's? If so, it passes quickly. In spite of his slurred voice, Quinlan methodically executes his plan-within-a-plan. He orders Grandi to switch off the light, which makes no sense to Uncle Joe because no one can see them anyway. Setting aside his cane, Hank puts on a pair of gloves retrieved form his pocket. He is prepared. His actions are premeditated. We watch his gloved hands cross over to the other side of the bed, near Susan's head. Does he intend to strangle her, the way his wife was killed? In an earlier scene he referred to strangulation as the safest method of murder. Grandi is puzzled. He asks questions he should have asked earlier. His illusion of being in control of their criminal partnership evaporates. A shot of Quinlan's gloved hands in the foreground pictures Grandi in the background. But instead of menacing Susan, one of those hands pulls out a gun and points it an Uncle Joe.

A moving high angle shot from Hank's point of view pictures the restless but still unconscious Susan as helpless. Next a low angle shot shows Quinlan forcing Grandi against

Touch of Evil. Hank Quinlan (Orson Welles) turns on his co-conspirator, Joe Grandi (Akim Tamiroff), while their victim, Susan Vargas (Janet Leigh), lies unconscious and helpless between them.

the wall and disarming him. Then another high angle shot pictures Hank looming over his shorter partner as he compels Grandi to phone Sergeant Menzies at the police station. From *every* angle Quinlan is visually dominant. Uncle Joe's threat to tell the police about their secret arrangement should Hank blame him for what happened to Susan is answered by Quinlan's sinister chuckle. Grandi still hasn't figured out Quinlan's surreptitious plan. Meanwhile, light streaming into the room through the window pulses on and off, like a heartbeat, building tension.

Though he is drunk, Quinlan's focus is chillingly sharp when he orders Menzies to "break" Sanchez into confessing to the murder of Rudy Linnekar. He is once again capable of conducting operations on two fronts at the same time. After he finishes with Menzies, his instructions to Grandi are crisp and sober. Music seeping in from across the street gradually grows louder and faster throughout this scene, matching the increasing clarity and violence of Hank Quinlan's actions. Locking the door to the room, Quinlan briefly appears smaller than Grandi, until he begins to stalk his victim. In a reverse angle shot we see only part of his body and little of his face, as though he were too big and powerful to be contained within the camera frame. Fragments of his figure hover over the retreating Grandi. From a subjective point of view we stalk the little man with Hank. Grandi flees in terror from us, his toupee as askew as his confidence. But there is no escape for him. Blinking light exposes him wherever he goes. A reverse angle shot depicts his stalker as enormous—so tall he has to duck under an angled portion of the ceiling.

Pulsing light, percussive music, rapid editing, extreme camera angles, fragmented images of body parts, and straining, awkward body movements add up to a potent impression of chaotic fear and controlled violence. Grandi's death by strangulation with one of Susan's nylon stockings is drawn out for dramatic effect. His struggle to escape death is both desperate and pathetic. There is nothing tidy about this crime. And, perhaps most importantly, through the strangulation of Grandi we can imagine some of the horror Quinlan's wife experienced. Particularly disturbing is a shot of Grandi's feet lifted off the floor, kicking wildly and uselessly in the air as he suffocates. Quinlan leaves him dangling over the iron railing at the foot of the bed, just above Susan's face.

The murder of Grandi serves Quinlan's agenda in several ways. It satisfies his desire for revenge against Vargas. It silences the only material witness to his involvement in the assault on Susan. And it indirectly avenges his wife's murder. Poor Uncle Joe is an unwitting surrogate for her long dead killer.

Quinlan's hulking figure exits the room. He turns and looks back at his handiwork, pausing for a moment. To contemplate Susan's undeserved fate? He looks dazed—emotionally and morally numb. The heavy door and door frame seem to surround and imprison him. When the door closes, the camera moves in to a close-up of a handwritten sign attached to the inside of the door. Placed there by the hotel management, the sign reminds guests not to forget to take their belongings when they leave. The larger significance of that routine institutional message dawns on us only in retrospect. Quinlan forgot to take his cane, as he has done on previous occasions. Like the music drifting in from across the street and the pulsing neon sign streaming in through the window, the sign on the door plays a dramatic role by *coincidental* alignment with the actions of the characters.

Henry Mancini's screaming *background* music reinforces the scene's local music when Susan awakens to see Grandi's grotesque face, with its eyes bulging and tongue protruding, hovering over her. We see what she sees, fitfully lit by another burst of light. Wrapping a bed sheet around her naked body, Susan retreats to the fire escape. She calls down to a crowd of passersby on the street below. The camera shifts to their point of view, from which Susan looks small and sounds even smaller amidst the din of music and automobile traffic. She cannot communicate her distress to the public. They wave at her and laugh, no doubt under the illusion that her lack of clothing proceeds from a very different cause than we know it does. Their reaction is a preview of the kind of public reception she and Miguel would get if the plot to destroy their reputations succeeds.

Worse yet, Susan's frantic husband drives right past the Ritz Hotel without noticing her. He honks his car horn in his impatience to get past other vehicles and pedestrians in order to find her. Ironically, his horn drowns out Susan's weak cries for help. He speeds recklessly through the crowded streets of Los Robles. Racing past the border customs checkpoint, he bumps into a pedestrian without stopping. The gentility and compassion and respect for the law he exhibited earlier are gone now, stripped away by panic and rage.

Vargas charges into Grandi's Rancho Grande in search of his wife. We view his arrival from a distance, and unusually framed. Sandwiched between the legs of a stripper performing in the foreground and painted images of alluring, smiling strippers on a wall in the far background, Miguel seems out of place. The setting doesn't match his anxiety. The larger world doesn't share his private concern, just as it did not share Susan's distress in the previous scene.

Vargas makes his way to the cabaret's smokey back room, where members of the Grandi gang sit drinking and playing cards. He yells at them in Spanish. The room goes silent. Vargas gets the attention he demands. Then loud rock and roll music commences on the jukebox and communal indifference is restored. Miguel wanders through the room, searching for someone. We watch him through beaded curtains hanging in the doorway. Like the music and the strippers in the other room, the glittering, festive beads mock his sober mission. He grabs a beer glass, smashes it to the floor, and shouts for attention. And gets it. The camera switches to a different angle, eliminating the intrusive, frivolous beads.

Pancho approaches Vargas and contemptuously blows cigarette smoke in his face. That largely symbolic attack is answered with real violence. Vargas grabs Pancho by the collar and slams his head into the jukebox, silencing both the arrogant young man and the distracting music. Risto, the boy who threw acid at him in an earlier scene, is Vargas's next target. When Risto fails to answer the questions put to him, Miguel grabs him by the front of his leather jacket, lifts him off the floor, and carries him half the length of the bar before slamming him into it. Such an act of violence requires great strength, and great rage to produce it. Another gang member tries to interfere but is easily swept aside. Risto's dangling legs recall a similar image of Uncle Joe's dangling legs as he was being strangled by Quinlan. The parallel between Hank and Miguel grows stronger. Both men are driven to violence by a passionate devotion to their wives. Welles's choice of camera angle, lens, set design, and lighting emphasizes the three-dimensional depth of the room, and thereby the raw power of Vargas's movements within it.

Miguel's outburst sends most of the cabaret's patrons running for the exits. Demanding to know the whereabouts of his wife, Vargas hurls the uncooperative Risto out of the camera frame. Then he is attacked from various angles by Risto's allies, but disposes of all of them. The cabaret is reduced to shambles. Like Charlie Kane tearing apart Susan Alexander's room, Miguel transforms Grandi's establishment into something resembling his own emotional state. Only the arrival of the police puts an end to his rampage. Al Schwartz is with them. He and Vargas stand next to the overturned bar that complements Miguel's mood. But a false, starlit ceiling hanging over their heads and a background wall painted with festive images counterpoint their grim conversation. Schwartz informs Vargas that Susan was picked up by the vice squad. The two men move to the entryway, where beaded curtains in the background clash with more bad news revealed by the Deputy District Attorney. Susan was found in a hotel room, half naked and surrounded by illegal drugs.

Miguel pushes angrily through the offensive beads and moves to another part of the nightclub. But there the decor is even less conducive to his fury. Figures of alluring, smiling strippers on the wall seem to mock him with reminders of the false public image of Susan that Grandi and Quinlan tried to create. But there is worse to come. Schwartz informs Vargas that Susan has been charged with murder. A close-up of Miguel and the back of Schwartz's head eliminates all visual contradictions as the stunning impact of Quinlan's corruption and Susan's peril hits home. This image of Vargas quickly goes out of focus, disintegrating like his emotional self-control.

At the police station the camera tracks with Vargas and Schwartz as they run down a corridor towards Susan's jail cell. Welles frequently uses his camera to give his audience a visceral feel for a character's state of mind. Mancini's background music reinforces the camera movement. Drawing on a variety of styles and played at varying volumes, the music runs a gamut of dramatic functions: sometimes adding an exclamation point to visual images, at other times quietly insinuating what is left unspoken or even unrecognized by the characters, and sometimes deliberately running counter to a scene or a character's prevailing mood. When Miguel reaches Susan's cell, the music settles down to an understated, bluesy, almost mournful jazz.

Miguel comforts his delirious wife in her jail cell. We observe him through the cell bars, which look dark and heavy in silhouette, as he defends her against accusations by the coroner, who stands outside the bars along with Sergeant Menzies. The coroner's cynical assessment of Susan's situation is exactly what Grandi and Quinlan counted on from the public in general when they framed Susan for crimes she did not commit. Looking like a prisoner himself, Miguel backs against the cell wall and lashes out verbally at the absent Quinlan. But Susan calls him back to her side, and his vigorous defense of her is cut short. Earlier in the movie he neglected Susan in order to pursue the Linnekar case. Now he must abandon Susan again to pursue *her* legal case. But this time it's much more difficult for him to leave.

Captain Menzies is a silent observer up to this point in the scene. He stands outside the cell, scrutinizing the prisoner and her husband inside. We read no sympathy in his face, and yet he lends no support to the coroner's assumption of Susan's guilt. When he sees Susan cling desperately to Vargas, Pete's resolve to remain detached evaporates. Subsequent close-ups of Miguel comforting Susan while Menzies observes contain no prison bars separating them, suggesting greater emotional intimacy between Quinlan's old friend and Quinlan's greatest enemy.

Vargas steps outside the jail cell. From *his* point of view we see Menzies in a frontal medium shot, through the cell bars, as though Pete were in prison too. The door swings open, metaphorically liberating the conscience-stricken Sergeant. What he does next is both an act of moral courage and, in his own mind, an unforgivable betrayal. The cell door opens up for him. But visible on the wall behind him, the shadow of prison bars seem to close on *his* shadow. The nature of his next action is irreducibly contradictory, in emotional and ethical terms. He motions for Vargas to follow him.

The camera tracked rapidly with an anxious Vargas at the start of the scene. Now it tracks slowly with a reluctant Menzies as he leads Miguel to an isolated storage room where they can talk privately. Mancini's background music echoes the grimness rather than the liberation of Pete's decision.

The storage room is a cramped, ugly place, with exposed ceiling pipes hanging over Menzies' head in a low angle long shot. Appearing much larger than Pete is part of Miguel's figure in the foreground. Again by showing only part of a character's figure Welles visually conveys that character's dominance over another. Avoiding the dreaded moment of truth, Menzies back peddles defensively, downplaying the seriousness of Susan's legal situation in order to avoid the pain of betraying Quinlan. Vargas, refusing to accommodate, approaches and confronts him. So Menzies sadly unveils Hank Quinlan's cane. Vargas takes that object in his hands and silently caresses it. The cop's crutch suddenly becomes the lawyer's key to liberating his wife and putting the cop behind bars. But the cane is merely a token representative of the despised Quinlan. It is not a *weapon* against Hank until Menzies approaches Vargas and, in an intimate close-up of the two men, reveals that he found the cane in the hotel room where Grandi was murdered. With a slight sigh of relief but no word of thanks, Miguel turns away from Menzies and walks out of that close-up. Pete will get no reward for doing the right thing. As Quinlan once noted, being a good cop is a dirty job.

Sergeant Menzies' face dissolves to an exterior shot of the front of Tanya's place. Vargas creeps across the screen, climbs onto Tanya's porch and peers through a window. Inside the house Quinlan sits in a chair, half stupefied from booze, listening to the pianola. A bottle lies within easy reach. His chair is the one Tanya sat in earlier, when for a moment we thought she too was contemplating her past. The fact that Quinlan is still drinking after having completed his mission, and sought out Tanya and her pianola for emotional succor, implies that, unlike the coroner, he is not comfortable with his cynicism. He is troubled by what he did to Grandi and Susan, even though he could not resist his urge to do it.

From a different camera angle we see a dirty, paint-peeled wall decorated with a stuffed bull's head, banderillas, several portraits of matadors, and a large mirror. In the mirror we see a reflection of Vargas looking into the house through a window. Positioned as that mirror is, Miguel's reflection becomes another matador portrait. Completing the metaphor, the camera pans right towards Quinlan, who upon seeing Vargas in the window rouses himself and stands up. His large head is pictured next to the bull's. He is the hunted now. Vargas is the hunter. And in spite of his many crimes and character flaws, it is difficult not to pity him. With his bloated face and blinking eyes he seems to only vaguely comprehend the forces closing in on him now. Like a bull in a bull ring, he is destined for slaughter. Dangerous but ultimately doomed.

Miguel silently withdraws from the window and recedes into the dark of night, like some lurking fiend in a horror film. Seated on a chair in front of the window is a white female doll, posed in a childlike yet elegant manner. It is a stand-in for Tanya, who would never consciously allow herself to be seen in such a pose, or openly express her softer emotions.

Vargas joins Menzies on the platform of an oil derrick across the street from Tanya's place. The camera cranes and tilts up as Miguel climbs some steps to reach the platform. Much of the action in this scene occurs on two levels: physically, tactically, and morally. Camera movement mimics that duality. Vargas and Menzies debate about how best to get Quinlan to incriminate himself on audiotape, via a concealed microphone worn by his best friend. Tanya's sentimental pianola plays softly in the distance, exacerbating Pete's emotional dilemma. He tries again to talk Vargas out of their plan, explaining away the drugging of Susan as a phony, staged event, and assuring Miguel that she's feeling fine. He even exploits Susan's desire to leave Los Robles as soon as possible as an argument for suspending her husband's crusade against Quinlan. Joseph Calleia's weary, plaintive delivery of Pete's lines make it a persuasive plea. But Vargas is determined not to let up "until my wife's name is clean. Clean!" He's right, of course. Not only for Susan's sake, but for the sake of Quinlan's previous and future victims. Still, there is unwitting irony in Vargas following "Clean!" with "What do you think you're carrying that microphone for?" He hates spying with a tape recorder, yet is willing to use such a morally repugnant means to achieve a righteous end. An end that is also self-serving. Welles seems to imply that such compromises are a slippery slope, potentially leading to the kind of corruption that long ago engulfed Quinlan, whose moral descent we see only its final, worst stage.

William Johnson, in an article entitled "Orson Welles: Of Time and Loss," notes the visual similarity between the bomb that killed Rudy Linnekar at the start of the film and the tape recorder that destroys Hank Quinlan at the end. In between those two incidents are numerous images of oil derricks. "Though Quinlan is the only character who has succumbed to the temptation of being a machine, nearly everyone in the film is under pressure to do so" (Johnson, p.24). Certainly Vargas comes close to it when he rages against the Grandis and knocks down an innocent pedestrian with his car in the wake of his wife's abduction. And in her habitual indifference to a world that has not been kind to her, Tanya too has become somewhat machine-like.

Vargas and Menzies bicker pointlessly about how to place their hidden microphone. The *real* issue dividing them resurfaces a moment later. Hating his betrayal of Quinlan,

Menzies describes Hank as the best friend he's ever had. Vargas interprets that assertion in a less positive light. "That's one reason for my staying" implies a lack of trust in Pete's moral integrity. Menzies resentfully fires back, reminding Vargas of who told him about finding Quinlan's cane next to Grandi's body. Vargas gets technical by pointing out that Menzies was legally obligated to do so. But Menzies matches him on that level too, suggesting that the cane could have been planted next to the body by someone else, just as Vargas claims that the drugs found on Susan were planted. Both men sound like lawyers now. And Welles seldom portrays lawyers in heroic terms. Vargas brings the argument back to common sense, appealing to Pete's honesty as a cop. The Sergeant concedes, in effect, by relaxing his belligerent posture. But as he looks sadly in the direction of Tanya's place, he makes a final, doomed effort to sustain the illusion of his best friend as a good man, claiming it was Hank Quinlan who made him an honest cop. Think of Bernstein defending the memory of Charlie Kane, or Eugene Morgan's unwaveringly sentimental view of Isabel Amberson. The depth of Pete's admiration and affection for Hank suggests that at one time Quinlan *was* a good man. But an unsympathetic Vargas is understandably preoccupied with Quinlan in the *present* tense.

David Thomson, in *Rosebud: The Story of Orson Welles*, argues that if Welles had made Quinlan "more ordinary, more amiable, more reasonable, more matter-of-fact," *Touch of Evil* as a whole might be a better movie — a "portrait of deranged duty and warped idealism" (Thomson, p.343). I disagree. Unlike Charlie Kane, whom we see during his dynamic, often generous young manhood as well as his increasingly selfish, autocratic later years, we see Hank Quinlan only at the end of his tether — the wreck of decades of physical and moral decay. Through Menzies and Tanya we catch fleeting glimpses of the man he was— the man Miguel Vargas still *is*. If we see Vargas's potential downfall in Quinlan, we see Quinlan's promising youth in Vargas. In spite of his grotesque surface, Orson Welles's Hank Quinlan, has very human, ordinary, matter-of-fact, even amiable *roots*.

Menzies sad face dissolves to a shot of Tanya's less sentimental gaze, shown from the same camera angle. She too looks in the direction of Hank Quinlan, while filling out some financial papers and smoking a cigarette. Another emotional smoke screen. In a reverse angle shot we see Quinlan, smoking *and* drinking to suppress *his* emotions, totter into the parlor and ask Tanya to tell him his fortune. A deck of tarot cards is visible in the extreme foreground, so large that they dwarf Quinlan, whose fate is both ominous and near at hand. Getting no response from Tanya, who seems reluctant to hurt him, he lumbers over to her table, looking very old and very fat. Smearing the tarot cards sloppily across the table, he again solicits his fortune. "You haven't got any," she finally answers, with a trace of regret. "You're future is all used up," she adds after he demands clarification. Like Joseph Calleia's Sergeant Menzies, Marlene Dietrich's Tanya packs a lot of emotion into a few understated facial expressions and lines of dialog. Clearly she and Pete have long and emotionally charged histories with Quinlan. But unlike the Sergeant, Tanya has tried diligently to sever those old ties. "Why don't you go home," she advises, gently but also perhaps selfishly. Seeing Hank in his present, pathetic state is painful for her, and she prefers to avoid pain.

Menzies hesitantly approaches the house. He glances back in the direction of the oil derrick he came from. Careful lighting highlights key objects and characters within the general blackness of the night. Menzies speaks to his co-conspirator through his concealed microphone. Vargas places himself on the derrick so he can get good reception with his tape recorder. His positions through much of the action that follows, whether he is perched on an oil derrick or slogging through a dirty river beneath a bridge, are indicative of what even he views as a compromise of his professional ethics. There is something cold, mechanical, and forbidding about the omnipresent, towering oil derricks. Like *The Magnificent Ambersons*, *Touch of Evil* is not a celebration of modern technology. Except, of course, the technology of movie making.

Approaching Tanya's place, Menzies is in a sense poised between the modern world (Vargas, tape recorder, oil derricks) and an antiquated world (Quinlan, Tanya, and the pianola). The sound of pumping oil mingles with the sound of piano roll music. Of course, a pianola is a *machine*, and as such is a magnificently contradictory symbol of both nostalgia and automation. Tanya and Quinlan live emotionally in the past, and are reduced to machine-like habits in the present. When Menzies reaches the porch, the pianola displaces the pumping sound and the camera repositions itself, replacing an oil derrick in the far background with a plant hanging from the porch ceiling in the near foreground. The plant, however, looks withered, if not dead, matching the moral decay and emotional corrosion of the two characters inside the house.

Menzies lures Quinlan out of Tanya's house by briefly showing himself in the doorway, stimulating the detective's curiosity. Quinlan initially mistakes his partner and buddy for Vargas. An understandable mistake, considering Hank's inebriation and Miguel's brief appearance in the same window earlier. Or maybe Hank's famous intuition is at work again. Menzies is secretly working with Vargas. So from Quinlan's intuitive point of view there is no longer a dime's worth of difference between them.

Viewed from a low frontal camera angle, Hank looks monstrously large as he walks out of the house through a tall, angular door frame. But his wavering gait and slurred speech belie any impression of power or intimidation his size might otherwise yield. Quite the opposite, the camera angle emphasizes his vulnerability, as it did Charlie Kane's while he paced around his deserted campaign headquarters after a humiliating defeat at the polls. Back inside the house, Tanya too seems vulnerable. She had told Hank to go home. But when he exits her parlor, she pursues him, not quite able to conceal her concern for his welfare. Thanks to a bit of re-editing in accordance with Welles's wishes, the two characters do not even get to share a final, mutual glance. For them it is too late for new beginnings.

Menzies and Quinlan discuss the Vargas case as they walk down a dark, deserted street. We observe them from high up on a distant derrick. But we *hear* them up close, thanks to the electronic bug Pete carries. The discrepancy between image and sound is oddly disorienting. And Vargas's twisting, turning movements as he repositions himself to maintain good audio reception yet simultaneously hide from Quinlan adds to that effect. In a subsequent shot Quinlan and Menzies, discussing what happened to Vargas's gun, appear as tiny specks in the background, dwarfed by yet another oil derrick looming behind them. In the near foreground is the antenna of the powerful arbiter of Hank's fate. Powerful, but not *all* powerful. Reception fades in and out, forcing Vargas to keep moving in order to record incriminating evidence against Quinlan. His temperamental tape recorder is a variation on Eugene Morgan's often malfunctioning prototype automobile in *The Magnificent Ambersons*. I suspect Welles might have enjoyed the breakdown and dismantling of HAL 9000 in Stanley Kubrick's *2001: A Space Odyssey*, if he had ever seen it. Eugene's undependable horseless carriage was good for a lark and a laugh, until it contributed to the downfall of the Amberson family and nearly killed George Amberson Minafer. Similarly, Vargas's unreliable tape recorder teeters between failure, which would have serious consequences for him and Susan, and success, which will destroy Hank Quinlan's career.

Viewed up close, the conversation between Menzies and Quinlan reaches a crisis. We hear their natural instead of their electronically filtered voices, except for a brief insert shot of Vargas, reminding us that this conversation between old friends is not as intimate as it appears. Hank deduces from what his partner says that Menzies has consulted with Vargas. Which makes Quinlan suspicious. "That explain that thing you're carryin' around now?" he inquires. Pete is too stunned to ad-lib a convincing reply. Has Quinlan's intuition alerted him to the hidden microphone? If so, the sting operation is a bust. It's a deliberate moment of suspense executed by Welles. But Quinlan is only referring to a metaphorical pair of "wings" Menzies has sprouted on his back. Hank is contemptuous of his partner's newfound self-righteousness. And he compounds that verbal disapproval with body language, walking away from Menzies.

Quinlan leads Menzies along a meandering route that takes them dangerously close to Vargas, who scrambles awkwardly to keep the other men in range yet remain concealed. Acoustical and visual perspectives shift constantly throughout this unusual chase sequence. By contrast, the debate between Quinlan and Menzies is cogent. Hank points out, with some justification, that "starry-eyed idealists" like Vargas are "the ones making all the real trouble in the world." He regards such men as "worse than crooks" because "you can always do something with a crook." Of course, Quinlan speaks from selfish motives. The idealistic Vargas is making "real trouble" for *him* rather than for the world at large.

At one point during their argument Hank directs Pete's attention to a nearby pumping oil derrick, where coincidentally Vargas lurks with his spy machine. For Quinlan the derrick represents greed, to which he has remained immune in spite of many professional opportunities to enrich himself. An extreme low angle shot from Hank's vantage point pictures the derrick as a towering structure reducing Quinlan (and his own brand of corruption?) to insignificance. Is it possible that Vargas, hiding inside Hank's metaphor for greed, comes from a family that made its fortune in oil? That is speculation unsupported by evidence presented within the story. But Vargas *is* engaged in a morally questionable form of law enforcement, in the manner of Quinlan before him. One way or the other, the derrick *is* a symbol of corruption.

Menzies, intruding himself into the camera frame with Quinlan, verbally intrudes on Quinlan's digression and re-directs their conversation back to the Grandi murder. Hank, not wishing to talk about it, walks away again. He describes himself as an honest cop who had no problems until Vargas came along, which is a lie. Menzies defends Vargas, which is a reversal of when he defended Hank against accusations *by* Vargas. Meanwhile, Miguel experiences difficulty keeping their conversation in range of his recorder as he crawls through and around various pieces of the oil pumping maze. For a short time even *we* can't get a fix on where the characters are in relation to each other. *Everyone* loses their way in this metaphorical maze of corruption and confusion.

Menzies becomes more forceful as the scene progresses, openly accusing Quinlan of murdering Grandi. Hank avoids the subject, digressing into the matter of his lost cane. Menzies pressures him about Vargas's gun. As he does so we see Miguel in the far background, creeping down off a huge oil tank. At one time or another all three characters in this scene are dwarfed by their surroundings—which include the physical world at large and the emotional forces battling within themselves.

Admitting nothing, Quinlan justifies his actions by accurately describing Grandi as a crook. Menzies retorts by describing Hank as a murderer. "I'm a cop," Hank answers back, clinging to his professional dignity while avoiding self-incrimination. Pete's attack weakens as he momentarily yields to sentiment. In another intimate tight shot, he half-excuses Quinlan's crimes as those of a crazy drunk still grieving over his dead wife. "What else is there to think about?" adds Quinlan, "except my job. My *dirty* job." That job is Hank's sole and obviously inadequate compensation for the loss of his wife all those years ago.

Intimacy disappears when Quinlan turns away from Menzies yet again, and the camera cuts to an extreme long shot of them. Pete accuses Hank of *making* his job dirty. Quinlan defends himself by referring to the official record, which portrays him as the honest cop he pretends to be. And by adding, "*Our* record, partner," he slyly implicates Pete in any crimes Hank committed. If Quinlan's career goes down in flames, so does Pete's.

Vargas catches up with Quinlan and Menzies as they walk across a bridge over a river dividing Los Robles, Mexico from Los Robles, U.S.A. Descending into the water beneath that bridge, he tracks them. Tossing aside his suit jacket, and along with it some of his professional ethics, Miguel gets down and dirty in the river's polluted water while holding his precious tape recorder above it.

Initially denying Menzies's charge that he framed suspected criminals in the past by planting evidence against them, Quinlan carelessly modifies his claim by insisting he didn't frame anyone *who wasn't guilty*. Pete now resents having been played for a sucker all those years. An overhead shot depicts the small, white figure of Vargas wading through black water as he tracks the larger, gray figures of Menzies and Quinlan. An image of honor and innocence in a corrupt world? But as a result of the machine Vargas carries, the electronically reproduced voices of Quinlan and Menzies begin to echo off the bridge's support structure. Menzies pretends not to notice. Hank, leaning over the side of the bridge, calls out Vargas's name. Even when drunk he is an astute detective. We see him in extreme long shot, yet the peculiar acoustics of the setting render his voice loud and clear.

The camera cuts to an intimate shot of the two men on the bridge. Quinlan's game leg alerts him to the conspiracy against him. He realizes he is being recorded. He turns aggressively on Menzies, who weakly denies the charge against him. Whatever tactical advantage Pete gained from his moral indignation over being used by Quinlan in the past disappears when his betrayal of Quinlan in the present is exposed. Their subsequent debate exposes the different ways in which they perceive their jobs. Quinlan accuses Menzies of working for Vargas. Menzies insists he is working for the police department. For Quinlan, personal loyalty is paramount. Menzies, on the other hand, sees a higher fidelity to the abstract ideal of justice. A quick overhead shot shows them standing on the bridge above a garbage strewn riverbank. Both characters try to claim ethical superiority in an ugly, corrupt world.

Anticipating trouble above, and putting Pete's welfare above his spy mission, Vargas lays his recorder on the ground and climbs up the riverbank towards the bridge. But before he can intervene, a struggle between Menzies and Quinlan over Vargas's gun ends in Pete getting shot. After remaining silent for so long in this scene, allowing the aural dynamics of voice, electronic broadcast, and vast landscape to play out without enhancement, Mancini's background music returns with a vengeance, exploding in a protest of brass at the ultimate betrayal of one friend by another. The big, empty world is suddenly filled with personal drama.

In vivid close-up, his eyes and mouth wide open, Menzies reacts with shock to what has happened. From a very low angle commensurate with his point of view, Pete drops to his knees. Hank removes Vargas's gun from the hand that murdered his best friend, only to have that same, guilty hand gripped by the bloody hand of his dying victim. Then from Quinlan's point of view we watch Menzies collapse, only to be visually replaced by Vargas approaching from the background. There is no escape for Quinlan in this nightmare. Everything he sees is bad. In an obliquely angled close-up echoing *his* nightmare, Menzies looks up in horrified disbelief as his own bloody hand. Killer and victim are each engulfed in his own, intensely private experience of this violence event. Meanwhile, Vargas scrutinizes them from an emotional distance. He observes Quinlan, especially, with a cool, curious look of disgust. Though not intentionally cruel or callous, Vargas has less emotional stake in the matter. *His* priority, to repair his wife's sullied reputation and, not coincidentally, preserve his own professional standing, has been achieved. Or so he foolishly assumes.

Ignoring Vargas, with whom he was so preoccupied moments earlier, and will be again soon, Quinlan fixates on his own bloodied right hand as he lurches off the bridge and down to the riverbank. Viewed in long shot by a tilted camera, he is a small, fragile human figure in an immense wasteland that resembles postwar Vienna in Carol Reed's *The Third Man*.

Vargas leaves the bridge in pursuit of Quinlan. Hank, in an extreme low angle shot taken from water level, reaches down clumsily to wash his friend's blood off his hand, in a river so dirty it seems incapable of cleansing anything. His face is puffy and his eyes look dazed. He rises, stumbles backwards, and falls heavily into a pile of garbage. A single tear trickles down his cheek. Then Vargas adds to his pain with a stabbing remark about Quinlan not being able to talk his way out of *this* crime. In a sense Vargas speaks for *all* of Hank's victims, past and present. And yet his comment seems needlessly cruel because he seems to comprehend nothing of Quinlan's self-imposed torment at betraying Menzies.

But if we are inclined to pity Quinlan, Welles is quick to temper that reaction. Not as helpless as he appears, Hank quickly recovers his will to survive and his passionate hatred for the Mexican. Verbally rising to his opponent's challenge, even as he remains seated in a pile of garbage, Quinlan replies, "*You* killed him, Vargas." True, in the limited sense that Miguel's exploitation of Menzies to incriminate Quinlan resulted in Pete's death. But Quinlan refers to something more literal, and dangerous. Looking bullish and belligerent in a big close-up, despite the heavy wrinkles around his tired eyes, he announces that he intends to testify that Vargas killed Menzies. After all, the murder weapon was Vargas's gun. Hank is confident that his still untarnished reputation as an honest cop will give his testimony credibility. Against this new tactical development Vargas's demand for the return of his gun seems naive and lame. From Quinlan's reclining point of view, the gun in his hand points up at his taller, younger, stronger foe, putting the Mexican at a disadvantage.

But Vargas is not entirely unarmed. Reminding the Captain that they are now in Mexico, not the United States, he disputes Quinlan's legal authority to arrest him. More importantly, as Miguel says this we see the Pete Menzies peering over the bridge railing far above him. It was Menzies who sacrificed his loyalty to Quinlan and rescued the Vargases from scandal and maybe even prosecution. And it is Menzies who bails Vargas out of a tough spot now. Quinlan ups the ante again by threatening to kill Vargas immediately for attempting to escape, rather than file murder charges later. Vargas by himself is no match for the ruthless Captain Quinlan, just as a younger, less experienced, less ruthless Hank Quinlan was no match for the criminal who murdered his wife.

The sight of Al Schwartz approaching the bridge with Susan in Vargas's car distracts Miguel from his confrontation with Quinlan. Acting on emotional impulse, Vargas runs to meet his wife. Quinlan fires a warning shot to stop him and turn him around, so he won't have to shoot the Mexican in the back. A last glimmer of honor in the otherwise thoroughly corrupt American cop? If so, it turns out to be a tactical error. Before he can shoot Vargas face-to-face, Quinlan himself is shot by Menzies, who dies immediately thereafter. A blast from the horn of his car draws Vargas quickly away from the scene. He is consumed with concern for Susan and has no time to waste on the drama that plays out between Menzies and Quinlan.

Pete's hat falls to the ground near Hank, catching the Captain's eye and informing him that it was his old friend who shot him. The gun drops from Pete's dead hand, falling into the river. Meanwhile, as he passes Schwartz on the bridge, Vargas hurriedly explains the deaths of Menzies and Grandi, and the recorded evidence incriminating Hank Quinlan for both crimes. A reaction shot of Quinlan overhearing Vargas's accusation shows him wincing in pain, from the gunshot wound no doubt, but also from the realization that his reputation as an honest cop is destroyed.

Separate actions overlap. Vargas reaches his car at the other end of the bridge and buries himself in Susan's embrace. Schwartz scrambles under the bridge and plays back a portion of Vargas's wiretap: the part where Pete accuses Hank of planting false evidence in criminal cases. Quinlan, lying nearby, hears that accusation by his best friend, whom he has just killed. These three actions, involving Miguel/Susan, Schwartz, and Quinlan, are shown in separate shots. The characters are emotionally isolated from one another. Then Welles *juxtaposes* separate emotions, to the same dramatic effect. The shadowy figure of Tanya, calling out to Hank in an open display of concern, runs past the comparatively brightly lit Vargases, embracing in their car. Happy and tragic relationships pass in the night, oblivious of each other. In the next shot Miguel and Susan drive away, towards "home."

James Naremore claims that Susan and Tanya "embody all the stereotypes of female sexuality in popular art." "Wildness" versus "domesticity." "Blonde and youthfully voluptuous" versus "dark and ageless." "Spunky, rational, and naive" versus "mysterious and world weary." "Wife" versus "prostitute" (Naremore, p. 156). Their only appearance together in the same shot brings this duality into stark focus. But who can say what Tanya *was* when she was Susan's age. Could they be mirror images of each other, like Quinlan and Miguel, separated only by the ravages of time and experience?

A close-up of the mortally wounded Hank Quinlan, listening to the taped playback of his final, lethal moments with Pete, includes Tanya calling out to him from the bridge in the background. He doesn't hear her. Rising unsteadily to his feet in an extreme low angle shot that accentuates his instability, he hears his own recorded murder of Menzies. A zoom-in close-up of the tape machine emphasizes its continuing role in the drama, long after Vargas abandoned it in favor of Susan and home.

From an overhead shot looking down over Menzies's body, we see Hank standing below the bridge, looking up. "Pete, that's the second bullet I stopped for you," he says, referring to the leg injury he suffered while saving Pete's life years earlier. A reminder of the debt Pete owed him. The "second" bullet was the one Pete fired into him to prevent the murder of Vargas. Conveniently overlooked by Quinlan is the bullet fired between the other two—the one with which he mortally wounded Pete, who can no longer debate the point. But blood silently dripping from Pete's hand down onto Hank's speaks eloquently for the dead man, undercutting Quinlan's desperate attempt to balance the score.

Clutching his guilty, bloody hand to his chest, Quinlan staggers backwards and falls dead into the river, where he floats, prominent belly up, amidst the debris there. Intercut with this tragic, pathetic resolution to Hank's life are a shot of Tanya reaching the riverbank a moment too late to comfort him, and Schwartz closing the cover of the tape recording that seals Quinlan's professional doom. In Hank's final moments of life everything he cared about either failed him, deserted him, or was stripped from him. Like Charles Foster Kane, he became a monster who had to be destroyed. But he was not *always* a monster. Earlier glimpses of a nobler Hank Quinlan allow us to mourn his passing.

In a kind of postscript, Schwartz and Tanya offer very different informal eulogies for Quinlan, still shown floating in the river. Schwartz reveals that Manolo Sanchez confessed to killing Rudy Linnekar and the stripper. Quinlan's intuition was right after all, making it unnecessary for Hank to have framed him, and set in motion his own downfall.

Tanya keeps her eye on Quinlan's floating body off screen. She is unmoved by Schwartz's summary of the Sanchez/Linnekar case, or the ironic implications it has for Hank. Having no faith in the legal system, she is more concerned with the dignity of an old friend and former lover. "Isn't somebody going to come and take him away?" Noticing her concern, Schwartz remarks, "You really liked him, didn't you?" But this is too intimate a question for the emotionally defensive Tanya. She deflects it by commenting that *Menzies* loved Quinlan, even though he killed him. She understands the horror and the courage of what Menzies did.

Schwartz sympathetically describes Quinlan as a great detective. Less sentimental, even in the presence of Hank's corpse, Tanya adds, "And a lousy cop." But Schwartz, like the reporters who press Thompson to provide them with a definitive assessment of Charles Foster Kane at the end of *Citizen Kane*, is not satisfied with Tanya's ambiguous assessment of Hank. "Is that all you have to say for him?" With no change in her facial expression, and without even glancing at the Deputy District Attorney, she offers a vague hint of much more. "He was some kind of a man," she says in an isolated close-up, as though speaking more to herself than to Schwartz. Antiquated pianola music emerges softly on the soundtrack, implying a thousand reasons why the usually cynical Tanya would say something so unabashedly sentimental about Hank Quinlan. Her reasons, like Hank's faded virtues, are buried in the past. We catch only a fleeting glimpse of them, as Bernstein does of his mysterious woman in white in *Citizen Kane*. Joseph McBride interprets Tanya's final attitude towards Quinlan as "laconic," with "neither sympathy nor condemnation" (McBride, p.139). On the contrary, I see in her a brief, nostalgic resurgence of the passion she was capable of feeling many years earlier. But it is a resurgence quickly snuffed out by the reality of Hank's death, which leaves her once again alone in a cold world.

Tanya, like Quinlan, Kane, the Ambersons, the Morgans, the Bannisters, Falstaff, and other characters in Welles's movies, is heavily burdened by the past. Knowing that opinions about people fade away and/or change over time, she undercuts her own tribute to Quinlan. "What does it matter what you say about people." Hank is dead, and Tanya arrived too late to let him know that she still gives a damn. She failed him.

Pulling her black coat (in effect, her mourning shroud) tighter around her to protect herself from the night breeze, Tanya turns and walks away from Schwartz, from the camera, from us, and from the world at large. Schwartz bids her a compassionate "Goodbye." She turns back briefly to acknowledge his kindness, then continues on her way. The pianola music that holds a thousand memories for her provides warm counterpoint to the blackness of the night, the coldly inanimate oil derrick ahead of her, and the bits of debris blowing across the road behind her. Also visible, far in the distance on the left side of the screen, is a tiny light. A light from Tanya's house? The Vargases return to their home after their nightmare. Tanya previously advised Hank to return home. Home is a small, imperfect haven in an immense, indifferent, sometimes inhospitable world. Tanya gradually disappears into the darkness, and presumably back into the fiercely guarded privacy in which Hank Quinlan found her earlier in the film. The camera cranes up slightly as we watch her go, adding to our melancholy sense of being disconnected from her life.

In the re-edited version of the movie, all of *Touch of Evil*'s credits appear at the end, overlayed by a repeat of some of Henry Mancini's darker music from the score, providing nice counterpoint to the sentiment expressed by Tanya and her pianola. The soundtrack and we return to the sinister, confusing, larger world from which Tanya and Hank Quinlan sought refuge.

5

The Trial: Waking into Nightmare

Orson Welles's 1962 adaptation of Franz Kafka's novel *The Trial* has garnered perhaps a wider divergence of critical opinion than any of his other movies. Some rank it at or near the bottom of his list of achievements: Francois Truffaut, John Russell Taylor, and Bosley Crowther. Others place it near the top: Peter Cowie, Frank Brady, and David Thomson. And a third group judges it either a qualified success or an interesting failure: James Naremore, Joseph McBride, and Peter Bogdanovich.

A quick reading of Kafka's novel after watching the film reveals a surprising degree of similarity between them. Much of Kafka's dialog and many of his scenes remain intact in the movie, though Welles freely reassigns that dialog and rearranges the order of those scenes. An extensive comparison between the two versions is beyond the scope of this book. But noteworthy are some of the changes Welles makes in the story to reinforce the guilt of the protagonist — not necessarily of the crime with which he is charged, whatever that might be, but of hypocrisy. For example, the characters of K's neighbor, Miss Burstner, and a cabaret singer/prostitute, as described in the novel, are combined in the film. K uses Miss Burstner's shady reputation to his own advantage on several occasions. Welles's protagonist is often a petty man. Sometimes he is more of a coward than is Kafka's hero, especially when groveling in the presence of his boss at work. On the other hand, sometimes he is more courageous than Kafka's original, as when he faces death at the hands of the state. The character of the Advocate, too, is more extreme at both ends of the scale in the movie than in the novel.

Regarding Welles's aesthetic choices in *The Trial*, critical opinion is again divided. Charles Higham quibbles, "The photography, which should be subtly gray, is merely flat and textureless" (Higham, p.161). James Naremore objects to the director's blending of multiple architectural styles resulting in a "nonspecific totalitarianism" that dilutes the film's satire (Naremore, p.201). David R. Slavitt, on the other hand, praises Welles's choice of settings as "truly Kafkaesque, sinister and whimsical, and all the more sinister for being whimsical" (Slavitt, pp.628–629). Ernest Callenbach likes the film's "melange" of old and new settings, describing it as "the landscape of totalitarian nightmare" and for the most part "stunningly successful" (Callenbach, p.40).

The same qualities condemned as inappropriate by some critics are applauded as highly effective by others. Which does not make fools of them all. It merely confirms that there are potentially many different ways to film a given story, and many different ways of perceiving and responding to those choices. Reacting to criticism by Peter Bogdanovich, Welles himself indirectly addressed Naremore's charge of nonspecificity. "I suppose the film's greatest weakness is its attempt at universality. Perhaps on one level a picture always loses by being deliberately universal" (Welles/Bogdanovich, p.281). This statement may read like a concession, but the words "suppose," "perhaps," and "on one level" subtly challenge those viewers who prefer their stories be tied to a specific time and place.

My own view is that Welles's polyglot settings, necessitated in part by a lack of money, contribute to his dramatic purpose in a least two ways. First, by broadening the movie's definition of totalitarianism through a certain amount of abstraction. The numbered, half-clothed prisoners standing outside the court building as K arrives for his official interrogation are ghostly reminders of not only the Nazi concentration camps, but of *all* such camps (Welles/Bogdanovich, p.281). Second, by generating in the viewer (at least *this* viewer) a feeling of disorientation commensurate with Joseph K's confused, frustrating dealings with the law and with his fellow individuals.

Tomasso Albinoni's "Adagio" plays over *The Trial*'s opening credits. Slow, somber, and unvarying, it sets a pessimistic tone before the story begins. Extending past the credits, it reinforces our impression of the Prolog as a parable of implacable Fate. Pin-screen images supply an abstract, static version of Joseph K's visually fluid nightmare to come. The parable features a Man and a Guard, whose antiquated costumes are vaguely drawn from a distant past. They stand before an arched opening in a symmetrical stone wall, through which bright light streams from a source on the other side. The wall, the gateway, and the light are simplified, metaphorical representations of the barriers to and promise of legal justice. Welles's solemn narration amplifies the imagery's mythical quality. We *feel* we are experiencing a fundamental truth about the human condition, just as *Citizen Kane*'s "News on the March" seemed, at first glance, a comprehensive and truthful portrait of Charles Foster Kane. Both of those impressions are challenged by subsequent events.

The Man, the Guard, and the Law are broad, generic categories which presumably explain the characters and situations portrayed in the larger story to come. But in that role they are inadequate. Joseph K does not always play the part of the Man seeking access to the Law. Sometimes he behaves more like the Guard, obstructing and browbeating others weaker than himself. And the Prolog as allegorical Truth is further called into question late in the film when it plays a specific role in the action rather than merely commenting on that action from a sanitary distance.

If the Prolog is not everything it pretends to be, it nevertheless offers insights into what we later see and hear. Losing faith in due process, the Man tries to bribe the Guard to let him through the gate. The Guard claims to accept those bribes not out of greed but as a favor to the Man, "so that you will not feel that you have left something undone." Corruption disguised as compassion. In the story that follows, Joseph K's lawyer, Hastler, similarly rationalizes selfish behavior. The Prolog's gloomy portrait of the power of Fate over the aspirations of individual man sets the stage for Joseph K's struggle against the State. Influenced by the Prolog, we *expect* him to fail. And for awhile he too embraces the myth of hopelessness.

Background music shifts from Albinoni to something modern, atonal, and vaguely sinister. The transition from one musical style to another is fuzzy, which is appropriate for a story about barely decipherable events, ambiguous motives, and fickle passions. The music fades out as the Prolog ends, but sneaks back in as the next scene begins, with "real" characters enacting a situation similar to the parable of the Man, the Guard, and the Law.

The narrator tells us, "It has been said that the logic of this story is the logic of a dream ... of a nightmare." In a nightmare the impression of reality is shaped by the anxieties of the dreamer. Anxieties that may echo legitimate concerns, but may also distort perception. The appearance of things in the story that follows is partly shaped by the emotions of protagonist Joseph K, whose point of view is not always shared by Welles.

Lying on a bed in his rented room, Joseph K awakens into rather than out of a nightmare he had no idea was possible in real life, despite later evidence that many of his fellow citizens have already experienced it. By seeing K in close-up, we share his circumscribed, self-centered point of view as he regains consciousness. By viewing his head upside down and from an oblique angle, we share his disorientation and bewilderment at the off screen disturbance that awakens him. Peter Cowie suggests that everything we see in the movie is presented through K's eyes, distorting our perception of otherwise normal people, events, and locations (Cowie, p.168). This would make *The Trial* similar to Robert Wiene's *The Cabinet of Dr. Caligari* (1919). Welles rejects that interpretation, but concedes that *The Trial* "is suppose to project a feeling of formless anguish, and that anguish is a kind of dream which makes you wake up sweating and whining," and to some extent distorts your perception of things outside yourself (Welles/Bogdanovich, pp.277 and 282).

Joseph K is awakened by the sound of someone entering his room through a door connecting it with the room of his neighbor, Miss Burstner. A low angle shot from K's vantage point conveys his apprehension. The door between the rooms towers over us in a threatening manner, thanks in part to high contrast lighting. A reverse angle shot of K sitting up in bed shows a painting of a nude woman on the wall behind him. Perhaps an indication of what he was dreaming about before his rude awakening. Later events suggest that he *is* preoccupied with sex, sometimes to the detriment of his legal defense, and in the present scene contributing to his false appearance of guilt.

Joseph K sits on the edge of his bed while the camera swings in behind him. We view the invasion of his room with him. The mysterious stranger pulls open the drapes, flooding the room with sunlight while verbally prying into K's private life. When K gets out of bed the camera's point of view changes. Now we scrutinize K, looking vulnerable in his pajamas and bare feet, partly from the perspective of the intruder, a plain-clothed police Inspector. K sits back down on the bed to put on his socks. The camera assumes a more detached point of view.

No less than imagery and music, dialog in *The Trial* evokes a world that is badly fragmented and inconsistent. Misunderstanding, evasion, and deception plague communication between characters. Upon hearing the door to his room open, K logically calls out the name of Miss Burstner. Who else would come through that door? The Inspector, as he does throughout the interrogation, answers a question with a question. He probes for information without providing any in return. And he frequently misinterprets K's words. "Miss Burstner frequently comes through that door during the night?" he inquires, implying something suspicious going on between them. It is a gross over-interpretation of K's innocent and reasonable assumption, and perhaps a deliberate tactic to confuse the suspect, rendering him more susceptible to further interrogation. Only by sheer coincidence does the Inspector touch on what we later discover to be K's sexual yearning for Miss Burstner. From K's point of view the eerily calm policeman seems almost a mind reader.

Miscommunication continues as K nervously calls out into the hallway for his landlady, Mrs. Grubach, to come rescue him from the intruder. "You were expecting Mrs. Grubach?" the Inspector asks, again implying something incriminating about K's behavior. Reacting to this disturbing presence in his private sanctuary, K alternately cowers and fights back in anger. He retreats to a shady, less exposed part of the room to change into his street clothes and thereby restore some tactical balance with his foe. The Inspector fires more questions at him from nearby, his dark figure etched against a sunbathed wall. The alarm clock on the dresser reads 6:14 a.m. Not a pleasant hour to receive an uninvited, inquisitive stranger.

Out of growing fear Joseph K defends himself by trying to divert police attention elsewhere. Informed that Miss Burstner is not in her room, K remarks that she often gets home late. "Very late, very late indeed. You are the police?" He not only informs the Inspector that Miss Burstner keeps unusual hours, he conveniently assumes that fact makes her a more likely target than himself for a police investigation. He cautions the Inspector not to jump to any conclusions about his neighbor, yet encouraged exactly that by mentioning her late working hours. And he helpfully adds that Miss Burstner will return home soon and then be able to answer any questions the Inspector may want to ask her. Clearly Joseph K wants to divert the spotlight of police scrutiny onto someone else. *Anyone* else. Even the woman he may have been dreaming about a short time earlier. But the Inspector refuses to play along with K's hopeful scenario. "Well, you certainly didn't come here to see me. Did you?" K inquires with a little too much surprise in his voice. Predictably, the Inspector answers a question with another question, exacerbating rather than soothing K's anxiety.

Feeling cornered again, K turns aggressive, questioning the legality of the Inspector's intrusion by pointing out that he hasn't shown K his identity papers. "Isn't that for *you* to do?" the Inspector calmly replies, transforming K's thrust into a counterthrust. K insists otherwise, yet tacitly yields the point by handing over his papers. Pursuing his advantage, the Inspector asks why K doesn't finish dressing, which is an unreasonable question since K pauses for only a moment while retrieving his identity papers for the policeman. But it makes K nervous anyway, sending him off on a verbal tangent about the disruption of his "regular habits." Like most of us, K is a creature of habit. And when his routine is disrupted, he loses composure.

Playing tag team, the Inspector is replaced by an assistant whom neither we nor K realized was on the premises. Both policemen wear suits, ties, trench coats, and hats. In appearance they could be American FBI agents circa 1962. Like his superior, Assistant Inspector 1 disorients K by misinterpreting what K says: in this instance about preferring not to get dressed in a cold hallway. K physically retreats from his new adversary while verbally confronting the policeman's challenge. But the policeman has already adopted a new angle of attack, informing K he needn't bother getting dressed because he isn't going anywhere. He is under arrest. K demands to know the charge against him. That would give him something solid to deal with. But the Assistant Inspector evades the matter by claiming that only his now absent superior is authorized to disclose that information.

As if on cue, Assistant Inspector 2 enters the room while quoting from the official rule book governing encounters between police and suspect. In effect, he reinforces his partner's evasion of K's question about the charges. K, tucking in his shirt, again walks away from a new challenge, until Assistant 1 comments enviously on the nice shirts in K's dresser drawer. K returns to the fray to defend his property, but quickly backs away again. Visually the two policemen surround him. They point out to him that since the property of an arrested suspect is routinely impounded, K's shirts will disappear in a sea of bureaucratic corruption, and would do him more good in the hands of friends than of strangers. Following the advice of Elsa Bannister in *The Lady from Shanghai*, the policemen have made terms with the wickedness of the world and have adopted some of its ways. One of them pokes K with his finger to reinforce his point. Intimidated, K makes a feeble, unsuccessful grab for his shirts, then retreats without them.

Avoiding eye contact with his adversaries, K tries to make the whole unpleasant affair go away by speculating to himself that it might be only a practical joke perpetrated by his coworkers from the office. Assistant Inspector 2 casually informs him that several of those coworkers are currently in Miss Burstner's room. So *is* the arrest of K just a practical joke? As it turns out, no. But for a weird moment anything seems possible. And the explanation offered by the police, that K's coworkers were brought along to make his late arrival at the office seem more "unabusive," does nothing to clarify the situation. Typically, Joseph K tries to restore meaning and order to his crumbling world by petulantly correcting the policeman's faulty vocabulary. But in his anxiety, K himself errs, replacing the faulty "unabusive" with "unobstrusive" instead of the correct "unobtrusive."

A frontal shot of the white-shirted protagonist opening the door to Miss Burstner's room includes the darker, sinister figures of the policemen bracketing him. But a reverse angle shot from K's point of view depicts his three coworkers, Rabenstein, Kublick, and Kaminer, as timid, unimpressive men, embarrassed to be caught examining a framed photograph belonging to the room's absent tenant.

Assistant Inspector 1 enters the shot of the coworkers and retrieves the photograph. K then enters the same shot and aggressively takes that photo from the policeman — something he failed to do with his shirts. Rabenstein averts his eyes from K, just as K earlier avoided his interrogators. The tracking camera, shooting from a low angle, effectively conveys the protagonist's boldness. In the next shot he again enters the camera frame from outside, but this time slowly, wringing his hands and averting his eyes even as he tries to challenge Assistant Inspector 2's poor grammar and logic. The other policeman now enters the frame too, riding to his colleague's rescue by undermining K's argument. K's coworkers too crowd into the picture. K is surrounded by the enemy. He tries to laugh off the whole episode as trivial. But the return of unsettling background music, plus a subjective shot, from K's perspective, of his three coworkers now looking dour and menacing, betrays his sudden loss of confidence. The pendulum of K's emotions keeps swinging back and forth. No sooner is he on the defensive than he turns aggressive again, demanding to know the identity of his accuser.

Ignoring K's demand, as they always do, the two policemen begin to search K's room. Flustered by their brazen violation of his privacy, K incriminates himself while trying to do the opposite. Denying the presence of any subversive or pornographic literature, he then inadvertently refers to his phonograph player as a "pornograph." Sabotaged by his own nervousness. Or maybe it's a Freudian slip, betraying his unspoken sexual preoccupation with Miss Burstner, at whose room he has just gotten an illicit peek while ostensibly defending its sanctity against invaders.

A misunderstanding occurs over the word "ovular," which Assistant Inspector 2 writers in his notebook to describe an oval shape in the floor, concealed under a rug. K objects to the corruption of the word "oval," as he did earlier to "unabusive." But Assistant Inspector 2 misinterprets K's objection as a denial of the very existence of an oval shape in the floor. So K explains that the oval is the outline of a dental chair once used by Mrs. Grubach's now late husband. He calls out to Mrs. Grubach, in the hallway off screen, to come and verify his explanation. But the police, whether to preserve their tactical advantage or out of obedience to police procedure, refuse her admittance.

Closing the door to Miss Burstner's bedroom, thereby isolating their conversation from K's coworkers, Assistant Inspector 1 offers K some confidential advice. K assumes he is being hit up for money, and refuses to play along. The policeman replies, "That's what they all say," which seems to confirm K's assumption. But when K openly accuses them of soliciting a bribe, the policemen vehemently deny it. Whether the accusation is true or not, the mere *hint* of public scandal gives K a tactical advantage over the two policemen. No longer intimidated by them, for the moment, he exits the room without their permission, reclaims one of his shirts from them, and heads for the kitchen. They meekly trail after him, reduced to addressing him indirectly, through Mrs.Grubach.

But as always, K's confidence blows hot and cold. In the kitchen, where Mrs. Grubach is preparing breakfast for him, K visibly wilts. Facing away from everyone, including the camera, he retreats to a corner, takes a deep breath, and rests his head against a cupboard for support. Off screen, though still audible to K, the policemen tell Mrs. Grubach that K's uncooperative behavior is damaging his case. Apparently he takes their words to heart. K has reclaimed his shirt but lost his nerve.

K and Mrs. Grubach initially avoid eye contact in the kitchen, but for different reasons. Few characters in *The Trial* help others in need without getting something in return. Mrs. Grubach tries to comfort her anxious tenant, presuming him to be innocent of whatever charge has been brought against him. But her every word, glance, and gesture betrays her infatuation with him. She insists a landlady should remain detached about her boarders' personal affairs, but admits that with K she cannot. And by telling him so she curries favor with him. Describing K's arrest as vaguely "abstract," she helps him verbally reduce his legal problem to something unreal, insignificant, and manageable.

Mrs. Grubach's dark-walled dining room seems a world away from the white-walled bedroom where K was interrogated. The landlady's compassion revives the protagonist's confidence. He dismisses his fear of the police as a consequence of surprise and disorientation, adding that "in the office, for instance, I'm ... I'm always prepared." The hitch in his speech betrays a remnant of uneasiness, in spite of his show of bravado. Worse yet, the way he describes his security at the office unwittingly betrays his hypocrisy. No one can "just crash in on me there. I should say not. People sometimes have to wait for weeks before they can get in to where they can speak to my secretary." In other words, K is to some of his clients what the police are, and his future attorney will be, to *him*. We're all tempted to play power games, regardless of our social status.

Self-assured to the point of arrogance now, K foolishly reduces his previous anxiety to his lack of a morning cup of coffee. That is ridiculous. But Mrs. Grubach, pursuing her own agenda, latches onto the topic of coffee to further ingratiate herself with the man of her middle aged dreams. "Coffee is always ready on the stove, Mr. K." Wearing a robe and a hairnet, fussing over K's breakfast and shirt, Mrs. Grubach looks and acts more like a doting mother than a would–be lover. Their separate motivations remain harmonious until clashing over the topic of Miss Burstner, for whom the coffee was originally intended. By criticizing Miss Burstner's "ungodly" work hours, Mrs. Grubach unwittingly betrays her jealousy of a potential rival for the apartment's resident male. Equally ignorant of his own selfish motives for doing so, K defends Miss Burstner as though on principle. More likely it is because he is fond of her — the same reason Mrs. Grubach defended *his* innocence. And yet earlier, in his bedroom, K chose to assume that the police had come to question Miss Burstner instead of himself. On that occasion self-preservation took precedence over physical attraction. Not wanting to antagonize K, Mrs. Grubach prudently yields the point about Miss Burstner. Peter Cowie sees Mrs. Grubach as one of only two "normal" characters in the movie (Cowie,pp.170–171). Welles himself claimed to agree (Welles/Bogdanovich, p.285). But however minor her crimes in comparison to the crimes of others,

Mrs. Grubach does victimize Miss Burstner, just as K is the victim of others, and others of K.

K's defense of Miss Burstner turns aggressive when he learns from his landlady that his coworkers still occupy her room. Outraged at their continued violation of her privacy, and emboldened by his easy intimidation of Mrs. Grubach, he storms out of the dining room and into Miss Burstner's room, where Kublick, Kaminer, and Rabanstein are indeed still rifling through her private things. He orders them to leave. Mrs. Grubach enters with coffee for the three strangers, mistakenly thinking to please K by pleasing his acquaintances. At K's request, though confused by it, she ushers the three men out.

Standing in a doorway leading to the balcony, K speculates that his uncommunicative coworkers are police informers. Visibly wilting under the burden of that new fear, he retreats out onto the balcony, where he finds the Inspector waiting for him. The surprise of that discovery shocks him out of his paranoia and turns him aggressive again. He is riding an emotional roller coaster, and the Inspector does not make the ride any smoother. Undermining the protagonist's newfound courage, he points out that K's behavior is attracting the attention of people in the adjacent apartment building. Curious, anonymous faces *are* watching him from behind the security of windows across the courtyard. The camera shows them only from a distance, emphasizing the emotional distance between neighbors. They may be entertained or even concerned about K's arrest, but not enough to get directly involved.

K demands the return of his identity papers, which he so meekly handed over to the Inspector earlier. The Inspector questions the wisdom of and motivation behind that demand rather than challenging the demand itself. And when K requests information about the case against him, the Inspector, walking away from the suspect, again avoids giving a direct answer. But K follows him, now *demanding* to know the charge against him. The Inspector deliberately misinterprets that demand as an implied claim of innocence. Frustrated, K affirms that claim, which is absurd because he doesn't yet know the charge. Then he transforms that weak defense into a stronger offence by threatening to bring charges of abuse and bribery solicitation against the police, and to enlist the help of a lawyer who happens to be a family friend.

Disdainfully walking away from the Inspector after issuing his threat, K is lured back by the policeman's announcement of Miss Burstner's arrival on the street below. Sex replaces moral outrage as K's new priority. Informed that he will have to accompany the Inspector to police headquarters in order to file his complaint, K dismisses the whole thing as unnecessary. He obviously prefers to stay and talk to Miss Burstner. But the Inspector will not let the matter drop, in effect transforming a tactical liability into an advantage.

Reading from a pad containing his handwritten notes and those of his colleagues, the Inspector remarks on K's use of the word "pornograph." This encounter between detective and suspect ends on a note of absurd miscommunication as they haggle over the word "ovular." Both men agree there is no such word, yet cannot agree on how it got into the Inspector's note pad, and what relevance it has to K's legal case. The Inspector departs apparently convinced that K, rather that one of his own colleagues, used the word first, in a misguided effort to deflect the investigation. K's attempt to correct that false impression results, to his enormous frustration, in the word making a *second* appearance in the official record, and again as *his* quote. Babbling something about K's "foolish babbling," the Inspector leaves with a false but intransigent impression that the suspect has seriously incriminated himself during interrogation.

During K's verbal joust with the Inspector, Mrs. Grubach joins them on the balcony.

Regarding her as an ally, K tells her to stay. Both landlady and tenant are dressed in light-colored clothing, matching the color of the balcony. The Inspector wears black. Visually he is the intruder here. But after he departs, the alliance between K and Mrs. Grubach founders once again on the topic of Miss Burstner. Unaware of K's attraction to the other woman, the landlady tries to score points with him by making excuses for the presence of so shady a character as Miss Burstner in their apartment. To her surprise the maneuver offends K, who may be no less a prude than Mrs. Grubach but whose sexual arousal overrides and may even be piqued by his neighbor's questionable reputation. Instead of admitting his attraction to Miss Burstner, he offers up a high-minded defense of her civil rights. Physically separating himself from Mrs. Grubach, just as the Inspector earlier walked away from *him*, K indignantly refuses to listen to her reasons for criticizing Miss Burstner. She claims she was only trying to protect the reputation of her house and of her other boarders. Which, like K's defense of Miss Burstner, is not entirely honest. She was also trying to curry favor with K by discrediting a potential rival. But it doesn't matter anyway, because K leaves the balcony and closes the sliding glass door behind him, withdrawing inside his room to finish dressing. He briefly returns to the door to defend his neighbor's honor, informing Mrs. Grubach that if she evicts Miss Burstner on moral grounds she might as well evict him as well. The insincerity of K's indignance (we see no evidence that he gives up his room with Mrs. Grubach after Miss Burstner is evicted) is humorously punctuated by Welles when K violently pulls down the window blind to cut off visual contact with the exiled Mrs. Grubach, and it collapses to the floor. Not only is K's defense of Miss Burstner selfishly motivated, it is less committed than it seems.

K's relations with Miss Burstner are as complicated by conflicting urges as are his relations with Mrs. Grubach. They meet in the hallway between their rooms. A claustrophobic ceiling and walls, contrasting patches of light and shadow, plus carefully chosen camera angles visually enhance the great emotional distance between their private worlds. K's timidity is one measure of that distance. Muted jazz plays on the soundtrack. Fading in and out, it is subjectively attuned to K's furtive attraction to Miss Burstner. The entire, extraordinary score by Jean Ledrut is made up of half-formed motifs in a variety of styles. Like the reasoning and feelings of the characters, nothing is fully developed or consistent.

K lingers in the hallway to talk with his neighbor, but cannot think of much to say. She generously provides him with a topic, revealing that today is her birthday. He bungles that opportunity by asking if that is why she arrived home later than usual. She is annoyed by his interest in her private affairs. K apologizes profusely. She seems pacified, even a bit intrigued by his shyness and sensitivity. But that interest competes with her fatigue after a long night's work. She bids him goodnight and retreats to her room, closing the door behind her.

Impelled by sexual attraction, and perhaps sensing from her forgiving smile that she might be receptive, K walks down the long hallway to Miss Burstner's room, knocks on the door, and then opens it without being invited inside. The unexpected sight of Miss Burstner undressing causes him to immediately withdraw, again with apologies. He returns to his own room and closes the door. Yet his mistake yields unexpected dividends. Answering a knock at his door, he finds Miss Burstner standing there in her nightgown. She took the trouble to follow him, and doesn't appear to be angry. K's fragile confidence recovers.

Joining Miss Burstner in the open doorway, K politely invites her inside. But she is offended by what she assumes to be a sexual overture. K stammers and fidgets but in a roundabout way defends himself by interpreting her knock at his door as a sexual signal. If that is true, why shouldn't she interpret *his* earlier knock at *her* door in the same way, regardless of his apologies to the contrary? The whole scene is a delicate negotiation between two very different people. K repeats his invitation to enter. Battling competing desires of her own, Miss Burstner contemplates accepting, then declines in favor of badly needed sleep.

Miss Burstner casually remarks on what a "long, hard night" it's been. K concurs, thinking of his own ordeal with the police. She is irritated by his concurrence, misinterpreting it as another intrusion into her privacy. He corrects that false impression. "I was talking about myself." She then appropriates *that* remark to make a cynical observation about *her* male customers at the nightclub, and perhaps about men in general. "That's what they all do. What else do they ever talk about. So give me a rest, will you." In a broader sense, Miss Burstner's complaint applies to every character in the story, including herself. They all exemplify Charlie Kane's jaded philosophy of love: "A toast ... to love on my terms. Those are the only terms anybody ever knows. His own."

In addition to fatigue, Miss Burstner sites fear of eviction by Mrs. Grubach as a reason for declining K's invitation. Both of them glance warily in the direction of their landlady's room. For a moment they are of like mind. But the moment quickly passes. Miss Burstner returns to her own room, saying she has forgotten what she wanted to ask K. He then transforms her excuse for leaving into an excuse to follow her, suggesting that the question might come back to her. "Nothing ever comes back to me," she complains, reshaping his specific point into a broader declaration of cynicism. Then she cynically mocks her own cynicism. "Big statement! Shut up, everybody!" she says as she flops into bed, too exhausted to sustain her train of thought.

The disconnected conversation continues as K misinterprets "Shut up" as a directive aimed specifically at him. Apologizing, he starts to leave her room, until she gives him an excuse to return. Weary of K's constant apologizing, she complains about it (*her* constant habit). Without thinking, he starts to apologize for apologizing too much, then realizes the absurdity of doing so and stops himself. He agrees with Miss Burstner's previous comment about nobody giving a damn. But then he turns that comment against *her*. "I know *you* don't." And yet while casting himself as her victim he surreptitiously, perhaps unwittingly, maneuvers to take advantage of her, closing her door to secure their privacy. Mindful of Mrs. Grubach's hostility, and not as wearily inattentive as K assumed, she orders him to leave it open. He obeys, at first. Then, ignoring the trouble it might cause Miss Burstner, he closes it again when she turns her back. He sits down next to her on the bed, without an invitation. The camera closes in to capture their growing intimacy. The ornate curtains, bedspread, and wallpaper in Miss Burstner's room suggest, perhaps falsely, a fuller life than do the bare walls of K's room and Mrs. Grubach's dining room. Scattered about the walls and dresser are many photographs, implying emotional attachments to family and friends. In that respect the room resembles Susan Alexander's first apartment in *Citizen Kane*. Through photographs and knickknacks Welles gives us a visual feel for the accumulated emotional baggage of the two women — baggage which neither Joseph K nor Charlie Kane know anything about. But Miss Burstner is neither as young nor as naive as Susan Alexander. She is more akin to Susan Kane at Xanadu, or the El Rancho. And to Tanya in *Touch of Evil*. Both of whom were loath to let anyone intrude on their jealously guarded privacy.

K and Miss Burstner are like two trains traveling along parallel sets of tracks for a short distance but only occasionally intersecting. Even when K agrees with one of her comments the sympathetic connection between them is soon broken because she soon forgets what that comment was. She attributes her forgetfulness to "lousy national champagne," which triggers a new line of conversation and, coincidentally, gives us a new piece of information about the sorry state of society as depicted in *The Trial*.

If K practices deception in this scene, Miss Burstner reveals her own expertise in that area by explaining that her inebriation is the result of a failed attempt to cheat a nightclub customer into paying liquor prices for her to drink tea. K pointlessly apologizes for her lack of success, then reflects on his habit, dating from childhood, of feeling guilty about things he did not do. James Naremore interprets this unwarranted shame as a sign of K's participation in his own dehumanization (Naremore, p.201). Ironically, the protagonist does *not* feel guilty, until late in the movie, about things he should. His confession to Miss Burstner is a rare, honest, brief moment of self-analysis. She lies quietly next to him, listening while offering no cynical counterpoint. Romantic music quietly emerges on the soundtrack. Taking advantage of her emotional and physical proximity, K leans over and kisses her. She responds warmly. But that moment too passes quickly.

When K's half of the conversation turns to the subject of his arrest, Miss Burstner is slow to comprehend. Basking in the glow of their foreplay, she pays little attention to what he says, dismissing it as the product of intoxication. The characters are slightly out of sync, interpreting each other's comments according to their own inclinations and concerns. Miss Burstner is intoxicated. Therefore if K says something that makes little sense to her, he too must be drunk. Until he discloses that he is under arrest. She stops caressing his face and sits up. We can almost hear her mind shifting gears. Romantic music disappears and is replaced by something more ominous and alienated, echoing the unpleasant dissolution of their brief romance.

Just as she earlier exhibited mixed feelings about K's shyness, Miss Burstner is alternately intrigued and put off by his arrest. At first she questions the truth of his claim. And she does so in terms rooted in her own experience. "It isn't something you suddenly notice, like bleeding gums" says more, in a grotesquely funny way, about her own problems than about K's. She speculates that K may have dreamt his arrest. He insists it is real, pointing out the disarray among photographs of *her* mother on the dresser. She takes offense at the mention of her mother by a comparative stranger. Obviously that is a sensitive, extremely private matter for her. Then her attention returns to K's arrest. She tries to rationalize it out of existence. Maybe it's a gag is the same evasion K tried earlier, reducing his arrest to a practical joke played by coworkers. Or maybe it's the result of a lie told about him by someone else. The point here is that Miss Burstner's view of her neighbor is in flux. Vaguely agreeing with her hypothesis, K assumes he is cultivating a sympathetic ally. Someone with whom he can share and thereby reduce his burden. Instead, he unwittingly feeds her fear of becoming involved with him. She sits on the bed while he sits in a chair. No longer embracing, they drift apart without realizing it.

Expanding on Miss Burstner's comment about lies, K speculates that one of his coworkers might have spread rumors about him. The eagerness in his voice suggests that he is, for the moment, more interested in getting closer to Miss Burstner than in discovering the truth behind his arrest. If so, his effort backfires. Fuelled by K's comment, Miss Burstner infers that his arrest, whether false or not, might involve politics. That thought clearly terrifies her, perhaps because in her profession she often clashes with the police. K tries to reassure her, but it is too late. Their fleeting intimacy collapses under the weight of fear. She pushes him away, angrily questioning why they are having a conversation at all, and why he is in her room. Such a cold rejection of a man she kissed only a short time ago.

So divided are their perspectives at this point in the scene that the two characters disagree about how they got together in the first place. K claims Miss Burstner invited him into her room, which is not true. He followed her there without an invitation. On the other hand, she tolerated his presence. "That's what *you* say!" she retorts. Attempting to restore harmony by casting Miss Burstner as a victim like himself, K notes that during his interrogation her mother's photographs were rudely handled by the police. He even gently props up one of those pictures that she, in her anxiety, accidentally knocks over. Bad move. Miss Burstner will permit absolutely no discussion of her mother, for whatever reasons.

Fear and anger impel Miss Burstner to evict K from her room. She offers an insincere apology for his troubles and then rudely pushes him out of her private sanctuary, slamming shut the double doors that once again divide their rooms and their lives. In his desperation to calm Miss Burstner, K expresses concern that their ruckus might awaken Mrs. Grubach—the same Mrs. Grubach he rudely locked out of *his* room earlier. Full frontal close-ups depict Miss Burstner's fury and K's consternation at this violent end to their briefly promising relationship.

Carrying a birthday cake intended as a peace offering for Miss Burstner, Joseph K enters the office where he works, wending his way between long, symmetrical rows of employees seated at their desks, typing. Anonymous cogs in an immense corporate machine, they are as oblivious of K's private concerns as he is of theirs. If there were communication gaps between K and various characters back at the apartment, they are dwarfed by our first impression in this scene. Pulling back from K as it tracks him through the office, the camera conveys the enormity of the business environment around him. Commenting on this mammoth display of collective conformity and personal isolation is Albinoni's "Adagio," playing loudly to match the din of a thousand typewriters clacking at once. But the discontent implied in the music is not consciously felt by the protagonist or his coworkers, who seem inured to the conditions of their employment. Visible on the floor above the army of typists are a large computer and its white-jacketed technicians—tokens of a new, ascendant technological order.

K curtly informs his secretary that he will attend to waiting clients later. Depositing his cake in a storage closet, K unexpectedly encounters the Deputy Manager there. K is awkward and servile in the presence of his boss, hastily explaining that he didn't want to bring the cake (a token of his private life) into the office and is therefore storing it out of sight. The two men engage in polite small talk about K's romantic problems as they emerge from the closet. K slavishly adopts his boss's stance (hands behind his back) and pace as they walk.

K's relations with the Deputy Manager, like his relations with everyone else in the movie, fluctuate rapidly. At first the boss is sympathetic about his employee's personal problems. But when he sees K's teenage cousin, Irmie, standing outside the office, behind a glass partition, eagerly soliciting K's attention, that sympathy contends with moral disgust. Incorrectly surmising that Irmie is K's mistress, the Deputy Manager is alternately titillated ("We'll have to keep an eye on you, old man.") and shocked ("My God!")—envious and disapproving. Unfortunately K undermines his own credibility by *acting* guilty (his old childhood habit), stammering while trying to clear up the misunderstanding.

Visible through the glass partition and behind Irmie is a row of clients who stand and deferentially doff their hats at K and the Deputy Manager. Like the high court officials who will ignore K's legal plight later in the story, K and the Deputy Manager do not even acknowledge the presence of their clients. So much for K's earlier promise to attend to them "in a minute." Innocent of what the Deputy Manager suspects, K is nevertheless guilty of other crimes, of which he is as yet blissfully unaware.

Embarrassed in front of the boss and perhaps fearful of losing his job, K vents his frustration not only on his waiting clients but also on his secretary, to whom he speaks rudely, and on Irmie, whom he refuses to see. Irmie's dismissal is caused by a misunderstanding between K and the Deputy Manager, for which she is not to blame. Just as K's rude dismissal by Miss Burstner was based on a misunderstanding that was not *his* fault. But K does not yet see the connection between being victimized by and victimizing others in the name of expediency.

The camera shows K's departure in a beautiful low angle long shot. He stands on a platform where his office is situated, elevated above the mass of typists in the background. Above him looms a massive bank of florescent lights. Dressed neatly in his conservative suit, K is at this moment the worst type of corporate man, both bully and bullied. The prominent light fixtures are visual emblems of bureaucratic size, power, and order. A couple years after *The Trial* was released, Stanley Kubrick achieved a similar effect with a huge florescent halo light fixture hanging above the heads of government officials in *Dr. Strangelove*'s War Room. K descends from the platform and walks away, through and past anonymous typists as indifferent to him as he is of them. Background music eerily echoes the emotional dissonance among K, his boss, his secretary, Irmie, and the typists.

Returning home after work, peace offering (cake) in hand, K sees Miss Burstner's packing trunk being dragged out of their apartment building by a Miss Pittl, whose task is made more difficult by a metal brace strapped to her malformed leg. The distant, off screen barking of a dog, repeated during the scene, echoes the hostility between the characters we see. In extreme long shot they are dwarfed by the massive apartment buildings behind them. The camera tracks with them across a barren stretch of open ground. We see other, similar apartment buildings spaced well apart. Sharply etched against the dusk sky, they are double metaphors of collective anonymity and individual isolation—contrary aspects of the human condition in the society depicted in this film.

After the mass emotional disconnection between K and the typists at the office, his one-on-one encounter with Miss Pittl seems like an opportunity for a little human contact and mutual understanding. But it is not to be. Trying to be helpful, K tells Miss Pittl to take his cake, intending to free up his hands so he can pull her trunk. She testily points out that she's got her hands full with the trunk. Either she misunderstands his intention, or pretends to misunderstand it in order to vent her anger at him. Either way, she sets a bad precedent in their brief relationship.

Making a second attempt to help, K offers to phone for a taxi. Miss Pittl declines, petulantly pointing out that not everyone can afford such a luxury. She also refers to K by name. Her hostility towards him is based on an impression she got before meeting him. Miss Pittl is as unjustly rude to K as K was to Irmie and his secretary, as the Deputy Manager and Miss Burstner were to K, and as K was to Mrs. Grubach. The noisy brace on Miss Pittl's leg is as much a symbol of her emotional dysfunction as it is evidence of a physical disability.

Miss Pittl refuses to explain her grudge against K. She deliberately misreads his offers to help her as a cruel attack on her physical disability. In short, she adopts the role of martyr without K having done anything to deserve it—that we know of. But if K is a victim thus far in the scene, he unwittingly turns aggressor when he speculates on why Miss Burstner gave up her room. Incorrectly flattering himself that she did so because he kissed her, K questions Miss Burstner's right to take offense at that kiss by casting aspersions on her moral character, describing her with vaguely defined scorn as a "woman of the world" employed in a nightclub. As though that said it all. He once scolded Mrs. Grubach for casting the same aspersions. But *then* he was defending the woman with whom he was infatuated. *Now* he is defending *himself*. Miss Pittl, in turn, challenges K's moral character by refusing to discuss his sex life in public. Ironically, she behaves as prudishly in defense of Miss Burstner as Mrs. Grubach did while attacking Miss Burstner. Both women, and K, exploit propriety for personal gain.

K raises his voice out of sheer frustration. Miss Pittl assumes, incorrectly, that he is yelling at *her*. Eventually K learns about Miss Burstner's eviction. "I guess I *am* responsible," he reluctantly concedes. Perhaps K brought about the eviction when he slyly closed the door to her room while remaining inside — a violation of the house rules. As their brief conversation comes to an end, K and Miss Pittl are shown in separate, reverse angle shots. No mutual understanding has been achieved. K doesn't even learn Miss Pittl's name. Thus even at a social level far beneath legal matters of state, miscommunication is rampant.

Shadows part like theater curtains to reveal, not a stage performance but an audience *watching* a stage performance. The audience is *our* show. Welles never shows us what is happening on stage. In a scene in *Citizen Kane* he shows us only what is happening *backstage*, and nothing of the audience. But we do get an *aural* impression of the stage production attended by Joseph K. It sounds like a musical comedy very much at odds with the grim circumstances of K's life and, judging by their facial expressions, the lives of other audience members. Like the stage comedy production in *The Third Man*, this one offers escape from personal troubles.

K is sandwiched between two older women. One is asleep. The other wears a sour expression on her face. No one is having much fun. Then an attractive young woman seated behind K taps him on the shoulder. Things appear to be looking up. But to his disappointment she only passes on a message from someone off screen. Worse yet, that someone turns out to be the Inspector, whom K joins in the theater lobby. Like most settings in *The Trial*, this one is both mammoth and dilapidated, dwarfing individual characters but also symptomatic of the sad state of public facilities and the bureaucracies behind them. The Inspector leads K out of the theater, through unrecognizable structures of brick, plaster, riveted metal, and wood, and into yet another giant room whose function is unclear. Parts of an endless and confusing labyrinth that is the State. And the human heart. There are no clear cut lines between private, corporate, entertainment, and government facilities in this film, any more than there are between the private and public lives of its characters. Everything overlaps. The raucous sounds of musical comedy are replaced by less congenial background music echoing that confused landscape.

Despite interrupting K's recreational outing, the Inspector claims to be doing K a favor by scheduling his appearance before the interrogation commission after working hours. He has filled out an official form in K's name and drawn K a map of the interrogation site. But these dubious favors are offset by his appointment of two plain-clothed policemen to accompany K to that site. Their silence and dour expressions give them all the charm of Hitler's Gestapo or Stalin's NKVD. Is it their mission to help K find the interrogation site or to make sure he gets there whether he wants to or not? K assumes they are spies. The Inspector's denial is not reassuring. "No. They aren't gonna follow you. That isn't their job" suggests an even more sinister assignment. Or is that *our* misinterpretation of the Inspector's phlegmatic manner and sinister looking face, which comes courtesy of some high contrast lighting?

A large statue outside the government building where K's interrogation is to be held is draped in a white sheet. Is it a statue of Justice, now irrelevant in this age of *injustice*? The shroud implies disuse, like a sheet covering a discarded piece of furniture. Does the statue depict a religious or political figure currently out of favor with the government? Welles once claimed that *The Trial* contains no symbolism, then conceded, "It's full of do-it-yourself stuff. You can make your own symbols if you want to" (Welles/Bogdanovich, p.278). The shrouded statue tempts us to speculate but refuses to verify. Like the mysterious monolith in Kubrick's *2001: A Space Odyssey*, it is a mirror held up to the audience.

Judging by its upraised arms, the concealed statue appears to be appealing for something. The camera tilts down to a crowd of mostly elderly, gaunt, mute individuals gathered at the foot of the statue, which now seems to offer a silent appeal on their behalf. Are these human figures K's fellow accused, inured to the hopelessness of their legal cases? Or are they already condemned and awaiting sentence? In either case they are reduced to living statues, martyrs to the confusion and corruption of the Law. Half-clothed, carrying bundles of their meager belongings (the rest no doubt confiscated by the State), and wearing numbered placards around their necks, they call to mind Holocaust victims awaiting their fate in Nazi concentration camps. They stare blankly, at nothing and no one in particular—each absorbed in a hell of his or her own. The sound of a breeze and visible ripples in the sheet draping the statue emphasize, by way of contrast, the frozen, hopeless aspect of these people.

K, still relatively hopeful about *his* case, weaves his way through this eerie, three-dimensional frieze of despair and towards the building where he will plead his case. This action recalls a previous image in which he obliviously weaved his way through a mass of lower caste coworkers at the office. He does not comprehend the despair of the people gathered at the foot of the statue, but at least he is vaguely disturbed by it. The connection between their fate and his is dawning on him. Albinoni's "Adagio" returns to the soundtrack. K's understanding is just beginning to catch up with its tragic impression of implacable Fate.

Like every other setting in the movie, the courthouse is a virtual maze. Inside that maze K encounters a woman named Hilda, the wife of a courtroom guard, washing clothes as though she were at home. Is this a private residence or a public building? Again the distinction between private and public lives is obscured. Partly for budgetary reasons, Welles filmed this and many other scenes at an abandoned railway station in Paris. It was an inspired improvisation. If the police can invade K's bedroom and a public theater, and later a storage room at K's office, why shouldn't a courtroom guard and his wife set up housekeeping in the courthouse? Many characters in *The Trial* exploit their public status for personal gain.

With no word of explanation, Hilda directs K to a nearby courtroom. We enter that room with K, via a tracking camera. The effect is intimidating. The courtroom is large and crowded. K, no longer the defiant, sarcastic rebel he played with the Inspector in the previous scene, reflexively backs away. But Hilda shuts the door behind him and a young boy (who is *he?*) pulls him by the hand towards the Examining Magistrate's rostrum. Both Hilda and the boy seem to know more about his legal situation than K does. And the unsympathetic stares of a crowd that seems to be expecting him do nothing to alleviate his anxiety. K is instructed to step up onto the rostrum. It is an awkward climb to a narrow, exposed perch that seems designed to put the defendant on the defensive. This has the look of a Stalinist show trial. But our initial impression of a vast conspiracy against K is suddenly dispelled when the Examining Magistrate identifies him as a house painter. Did the police arrest the wrong man? Was it all just a monstrous, bureaucratic snafu? K declares that he is not the expected house painter. The crowd erupts in laughter. The same crowd that seemed so hostile and intimidating to K when he entered suddenly becomes a source of emotional comfort and tactical advantage to him.

Emboldened by his adversary's blunder, K openly challenges the legitimacy of his arrest and interrogation. Speaking loudly, K solicits public sympathy for his cause. And he gets it, like Charlie Kane at the campaign rally. He informs the crowd of the police attempt to bribe him. Then he falsely describes his own demeanor under police interrogation as "calm," making himself look braver than he really was. And he implies the existence of a government conspiracy against him. Like Marc Antony's eulogy for Caesar in Shakespeare's *Julius Caesar*, K's oration is a bit disingenuous. "What's happening to me is of no great importance. But I think it is representative of what's happening to a great many other people as well." The second point is probably true, judging from the pathetic crowd gathered at the foot of the statue outside the courthouse. But what happens to K is, naturally, of paramount importance to himself. By pretending otherwise he merely postures for political gain.

Shots of K from various crowd vantage points reflect the fact that his audience too consists of multiple and contradictory perspectives. Like the Roman masses, their loyalties are fickle. They are easily distracted from K's predicament by the unexpected, lurid spectacle of Hilda being sexually mauled by an unidentified man at the back of the room. Noting that the Examining Magistrate appeared to signal someone just prior to the disturbance, a frustrated K accuses his inattentive audience of participating in a conspiracy against him. More likely the signal was directed at the man forcing himself on Hilda — a man who turns out to be a law student with connections to the Magistrate. Public opinion is a pawn manipulated first by K and then by the Examining Magistrate. K jumps down from the rostrum, which for a moment he had transformed into his bully pulpit, and enters the crowd. They stare stupidly back at him, less offended by his insults than fascinated by the spectacle of his outrage. It is unlikely they conspired against him. To them he is little more than a brief, entertaining diversion.

Taking advantage of K's estrangement from the crowd, the Examining Magistrate declares publically that K has "thrown away all the advantages which an interrogation invariably confers on an accused man." Posturing no less than K did moments earlier, and for equally selfish reasons, he removes the burden of injustice from his own shoulders and places it squarely on the accused's.

In a subjective shot from K's point of view, the Examining Magistrate and his unkind remarks are amplified by the stares of the crowd. To K it must indeed seem like a vast conspiracy. But we have already seen the fickle nature of the crowd's loyalty. Our image of them now is perhaps distorted by the protagonist's fear. K fights back, warning, "Just you wait!" But when he exits the courtroom he is dwarfed by its lofty doors, which seem designed for a world of giants. His parting threat seems puny by comparison.

K's situation gets no clearer when he returns to the office. Upon entering he spots the three coworkers whom he earlier encountered in Miss Burstner's bedroom. Elevation often implies power in *The Trial*. The Examining Magistrate's rostrum, K's office, and later on the Advocate's raised bed and Totirelli's lofty apartment are four examples. Standing on a catwalk above him, the three clerks bow in tandem. Their bows suggest respectful subservience, but their elevated position implies tactical superiority. Are they spies for the police? Are they part of the vast conspiracy against K? Or is K just being paranoid? Welles envelopes us in K's confusion and inconsistency. The music of alienation comes and goes throughout this scene, echoing K's inability to make sense of what is happening.

K hears groaning from a storage room. He enters and is surprised to find the two Assistant Inspectors he met earlier now being flogged by a third policeman dressed in leather. The storage room is where K stashed Miss Burstner's birthday cake — a bribe intended to get him back into her good graces. The Assistant Inspectors are being punished for the bribes they allegedly solicited from K, even though he never filed a formal complaint at police headquarters. He did, however, mention the bribe in court. Maybe his *personal* embarrassment of the Examining Magistrate now results in the punishment of the Assistant Inspectors. In which case the storage room masks the private motives of both K and the Examining Magistrate.

K is shocked by the violent consequences of his accusation. Tight camera shots render the storage room claustrophobic, bringing those consequences much too close for comfort. Short, rapid-fire bursts of overlapping dialog assault K. While attacking his victims, the Man in Leather bumps an overhead light fixture. It bounces and swings, its erratic illumination intensifying our and K's impression of the violence. An echo from the cellar scene in Hitchcock's *Psycho*?

Typically, K tries to rationalize away his guilt. "Well, it wasn't anything personal. I was just defending a principal." Actually, he was defending himself, and rightfully so. But even a righteous act can produce unforeseen, unwanted results. Previously the Assistant Inspectors were just creepy, crude figures of police corruption. Now we get glimpses of their private lives. One is married and has children. The other is engaged to be married. Both are poorly paid by the State. The victimizers become victims. Which doesn't necessarily make them admirable. The men plead poverty and tradition as excuses for soliciting a bribe from K. One of them complains that even if they are guilty, they would not have been punished if K hadn't denounced them in front of the Examining Magistrate. In other words it wasn't their corrupt actions that brought about their current suffering, it was K's public disclosure of their corruption. Morally myopic, they recognize only the evil of their pain, and not of their behavior. Under the strain of torture they cannot even maintain a united front. Assistant Inspector 1 points out that until now he and his partner have had clean job records—"especially me." A small crack in their alliance. Later his partner makes a desperate plea to divert punishment away from himself and onto his partner. Pain and fear are not an edifying spectacle. They do not always bring out the best in people.

Horrified by the violence he indirectly caused, K clumsily bribes the Man in Leather to cease. In other words he does what the victims did earlier to him. And he does so less to spare them from pain than to soothe his own pangs of guilt. In order to make the victims seem less deserving of punishment K shifts blame for their corruption onto higher law enforcement authorities who are conveniently absent. He even offers to pay extra for the Man in Leather to whip those higher officials, which is ridiculous since K would be just as squeamish witnessing *that* violence. But the Man in Leather refuses to cooperate anyway, so K simply avoids responsibility by fleeing the torture room. Welles gives us striking shots of one of the victims, bare chested and vulnerable, clinging desperately to K while fending off the whip. K just as desperately pries himself loose from *his* source of pain, shoving the victim's grasping hand back inside the room and shutting the door. K locks his horror and guilt inside the closet.

K escapes the torment of his conscience by seeking sanctuary in his office. The "Adagio" returns, lamenting K's flight from responsibility as well as the ignorance and indifference of his coworkers visible on the floor below his elevated platform, and blissfully unaware of the violence occurring a short distance from their desks.

Waiting for K in his office is his Uncle Max, who expresses mild concern over K's arrest. Only when he learns that the arrest involves a criminal charge does his concern become acute. Such a charge could damage the family's, and therefore his own, reputation. Now he aggressively chastises K for refusing to see Irmie, who informed Max of the arrest.

Still agitated from the storage room encounter, K tries to fend off Max's annoying criticism by quoting a company rule forbidding lengthy conversations with relatives during working hours. Sometimes the rules work to K's advantage, and sometimes they don't. Max switches tactics, playing the victim of K's callous disregard. "Now my only thought when I made this long, exhausting trip was just to try to help you" is self-serving propaganda intended to instill a sense of obligation in K. Max even lays claim to being K's surrogate father. And K's reaction of disgust suggests that Max has played that card before.

Moments after K quotes company regulations in order to fend off Max, that defense is undermined by a company bell signaling an end to the work day. Hundreds of workers stand as one and noisily head for the exits. They seem to betray the protagonist. But of course that impression is an illusion based on coincidence. They know and care nothing about his situation. Also disturbing, in a more general way, is their Pavlovian response to the closing bell. Welles's high angle shots and tracking camera combine a critical detachment (height) with a visceral involvement (movement) in their exodus. The "Adagio" returns briefly, adding to the somber mood of the imagery. One is reminded of the mass movements of workers in Fritz Lang's *Metropolis* (1926) and, on a lighter note, in Billy Wilder's *The Apartment* (1960).

Max tags along with his fleeing nephew, babbling about their need for competent legal aid. K is momentarily distracted by the sight of the storage room, reminding him of his other burden. Then Max is distracted by the company's enormous computer. K, in turn, allows himself to be diverted from the storage room horrors by his Uncle's inspiration to use the computer to help solve K's legal problems. In spite of his earlier, convenient fidelity to company rules as a means of avoiding a debate with Max, K is now willing to overlook a regulation forbidding the use of company assets for personal gain. Max and K are divided in their opinions about why computers, like ships, are referred to as "she." And they are divided again by the sound of muffled cries of distress from the storage room, now below them. K is again distracted by those cries. But he conceals his guilt from Max by describing them as coming from a dog in the courtyard. Opening the storage room door, he finds Assistant Inspector 2 applying tape over his own mouth in an effort to spare K the unpleasantness of hearing him scream. This bizarre vignette illustrates the extent to which a person will debase himself in order to curry favor with anyone who might be able to help him. Revolted by this exhibition of self-debasement, K closes the door and returns to the lesser annoyance of his Uncle.

K rejects Max's plan to exploit the company computer. Max agreeably accommodates himself to that rejection. By the end of the scene he claims it was K's silly idea in the first place. By selective amnesia he casts himself in a more favorable light.

With K in tow, Max seeks out an old lawyer friend, Albert Hastler, for legal advice. Ignoring the objections of Hastler's assistant, a young woman named Leni, he aggressively invades the Advocate's maze-like apartment. A tracking camera involves us in this bold intrusion. K, meanwhile, is distracted from his Uncle's mission, and therefore his own legal defense, by Leni's physical beauty, just as he was earlier by Miss Burstner's.

Apparently ill, Albert Hastler lies in a huge, ornately decorated bed on a raised platform. A wounded king on his throne. Because the bed is shown initially from a low camera angle, we cannot see its occupant. Smoke from his cigar further obscures him. Inaccessibility is a tactic he uses to manipulate clients. Intensifying the atmosphere of isolation surrounding Hastler is a thunderstorm rumbling outside. Think of Thompson's encounters with Susan Alexander and with Bernstein in *Citizen Kane*. Everyone occupies his or her own little world. Lightning flickers through windows and skylights. Electric lights have failed, further isolating individual characters from the decaying society that should surround, link, and protect them. Max refers to "a power failure, of course," implying that such outages are common.

Max is puzzled about Leni's role in Hastler's life. Is she a maid? A nurse? A mistress? Her role is as confusing as the maze of rooms that make up Hastler's residence. Placing a hot towel over the Advocate's face (another visible barrier between lawyer and client) and whispering something in his ear, she receives an affectionate pat on the rump in return. Defending her boss's need for peaceful rest, she is rewarded by his permission to stay when Max suggests that she leave. Add secretary and guard dog to Leni's list of duties.

The Advocate's indifference to if not annoyance with his uninvited guests turns to keen interest when he discovers that Max's business with him concerns Joseph K's legal case. Sinister background music echoes Hastler's predatory demeanor. Sitting up in bed, he removes the hot towel that hid him from view. Steam rises from his head, giving him a demonic aspect. And he will live up to that metaphor. Earlier, Max told K that Hastler "had quite a reputation in the past." If the ailing lawyer's career is in need of resuscitation, K's legal case may be just the ticket. He seems aware of its significance before any details are revealed by Max or K.

The Advocate gets out of bed to greet his new client. Max's demeanor suddenly changes from bold to cautious. He recognizes this as a delicate moment of negotiation between lawyer and client. But K is in a more belligerent mood. Despite standing below Hastler's raised platform and under a chandelier that is one measure of Hastler's prosperity and prestige, K sharply questions the Advocate about his prior knowledge of K's legal case. Hastler is evasive, feigning only *casual* interest in the case so as not to appear needy in the eyes of a prospective client. He claims to have learned about it through routine conversation with his professional colleagues. And while under interrogation by K, Hastler solicits Max as an ally by disguising his professional desperation as compassion and loyalty to an old friend. Max endorses that false front in the face of K's suspicion that Hastler is a bit too friendly with court officials who have treated K unfairly.

The movements of characters in this scene are a choreography of tactical maneuvering. Max leads the way by charging uninvited into the Advocate's bedchamber. Then K challenges Hastler face-to-face while Max hangs back. Hastler responds by retreating from K and circling around Max, using the latter as a shield. Framing, camera movement, and staging capture the fluidity of human relations: Max and K versus the Advocate; K versus the Advocate; The Advocate and Max versus K; the Advocate and Leni versus K; and so forth. At one point K rolls his eyes in disgust at Max's increasing servility towards Hastler. Yet K was no less obsequious towards the Deputy Manager back at the office. It is so easy to recognize fault in *others*.

The Advocate seeks to transform his close relations with officials of the high court into an asset instead of a deficit by introducing Max and K to the Chief Clerk of the law courts, seated unobtrusively at the far end of the room. We didn't notice him before now. Viewed initially in extreme long shot, the Clerk is as remote from the other characters as Kane and Susan often were from each other in the vast expanse of Xanadu. Padding his own tactical position, Hastler contrasts the rudeness of Max and K, who "burst in and took us by surprise," with the good manners of the Chief Clerk, who discreetly "preferred to withdraw."

Placing a burden of debt on K and Max while demonstrating his own influence with the court, Hastler asks the Chief Clerk to take a few moments out of his busy schedule to advise the other guests on their legal problem. Grabbing his lapels, the Advocate strikes a self-important pose. But his tactics unexpectedly backfire when he asks the Chief Clerk to confirm Hastler's impressive record as a defense lawyer, thereby bolstering his reputation in the eyes of a prospective client. By remarking that Hastler "partially" won a few of the many legal cases he has defended, the Chief Clerk unwittingly undermines that record,

The Trial. Left to right: Joseph K (Anthony Perkins), the Advocate (Orson Welles), and K's Uncle Max (Max Haufler) maneuver around each other seeking a tactical advantage as they discuss K's court case in the Advocate's bedroom.

reinforcing Max's earlier hint that the Advocate's reputation is a thing of the past. Hastler quickly changes the subject. But he need not worry. Max is too awed by the Chief Guard's rank to catch any subtleties in their conversation. And K, pursuing an urge momentarily stronger than concern over his legal situation, isn't even listening.

Earlier in the scene Leni playfully flirted with K, buckling his knees by bumping them from behind with her own. When the Advocate introduced the Chief Clerk and then tried to elicit gratitude from K, Leni stood by her boss's side, grinning up at him. It is difficult to say whether her romantic distraction of K from the discussion of his case is motivated by a genuine attraction to him or by devotion to Hastler and his attempt to manipulate a difficult client. Maybe both. She could be as divided in her priorities as the protagonist himself. Hastler orders her to leave his bedchamber, raising the possibility that her subsequent actions are under his direction. K wants to pursue her, but hesitates, divided between a desire for her and worry about his legal case. The sound of breaking glass from off screen gives him an excuse to follow her out of the room.

The camera tracks with K as he pursues Leni through the labyrinth of Hastler's apartment. Stacks of books are circumstantial evidence of the Advocate's vast legal expertise. But his is also a disorderly world, implying scattered focus and perhaps neglected obligations.

Bunches of lit candles, in addition to compensating for the State's defective electrical grid, give Hastler's apartment the look of a religious shrine. It may be no coincidence that his final confrontation with K will occur in a cathedral, where the Advocate displaces the authority of a clergyman. Followed by the camera, K passes by a wall of mirrors reflecting Hastler's collection of law books. He comes upon Leni standing in the place of a mirror she broke in order to attract K's attention. For a moment we are not sure if she is real or merely a reflection of Hastler's world. Is she the Advocate's agent provocateur, or does she pursue her own agenda with K? Though more economical, the visual confusion in this shot recalls the Maze of Mirrors scene in *The Lady from Shanghai*, where three characters find it almost impossible to distinguish real from unreal.

Complaining that K did not follow her soon enough, Leni betrays her selfish desire to control him. K defends himself by pointing out that it would have been impolite for him to leave the others too abruptly. Insisting that K did exactly that, Leni contradicts her previous complaint in order to flatter herself. She wraps K in the Advocate's huge overcoat, ostensibly to protect him from the storm outside when he leaves, but on a less literal level to imprison him within the Advocate's world, whether to service her own needs or her boss's. Leni raises the ante by announcing her intention to make love to him and pouting like a child that he doesn't like her. Rummaging through the Advocate's coat pockets, K finds a flask of alcohol. Hastler's drug of choice to relieve depression caused by ill health and a career in decline? Is the Advocate another Susan Alexander?

Assuming she is not giving a phony performance to enslave K to the Advocate, Leni behaves like a person fundamentally insecure, clinging and constantly demanding reassurance. Perhaps the Advocate is a source of power she latched onto. Now, in the wake of his diminishing status and health, echoed by the electrical outage in his apartment, she shifts loyalty to K. She stares obsessively up at him, as she did earlier at Hastler. Jealous, as the insecure often are, she accuses K of having a girlfriend. Displaying insecurity of his own, he shows her a photograph of Miss Burstner and pretends she is his girlfriend. Did he steal the photo from Miss Burstner's room? Leni criticizes the woman in the photo as old, hard, and selfish, incapable of sacrificing for K. She may be right, but her motive for attacking her phantom rival is entirely selfish.

In a bizarre attempt to entice K away from Miss Burstner, Leni shows him her physical defect. Pulling him into another room further away from the distraction of Hastler, the Chief Clerk, and Max, Leni reveals the webbed skin between her fingers. A web within which she intends to snare K, since she has no confidence in her ability to win him by more legitimate methods.

The hideaway to which Leni lures her prospective lover is a large room haphazardly strewn with legal files. Perhaps the flotsam of Hastler's old cases: lost, "partially" won, or never to be resolved. While the storm rumbles outside, the lovers recline cozily together on a mountain of legal debris that is both a testament to the Advocate's long, uneven career and a visual reminder of the bureaucratic Mt. Everest confronting K in his legal battle.

K and Leni enjoy a private interlude of romantic sanity amidst the clutter of a legal system gone mad. They embrace, kiss, and defy the Advocate's mess by rolling around in it. Then, suddenly, she tells him to leave. To keep him off-balance for her boss? Or to spare K the sad plight of becoming Hastler's client? She offers him a key to Hastler's apartment so that he can return to her whenever he wants. The lovers look and sound like co-conspirators (you and me against the world) as they cuddle under the Advocate's big coat and make fun of a court official depicted in a painting lying on the floor below them. Leni explains that the model for that portrait is in reality a vain man not at all like the image he ordered the artist to paint. He isn't even a judge — only an examining magistrate. She demystifies part of the legal system for K, who initially accepted the portrait at face value. The Advocate, by contrast, tries to persuade his clients that the law is beyond their comprehension and therefore they need *him* to defend their legal interests.

But if Leni enlightens K about the vanity of high court officials, she playfully reminds him, and us, that she too is vain. She bites him on the lip to get his wavering attention, then accuses him of brooding too much about his case. Neither of these actions is harsh enough to break their intimacy, but they do remind us that these two characters have very separate lives and agendas. Leni debunks the court one moment, then inflates its reputation the next by advising K to be more cooperative with the court, confess his guilt of whatever crime he is accused, then rely on outside help to get him out of it. Presumably she means the Advocate's help. So their romantic dalliance ends on a note of doubt, just the way it began. Is Leni offering K an honest, concerned, if pessimistic assessment of his case? Or is she jerking him around for Hastler's benefit? Throughout this part of the scene she and K frequently shift positions on top of the paper mountain — a physical reflection of their continual emotional and tactical realignment.

The voices of Hastler and Max, as they escort the Chief Clerk to the exit, intrude on the private world of Leni and K, who scramble out of their love nest and separate. Visible as silhouettes on the other side of a glass partition, Max and the Advocate discuss the indignities inflicted on all lawyers by the court. Hastler unwittingly betrays his caste mentality by complaining that a hole in the floor of the advocates' waiting room leads to the room where their clients have to wait. What a shame, having to keep such close company with one's inferiors. Meanwhile, K removes Hastler's coat and hangs it on a door, which is not where Leni got it from in the first place. Hastler notices the coat as he passes by, and is puzzled. Completing a comment he was making to Max, he says, "Yes it's all ... very humiliating." But the last two words are said in the context of his discovery of the coat, giving the entire line a new meaning. Does he suspect Leni of cheating on him with a client? If so, he would have a motive other than greed for mishandling K's legal case. And K would not be quite so undeserving of that ill treatment. Just as Michael O'Hara was not entirely deserving of Arthur Bannister's poor legal efforts in *The Lady from Shanghai*.

Tracking shots follow K as he sneaks through the twists and turns of the Advocate's residence. He unexpectedly comes upon a middle aged man, looking weary and forlorn, tucked away in a tiny room far from the Advocate's bedchamber. This is Rudy Bloch, one of Hastler's clients. Though K does not yet know about that relationship, he backs out of the room without a word, as though he were looking at a ghost. A specter of his own possible future. Albinoni's "Adagio" evokes a fatalism that Rudy Bloch visually embodies, and it haunts K as he searches for a way out of the Advocate's maze.

As surprising as his encounter with Bloch, K finds himself reunited with Leni in the big room they occupied earlier. Which means Bloch was very near the scene of their romantic interlude, and in retrospect undermining some of the credibility of that interlude. The romantic spell is broken. K is too nervous to accept Leni's invitation to resume their lovemaking. He insists on leaving. And he badgers her about the mysterious man he encountered. Leni reluctantly admits that Bloch is one of the Advocate's clients, but dismisses him as insignificant. Not a reassuring thought for a *new* client. As they part company Leni hands K the keys to the apartment, reaching through wooden struts in the wall to do so. The prison bar imagery is appropriate. Leni obediently heeds the Advocate's verbal summons from off screen. She is as much a slave as is Rudy Bloch, if better treated. And the key she offers to K opens the door into, not out of, that cage.

K rejoins Uncle Max outside the apartment building. A low camera angle, high contrast lighting, and falling rain highlight the external despair of the Advocate's residence, in keeping with the general state of society. Max knows about K's involvement with Leni, and accuses him of jeopardizing his legal case. Of course, Max's interest in that case is mostly selfish. Unable to deny his Uncle's charge, K ignores him and walks away.

K returns to the law court building, where he finds Hilda at her sewing table. Determined to settle his case without the Advocate's help, K is disappointed to learn from her that court is no longer in session. Neither its procedures nor its schedule are ever made clear to him, making it impossible for him to mount a proper defense. Frustrated, he barges into the interrogation room, searching for useful clues about the Examining Magistrate and the legal system. Protesting his unauthorized entry, Hilda pursues him. She appears to be another conformist, accepting on faith the authority and validity of the court's high priests. The sheer size of the room visually dwarfs the two intruders, reinforcing Hilda's orthodox viewpoint. But neither Hilda nor the trappings of the Law are entirely what they appear to be at first glance.

K is surprised to learn from Hilda that the man who kissed her and disrupted his protest speech earlier in this room is a young law student rather than her husband. K seems more offended by her infidelity than by the possibility that her action was a deliberate attempt to sabotage his self-defense. This is a little hypocritical in view of K's recent dalliance with the Advocate's mistress.

Ignoring Hilda's protests, K climbs up on the rostrum to examine law books on the Magistrate's table. He looks like a child in an oversized, adult world. But at least he challenges its power to control and ruin his life. "How dirty they are," he comments as he blows dust off one of the books. Inside the book he discovers a photo of a naked woman. "Dirty" acquires a second meaning. Once again private concerns have invaded the precinct of public business. K's discovery presages our discovery of erotic photos and a cowboy hat in an official, top secret safe on board Major Kong's B-52 in Kubrick's *Dr. Strangelove*. Both movies deals in the crosscurrents between private and public lives.

Miss Burstner yielded to K's comparatively gentle charms in a moment of weakness, on the occasion of turning another year older and after an evening of being ogled if not mauled by inconsiderate male clients. Leni's attraction to K, if genuine, was equally rooted in insecurity. Hilda's romantic interest in him now seems stimulated by its being illicit, which may also explain her involvement with the Law Student and the Examining Magistrate. Perhaps it is *her* form of escape from the domestic chores which are the only thing we see her doing. Like Leni, Miss Burstner, and K himself, she acts on contradictory impulses. After objecting to his unauthorized ascent to the Magistrate's table, Hilda reaches up to touch K's leg while he examines the forbidden law books. She offers to help him with his legal case, claiming "That's why I came in here," which is not what she claimed in the first place.

Distracted once again from his legal battle by the prospect of sex, K sits down on the rostrum and allows Hilda to caress his legs. He wisely advises her not to get involved in his case because it might cause her trouble, but in the next breath tries to impress her with his bravery and thus encourage her attraction to him. "The truth is I don't care how it all comes out" is not true. Not yet, anyway. "And if they sentence me I just laugh at them" is false bravado, although he will eventually do exactly that at the end of the movie.

Leading K to a bench at the back of the room, concealed behind the Examining Magistrate's rostrum, Hilda responds to K's bragging with some of her own, likewise intended to stimulate romantic interest. She gives K the impression that the Examining Magistrate is both preoccupied with K's case and romantically fixated on her. Hilda is flattered by the attention of powerful men, which in a sense makes *her* powerful. She hints to K that she could be a useful ally in his legal battle. Hiking up her skirt to reveal the stockings allegedly given to her by the Magistrate conveniently serves two purposes: convincing K that she has influence with the court and showing off her pretty legs to him.

The arrival of Hilda's *other* illicit lover, Bert the Law Student, complicates her seduction of K. From K and Hildas' vantage point we watch Bert slowly approach from a great distance, visible through the maze-like pattern of struts supporting the rostrum. Figuratively speaking Bert too is a strut, procuring Hilda and performing other menial tasks for the Examining Magistrate. Viewed from a low camera angle, Bert's eyes look menacing as he emerges from the tangle of struts to confront Hilda and K. But before he reaches them, Hilda makes fun of his physical attributes and tells K that when she gets back from wherever the Law Student takes her she will go away with him and do whatever he wants. In other words, she offers to be K's future slave while demonstrating her current enslavement to Bert and the Examining Magistrate. K's suspicions are understandably aroused. He fears a trap is being set for him by the other three players in this bizarre arrangement. But his wariness competes with the exciting prospect of getting revenge on the Magistrate by stealing his mistress. A plan which, by the way, reduces Hilda to nothing more than a useful tool, and contradicts K's earlier expression of concern about involving her in his private problems. There is no indication that K recognizes the hypocrisy of his shifting attitude. He is a long way from the understanding he will acquire at the end of the film.

Arrogant, perhaps because of his alliance with the Examining Magistrate, Bert expects K to treat him with deference. There is counterpoint between imagery and dialog in this encounter. Sternly advising K to leave, Bert looms large and dark in the foreground while K and Hilda appear smaller and lighter in the background. But when he follows suit with "You should have left the minute I came in," Bert appears shorter in the background than do K and Hilda in the foreground. With K's insolent reply, dialog catches up with imagery. But then another shot of Bert again visually dominant counterpoints K's verbal defiance. K moves away from Hilda's side, distancing himself from Bert as well. All alliances are in flux.

Bert settles the dispute by simply hoisting Hilda over his shoulder and hauling her away like a side of beef, to a rendezvous with the Magistrate. K follows them, protesting in vain. Welles's tracking camera conveys both Bert's intimidating power and the confusion of the court building they traverse. In several shots we catch a glimpse of Bert and Hilda through gaps between portable bulletin boards plastered with legal notices. Now you see them, now you don't. The characters blend in with the corrupt, confusing bureaucracy to which they are enslaved, as Leni did with the mirrors in the Advocate's apartment.

Mustering his courage, K places a restraining hand on the Law Student. Like a rabid dog (he *is* the Examining Magistrate's guard dog), Bert snarls and bites him. K is shocked by such behavior, but even more so by Hilda's unexpected objection to his rescue attempt. Moments after complaining about the Law Student and the Examining Magistrate, and offering to run away with K, she now perceives K as a threat to her fragile social status, "You want to ruin me?" And she executes that reversal of attitude, like so many other characters in the movie, without the slightest awareness of her inconsistency. Even the background music in this scene jumps back and forth from sinister to erotic to fatalistically somber. Adding to his confusion, K is surprised to learn that the seedy location at which they have arrived, and where Hilda and the Magistrate are to have their illicit rendezvous, is part of the law court offices. Bert carries Hilda into a room and locks the door behind them. K still cannot gain access to the legal system.

The Trial. Joseph K (Anthony Perkins, right) tries to rescue Hilda (Elsa Martinelli) from Bert (Thomas Holtzmann), the snarling Law Student who kidnaps her for the Examining Magistrate.

K's bewildering series of encounters with people linked in one way or another to the law continues. It's like a bizarre dance in which he changes partners every so often. His next dance partner is Hilda's husband, a courtroom Guard bitterly aware of his wife's infidelity and of the conspiracy between Bert and the Examining Magistrate to keep him out of the way by exploiting the legal system of which they are all parts. He encounters K while returning from a pointless official errand on which he was sent in order to facilitate a tryst between Hilda and the Magistrate. We first observe the Guard approaching along a wooden walkway surrounded by struts supporting a ceiling. Like Bert, he is shown bent over, coming towards the camera from a great distance. Their posture reflects their servility. Both are *human* struts, blindly supporting the legal structure above them. In a rear view close-up of the Guard, K seems to step out of out of the man's head. The two characters will prove alike in some unflattering ways.

Like Leni, Hilda, and the Advocate, the Guard is aware of K's public reputation as a rebel against the legal system. They are both victims of that corrupt system. One particular low angle shot of the two men renders them mirror images of each other. But if the Guard is exploited by Bert and the Examining Magistrate, he in turn tries to exploit K in order to get revenge on them — the moral equivalent of K contemplating a sexual relationship with Hilda in order to humiliate the Magistrate.

The Guard wants K to physically attack the Law Student. He would do the job himself, he insists, but is afraid of losing his job. What about the legal consequences for K? Typical shortsightedness. As is his reflexive, contradictory *defense* of the legal system against K's charge of prejudice. "It's a rule. None of our cases are prejudiced!" Unable to acknowledge the evil in an institution he serves, the Guard nevertheless resents being victimized by its corrupt higher officials. His imagination doesn't grasp the possibility of K being a victim of that same corruption. He cannot see that the Emperor has no clothes.

K is at first reluctant to participate in the Guard's revenge plot, fearing it might jeopardize his court case. Playing off K's vanity by describing K's protest speech as an example of courage under fire, the Guard in effect taunts K to live up to his rebellious billing. He exploits K's weakness for his own gain. The two characters walk parallel to each other through a cluttered setting that reflects the confused state of all human relationships in *The Trial*. Physical distances, exaggerated by camera angle and lens choice, echo emotional and intellectual distances. The Guard rejoins K to propose an alliance. K is intrigued. When the Guard walks away, he follows, his body language signaling interest even as he worries out loud about challenging the Examining Magistrate. The Guard rejoins him to flatter and encourage. K walks away, claiming to be unafraid but prudent. But he doesn't go far, and the Guard moves in close to him again. They form common cause out of separate, selfish interests. When the Guard departs, K follows. They are a team now. But when they reach the law court offices, the Guard is puzzled to discover that his keys do not fit the lock on the outer door. As was pointed out in the Prolog, there are guards of various ranks standing between defendants and the Law. Obviously *this* Guard is one of the less powerful.

An extremely low angle shot of K and the Guard moving along an elevated walkway visually emphasizes the height of the law court office windows looming above them, and to which they aspire. Gathered far below them is a crowd of timid people seeking access to the Law. Distracted from the Guard's mission of revenge, K joins them. He is more curious about them then he was earlier about the group of apparently condemned prisoners gathered at the base of a statue outside the building. He is beginning to feel a connection with the plight of other victims of the Law. But his relative cockiness sets him apart from them. They are wary of K, unsure of who he is and of what impact he might have on their own law cases, with which they are understandably preoccupied.

Seeking information about the elusive legal process, K targets an elderly man for interrogation. The old codger is seated apart from the others in an enormous, vaulted corridor. The man's age and isolation make him easy to intimidate. Speaking harshly, K demands to know, "Why are you here?" K's own fears shape his actions. The Old Man is a specter of K's possible future. And that future frightens K. The Old Man meekly explains that he is awaiting results of various affidavits he filed with the court. K browbeats him about it, implicitly criticizing the Old Man's timidity by crowing about his own rebellious indifference to legal problems. Instead of recognizing the Old Man as an ally deserving compassion, K treats him like an enemy. This is a very uncomfortable encounter to witness, because the character with whom we most identify is behaving much like his own tormenters in previous scenes.

Further dividing the two characters, K interprets the Old Man's submissiveness as a sign that he mistakes K for a judge instead of a fellow defendant. But who can blame the Old Man? K's bullying is not typical behavior for someone under arrest. By standing up and removing his hat out of deference, the Old man unwittingly undercuts K's attempt to intimidate him, transforming a tactical weakness into a strength. Whether ashamed of his own bad behavior or, more likely, terrified that he might some day be as beaten down and pathetic as the Old Man, K flees this disturbing encounter. Solidarity is not achieved.

Welles himself pointed out the suitability of using an abandoned train station as the setting for many of the film's scenes because it is by design a place where people *wait*, sometimes for long periods, sometimes delayed by bureaucratic red tape, and sometimes to be taken to unhappy destinations (Welles/Bogdanovich, p.247).

K's conversation with the Old Man draws a curious crowd of other accused individuals. The Guard, speaking from the elevated walkway that reflects his superior status and power, sternly orders them to clear the passage. He is, like K, a victim who exhibits no pity for *other* victims. They silently obey, doffing their hats to him as the Old Man did to K. But stepping out from that groveling mass of humanity is K, who is not so passive. A low angle shot from behind K, with the Guard visible far in the background, magnifies the gap between them. They are no longer allies of convenience.

Surrounded and overwhelmed by evidence of the hopelessness of his situation, and on the verge of panic, K asks the Guard to escort him out of the court building. But because K is no longer useful to his revenge scheme, the Guard refuses to waste more time with him. He even transforms an old disadvantage into a new advantage by pointing out that he still has an official message to deliver. The same phony errand he was assigned by the Law Student and the Examining Magistrate so they could dally with his wife is now a convenient excuse for him to dismiss K. But K fights back, turning his own inferior position into an asset. By *loudly* demanding the Guard's help, K threatens to disturb the peace of higher court officials presumably nearby. The Guard is tasked with maintaining that peace, and might be punished for K's disturbance. The Guard tries re-take the offensive by pointing out that those officials, if drawn to the scene of disturbance, might question K as well. But for the moment K's need to escape the depressing spectacle of the Old Man outweighs all other concerns. "I just want to get out of here and be alone." The Guard yields, providing direction to the exit. The whole scene has been a kaleidoscope of shifting emotional, ethical, and tactical alliances.

As K makes his way out of the court building, the specter raised by the Old Man is repeated and multiplied. The camera tracks by rows of accused men who stand respectfully as K passes by. They too apparently mistake him for a judge. But the last man in line is one of the two plain-clothed policemen we saw with the Inspector outside the theater. K panics and flees, stumbling through hallways filled with endless shelves of legal paperwork, and past more people under arrest who again rise and greet him in silent, misdirected pleas for mercy. The camera tracks him at close range, matching his unsteady gait and claustrophobia. He passes cubbyholes stuffed with masses of legal papers: in binders, in boxes, tied in bundles, piled high, crumpled up. Impossible to sort out or decipher. How different this impression of bureaucratic chaos is from the orderly vault of case files in which Miguel Vargas locates evidence of Hank Quinlan's corruption in *Touch of Evil*.

K is rescued from this madness by the most normal character in *The Trial*. In Welles's final cut of the movie, a female law clerk helps K with no ulterior motive for doing so. She comments on the wet laundry hanging in law court corridors, contributing to the dank atmosphere that adversely affects K's breathing. Tenants, she asserts, must be allowed *some* rights. Again the dividing lines between private and public life are blurred. Is the legal system encroaching on the individual citizen? Or is the individual encroaching on the system. In either case the clerk declines to accompany K outside the building, admitting," I'm not used to the fresh air." She has adapted *too* well to the stifling atmosphere of the Law. Perhaps she is not as "normal" as she seemed at first glance.

As K exits the law court building the architectural facades around him change from dilapidated industrial to an older, classical, more elegant style. Yet K, as shown from numerous camera angles, is dwarfed by *all* institutional structures. Church bells ring, but cannot dispel strains of uneasiness and melancholy in the background music, or in the protagonist himself. Emerging from behind a massive pillar (the individual hidden within the institution), cousin Irmie looks, acts, and talks like a typical American teenager of the early 1960's. Another deliberate anachronism. Welles's movie depicts a polyglot world drawn from various historical periods and places. Which is not all that abstract an idea, since any social order at any given moment in time is made up of structures and customs and fashions from different periods of the past, as well as new trends pointing towards the future. As K and Irmie walk through city streets, classical architecture yields to a clean, modern skyline.

K correctly deduces that Uncle Max sent Irmie to spy on him. But like everyone else, she pursues a private agenda within her official mission. She is infatuated with K. And that attraction, like Leni's, is partly based on her assumption that he is guilty of whatever charge has been brought against him. Trying to appear worthy of K's outlaw affection, she tells him that she often plays hooky from school. But she makes her case to a divided jury. K, sometime rebel and sometime conformist, scolds her for skipping school, and for using crude language. She retaliates by placing blame on him, insisting she wouldn't be here if K hadn't gotten himself in trouble, which again implies her assumption of his guilt. Except that this time she *admonishes* rather than admires him for it. Like K, she is both rebel and conformist, depending on what role suits her transitory emotional needs.

Perhaps secretly flattered by the adoration of his cousin, K puffs up his outlaw reputation, just as she did her own to impress *him*. K did the same thing earlier, for various reasons, with the Guard, Hilda, Leni, and Miss Burstner. But his self-confidence seems insignificant when measured against the massive skyline we see above his head in low angle shots and the geometric patterns of light and dark formed by concrete steps at his feet in high angle shots. Even his words contradict each other. In one breath he proclaims, "Influence — that's all that counts in the long run." In the next he brags about using his work skills to solve his legal problems.

A tiny indication of K's capacity for unselfishness, so rare for any character in this movie, is his concern about Irmie returning to school on her own. Like his fitful expressions of concern for Miss Burstner, the tortured Assistant Inspectors, and Hilda, it is a spark of conscience that catches fire by the end of the movie. But Irmie is not grateful for his compassion. Like most teenagers, she is annoyed at the prospect of her classmates seeing her escorted back to school by an adult. But when K in turn protests that he is, after all, her cousin, Irmie reverses attitude and transforms that fact into a romantic overture. "Cousins get married." Her adolescent need for independence from adults battles with her adolescent crush on one adult in particular.

Determined to assert himself, K almost swaggers down a long, dark hallway leading back to the Advocate's apartment. His knock at the door is deliberately bold. He forces an entry. But once inside he is upset to discover Leni dressed only in her slip while in the company of Rudy Bloch, the Advocate's other client. Tracked by the camera in a low angle shot, Leni runs from K with a look of panic on her face. Is she ashamed of being caught with Bloch because she really likes K? Or is she afraid that K's discovery of her double-dealing might adversely affect his (and therefore her) relationship with Hastler?

Jealous, K browbeats the older, shorter Bloch. Unaware of his hypocrisy, K challenges everything Bloch says, in the same way K's responses were challenged by the policemen who interrogated him in the first scene. When K snoops among the papers on Hastler's desk and Bloch sneaks a peek over his shoulder, K rudely conceals them. In short, K takes out his frustration with the Law on a more helpless victim of the same system. Bloch, on the other hand, takes advantage of K's boldness to do something (snoop) he hasn't the courage to do on his own. Further debasing himself, Bloch cravenly agrees with everything K says, even when K contradicts himself. At one point K chastises Bloch for overestimating the rank of the court official depicted in a painting behind Hastler's desk. Yet K did the same thing earlier, until Leni told him the truth about that official. K now exploits that truth to demonstrate his superiority to Bloch. Instead of commiserating with his fellow client, K is jealous, cruel, deceptive, and petty. He grabs, pushes, and intimidates Bloch, forcing the older man to take him to the kitchen, where Leni is preparing food for the Advocate. Only a few steps ahead of them, Leni slips into a white dress as she rushes past a wall of windows and mirrors. Now you see her, now you don't — a perfect visual metaphor for her fickle allegiences.

Large and uninviting, the kitchen serves as a battlefield of shifting alliances among the three characters. K exiles Bloch to a corner chair in the far background, just as Hastler exiled Bloch to the maid's bedroom. More chairs situated along the wall seem to be waiting for more clients. Leni guiltily buttons her dress as K accuses her of having sex with Bloch. Then she starts to *un*button K's suit coat, and kisses him. She insults Bloch to his face, assuming this will pacify K's jealousy. She insists she must show Bloch *some* attention because he is one of the Advocate's "best" clients—"best" meaning most profitable and least troublesome. But why shouldn't K assume that her displays of affection for himself are just as phony, since he too is just a client?

A shot of K in the foreground scrutinizing Bloch off screen while Leni works over a stove in the background spaces the three characters very far apart from each other. A reverse angle shot from K's point of view shows Bloch, knees and hands meekly pressed together, sitting in the corner, passively awaiting judgement. K closes the immense gap between them and stands looming over his fellow client. Bloch looks like a trapped animal. When Leni exits the kitchen to take the Advocate his meal, Bloch starts to follow her, preferring their tyranny to K's. But K orders him to remain. Closing the emotional gap between them, he sits down next to Bloch, casually tucks one leg under the other, and softens his tone of voice. In response, Bloch too relaxes. A new camera angle shows them on the same level. Having removed his suit coat, K is now dressed the same as Bloch, visually reinforcing their new comradery. Leni's prior attempt to seduce K, starting with the removal of his suit jacket, ends up promoting an alliance between two men whom she can better manipulate when they are apart. In her absence they are free to discover how much they have in common as clients of the Advocate, rather than what divides them as sexual competitors for Leni.

K and Bloch compare notes on their legal problems and on the Advocate's shortcomings as a defender of their interests. Speaking in conspiratorial tones, and seated close together now, they laugh and giggle in a manner reminiscent of K and Lenis' romantic interlude from an earlier scene. Bloch grows secure enough to confess blasphemy. In exchange for K's promise to reveal one of his own secrets, presumably making the two men equally vulnerable to each other, Bloch admits that he has hired other advocates besides Hastler. Background music takes a break during this conversation. The sound of anxiety and sadness yields momentarily to the rare good cheer of open and honest communication.

Leni's return complicates this new alliance. Initially appearing far across the room, and visually aligned with a portrait of a high court official hanging on the wall, she approaches and tries to reassert dominance over K, luring him away from Bloch and encouraging his sense of indebtedness to the Advocate. And while protecting Hastler's agenda, she pursues her own. "I want you to be fond of me," she coos. But K turns away from her, complaining about the difficulty of getting an audience with Hastler. Bloch re-enters the camera frame, after his brief exile, and explains why the Advocate *will* see K. It is because K's case, unlike Bloch's, is still at the hopeful stage. This is spoken in an intimate close-up of Bloch and Leni. Glancing furtively at him, she seems almost ashamed of herself as Bloch bemoans the hopelessness of his case. But in a wider shot Leni is shown fiddling with Bloch's vest buttons, trying to control him through sex the same way she tries to control K. Failing that, she turns back to K, resumes playing with *his* buttons, and tries to transform Bloch's honesty into a flaw by pointing out that his talkativeness is why the Advocate won't see him anymore. The implied lesson is that if K wants to see the Advocate he should keep quiet. More close-ups of the three characters capture a remarkable confluence of separate but interlocking perspectives. Bloch sadly remarks that he has to be on hand at all times in case the Advocate, on a whim, decides to see him. "That's why I let him sleep here," Leni adds, trying to appear generous. But K is more inclined to see things through Bloch's eyes, so Leni attacks the *root* of Bloch's complaint. "The truth is, he likes it. Maybe not the waiting, but you do enjoy spending the night." Bloch's sheepish expression confirms as much.

The contrary prospects of sexual pleasure and humiliation battle each other inside K as he nervously accepts Leni's whispered invitation to see Bloch's room. In close-up she looks like a classic movie femme fatale. Would it really be so bad, she implicitly asks K, ending up like Bloch? The answer comes in a lingering, low angle shot of K, Leni, and Bloch standing close together in the open doorway of Bloch's little cell. Claustrophobic walls and door frame oppressively envelop them. Disturbing music returns, along with K's awakening from sexual temptation. Sober now, he remarks that this is the *maid's* room. Less sober, Bloch puts a more pleasant spin on his imprisonment, indicating the room's convenient location. Leni, standing between them, quietly monitors their reactions. Reinforcing her sexual hold on K, she tilts her head back and leans on his shoulder. A look of understanding passes between K and Bloch. Rudy once faced the choice K now faces. But if Bloch's meaningful glance is meant to encourage K's participation in sexual subservience, it has the opposite effect. Telling Leni to put Bloch to bed (like a child), K walks away. Bloch follows him, suddenly terrified that K intends to betray his secret about hiring other lawyers. This fear momentarily outweighs Leni's sexual authority over Bloch. She tries unsuccessfully to restrain him. But when Bloch and Leni learn of K's intention to dismiss the Advocate, they form common cause again, attempting to restrain *him*. Unable to stop K from barging into the Advocate's bedchamber, Leni executes damage control by at least locking out Bloch, whose presence might complicate things for her boss.

The Advocate's commanding voice puts a stop to Leni's efforts to restrain K. Sitting up in bed, he confronts the challenge directly rather than through an agent or from behind a mask. So confident is Hastler that he retains the upper hand over K that he explains something of the parasitic relationship between himself and Leni. She has a peculiar attraction to accused men. For amusement he occasionally allows her to tell him about her affairs. In other words, Leni feeds off the Advocate by taking sexual advantage of his enslaved clients, while Hastler feeds off Leni by using her as bait to keep his clients under control and by receiving titillating accounts of her sexual exploits. By inserting the phrase, "when I *allow* her to," he asserts his own supremacy in that cynical arrangement.

His head appearing larger in the foreground while Hastler appears smaller and lower in the background, K dismisses the Advocate from his case. He does, however, soften the blow by expressing polite appreciation for Hastler's efforts on his behalf, which flatly contradicts his earlier claim that "Hastler's done nothing." The Advocate calmly dismisses K's dismissal, counseling patience and negotiation instead, and claiming to have heard it all before. But K's defiance stiffens rather than weakens. The Advocate's reaction is surprising. "It's true, you know. Accused men *are* attractive." Is this base flattery, calculated distraction, or honest observation? For a moment Welles seems to step out of character to ponder a contradiction in human nature. "It can't be a sense of guilt. We can't all be ... guilty. Hmmm?" The Advocate seems to believe so, and to embrace that idea so passionately that it becomes his excuse for behaving as wickedly as he chooses in a thoroughly wicked world. Like Harry Lime in *The Third Man* and Elsa Bannister in *The Lady from Shanghai*. And that is his greatest threat to the protagonist. In addition to manipulating K for his own gain, Hastler wants to infect K with his cynicism about the Law, about human nature, and about Fate. He tempts K to abandon all hope and the better elements of his own nature. He plays Iago to K's Othello, Quinlan to K's Vargas, the Bannisters and Grisby to K's O'Hara.

Nudging K to give up all hope of goodness or justice in the world, the Advocate summons Rudy Bloch to his bedchamber and gives K a demonstration of how low human beings can sink. In effect he stages a short play, like Falstaff in *Chimes at Midnight*. Hastler facetiously claims that as an accused man even Bloch is attractive, which is so obviously not the case. Leni, equally unappealing now, flinches like a whipped dog at the sound of her master's voice commanding her to "fetch" Bloch. The Advocate pulls the bed sheet over his head, erecting an artificial barrier between himself and Bloch. That barrier, plus his antagonistic tone of voice, puts Bloch on the defensive. K, who is Hastler's audience of one, observes the action while hidden behind a dressing screen.

Standing at the foot of Hastler's elevated bed, Bloch is little more than a puppet controlled by the Advocate. Book-laden shelves on the wall behind the bed are visual testimony to the Advocate's presumably vast and unimpeachable knowledge of the Law. Hastler keeps his victim verbally off balance with lengthy pauses and sudden outbursts to which Bloch can only babble semi-coherent responses. "What do you want?" Hastler demands, as though Bloch had initiated this encounter instead of the other way around. "You were sent for, weren't you?" is Hastler's illogical follow-up when Bloch predictably fails to answer the first question. Then a third comment," You've come at the wrong time!", contradicts the second. Nothing Bloch can say would satisfy the Advocate because Hastler's intention is to generate false antagonism and thereby frighten and humiliate his client. "You're here, aren't you? Then stay!" contradicts "you've come at the wrong time." The Advocate both commands Bloch's presence and makes Bloch feel guilty for obeying that command. It's a lose/lose situation for the client.

Peeking out from under the bedcovers, and softening his voice, the Advocate seemingly makes himself more accessible to his client. But that impression is offset by the content of Hastler's status report on his client's legal case. Forcing Bloch to beg for scraps of information, the Advocate reveals just enough to suggest that he is the client's only hope of successfully resolving legal problems far too complex for the client to understand. "I saw my friend, the Third Judge" implies influence with high court officials, while description of an ongoing debate among those officials about whether or not the sounding of a bell marks the official start of Bloch's trial hints at a monumental complexity in the law which necessitates the help of a lawyer.

Some nearly subjective shots from the Advocate's perspective depict Bloch off to one side, looking insignificant. He drops to his knees under the emotional burden dropped on him. Defending his own dignity by proxy, K rushes in from off screen and tries to stop Bloch from abasing himself. K tells him to stand up. Leni tries to stop K from interfering, even resorting to the childish tactic of biting him. In the manner of terrified show trial victims who condemn allies and praise persecutors, Bloch desperately rejects K's rescue attempt.

Retreating back behind his sacred sheet, the Advocate tells Bloch," Do what your conscience tells you is right." That sounds reasonable, when isolated from the rest of his dealings with Bloch. But Hastler knows very well that Bloch's confusion and fear make him a slave. Bloch will "freely" chose slavish loyalty to the Advocate over rebellion with K. The two clients get into a minor slapping fight over that choice. Former allies of convenience, back in the kitchen, are now enemies, with the former object of their mutual contempt (Hastler) now the godlike champion of one of them.

Fearing abandonment, Bloch creeps onto the Advocate's bed on hands and knees. Prompted by Leni, he kisses the lawyer's hand, which is shown in close-up, isolated from the rest of Hastler's body. The Advocate attains divine status in the mind of his client. The hand itself is transformed into a religious icon. Bloch then meekly backs off the bed, his retreating backside a particularly undignified image.

Leni performs her own self-abasing acts of worship by rubbing lineament on the chest of her ailing boss and reporting to him on how she kept Bloch in line all day, locking him in the maid's room and giving him a bit of food and water for sustenance. She even permitted Bloch to pass his time reading one of the Advocate's law books, though in poor light. Assured by Leni that Bloch never progressed beyond the first page, Hastler openly admits that he grants his client a glimpse of the legal "scriptures" only to encourage in him a greater appreciation for the Advocate's efforts on his behalf. He and Leni discuss Bloch as though he were not present, adding their contempt to the burden of his humiliation. With crudely deliberate irony, Hastler tells Leni she has given Bloch too much praise, making it difficult for Hastler to tell his client the unpleasant truth about his case. In fact the only thing about Bloch that Leni praised was his subservience.

Sitting up in bed and revealing his face to Bloch, the Advocate adopts a carrot and stick method while discussing recent developments in Boch's case. Hastler claims he challenged a Judge's unfavorable opinion of both Bloch and Bloch's case. But his compliments to his client are always backhanded, either accompanied by insults or undercut by the qualifier "deliberate exaggeration." Again allegedly quoting the Judge, Hastler accuses Bloch of manipulating the case. The reverse, of course, is true. The Advocate manipulates both Bloch and the case to his own advantage. What greater demonstration of power can there be than to foist your own crime upon your victim, making *him* feel guilty about it. Finally, and viciously, Hastler twists the knife in his client by revealing that Bloch's trial has not yet even begun. The fear, the torment, and the enslavement are never-ending.

Always in the wrong, the sobbing Bloch is sharply rebuked for doing exactly what the Advocate wanted him to do, which was to act out his enslavement to Hastler. He is denied both the right to rebel and the right to submit. "Have you no shame, to behave like that in front of my client? You're destroying his confidence in me." On the contrary, the Advocate has manipulated Bloch's performance in order to break K's occasionally rebellious spirit and encourage K's despairing dependence on the Advocate.

Disgusted by Hastler's sadomasochistic stage production, K walks away, firmly repeating his dismissal of the Advocate's services. Sitting up in bed, with the prostrate Bloch visible below him, Hastler confronts K without benefit of distancing devices. His cynical challenge offers K no shred of dignity in pursuit of security. "To be in chains is sometimes safer than to be free." But K increasingly demands more for and of himself. He wordlessly departs (Hastler having devalued all words during their confrontation), pursued by the Advocate's mocking laughter.

Leni follows K to make a last ditch effort to change his mind. Failing that, she advises him to contact a man named Titorelli, the official court painter who presumably has influence with the judges whose portraits he paints. She is careful to offer this advice out of Hastler's earshot. Does she really care about K? Or is she again acting as the Advocate's agent, setting K up for yet another disappointment, so that in despair he will crawl back to Hastler. Neither we nor K are sure of her motive. James Naremore suggests that the negative portrayal of women in *The Trial* result from Welles's "reactionary attitude toward women" in general (Naremore, p.213). Possibly. But it is *K* who tried to seduce Miss Burstner, not the other way around. And he is a willing participant in the attempts of Leni and Hilda to seduce him. Determined to free himself from the Advocate's clutches, K smashes open the door and leaves.

Titorelli, the court painter, is a celebrity adored and hounded by hordes of teenage girls. Among them is a girl with a hunchback, suggesting emotional neediness as a characteristic of fanatical devotion. Rudy Bloch was no less needy in his groveling behavior towards the Advocate. Titorelli is *any* artist who climbs into bed with the power of the State. His residence, constructed out of ill-fitting slats that do little to guard his privacy, resembles a prison, and is surrounded by fans relentlessly pressing in on him. It is perched at the top of a long and winding staircase, above what appears to be a giant boiler. The proverbial pressure cooker. Like any artist whose social status depends on the approval of powerful public officials, Titorelli's situation is precarious. The camera follows K's dizzying journey up the staircase, in the company of the artist's screaming fans and loud, fast jazz on the soundtrack. The fans' interest in K is sparked by their belief that he wants Titorelli to paint his portrait. Since the artist specializes in painting prominent officials, K must be someone important. At first K is intrigued by the attention he receives from the girls, smiling as they grab at him. But the hothouse thrill of celebrity quickly cools as he discovers its drawbacks, echoed by a change in background music when he enters Titorelli's cage. Throughout the remainder of the scene K feels increasingly hot and claustrophobic, particularly under the ceaseless scrutiny of numerous, anonymous eyes staring at him through the slats. I am reminded of the newsreel camera peering through gaps in a wooden fence to spy on the elderly, wheelchair-bound Charles Foster Kane.

Despite the appearance of prison bar-like shadows everywhere in Titorelli's apartment, including across his shirt, the artist has adapted well to his gilded captivity. He forcibly ejects some of his more ardent fans, and complains to K of their constant intrusion. But there is sexual innuendo in his words. Perhaps he has enjoyed the benefits as well as suffered the annoyance of their zealous attention. Light streaming in through the slats throws striped shadows across K's face and clothing. Laughing girls poke at him. A striped sheet is draped over one of Titorelli's paintings. Art too, as well as the artist, is a prisoner here. K asks for the painter's legal advice. Titorelli slyly implies that the price of that advice is the purchase of one or more paintings. The paintings becomes a device for K's enslavement to Titorelli.

Titorelli's artistic enslavement to the court becomes clear when he tells K that he paints judges according to their instructions rather than his own artistic vision. The subject of Titorelli's latest work-in-progress wanted wings painted on his feet, combining Justice with the Goddess Victory. K comments that the result looks less like Justice than it does the Goddess of the Hunt "in full cry." Not a reassuring image of the Law for an accused man to have. In his arrogance and vanity the Judge chose to have Justice, meaning of course himself, portrayed as a symbol of naked power rather than of fair play. By following the Judge's instructions, Titorelli *coincidentally* painted his subject accurately, as a predator. But the artist seems unaware of that irony.

While he and K continue to fend off his intrusive fans, Titrelli casually remarks that the girls belong to the court. "Practically everything belongs to the court," he adds. Are the artist's fans hired by the court to flatter and perhaps even sexually satisfy him? Or are they spies sent to monitor his behavior? Or is Titorelli merely being paranoid about them, as K was earlier about the fickle crowd at his interrogation by the Examining Magistrate?

Titorelli's influence over the legal process is less than K hoped. The best he can do is to get K an "ostensible acquittal," which would merely return K to square one, susceptible to yet another arrest and another trial. "Definite acquittal" is so far beyond Titorelli's influence that he's never even heard of one before. If the painter, along with the police inspectors, the Guard, and the Advocate, are intermediaries between K and the Law, like the Guard in the Prolog parable, they are only peripheral figures of power at best. K will never gain access to the Law's inner sanctum, if indeed there is one.

Titorelli's matter-of-fact description of the Law's endless complexities and absurdities, much like the Advocate's description of Rudy Bloch's legal case, drain the hope out of Joseph K, who gradually succumbs to panic. Staring eyes and pitiless grins press in on him through prison-like walls. The faces of Titorelli's fans seem less human and more frightening by appearing to us, and to K, in fragments. Titorelli's earlier description of waking up in the morning and being startled by the presence of a judge in his room recalls K's first encounter with the Inspector, and Hilda's with the Examining Magistrate. Not even the sanctity of home is guaranteed. But K and Titorelli are not equals in the present scene. The artist has a tactical advantage over his guest, who by now wants only to get out of the celebrity's cage. Before letting him go, Titorelli exploits K's weakened condition to sell him several paintings K does not really want, and to subtly threaten K with scandal at his work place should K try to renege on their business arrangement.

Surprisingly for K, but not for Titorelli, the back door leading out of the apartment leads *into* the law court office, lending credence to Titorelli's earlier claim that almost everything belongs to the court. He accepts it as a permanent fact and accommodates himself to it, compromising his artistic as well as his moral integrity along the way. Oppressed by the rather jolly cynicism of Titorelli's confinement, K flees from it, and figuratively from the "Adagio" that by now subjectively expresses his own growing fatalism.

In a long corridor lined with bulging drawers and piles of legal documents, K encounters more of his fellow accused, who again stand to greet him. In an earlier scene he believed they did so because they thought he was a judge. Now, in panic and influenced by an old superstition told to him by the unreliable Rudy Bloch, he interprets their deference as fear, rooted in their assumption that the shape of K's mouth marks him as a condemned man. K's perception of the same phenomenon changes over time, in accordance with changes in his emotional state.

Fleeing from people who should be his allies, K finds himself in a corridor lined with the same ill-fitting slats that lined the walls of Titorelli's residence. A mob of the painter's screaming fans pursues him from just beyond those slats, their youthful frenzy enhanced by slightly fast motion photography, fluid tracking shots, and a distorted soundtrack. K runs from them like a deer hunted by a pack of wolves. Are they agents of the State? Or do they mindlessly chase the fleeting celebrity that rubbed off on K as a result of his encounter with Titorelli? Could he turn this horde of Irmies into an army for his cause? No. His panic precludes it. At one point during the chase the camera pans rapidly with him as he passes by. The lighting pattern of stripes across K's face and body becomes so severe that we cannot make out his real shape. He becomes the invisible man, disappearing into the overwhelming pattern of his environment. This moment is the apex of K's fears and the impact of those fears on the partly subjective imagery of the movie. Terror reduces him to an inhuman abstraction. Subsequently running through what appears to be a concrete sewer, he chases his own shadow. The demons he runs from are both external and internal.

Eventually K eludes the mob. A tracking/traveling shot of the girls reaching in through openings in the stone wall to get at K cuts to just a traveling shot moving past tall church windows in a different wall. One image of worship segues to another. In extreme long shot K stands on a bare floor in a cavernous room lit by a few hanging light fixtures. A tall, riveted iron pillar is visible to his right. Is this a church or a factory? A godlike, off screen voice calls him by name. It belongs to a Priest. What began as a high angle shot emphasizing K's smallness within a huge setting now becomes a low angle shot of him looking up at a clergyman in a pulpit. Both camera angles show the protagonist at a visual disadvantage.

The Priest is surprisingly well-informed about K. He knows K's name, that K is charged with a crime, that K's case is going badly, and that K's guilt is already presumed proven. It is not a sympathetic voice. Reinforced by Albinoni's "Adagio" and a low camera angle that gives the Priest an air of authority, it is more like the voice of doom. Even after he descends from the pulpit and joins K on the floor, the Priest exhibits little compassion. K defensively retreats behind a fatuous, self-serving generality: "How can any man be found guilty? We're all simply men here, one as much as the other." The Priest fires back, "The guilty always talk like that." Neither character is particularly admirable in this confrontation. K evades all responsibility while the Priest arrogantly presumes guilt.

Though he has done nothing to earn K's trust, the Priest asks K what his next move will be. Nervously edging away from the clergyman, K announces in a voice more confident than his body language that he intends to get more help. Pursuing K, the *voice* of the Priest criticizes K's excessive reliance on outside help — especially from women. This is an odd statement, perhaps reflecting the Priest's own view of women. K sees a tactical opening and returns fire, pointing out that women have influence with powerful public officials. He adds, sarcastically, that the Priest wouldn't know much about that (sexual) aspect of the court.

K attempts to withdraw from the confrontation on this minor note of triumph, using his job as a convenient excuse to leave. The grim "Adagio" fades out. But escape is not that easy. K slips behind a curtain like an actor leaving a stage. But he finds no exit there. Groping his way blindly along a wall, K grows anxious again. And in this moment of vulnerability he is approached by the Advocate, who has left his sick bed to persuade the protagonist to re-hire him. K himself remarks on the film's confusing intermingling of different public settings when he asks what the Advocate is doing in a church. "Or am I still in church? Or is this part of the law offices?"

Hastler's appearance outside his own apartment is strong evidence that K's case is important to his career. Perhaps even vital, considering earlier hints of his declining reputation. With close-cropped hair and a full face, there is something starkly brutal about Welles's appearance in this scene. No longer posing as indifferent or amused, he now actively *hunts* his prey.

Pursued by Hastler, K flees towards a light, still searching for a way out of the institutional maze in which he feels trapped. Instead he bumps into a table on which sits a slide projector. Appearing as if by magic, it is a visual aid serving the Advocate as a tool of propaganda. Striding out of the camera frame and away form the Advocate, K contemptuously dismisses that propaganda. "Lectures and sermons" lumps State and Church together as institutional forces attempting to coercively shape his perceptions and determine his fate.

Backed by eerie music of disorientation, Hastler projects his slide show on a screen behind the protagonist, who appears visually trapped within it. K turns to watch the show, which consists of the same images used in the Prolog. Noting that the parable of the Law is derived from writings which preface the Law, the Advocate uses the parable to discourage K from thinking he can successfully defend himself in court. The return of the Prolog in this scene changes its dramatic status from a general statement of pessimism about the Law and Fate by film maker Orson Welles to a more narrowly defined instrument of intimidation and persuasion employed by the Advocate. Instead of underpinning and informing the drama as a whole, the parable is reduced to a dubious piece of propaganda linked to a flawed character. And it is no coincidence that the slide show images up on the screen resemble movie images. Like Stanley Kubrick in *Dr. Strangelove* and *A Clockwork Orange*, Welles implicates his chosen art form in the crimes of political oppression. Michael Anderegg observes that Welles liked to play characters who "recite pointed moral tales" (Anderegg, p.147). Like Harry Lime and Mr. Arkadin, among others, the Advocate tells his tale for tactical reasons. In *The Stranger* FBI detective Wilson shows Mrs. Rankin, the unwitting wife of a Nazi criminal, a film of Nazi concentration camp horrors in order to persuade her to betray her husband. Wilson is willing to put Mrs. Rankin's life in danger in order to achieve his goal. The Advocate's reason for showing and telling K the parable of the Law has no such patina of morality. He simply wants to line his own pockets and promote his own reputation. Late in *F for Fake*, narrator Welles undercuts himself by exposing as fraudulent a story he told earlier. He *wants* us to be aware of the deceptive as well as enlightening potential of art.

The slide show is a parable of Fate's unconquerable power over the individual. A shot of K's silhouette walking towards the illuminated screen creates the visual illusion that he is walking in place, unable to get any closer to the gateway which provides access to the Law. But at the same time he *verbally* rejects the grim lesson visually offered to him. "I've heard it all before. We've *all* heard it" suggests that the parable is a collective myth, perhaps force fed to school children. Continuing with the parable in a hushed, portentous voice, the Advocate announces the Guard's intention to close the gate, ending all hope of the Man gaining access to the Law. But as Hastler narrates the tale we see a close-up of his hand changing slides in the projector. By showing us the *mechanism* of the parable, Welles distances us from its *content*, as he did with "News on the March" when he showed us the projection booth from which it emanated in *Citizen Kane*. It's all sleight-of-hand. A magic trick. Which doesn't necessarily make it meaningless or false. But it does make the audience aware of that "man behind the curtain" manipulating the show, as Dorothy discovered in *The Wizard of Oz*.

The Advocate annotates his parable, noting that other commentators have pointed out that the Man approaches the door to the Law voluntarily. The implication is that he has only himself to blame for the disappointing results. A medium close-up of K standing in front of the projected doorway includes Hastler's shadow standing off to one side. Hastler has, in effect, inserted himself into the parable. But K, unlike Rudy Bloch, has learned to question what he is told and shown. "It's all true?" he asks in a mocking voice. Hastler counters with, "We needn't accept everything as true. Only what's necessary." Necessary for what? For whom? To sustain myths which provide an advantage to people like the Advocate? K sees through this smokescreen. "God, what a miserable conclusion. It turns lying into a universal principle." Like Charlie Kane, Hank Quinlan, and Harry Lime, who all combine ambition and egotism, Hastler cannot help but project his own needs onto his view of the world. Rejecting such self-serving cynicism, K walks away from the projection screen, his silhouette becoming larger than the Advocate's. He takes himself out of Hastler's projected reality, which he no longer mistakes for truth.

K approaches the projector and removes the slide depicting the closed gateway, leaving a blank, white screen. Hastler's shadow appears now in front of that screen, in effect trapped in *K's* magic lantern show. Changing tactics, the Advocate tries to discredit K's defiance by re-defining it as a ploy to set up an insanity plea based on delusions of persecution. The two men face off, with the now blank slide show screen visible between and behind them. Painting conflicting portraits of their struggle, they in a sense contend for control of that screen. The Advocate offers K a chance to play the role of "victim of society," which would make the protagonist as self-serving as Hastler. K is now shown standing by himself in front of the blank screen, on the verge of allowing Hastler to define and control him. But again he rebels. "I am a *member* of society," is an acknowledgement of personal guilt, though not necessarily guilt of the unspecified, official charge against him. K refuses to disassociate himself from the corrupt society around him, and therefore accepts at least some of the blame for its corruption. Which is only right, since we've seen him treat other people quite badly at times. K again walks away from his adversary and the slide show screen.

Unable to comprehend K's uncynical attitude, the Advocate dismisses it as another gambit to convince the court of his insanity. But K brilliantly undermines that argument by turning it on its head, accusing the court of *wanting* him to believe he's insane because it makes him easier to intimidate and control. That is also what the Advocate wants, because it would keep K, like Bloch, hopelessly dependent on him.

The projector light fades out, extinguished by the force of K's rejection of the Advocate's and his own illusions. "It's all lost" he sadly acknowledges, referring to his legal case. But he no longer projects his private burden onto the rest of the world. "So what? Does that sentence the entire universe to lunacy?" Rejecting cynicism in the face of personal defeat is K's triumph over the Advocate, who long ago succumbed to that cynicism in himself. Declaring his liberation, K is shown in close-up, his face half in shadow and half in light. Despair is not dispelled entirely, but it does not consume him either. Like O'hara escaping from Elsa's cynicism in *The Lady from Shanghai*, K evades the Advocates.

Leaving Hastler and resuming his search for an exit, K pays his final disrespects to the Priest, who approaches him with yet another challenge. "Can't you see anything at all?" Locating an open door through which light enters, K finds his *own* exit from despair after, paradoxically, being denied access to institutional justice. He answers the clergyman's challenge. "Of course I'm responsible" sums up his change of heart since the beginning of the film, when he denied *all* guilt. The Priest patronizingly refers to K as "my son." K rebuts, "I'm *not* your son," rejecting the Priest's presumption of authority over him. Then he exits through the door. Albinoni's dirge continues on the soundtrack. But by implication K now rejects its grim message too.

Outside it is night. K emerges from the cathedral. Though visually dwarfed by its enormous facade, he strides triumphantly away from the church and towards the camera, whose frontal angle emphasizes his determination. But a reverse, low angle shot pictures the two plain-clothed policemen, seen earlier in the film, stepping out from the imposing facade of another large building. Perhaps another government building. Victory over one's self does not necessarily translate into victory over the outside world. The "Adagio" continues to haunt the protagonist. From one particular camera angle the policemen seem to emerge out of K himself, just as K seemed to emerge out of the Guard many scenes ago. They are all variations on each other, each capable of being tormentor or victim, deluder or deluded.

K's mysterious escorts manage to look ordinary and sinister at the same time. With no word of explanation they hustle Joseph K through deserted city streets. K offers no protest or resistance to his abduction. He seems to know *his* battle against the State was bound to end this way. In extreme long shot the camera, like a timid pedestrian out after curfew, peeks at his obscure kidnaping from around the corner of a building. K's is a classic disappearance in the night, concealed from public view. The trio moves past urban facades old and new, but always massive. Along the way they pass by the still shrouded statue of ... Justice? Their oppressively silent journey takes them to the city's outskirts. Past a placid river that mirrors the slumbering, perhaps willful ignorance of K's fellow citizens. Ignorance that K once shared. The disruptive protagonist is to be discarded like so much garbage.

The site of K's execution is an abandoned rock quarry dug into a flat, littered wasteland. A stationary camera pictures K and his abductors receding far into the distance, again highlighting the terrifying obscurity of K's grim fate. Nature too, in the form of a dawn sky, visually overwhelms him. One of the policemen tries to remove K's jacket, but K insists on doing it himself, retaining a sliver of control in a hopeless situation. He is rudely shoved into the quarry pit, where he calmly and neatly sets his jacket aside and then removes his vest, tie, and shirt.

The policemen reluctantly follow K into the pit to complete their assignment. They lay K's head gently down on his rolled-up jacket. From out of a case that conveniently disguised its contents they retrieve a large butcher knife. While K passively though nervously watches them, they pass it back and forth, neither wanting to play the role of executioner.

K takes advantage of their hesitation. Refusing to commit suicide for their convenience, he forces them to take personal responsibility for the deed. In other words he tries to do for them what he finally did for himself. So they too are human — capable of contradictory feelings. Devotion to duty duels with repugnance and shame. They flee from their dilemma, as K did from the storage room where two policemen were being tortured as an indirect result of his accusation that they solicited a bribe form him. K stands, taunting his executioners with words and laughter as they climb out of the pit. Has he won? No. The executioners merely distance themselves from their victim. Instead of stabbing him to death, they toss a lighted stick of dynamite into the pit and run away. Crouching on the ground at a safe distance, and viewed from the rear, they look as undignified as Bloch did while prostrating himself before the Advocate.

A moment before the dynamite explodes, K bends down, picks up something, and starts to hurl it out of the pit. Is it the dynamite? Does K actively rebel by turning the weapon back on his oppressors? The ambiguity of K's final act can be measured by the diversity of critical interpretations of it over the years. James Naremore (Naremore, p.201) and Peter Cowie (Cowie, p.175) see K reaching for the dynamite before it explodes. Ernest Callenbach suggests that K kills his executioners with it (Callenbach, p.42). And Joseph McBride views the "mushroom" cloud resulting from the explosion as an indication of K's "tragic decision to be the agent of universal destruction" after passing judgement on the wicked world (McBride, p.147). That would mean that K finally embraces the Advocate's cynicism. At the other end of the spectrum, Peter Lev contends that K "insists on his dignity, but does not take up arms against his oppressors" (Lev, p.182). Strangest of all interpretations is that of Charles Higham, who sees Joseph K blowing *himself* up with the dynamite, despite earlier refusing to kill himself with a knife (Higham, p.165).

The way I see it, the explosion comes from the pit, not from the flat ground surrounding it, where the executioners crouch. And K's laughter ceases the moment of the explosion.

He is dead. Whether or not he died in the act of taking up arms against his enemies is left vague by Welles, who may have wanted his audience to ponder for themselves the moral implications of K's situation. What is *not* vague is that we witness the explosion from a comfortable distance equivalent to the executioners' perspective. The executioners who in the end could neither disobey orders no face up to the gruesome consequences of obeying them. K dies out of sight, anonymously. Only the cessation of his laughter marks his termination. Until Welles inserts music to cry out *for* him.

As smoke from the explosion rises out of the pit, Albinoni's "Adagio" returns to the soundtrack, but in a different form and to a different effect than earlier. Previously a muted, melancholy, and passive ode to grim Fate, it now *screams* out of the soundtrack, passionately protesting the injustice done to Joseph K and the cowardice of his executioners. In order not to disrupt the powerful counterpoint of sound and image, the movie's final credits are spoken rather than shown by Welles. But during that narration the "Adagio" settles back into its passive, fatalistic mode and the screen freeze frames, lingering on the now vaguely mushroom-shaped remnants of the explosion that killed K. Despite Welles's protest to the contrary (Welles/Bogdanovich, p.275), there is a whiff of nuclear menace in that image, as though K's personal triumph over cynicism were displaced by a much bigger reason for despair. A looming threat to the entire world instead of to one man. But tempering that gloomy, apocalyptic impression is Welles's voice reading the final credits, reminding us that this is a movie — an imaginative exploration of possibilities rather than an unimpeachable prophecy of the future.

The second to last image in *The Trial* is a close-up of the slide projector, with a glaring image of the door to the Law visible on the projector lens. Suddenly the glare is removed and the tiny slide image becomes clearer. Then comes a full shot of the door, minus all traces of the technology (projector) that brings it to us. The door is almost closed. But whether the door is optimistically half open or pessimistically half shut, Welles reminds us that the image is after all just a metaphor — a metaphor fashioned by someone for a purpose. Just as Charlie Kane fashioned a glass ball paperweight scene into Rosebud.

6

Chimes at Midnight: Rough Winds

Two tiny, silhouetted human figures far in the distance walk slowly across a wintry rural landscape. The larger figure limps and uses a walking stick. The smaller one carries himself with arthritic caution. They disappear behind a much larger tree trunk in the foreground — human fragility and mortality overshadowed by the comparative solidity and permanence of nature. It is the winter of their discontent. But this is not *Citizen Kane*, with its grim introductory portrait of decay and death. A sprightly tune played on recorder accompanies the two anonymous figures on their laborious trek, suggesting a rather lighthearted attitude towards the ravages of time. Image and sound gently counterpoint one another at the start of the remarkable *Chimes at Midnight*. How Welles was able to make two such stylistically contrary movies, *The Trial* and *Chimes*, back to back, and do them both justice, is something of a marvel.

The film's second image gives identities and voices to the characters. They are fat Sir John Falstaff and skinny Robert Shallow. The camera remains stationary, highlighting their difficult progress through and out of the camera frame. But if their bodies are worn out and even the sprightly recorder music now deserts them, Shallow's nostalgic reminiscences warm their path. "Jesus, the days that we have seen," he boasts to his more subdued companion, who gently reprimands, "No more of that, Master Shallow." One can imagine old Charlie Kane and old Jed Leland (or even old Orson Welles and old Joseph Cotten) engaging in similar banter, had they been able to overlook each other's many faults and reconcile in *Citizen Kane*. In *Touch of Evil* Hank Quinlan and Pete Menzies share a similar remembrance of things past. Certainly Falstaff has as many faults as those four characters. But they are not *fatal* flaws, and his spirit is more generous, more forgiving.

The old men find shelter in a building, moving towards and past a crude furnace blazing in mid-foreground. Typical of a Welles movie, deep focus photography and character movement from background to foreground heighten our visual sense of the distances between objects, and therefore our appreciation of the movement of those objects either towards or away from each other.

Shallow inquires about a mutual friend whom he has not seen for a long time. "She lives," Falstaff replies succinctly, his tone of voice implying that the *quality* of her life nowadays leaves much to be desired. Shallow pumps him for details. Falstaff supplies the only detail that matters. "Old, old, Master Shallow." A church bell chimes in the distance, figuratively tolling for the passing of an entire generation. Visually dwarfed by Nature in the movie's first shot, the old men are now diminished by the lofty interior of Robert Shallow's house. "She cannot choose but be old," Shallow cheerily replies to Falstaff's cheerless observation. In Sir John we detect a deeper sensitivity to the ravages of time and loss. A sensitivity which inspires in him both an existential defiance of death and a tolerance for the vicissitudes of life. His relatively somber mood in the Prolog adds emotional depth and foreshadowing to the carefree, witty Falstaff we encounter after the opening credits. Just as Charlie Kane's death at the beginning of *Citizen Kane* tempers later scenes depicting his youthful vitality.

Falstaff and Shallow retreat to a corner of a cavernous room and seat themselves in front of a roaring fireplace. By moving his camera and having the characters crouch under a heavy wooden beam to reach the bench, Welles intensifies our impression of the warm coziness of their little sanctuary. Cut to a big close-up of their faces. Lit by flickering firelight, the two old friends regard each other affectionately as they reflect on their long acquaintance and many adventures together. Falstaff sums it up best, echoing the metaphor of the church bell still ringing in the distance. "We have heard the chimes at midnight." Shallow heartily agrees, but fails to catch the melancholy note in his companion's remark. Falstaff glances at his foolish friend with fond indulgence. For all their difference in stature, these two old gentlemen are a matched set — another Laurel and Hardy. But in spite of similar ages and shared memories, they see themselves differently. Shallow has emotionally taken up residence in the past, remembered or imagined, like Charlie Kane fixating on Rosebud. Falstaff, as we shall see, still resides joyously in the present. He sees too clearly the tricks behind the fantasies we employ to ward off fear, regret, and sorrow. Yet at the time of his appearance in the Prolog, he is much closer to his dotage than he realizes. The wistful quality of Falstaff's voice as he speaks of hearing the chimes at midnight conveys a lifetime of experience and memory. What a difference there is between his ancient, wizened face and the ravaged, tormented face of Hank Quinlan at the end of *his* days in *Touch of Evil*.

By means of a gradual progression from the beginning to the end of the Prolog, the camera moves from extreme long shot to big close-up of Sir John Falstaff—from an objective recognition of his insignificance and fragility in the larger order of things to a warm intimacy with his wisdom, affection, and tolerance. The Prolog from *Chimes at Midnight* exemplifies Welles's filmmaking at its best. And though he clearly relishes Shakespeare's hyper-articulate dialog, which requires neither concrete imagery nor even (blasphemy!) actors to achieve dramatic eloquence, Welles prunes the Elizabethan rhetoric sufficiently to allow his camera and his non-verbal soundtrack to often speak volumes for his characters. Unlike Welles's *Macbeth* and *Othello*, *Chimes* is an amalgam of re-fashioned fragments derived from several Shakespearean plays rather than an adaptation of one, coherent story line. The enthusiasm and aesthetic joy that exudes from this filmed mosaic is no doubt a product of the creative freedom Welles must have felt in making it. He could at once pay tribute to, exploit, and remain independent of his favorite playwright. In short, Welles had his cake and ate it too.

Prolog concluded, the film's opening credits roll by to the accompaniment of Angelo Francesco Lavagnino's vigorous martial music. That title music yanks us out of Falstaff and Shallows' fireside chat and thrusts us into a broader world of kings, armies, and politics. Reflection cedes to action. The camera follows suit, cutting first to an exterior shot of Falstaff's favorite hangout, the Boar's Head Tavern in Eastcheap, then to a shot of the tavern together with the massive, fortified stone wall of a castle in the distance, and then to a shot of the wall alone. Step by step we are drawn away from Falstaff's private realm and into the realm of public affairs. All three exterior shots contain men riding by on horseback, no doubt on some momentous business of state.

Cut to a low angle long shot of a dark line of peasant foot soldiers trudging up a hill, in the face of a strong wind. The oblique angle of their trek across the screen accentuates their numbers and their physical exertion. High over their heads hangs a large white cloud, visually diminishing them. Outfitted mostly in ordinary peasant garb rather than formal battle gear, many carrying implements more suited to farming than to fighting, they appear out of their element. A quick lap dissolve carries us to the end of their loose column. The helmet of a man bringing up the rear is blown off by a gust of wind. Moving gingerly, like Shallow and Falstaff in the Prolog, he turns back to retrieve it. His feeble movements counterpoint the martial music. He looks ill-suited to the life of a soldier.

That impression is in turn counterpointed by another that immediately follows it. The final image under the opening credits is a long shot of what look more like *real* soldiers. They stand facing the camera, with their feet planted firmly apart, and brandishing weapons. Visible to the right of and behind them are bodies dangling from makeshift gallows. Enemies of the State? *Macbeth* contains a similar image. Nor was punishment any less extreme in *Othello*.

The makeshift gallows are abstract in appearance, the tallest ones looking similar to the "Y" tipped staffs of the witches in *Macbeth*. On the other hand a crossbeam on one of the structures, just under the split in the "Y," resembles the crucifix-tipped staves also featured in *Macbeth*. An ironic symbol mixing Christianity and pre-Christian violence, reminding us of the contradictory nature and practice of royal power.

By positioning the foot soldiers at varying distances from the camera, and timing his shot so the sky in the background is lighter than the sky overhead, Welles adds visual depth to the image, emphasizing his recurring point that the world is very large and the individual very small.

Music fades and the screen goes blank. The emotionally detached narration of Ralph Richardson broadly sets the scene for events to follow. King Richard II has been murdered, rumor has it at the instigation of Duke Henry Bolingbroke, who is now King Henry IV in spite of the more legitimate claim of Edmund Mortimor, currently a prisoner of Welsh rebels and unlikely to be rescued by his rival. In other words at the highest level of state affairs the situations in *Macbeth* and *Chimes at Midnight* are nearly identical. Whatever qualities of honor, duty, compassion, and sobriety may later be exhibited by Henry and his eldest son, the Prince of Wales, their prestige and power are built on a foundation of murder and greed.

At the start of Richardson's brief narration the screen is blank, as in a cloudless sky. Suitable to the airy detachment of the narrator's vantage point. But as he describes the morally dubious circumstances of the present King's rise to power the camera tilts down to show Henry's royal residence, Pomfret Castle, circa the winter of 1400. In ethical terms we descend from the comparatively petty sins of Falstaff and Shallow to the more consequential crimes of the King.

Inside the castle's dark interior, which as James Naremore notes bears an atmospheric resemblance to the Thatcher Memorial Library in *Citizen Kane* (Naremore, p.222), we look up at a large window through which rays of sunlight stream down upon the new monarch. Seated on his throne, shielded by a row of uniformed soldiers, King Henry IV appears to us at first as an anonymous abstraction — a tiny, isolated, albeit splendidly illuminated portrait of frozen majesty. Almost a prisoner in an enormous dungeon, confined rather than protected by armed guards. That impression is partly false. Henry is master of the throne room, as the remainder of the scene bears out. But in another sense he *is* a prisoner of his rank, desperately guarding against potential usurpers who would do to him what he did to his predecessor, and constantly needing to maintain a rigidly formal, flawless public image bearing little resemblance to the untidy realities of human nature.

Relatives of the abducted Edmund Mortimor have come to Pomfret Castle to plead for the King's intervention on his behalf. The narrator accuses one of them of a different agenda: "to procure malice, and set things in a broil." Choosing between right and wrong in this dispute is like choosing sides in a cockfight. Everyone is stained with ambition, greed, betrayal, or brutality.

Shown from a low, oblique camera angle, the relatives of Edmund Mortimor cross from right to left. Towering stone arches and a line of guards armed with tall spears are visible behind and above them. The Earl of Northumberland, his son Hotspur, and the Earl of Worcester approach their new sovereign at a tactical disadvantage. Visually their procession recalls that of the foot soldiers in the previous scene, with stone arches and tall spears substituting for massive clouds.

From over the King's right shoulder we look down on Northumberland, who approaches the throne humbly but is rebuffed harshly. We do not see Henry's face (a distancing technique that enhances his majesty) as he loudly brands Mortimor a traitor. His advantage over the petitioners echoes that of Macbeth, who is shown from a similar angle during a royal audience. Henry looks and sounds every inch a king — all royal crown and resounding vibrato.

Hotspur rises to Mortimor's defense more forcefully that did his father, thereby earning a medium close-up. Moving out of the tilted camera frame, he appears to boldly charge uphill to confront the King. In an oblique side shot of the combatants, he matches Henry in height, which Northumberland failed to do. But the bright shaft of sunlight from above falls solely on the King's face. The contest is uneven.

Worcester, predictably, lets his companions test the waters first before presenting his petition. We watch him ascend the steps towards the throne. For a moment he attains the camera's level, but then the camera pivots to adopt roughly *his* vantage point, looking *up* at the King, whose crowned head is bathed in sunlight. The contest is still uneven. Worcester's appeal, however, is notably different from those of his companions. He reminds the King of the material contributions his family has made to Henry's current "greatness," appealing to the King's political rather than moral sensibilities. This is a cold, cynical business. Fittingly, Henry's breath is visible in the chilly February air.

Worcester's appeal fails. Shown at a disadvantage, from behind the King's head, he bows in submission and withdraws. But his manner of doing so is calculated, self-conscious, almost a parody. Northumberland makes a feeble last effort to change the King's mind, but is ordered to leave, along with his son. For the first time we see Henry's face close up. The regal lighting effect and royal crown are still in place, and the camera is reverently low, but he now appears more human being than abstract icon.

Hotspur advances towards the throne as if to take it by force, then returns to his senses, bows curtly, and withdraws. On their way out of the throne room he and his two companions are again dwarfed by the castle architecture and the spears of Henry's royal guards.

Just as their approach to the throne occurred in staggered, separate movements, so does their retreat from it. They make up an imperfect alliance. Worcester waits for Northumberland and Hotspur at the entrance to an anteroom. Hotspur, recklessly defying the King's command not to speak of Mortimor, pauses briefly beside Worcester, then angrily storms ahead of him. Worcester follows, urging caution. The three men huddle again, until Hotspur, full of sound and fury at Henry's defiance of Richard II's proclamation that Edmund Mortimor be his successor, bolts away again from his timid companions. And again Worcester follows in an attempt to calm his young, headstrong ally. As usual Northumberland lags behind, avoiding contention. Ironically, when Hotspur turns to face his companions and accuses them of cowardice, Northumberland appears much larger in the foreground. We see only part of his body—a visual technique Welles uses elsewhere (e.g. Hank Quinlan stalking Grandi in *Touch of Evil*) to convey dominance rather than weakness. Worcester, occupying the middle ground, is next in size. Dynamic Hotspur, in the background, is the smallest.

Like the King, Hotspur cares about public opinion, both in the present and in a longer term, historical perspective. He says as much in his condemnation of Northumberland and Worcester. He may well be "the last of the true knights" who "could never betray a friendship," as Welles himself claimed (Welles/Bogdanovich, p.102), but he is not immune to the Machiavellian spirit of King Henry IV and the Prince of Wales. On the other hand, his passions often overrule his cold calculations. In that respect he resembles Falstaff. Hotspur's vision is more far-reaching than either Worcester's or Northumberland's, but it is also less pragmatic. His treasonous outburst is well within earshot of royal guards visible in the background.

Hotspur describes dead King Richard as a "sweet, lovely rose" compared to Henry,"this thorn, this canker." It is a contrast emotionally suited to support his argument for rebellion, and to fire his indignation into action. But Richard II was not universally viewed through Hotspur's rose-colored glasses. Among other grievances against his reign was a despised poll tax used to extract money from the poor in order to finance his war against France. Hotspur's unstinting praise of Richard is of the same dubious kind as George Minafer's belated regard for his dead father in *The Magnificent Ambersons*. Both are more politically convenient than heartfelt.

When Hotspur deserts his companions for the third time, the camera tracks with him in a close-up profile. His head rushes past a variety of visual patterns in the background that echo his agitation. He reverses direction, changes pace, and ignores Worcester as he walks past him. Railing against the "half-faced fellowship" of his allies, he speaks of performing seemingly impossible tasks to restore honor to the world, and not coincidentally pride to himself. Hotspur is the embodiment of the "starry-eyed idealist" on whom Hank Quinlan blamed most of the world's troubles in *Touch of Evil*.

Shown in a static shot matching his calmer state of mind, Worcester dismisses his young cousin as distempered. Now it is *his* turn to walk away in disgust—a calculated maneuver to gain the upper hand in their contentious alliance. Hotspur follows, apologizing for his rashness. Passive Northumberland, as usual, brings up the rear.

Impulsively charging past Worcester, Hotspur finally turns to face him in a shot similar to an earlier one, when he scolded his older companions for their passivity. This time Worcester is the large, partial figure in the extreme foreground. And this time Hotspur, looking small in the background, pleads for understanding rather than chastises. In a low angle reaction shot Worcester's new advantage is suddenly clear. Shafts of sunlight beam down near his head from a window above and behind him. Towering archways reinforce rather than diminish his stature. Northumberland, much smaller in the background, discretely positions himself behind Worcester, allowing the latter to fight his battle for him. Only when Hotspur calms down does his father emerge from behind Worcester's robes.

Hotspur contritely yields the floor to Worcester, who steps closer to him and speaks in conciliatory terms now. Displaying generosity *after* he gains the upper hand in their relationship, he even invites the impetuous young man to continue his former tirade. A new tactical arrangement reveals itself in another deep focus image of all three men. Linking passion and courage with status and political connections, Worcester leaves Hotspur in the far background and approaches Northumberland in the foreground, soliciting the latter's influence with the Archbishop of York in a scheme to build a military alliance against King Henry. The otherwise spineless, indecisive Northumberland is now a source of power to be wooed. Hotspur joins his two companions, re-forming the alliance they presented at the start of the scene. Sunlight seems to shine down benevolently on them. But they are not equal partners. Advising deception, which is *his* tactical forte, Worcester departs, leaving his partners smiling in admiration after him.

Northumberland is cautiously optimistic about Worcester's plot. Hotspur, as passionately optimistic now as he was pessimistic moments earlier, brims over with confidence. He gleefully ponders not only the overthrow of a King, but the murder of the King's drunken heir, the Prince of Wales, with a pot of poisoned ale. Poison? What happened to all that high talk about restoring honor to the kingdom?

Direct cut to the aforesaid Prince of Wales, imbibing from a mug of *un*poisoned ale in the cellar of the Boar's Head Tavern. A low ceiling counterpoints the lofty ceilings of Pomfret Castle, visually complementing the differences between low and high society. In spite of those differences, and of their brewing political antagonism, Hotspur and the Prince are alike in their youthful impetuosity. The camera wheels about rapidly as it follows young Hal, who tosses his drinking cup to Falstaff's young page, embraces several young women standing nearby, and trots up a narrow stairway to an upper floor. At the top of the stairs he encounters several older comrades sleeping off the effects of a drinking binge. The Prince, by contrast, has recuperated quickly. Unlike the mentor he presently seeks.

The tavern is a maze of rooms built out of asymmetrical slabs of wood, architecturally reflecting its multidimensional, flawed, very human inhabitants. As such it is very different from the spacious, symmetrical, and rather singular splendor of Pomfret Castle, which matches the *public* image of its reigning monarch. Before we encounter the King of Boar's Head Tavern, Sir John Falstaff, we learn that his pocket has been picked by an acquaintance named Poins. Hal shares in the fun of that prank by compounding it with one of his own. Who would dare joke in such a manner with King Henry? The tavern is a comparatively egalitarian kingdom.

Prince Hal is about to pour some ale on the exposed foot of his sleeping, snoring mentor when that same foot, by accident or design, rises up and kicks the cup out of his hand. Hal is surprisingly delighted by this foiling of his prank. Poins, however, left the vicinity before the prank commenced. He is both afraid of Falstaff and envious of the old man's ties to the powerful Prince of Wales.

Chastising Falstaff for laziness, but obviously admiring him for it at the same time, Hal leaps into bed beside his mentor, who slowly revives from a long sleep preceded by their drunken revelry. A low level shot of the two men from the foot of the bed might suggest a portrait of lovers. But the image is more maternal than sexual. James Naremore notes that Sir John is something of a surrogate mother to the young Prince, supplying warmth, love, and physical contact to counterbalance the stern, remote, fatherly lessons in honor, duty, and realpolitik that Hal receives from the King (Naremore, p.219). In another sense Hal and Falstaff are the youthful and aged faces of the same carefree, roguish personality. The contrast between youth and age is striking. Hal is slim, young, dark-haired, and vigorous.

6. Chimes at Midnight 223

Chimes at Midnight. Sir John Falstaff (Orson Welles, left) and Prince Hal (Keith Baxter) — decrepit old age and youthful vitality — make strange yet oddly sympathetic bedfellows at the Boar's Head Tavern.

Falstaff is fat, white-haired, wrinkled, and ponderous. Flash back to an image of Hank Quinlan and Miguel Vargas face to face, arguing legal ethics in Vargas's hotel room in *Touch of Evil*. Of course Hank and Miguel were too much at odds from the beginning of their relationship to forge a friendship. Sir John retains a zest for life which long ago deserted Quinlan. For every insult the Prince of Wales aims at the old man's self-indulgent, semi-legal lifestyle, Falstaff effortlessly conjures up a witty and sometimes wise retort.

King Henry answered opposition in the previous scene with ruthless authority. When Falstaff discovers his pocket has been picked he reacts with bluff, bombastic outrage. He even pauses before expressing that outrage, pondering what sort of reaction would have the greatest theatrical effect. For Falstaff, all the world's a stage, not to be taken too seriously. He knows too well that power and fame inevitably succumb to decay and death. So why not hang on to the only transitory things worth a damn — friendship and good times.

Falstaff's royal tirade is immediately challenged by Mistress Quickly, the tavern's Hostess, who denies his bombastic charge that her "bawdy house" harbors thieves and prostitutes. That charge is self-evident. Before discovering that his own money is missing, Falstaff confessed that *he* is a thief. His show of moral outrage now is pure hypocrisy, as was King Henry's condemnation of Edmund Mortimor as a traitor. But Henry's crimes are far greater than those of his Boar's Head counterpart. Falstaff's hypocrisy is full of overstated humor and self-awareness. The King, by contrast, admits nothing of his faults in public. Nor would he tolerate the Hostess's uppity retorts. So withering is her counterattack that Sir John briefly retreats from their contest, waged from opposite ends of a long, narrow staircase that exaggerates the distance between them. In this instance the imagery is deceptive. The two combatants are not so alienated from each other as they appear to be. Their argument is more for sport than for real.

Retreating to the main hall on the ground floor of the tavern, Falstaff instinctively seeks out an audience for his performance. He is, above all, an actor. And the Prince of Wales is often his biggest fan. The main hall is long and lofty, comparable in its crude way to Pomfret Castle's throne room. Our first glimpse of Falstaff in this setting is from a great distance, as was our first glimpse of King Henry. Sir John sits on a large chair resembling a crude throne. The camera looks up at him reverentially. But Falstaff's royal court, so unlike Henry's, is full of *mock* conflict and genuine laughter. He may boast loudly of "mine ease in mine inn," but his joy is shared with everyone. Including Mistress Quickly, at whose expense he jests.

Hal, from an equal or even higher visual plane, attacks Falstaff's credibility and thereby tilts the contest in favor of the Hostess. He flaunts an unpaid bill taken from Sir John's purse, validating the Hostess's charge that Falstaff owes her money. The victim of this attack swills from a cup of sack supplied to him by his faithful page. He is unfazed by Hal's betrayal, because it's all in good fun — most of the time.

Poins emerges from concealment at the very moment Hal declares Falstaff the quarrel's loser. Aping Hal's triumphant inventory of Falstaff's debts, Poins circles the besieged knight while attaching himself to the Prince. Craven and cunning, a discount version of *Othello*'s Iago, he seeks advantage wherever he can find it. The Prince of Wales is, for the moment, a source of considerable advantage.

Bested by evidence of his debt to the Hostess, Falstaff wisely seeks reconciliation with her. But reconciliation for him is just another avenue to victory. "I forgive thee" is no apology. Slapping her backside affectionately, he sends her off to fetch him more sack. And she happily obliges. With a bit of showmanship Falstaff triumphs over the minor setbacks in his life. And the laughter of his tavern audience affirms that, in this instance, everyone comes out a winner.

Leaving his throne to do verbal battle with his principle enemy (if "enemy" is applicable to a contest in which both sides win so long as they are entertained), Falstaff joins Hal in a quiet corner of the room. There, in an intimate tight shot, he accuses the young Prince, with mock sobriety, of leading his poor mentor into a life of wicked self-indulgence. To Hal's great amusement Falstaff deliberately undercuts his own argument with pregnant pauses and ironic qualifiers. The fun of it is that both characters *know* it's a performance. They all but dance around one another, with the camera (us) as their third partner, while Falstaff pretends to bemoan his own lack of virtue.

Poins re-joins them, transforming their duet into a trio. He proposes their next adventure be a robbery. Sir John agrees to it. Hal points out the obvious irony of Falstaff vowing to repent in one breath and plotting a crime in the next. But with a little verbal trickery Falstaff translates thievery into a respectable "vocation." He does so, however, while retreating from Hal, his body language conceding the flimsiness of his argument.

Huddled in a close-up and speaking in whispers to conceal their discussion from the other tavern patrons, who no longer play a role in their game, the three men plot their crime. A robbery of wealthy religious pilgrims and prosperous traders who are scheduled to pass through the area the following day. Hal initially grins in approval of the idea, then balks at participating in it. Falstaff reprimands him by, absurdly, accusing him of lacking such conventional virtues as "manhood," "honesty," and "good fellowship." More twisting of words and their meanings in order to further one's own interests, just as Hotspur did to bolster his courage and moral outrage in opposition to the King. The difference is that Hotspur was not aware of his own trickery. Falstaff is. He even sneaks in a jab at royal hypocrisy by insisting that Hal cannot be of royal blood if he cannot bring himself to steal from his fellow man. We've already learned that King Henry stole the crown from Richard II and Edmund Mortimor. Sir John is, among other things, an agent of satire held over from a dying era to puncture the rhetorical pieties of its successor. In the words of James Naremore he is "old Medieval Vice" now "brought into contact with the new politics" and become a "critic of the state" (Naremore, p.216). Like *Touch of Evil*'s Hank Quinlan, minus the heavy baggage of murder. Welles often sets up a conflict between opposing lifestyles, philosophies, and/or aesthetic values in which each side illuminates the other by direct or implied criticism. In *The Magnificent Ambersons*, for example, George versus Eugene is an uneven contest between spoiled brat and compassionate adult, counterbalanced by a lifestyle contest between George's elegant horse and buggy and Eugene's unreliable, polluting automobile.

Hal threatens to return to his father rather than participate in a robbery. Falstaff speculates that he himself will be branded a criminal when the prudish Hal becomes King. Betrayal is perhaps the worst crime between friends. Falstaff expresses bluff indignation by walking away from Hal, who follows him while protesting "I care not!" But Hal's flustered manner and the fact that he follows Sir John to dispute the point suggest otherwise.

Poins re-enters the camera frame from which Falstaff departed. Sensing an opportunity to curry favor with the heir apparent, at Falstaff's expense, he detains the Prince with a whispered jest about the old man. Grinning at the chance to reverse his recent defeat, Hal now *runs* to Falstaff, laughing and hugging Sir John and agreeing to participate in the robbery. Falstaff, unaware of the plot just hatched against him, dotes on the young Prince like a proud father. Poins joins them in a celebration of fellowship. Hal heads for the exit, exuberantly kissing a young woman and then passing her off to Poins, who departs off screen with her. All for one and one for all. The three scoundrels seem to share everything, from the contents of Falstaff's purse to the tavern's prostitutes.

Jed Leland began a negative review of Susan Alexander's operatic debut in *Citizen Kane*. Charlie Kane completed it, then fired Leland. It was, in their eyes, a mutual betrayal from which their friendship never recovered. In *Touch of Evil* Pete Menzies and Hank Quinlan ended up betraying and killing each other. Hal's participation in Poins's plot against Falstaff is a *mock* betrayal, well within the moral parameters of their friendship. It is an amusing charade rooted in rather than violating mutual trust.

Bidding farewell outside the tavern gate, Falstaff proves oddly prescient by advising the future King to remain indulgent of thieves like his old friend. In eloquently vague terms he defines himself as a romantic scoundrel a la Robin Hood. Falstaff describes his kind in general as "minions of the moon," like the fanciful characters populating Shakespeare's *A Midsummer Night's Dream*. He makes his gentle appeal while pictured in front of the tavern—home to a happy assortment of rogues. We view him from over the shoulder of the Prince, who stands some distance away and then turns his back on the old man. Shown in close-up, glancing up at the same bright sun that illuminated his father's face in an earlier scene, Hal speaks quietly and soberly of the need to awaken from Falstaff's dream world. Soft organ music plays in the background, lending conviction to his words. Visually framed by a tree trunk, the tavern's wooden facade, and Sir John's white-haired face, the Prince nevertheless makes a convincing argument that idle sport without hard work eventually becomes as tedious as the reverse. Turning to face his mentor, he betrays something of his more cynical view of life. He vows to reform his own character in a manner tailored to impress his future subjects, who will be pleasantly surprised by a display of moral strength from him. In other words he'll have his cake and eat it too: enjoying the fruits of Falstaff's idle lifestyle, then exploiting that very lifestyle in a public bid for credibility as a paragon of conventional virtue. Is Hal's friendship with Falstaff a sham? A mere staged event to further his political ambition in the long term? While thus challenging Sir John, the Prince is visually backed by an enormous stone wall in the distance, which symbolically stands in for his father's castle and for the conventional confinements of honor and propriety that Falstaff largely ignores.

Time for another reversal. The Prince of Wales undermines his declaration of realpolitik with a broad wink before departing into a broad, sunlit landscape, with the confining wall in the distance. Reassured, for now, that Hal's harsh words were spoken in jest, Sir John jokingly inquires if thieves will be hanged during the Prince's upcoming reign. Hal, replying in kind, offers to appoint his mentor as hangman of such thieves. Which is a clever way of saying "yes" while making it sound like "no."

The Prince of Wales skips merrily away from the tavern as Sir John fondly watches him go. The camera, situated above and well apart from both characters, but closer to Falstaff's point of view, pictures the sunlit landscape and the distant stone wall framed snugly within the tavern's open gate. For the time being Falstaff remains the spiritual father of young Prince Hal, whose fitful tilt towards King Henry will occur later. But we already sense the emotional pull of that forbidding wall and its King.

The frivolity by which Hal masks his puritanical side from both Falstaff and himself is counterpointed by the pomposity that underlies and undermines the seriousness of Hotspur's determination to depose Hal's father. A scene at Hotspur's castle is introduced and then repeatedly punctuated by an elaborate trumpet fanfare played by musicians standing high up on the battlements. Matching that fanfare, which seems to come at us from every angle, is Hotspur's rhetorical bombast as he reacts indignantly to a letter from a potential ally rejecting an appeal to join his risky crusade against King Henry. Two suits of armor, one with absurdly broad shoulders, stand behind him at left and right, reinforcing his hot rhetoric and the trumpets' blare. Between and behind the armored suits, Lady Percy struggles to get her husband's attention.

While Hotspur rants and raves the camera pulls back from him, revealing his pulpit to be a steaming hot bathtub. His fist-clenching call to courage is less convincing when spoken from such a position of leisure. The steam we could almost have believed spouted from the moral rage within his very pores is merely a token of comfort. Two servants rush into the camera frame to dry their master with towels as he emerges from the tub. Further offsetting Hotspur's tirade is some lightly festive background music, opposing the local trumpet fanfare. Approaching her husband, Lady Percy momentarily disappears behind the helmet of a suit of armor that embodies the dedicated, single-minded, rather mechanical warrior Hotspur aspires to be. Even in a story set in 1400 Welles finds a mechanical metaphor for the kind of automated, unthinking, dictatorial behavior he so distrusts. Like the pumping oil derricks in *Touch of Evil*, the statues decorating the church clock in *The Stranger*, the clacking of a thousand typewriters in *The Trial*, and automobiles in *The Magnificent Ambersons*.

Drying his genitals, discreetly below the camera frame, Hotspur enthuses, "By the lord, our plot is a good plot as ever was laid." The double entendre is obvious. Hotspur invests his sexual passion in his political crusade — a fact later confirmed by Lady Percy, who complains of being banished from his bed for the past fortnight. By way of contrast, Falstaff boasted to Hal that he had not visited a bawdy house but once in a quarter of an hour. An exaggeration, to be sure. But clearly he prefers sex to battle. Behind the smiling, metaphorically masturbating Hotspur one of the suits of armor stands with its legs knock-kneed, looking ridiculous.

Hotspur's plot against King Henry parallels the plot hatched by the Prince of Wales and Poins against Falstaff. But the serious consequences of the former contrast with the comparative harmlessness of the latter. Hotspur's unbounded, adolescent enthusiasm for war recalls Charlie Kane's eagerness to start a war between Spain and the United States. Or the puerile, sexually reinforced, eventually obscene enthusiasm for nuclear war displayed by several characters in Kubrick's *Dr. Strangelove*.

Hopping about in his bath towels and with his leggings pulled up only halfway, Hotspur rails against the fickle ally who rejected his call to arms. Actor Norman Rodway looks and sounds a bit like Laurence Olivier in this scene. Could Welles be mocking some of Olivier's lively interpretations of Shakespeare? Still struggling with his clothes, and yelling an overwrought "What, ho!" in close-up, Hotspur impatiently bolts into the courtyard to inquire about his horse. The doorway he passes through is covered in shadows resembling prison bars. A metaphor Welles uses also in *The Trial*, *The Lady from Shanghai*, and other movies. Serious matters underpin the comic surfaces of this scene. Hotspur is a prisoner of his own passions, including his notions of honor, which will eventually cost him and many other men their lives. But for now he plays the comic fool. Even his frustrated wife is amused. In an extreme long shot that diminishes his presence, he boasts that his horse will be his throne, then loses his grip on the towel around his waist, briefly exposing his backside. Rhetorical bombast and corporeal reality clash, as they often do in a more self-conscious manner with Falstaff.

Brisk editing in this part of the scene complements Hotspur's excitement. He returns inside the castle to finish dressing, attended by his amused wife. Worcester and several other men arrive outside, carrying a letter from Hotspur's father, who pleads illness as an excuse for inaction. Single minded of purpose, Hotspur interprets Northumberland's passive evasion as active betrayal, accusing his father of revealing their plans to the King. Fanaticism renders Hotspur intolerant of weakness in others. He pronounces judgement on his father while viewed from a distance and through a small window, which emphasizes the narrowness of his vision. It is as if Falstaff were directing this scene, aesthetically sabotaging Hotspur's passionate rhetoric at every turn.

Hotspur's moral disgust with his father parallels King Henry's moral disgust with his son, the Prince of Wales, who in turn is alternately disgusted with and pleased by his surrogate father, Sir John Falstaff. Ironically, one imagines Hotspur could more easily adapt to the extremes of *either* Falstaff or King Henry than to the noncommital, wishy-washy Northumberland. Perhaps Sir John adopted the wrong son.

Helping her husband get dressed, Lady Percy caresses him and complains of neglect. In several close-ups she is visually backed by a flaming fireplace — the lure of hearth and home. Hotspur's determination falters for a moment. Then he bolts from her and heads for the courtyard. She pursues him, briefly delaying his departure by physical force. In a tight shot her long hair eclipses his face. But he soon breaks free of her grasp and the camera cuts to a long shot.

Servants attend to Hotspur's shoes and cape. He roughly pushes them aside and rudely rebuffs his wife, "I love thee not, Kate. This is no world to play with mammets and to tilt with lips." And yet he appears dependent in many ways on those he turns aside in this scene.

His boast of independence rings hollow. He storms out of the camera frame, pursuing a world of "bloody noses and cracked crowns." Neither his words nor his delivery of them do justice to the carnage of battle he shortly instigates. Hotspur's understanding of the consequences he now so honorably and idealistically sets in motion is tragically inadequate.

Lady Percy employs her considerable charms to divert her husband from his mission. The playfulness of their banter undercuts the seriousness of that crusade. It's all a great, abstract game to him. With a fond, frivolous goodbye kiss—their *last* kiss, as it turns out—Hotspur departs, leaving his wife with a promise of great rewards to come. Royal crowns for both? With a smile and a casual shrug, she agrees to be content in his absence. They have no idea what lies ahead. In the scene's last shot we see them from a distance, framed overhead by a dark, ominous archway that foreshadows tragedy to come.

The excitement and confidence, however misplaced, of Hotspur's preparation for war is matched by preparations for another great undertaking in the scene that follows. Both adventures involve attempted robbery, though on vastly different scales.

In the woods at Gad's Hill, Prince Hal helps dress Falstaff in a white friar's robe, experiencing as much difficulty as Hotspur did putting on *his* clothes. A low camera angle emphasizes Sir John's vast bulk and Hal's struggle against it. Falstaff complains that he was thin when a young man, but that sighing and grief made him fat. We've seen little evidence of either. We *did* see evidence of prolonged grief in *Touch of Evil*'s Hank Quinlan, who by the time we joined his story had long since lost the capacity for tolerance, self-scrutiny, and good humor that Falstaff possesses.

There is a practical reason for the white robes worn by Falstaff and his co-conspirators in this scene. Posing as clergymen, the thieves mask their intentions from their intended victims. They are wolves in sheep's clothing. But when Sir John learns they will be outnumbered two-to-one by their victims, he fears an unintended reversal of roles. So much for reckless courage—the one quality Hotspur possesses in excess.

In a landscape filled with the slim trunks of tall trees, the wide, white-robed figure of Falstaff stands out like a polar bear in a tropical jungle. He calls for his horse, as did Hotspur, but is denied it. Unlike the prideful Hotspur, Sir John acknowledges his shortcomings and even abets the Prince's insults. Hal tells him to lie down with his ear to the ground and listen for the approach of their prey. "Have you levers to lift me up again?" Falstaff inquires, only half in jest. The whole undertaking is a fiasco, yet very entertaining, especially for the Prince. Not since Kane, Leland, and Bernstein invaded the staid offices of the *New York Inquirer* has Welles given us such an undiluted scene of friendship and good fun. And the site of this revelry is every inch a magical Shakespearean forest, even without the sprites and nymphs. The snowy, leaf-covered ground, dark tree trunks, and dappled sunlight create a visually idyllic forest. A wintry variation on Puck's playground, befitting Falstaff's late stage of life.

Posing as pious friars, Falstaff and his henchmen wait until their victims get within range, then draw their swords and chase them off. No one gets hurt or killed. Symbolic convention is overturned as the white-costumed thieves play our heroes while their dark-costumed victims play villains who were transporting money to the King's exchequer. Prince Hal and Poins, observing the robbery from a distance, exchange their white robes for black hats and capes, reversing their previously heroic roles. Hal, very conscious of the spirit of play, makes his costume switch with exaggerated theatrical flair—like a villain in a silent movie melodrama. He and Poins creep across the screen on sinister tiptoe while *their* victims, in white, collect their spoils in the background.

Falstaff holds two bags of stolen loot in his right hand. Snatching a third bag from

Bardolph, he complains, "Come, my masters, let us share." All for one and none for all, it seems. Falstaff frequently asserts the opposite of what is visibly true, yet his broad, self-conscious manner of doing so deceives neither himself nor anyone else. Expanding his self-righteous bluff, he complains about the absence of the cowardly Poins and Hal. A nearby donkey brays, as though laughing at Sir John's ludicrously hypocritical display of moral outrage. Then, suddenly, the "cowards" return, disguised as "real" thieves and noisily attacking Falstaff's little gang of not-so-cutthroats.

Sir John, moving with surprising agility, predictably *leads* his band of phony friars in retreat. The background music perks up and the camera tracks with these somewhat abstract, black and white, comical figures dodging and weaving among the tree trunks. Quickly falling behind, the fat man attempts evasive maneuvers and waves his sword ineffectually at his pursuers. He is what he accused Hal and Poins of being moments earlier — an errant coward. Later in the story, however, we see the grim consequences of *real* courage operating in a bloody cause.

Finding himself at the rear of his retreating troops, Falstaff jettisons his bags of loot and kicks them away in hopes of diverting his pursuers. Lingering behind with Hal and Poins, the camera observes Sir John's ignominious flight with cool amusement. The Prince and Poins, discarding one fake identity (dark capes and hats) for another (white friar capes), laugh uproariously while retrieving the discarded loot. They walk away, into the depths of a magical Shakespearean forest where adventure has no ill consequences.

Prince Hal's carefree departure from Gad's Hill is contrasted, by direct cut to the next scene, with his father's stiffly formal arrival in one of the large rooms of his royal castle. Henry's robes are dark. He wears his crown and speaks solemnly. The Christian cross hanging around his neck is not there for sport, though it conceals a multitude of sins. The white robe worn by his son in the previous scene was, by contrast, a deliberate and frivolous charade.

Accompanied by his younger son, Prince John of Lancaster, Henry complains of the "unthrifty" Hal. But what Hal stole from his father by way of Falstaff (the money intended for the King's exchequer) is trivial compared to what the King stole from Richard II. Word comes of large armies raised by Hotspur and Worcester to depose him. Yet he is much more disturbed by the *personal* dishonor inflicted on him by his wayward son. So great is that burden that he expresses envy of Northumberland, and wishes he could by magic exchange the Prince of Wales for Hotspur. It matters less to him what treasonous cause Hotspur espouses than that Hotspur's sense of honor drives him to follow it. That is the starry-eyed idealism Hank Quinlan condemned in *Touch of Evil*. But the earlier film deals with the horror of corruption. In *Chimes at Midnight* the scales are somewhat reversed, with the horror and hypocrisy of idealism matched against a kinder, gentler, wiser brand of corruption.

Tracked from directly in front by the humbly retreating camera, followed at a respectful distance by members of his court, and flanked by obedient, machine-like soldiers, King Henry walks down a passage while pondering his paternal curse of a debauched son. He speaks of the Prince's lowlife companions, "as stand in narrow lanes, and beat our watch and rob our passengers." It is probably no coincidence that the passageway King Henry walks through at this moment is both lofty and narrow, like his notions of masculinity and virtue. He contemptuously describes Hal as "wanton and effeminate"—the kind of effeminacy that Hotspur, preparing for battle, rejects in his wife and that Hal will eventually reject in himself and in Falstaff. But the corridor down which Henry walks grows darker and darker, foreshadowing not only the darkness of his approaching death, but also reflecting the moral darkness resulting from *his* notions of honor and duty.

The grand architectural symmetry of King Henry's castle is counterpointed by the more ragged contours of buildings along a street in Eastcheap. Prince Hal and Poins ride by on horseback, looking anything but effeminate, as Henry accused them of being. Tracked by a sympathetic camera, they enter Boar's Head while celebrating their easy victory over Falstaff in the forest and anticipating more entertainment to come when Sir John tells his inevitable lies about what happened there. They don't have long to wait. Falstaff enters, brandishing his sword at a keg of ale — something he did not do very effectively in the face of what he thought was *real* danger. He loudly damns all cowards while his beaten comrades slink into the tavern behind him, moaning and groaning in defeat. Sir John continues his tirade against cowardice while making a beeline for a cup of sack. What a contrast between words and action, like the visual contrast between Falstaff's white robe and his black hat and gloves. By placing his camera near the cup of sack, Welles humorously emphasizes Falstaff's resolute, straight-line movement towards it.

As soon as Hal and Poins reveal themselves, Falstaff spits the sack out of his mouth, throws down his sword in an exaggerated show of disgust, and repeats his curse on all cowards. His bluff ire momentarily displaces his thirst. But even as he verbally jousts with Hal, he pours himself another cup of sack. In *The Magnificent Ambersons* Welles simultaneously celebrates and demythologizes a bygone age. Similarly, Falstaff now complains that "good manhood" has been forgotten in modern times, adding that he is one of only three good men left in England. Having witnessed his behavior at Gad's Hill, we know better. But Sir John's boasting mocks itself anyway. He's full of blarney, but he knows it. The King's and Hotspur's complaints about dishonor are spoken without self-conscious irony. Falstaff's diatribes, in effect, parody theirs.

Reclining with Poins in a corner of the room, Hal challenges his mentor's boasting. Opposing sides in this conflict are shown in separate shots at first, emphasizing their contrary points of view. Leaving off re-filling his cup with sack, Falstaff takes up the challenge. With narrowed eyes and a slightly more serious tone of voice, he advances on the backtracking camera and his off screen foes while threatening to thrash Hal and put his subjects to flight. It is an empty threat, but delivered with a touch more bite than we are accustomed to from him. No doubt it is rooted in Sir John's false assumption that Hal and Poins behaved as cowards at Gad's Hill.

The Prince and Poins remain in relaxed postures. But Hal's facial expression is now serious, almost menacing. It is no trivial thing for him to have his honor challenged, even in apparent jest. Communication between characters in a Welles film often balances precariously between different outcomes. Mood is mercurial, partly because the intent of one character does not fully match perception in the other. After another exchange of insults Falstaff sits down at a table, contemptuously turns his back on his foes, and again proclaims them cowards. They appear in the far background while he looms large in the foreground — an image reflecting his feigned low regard for them.

Poins rises to the challenge, approaching Falstaff and enlarging his visual presence within the camera frame. Falstaff backs off his previous accusation of cowardice, only to re-state it in a roundabout way. "I would give a thousand pounds if I could run as fast as thou can'st." Wit is always Sir John's best weapon. The only one he wields with any authority. And he is not afraid to aim it at himself.

Prince Hal, better armed than Poins to engage the master in a war of words, approaches Falstaff on the other side. Feigning astonishment, he encourages Sir John to elaborate on his adventure in the forest. Predictably, it becomes a tale of great danger and courage, featuring a lengthy duel with many cutthroats — twelve taken on by Falstaff alone. Multiple, death-defying wounds and the loss of his stolen loot was the price paid. Hal eagerly attends to other members of Falstaff's gang when they are called upon to validate their leader's story. Then he turns back to face Sir John, sits down at the other end of the table, folds his hands, and solicits more details. The big man takes the bait, increasing his tally of beaten opponents from twelve to fifty. In a shot of Hal from Sir John's point of view we see the Prince looking small and humble, framed by the architecture and furnishings of Falstaff's domain. A reverse angle shot depicts Sir John as big and powerful as he points his finger at the camera, us, and Hal while bragging of killing two, then four, then seven foes. He does not realize that the Prince in front of him and Poins standing behind him have him tactically surrounded. As Sir John's tall tale stretches even taller, Hal closes range until Falstaff appears, and begins to feel, uncomfortably hemmed in.

But if they enjoy an advantage, Hal and Poins are not always a harmonious alliance. Outraged, Poins questions Falstaff's story. Hal pulls him aside to shut him up, insisting that their triumph will be sweeter by granting Falstaff more time to make a bigger fool of himself.

Speaking from his throne-like chair, with his humble subjects silently observing him from far in the background, Sir John inflates his tally of victims from seven to nine to eleven. But he has to twist awkwardly in his chair to address Hal and Poins, who are behind him. He does not appear as regally dominant as did King Henry when dealing with the challenges of Northumberland, Hotspur, and Worcester. But then, King Henry's court was not half so much fun as Sir John's.

Choosing one of his many inconsistencies to pounce upon, the Prince and Poins crowd around Sir John and commence their counterattack. Hal, predictably, leads the charge, with Poins following suit. In close-up Falstaff appears trapped on two sides, just as he falsely claimed to have been during the Gad's Hill battle. Deserting his now vulnerable throne for some breathing space, he tries to turn a disadvantage into its opposite by indignantly refusing to account for the discrepancies in his story, even under pain of torture. Magically, his inability to prove his courage at Gad's Hill becomes proof of his courage now. Of course, in the comparatively safe world of the tavern Sir John knows he will not have to face the torture he so valiantly defies.

Frustrated by his mentor's slippery tactics, Hal rails in protest, turning away in disgust only to return in outrage a moment later. He attacks Sir John's cowardice and physique, as though the two were linked. And he prefaces his assault in a curious manner. "I'll no longer be guilty of this sin. This sanguine coward." The emphasis on "I" suggests that *Hal* is the sinful one, that Falstaff represents his sin, and that the Prince intends to purge himself of both. Falstaff tries to return fire in kind, attacking the Prince's *slim* physique with so many unflattering metaphors that he runs out of breath. But they are empty insults. Unscathed, Hal scornfully encourages the old man to resume his attack after he catches his breath — another jab at Falstaff's age and poor physical condition.

Picking up the sword that Falstaff earlier tossed aside as an expression of contempt for *Hal's* cowardice, the Prince now offers a concise, convincing revision of Sir John's wildly distorted account of the Gad's Hill battle, as evidence of *Falstaff's* cowardice. The big man silently sits back down on his throne. From far across the table, near Hal's vantage point, we now see Falstaff looking insignificant, as we earlier saw the Prince from Sir John's perspective. Supplementing his verbal assault with a visual aid, Hal instructs Poins to drop a bucketful of coins on the table in front of Falstaff. It is the loot Sir John discarded in panic.

Recollecting another previous image, Hal and Poins crowd around their seated victim, daring him to answer their charges. After only a moment's hesitation he does so, casually claiming he knew all along they were the disguised robbers who attacked him. And that so knowing, he could not bring himself to harm them. The outrageousness of his claim transforms his opponents' scorn into appreciative amusement, though Poins first glances at the Prince for guidance as to how he should react. Falstaff heartily embraces both of them. No one believes Sir John's clever apology for cowardice, but all admire his inventiveness of wit. So in a sense, Falstaff in this scene escapes entrapment, as he *falsely* claimed to have done at Gad's Hill.

Restored fellowship is rudely disrupted from outside an intimate medium shot of Falstaff, Hal, and Poins. The Hostess rushes in, announcing the arrival of a messenger from the King who wishes to speak with the Prince. Visible behind her, through the open tavern doors which mark the border of Falstaff's kingdom, are royal soldiers racing by on horseback. They look like creatures from a different world.

Now that he and Sir John are reconciled, the Prince insults his real father's representative with a witty turn of phrase after the fashion of his surrogate father. Mistress Quickly is amused. She is loyal to Falstaff, in spite of their occasional spats. The Prince now sends *his* representative, Poins, to dismiss the King's. Basking in the sunshine of Hal's loyalty, Falstaff gathers his many friends around him, orders the gates to his kingdom closed, and proposes more entertainment in the form of an improvised play. The entertainment is also to serve a practical purpose, helping the Prince prepare for what will no doubt be an unpleasant audience with King Henry the following day. Intercut with this image of fellowship is a shot of Poins far in the distance, glancing back at Falstaff and Hal as he exits the tavern. Perhaps jealous of their intimacy, he looks like a man apart from rather than allied with Falstaff's merry band of revelers.

Quick cuts, a wheeling camera, and festive yet wistful background music, which both celebrates and laments the fragile world of make-believe, contribute to our impression of joyful activity as the tavern stage is erected. Hal, who is to play himself, grabs Falstaff's hat and puts it on his own head. This reinforces, albeit in happier terms, the mixing of their identities that we witnessed earlier in the scene, when Hal equated his own sins with Sir John's. Falstaff, meanwhile, transforms a seat cushion from his own chair into King Henry's royal crown — a nifty little insult to his rival for Hal's affections. And the chair that we formerly perceived as Falstaff's throne now represents King Henry's, raised appropriately to the top of a table.

Everyone gets involved in the production as the camera crosscuts furiously among different facets of preparation. An audience of patrons and prostitutes gathers in front of the impromptu stage. Props are assembled. Costumes and music are improvised. Welles places us nearly everywhere at once in what initially looks like chaos but soon develops into an organized enterprise. Falstaff looks even larger than usual in his makeshift crown. He is a bloated lampoon of royal dignity and authority. Prince Hal removes his friar's robe, which dates from a prior escapade, and appears again in his regular clothes to play himself in a *new* comedy. But when Poins returns with grim news from the real world outside the tavern, a contrary aspect of Hal's personality takes center stage.

Instead of rejecting the King's messenger on behalf of Hal, Poins *becomes* the King's messenger, spoiling the revelry of Falstaff's realm by reminding Hal of his neglected duties in the larger world. Pondering Hotspur's recent change of character, putting off the "quiet life" for "work," Hal walks away from Poins and into a shot with Falstaff, who remains in costume for the play and therefore looks ridiculous standing behind the uncostumed, now grim Prince. Trying to kid Hal out of his sudden fit of sobriety, Sir John inquires if the Prince is not afraid of the terrifying Hotspur. Bad timing. Hal reacts with a jest, but it is an *angry* jest that targets Sir John's and therefore indirectly his own cowardice. He also knocks off Falstaff's phony stage crown, signaling the end of make-believe. For a moment.

Suddenly recoiling from his own critical self-examination, Hal throws himself back into the spirit of play. He grabs, partially disrobes, and kisses the nearest available woman. Sensing that this might be his last hurrah with Falstaff, and therefore with his own lighter side, he abandons himself to revelry. Meanwhile a jubilant Sir John re-crowns himself, this time with a metal pot. Anything will do. He calls for a cup of sack in order to redden his eyes for his fierce performance as King Henry. It is, of course, a convenient excuse to have another drink. Poins is visible behind and above him, smiling now and apparently in full sympathy with the spirit of the occasion. Shown from a low angle, Sir John once again appears to be sovereign of the tavern. Shown from a slightly high angle, the smiling, enraptured Mistress Quickly reverently takes her seat in the audience.

With great effort, to the vast amusement of the gallery, Falstaff is hoisted up onto his newly elevated throne. Audience members in the cheap balcony seats are above him. They are as much a part of the festivities as he is in this relatively democratic production. Nevertheless, the mocking parallels to King Henry's first scene in the film are evident. Sunlight from a high window glints off Falstaff's pot as it did off Henry's crown. Sir John mocks the King's quavering voice, yet remains fundamentally himself by dipping his finger into a cup of sack and then sucking on it. Along with Hal, we kneel before him. The bogus King passes severe judgement on his heir apparent. Laughter from the Hostess disrupts his performance, and distracts Prince Hal. Sir John grumbles about the interruption, then merrily returns his attention to the play. By contrast, *his* disruption of *Hal's* play, the coronation near the end of the movie, will not be so well tolerated.

Employing elaborate wordplay, Falstaff comes close to labeling the Prince of Wales a bastard, then insults King Henry in the process of backing away from insulting Hal. Sir John is Shakespeare, deftly manipulating words and meanings for the sheer pleasure of doing so. He launches into a mock critique of the villainous company Hal keeps—something the real King has already done in all seriousness. But then he transforms that critique into a shameless celebration of his own virtues. It is quite an achievement to champion one's self while posing as one's greatest rival and harshest critic.

A change in camera shots brings Hal back into view. After weeping bogus tears of shame at his bogus father's rebuke, the Prince now challenges Sir John's self-serving praise. We observe Hal from a high angle shot taken near Falstaff's head, placing the Prince in an inferior position. But the absurd pot handle of Sir John's stage crown reminds us of the illusory nature of Falstaff's advantage.

Speaking in a resonant voice, Sir John sternly advises his son to retain the friendship of the virtuous Falstaff. With a dismissive wave of his royal hand he further commands Hal to banish his other lowlife companions, who from the audience cheer their own exile. They know this is only a play, with no ill consequences for themselves. Yet Sir John's mock banishment of them eerily foreshadows the very real banishment *he* will suffer at the hands of Hal.

Upstaged by his mentor's performance, the jealous Prince executes a role reversal even before the audience laughter fades. He strips Falstaff of royal robe and crown, puts the crown on his own head, and ascends to the makeshift throne. He does not, however, appropriate Falstaff's white friar's robe nor the relative innocence of spirit that went along with Sir John's performance as King. Shown in long shot during this rapid turnabout, Falstaff looks like a helpless manikin. But he adapts quickly, appropriating his page's cap to help him impersonate the young Prince of Wales. It is not a flattering wardrobe choice, from

Hal's point of view. After all, this is still a contest of egos, even if it is friendlier and gentler than King Henry's confrontation with Hotspur. In one particularly striking shot Falstaff dons his page's cap and rises up to challenge Hal while Hal wraps himself in his new royal robe and sits down on his throne. The plastic interchangeability of roles in this magical realm of make believe is beautifully illuminated in this image. But quicksilver changes in make-believe relationships sometimes reflect the same in *real* relationships.

The previous interplay between Falstaff and Hal is now re-enacted and revised, with roles reversed. Hal adopts his father's vocal vibrato and theatrical flair while reciting the many faults of his eldest son. Unwilling to be upstaged, Falstaff turns away from Hal to joke confidentially with the tavern audience and with us, via a camera situated in that audience. The laughter he inspires disrupts the newly ascended King, who then re-directs that laughter and re-takes the offensive by unleashing a flurry of insults at Sir John. At one point during this tirade he stands and raises his voice, playing his role dangerously close to straight. What he says as King Henry is very close to what he feels as Prince of Wales. Through his critique of Falstaff, the emotionally divided Prince condemns that part of himself that most resembles and admires Sir John. Soon the laughter of the audience falls out of sync with the Prince's increasingly serious rhetoric. Meanwhile the object of his verbal abuse turns away from him and looks at the camera/tavern audience. He appears amused at first, then puzzled. What began as a parody has become a serious play embedded within a parody.

Sir John gently prods Hal to name the villain of whom he speaks, but the reply is not so gentle, in spite of continued laughter from the spectators. "That old, white-bearded Satan," Hal declares. An accommodating Falstaff adopts a rather satanic facial expression in response, though he doesn't show it to the Prince. Hal's inventory of Sir John's many faults is undeniably accurate. But his characterization of them as satanic is grossly exaggerated, and slyly challenged by Falstaff, beginning in a high angle shot of him standing at Hal's feet. Tossing aside his page's cap, and along with it the submissive role he *was* playing to Hal's King Henry, Sir John mounts a serious counterattack while remaining outwardly jocular. Edging away from the Prince and closer to his tavern audience, including us, he turns to face his accuser and declares, in so many words, that to be what the Prince condemns is to be *human*, not satanic. Drunkenness, gluttony, vanity, villainy, and old age are counterbalanced by sweetness, kindness, loyalty, and valor. A mixed bag of attributes even in the best of men. Pleading his case remarkably well, Falstaff vehemently denies that he is Satan. His audience applauds their concurrence, despite cheering its opposite moments earlier. Like most audiences, including the courtroom spectators at Joseph K's interrogation in *The Trial*, or the Roman mob at Caesar's funeral in *Julius Caesar*, this one is fickle.

Even at his noblest, Welles's Falstaff is flawed, proving his point about humanity being a mixed bag of good and bad. He pleads not to be banished from Hal's presence, but does so at the expense of his comrades. Yet in the midst of displaying selfishness, Falstaff displays wisdom too. Pausing significantly between "banish" and "Poins," he intimates a knowledge of Poins's *truly* villainous ways. Ways with which Hal was more than willing to ally himself when it suited his purpose.

Climaxing his self-defense with a mountain of good will, Falstaff pleads, in close-up, "Banish plump Jack, and banish all the world." His argument exceeds himself, philosophically embracing the whole of humanity. Visible above and behind him are the rough-hewn ceiling and crossbeams of the tavern — visual metaphors of that flawed humanity. To condemn Falstaff so thoroughly as did the Prince of Wales is to reject human nature. Recognizing themselves in his performance, Sir John's audience erupts in applause. But then the

Prince's head thrusts into a shot of that audience, undercutting their concurrence both visually and verbally. "I *do* [banish you]," he declares. As the applause fades the camera cuts to an intimate shot of Hal and Falstaff, now appearing on the same level in face-to-face confrontation. No more play-acting. The Prince, aggressively invading the camera frame, quietly reiterates, "I will," for Falstaff's ears alone. The silly pot on Hal's head cannot mask the serious look on his face.

Sir John is surprised and confused. As Samuel Crowl has remarked, "For all of Falstaff's Orwellian alertness to the sham hollowness of political rhetoric ... the one person he does not see through is his own pupil — the most powerfully shrewd character in the play" (Crowl, p.376). Before Sir John can formulate a reply to Hal, the Hostess interrupts their confrontation with news of the Sheriff's arrival. The Sheriff had knocked at the tavern door earlier, during Falstaff's passionate defense of himself. An example of overlapping events common in Welles's movies. No matter how passionately involved we may be in something Welles shows or tells us, he encourages us to be aware of outside, even contrary matters. The resolution of the story's primary conflict, between Sir John and the Prince, is conveniently delayed. Hal removes his improvised crown. Falstaff asks the Prince to remain in character as the King so that he, Falstaff, can continue to plead on behalf of *his* character, the Prince of Wales. But their tavern audience is already scattering at news of the Sheriff's invasion. The realm of make-believe, already attacked by a dose of reality from within, is now destroyed by an assault from without.

Caught in the mayhem of their fleeing audience, Hal eludes Falstaff's attempted embrace. Rapid editing and a moving camera depict general panic in all directions as tavern dwellers flee the law. Martial drum music displaces the more relaxed incidental music that accompanied the play. The Sheriff invades with his goons. The camera, as though it too were hiding, initially shoots them from under tavern tables, showing only the soldier's legs and their vicious dogs advancing aggressively through the room. Thus fragmented, the Sheriff's men look less human, more mechanical, and more menacing. In the broad context of Sir John's and King Henry's battle for Hal's soul, the King now strikes back.

Upstairs Hal hides himself in bed with a prostitute. In the same room Falstaff slips under the floor through a trap door, as though making a magical exit on stage. For him *life* is a play. Before doing so, he and Hal exchange a few words of encouragement. Allies again, just like old times. Falstaff even admits that his "true face and good conscience are things of the past," which is a clever way of confessing his cowardice.

The Sheriff enters and, remaining at a respectful distance, asks the Prince the whereabouts of a "gross fat man" wanted for robbery. Hal orders him to leave. The Sheriff and his goons reluctantly depart. Hal remains loyal to Falstaff by shielding him from the Sheriff. But because Hal himself played an indirect role in the robbery, he is shielding himself as well as Sir John. The Prince's mixed feelings about the whole affair are evident in his behavior after the Sheriff departs. Leaving the bed and the woman, he heads resolutely for the exit. Falstaff pops his head up through the trap door. Hal, who has already passed him by, remarks in a perfunctory manner that they must all be off to the war. There is no more time to waste on improvised stage plays or frivolous forest adventures.

One strong impression deserves another that contradicts it. Leaving Falstaff behind, the Prince walks out into a corridor overlooking the main hall. From the floor below the Sheriff glances up at the Prince and facetiously bids him goodnight. Reflexively intimidated by the lawman, because part of him still identifies with his outlaw mentor, the mighty Prince of Wales retreats a step, awkwardly bumping his head on a low wooden beam. It is not as easy to banish the Falstaff in his soul as it was earlier to banish Sir John in the context of an improvised stage play. But the Prince quickly recovers self-control, reasserting his *other* father's legacy by stepping forward again to challenge the Sheriff. Put in his proper place, the Sheriff meekly withdraws.

Sir John approaches Hal, enthusiastically echoing the Prince's call to arms, but in the next breath calling on Mistress Quickly to bring him breakfast. Emotionally and physically he hasn't the stomach for war. There are more pleasant things to command his attention, especially in the limited time left to him. The Hostess pursues him down the hallway and harangues him about his unpaid debt to her. Falstaff reacts by imbibing more sack, which he seems to have stashed in numerous locations throughout the tavern, like an army with multiple supply depots. Hal follows his bickering companions, encouraging their dispute for his own amusement. Slipping into a room adjacent to the hallway, he observes their argument through an open window, like an audience watching a stage play through a proscenium arch, detached and amused. Until the Hostess verbally drags him into the dispute, at which point he rejoins them in the hallway, becoming a player instead of just an observer. The Hostess solicits Hal as an ally by disclosing a lie Falstaff told about him. Sir John deftly defuses the matter with a verbal sleight-of-hand. The two men hug affectionately. All is as it was in their first scene together. But then Falstaff carelessly oversteps the boundaries of their friendship.

Michael Anderegg claims that Falstaff "distrusts words" and "wants to deny the efficacy of language" (Anderegg, p.134). Sir John parodies the rhetorical flourishes of King Henry, and tells lies so outrageous that no one believes him. He frequently contorts language in such an extreme manner that it conveys the opposite of its literal meaning. No wonder he fails to anticipate the wound he now unwittingly inflicts on Hal's pride. Because Hal sometimes *does* take words seriously.

Falstaff compares King Henry to a fearsome lion and the Prince of Wales to a harmless cub. While doing so he casually withdraws into the adjacent room from which Hal emerged moments earlier to challenge *him*. In Hal's mind, Sir John's casual display of disrespect will validate the King's later warning of the danger of a monarch getting too close to his subjects. The Prince does not follow Falstaff into the side room to debate the issue. Instead, by way of a reply, he turns to Mistress Quickly and promises to compensate her for Sir John's unpaid bill. He will undo Falstaff's injustice to her, which after all is a sovereign's responsibility to his subject. In other words, he will no longer play the role of Falstaff's understudy. The Prince departs without speaking another word to Falstaff.

Chimes at Midnight contains many moments when Hal seems to break ranks with Falstaff, rebelling against his surrogate father just as at some point before the movie began he must have rebelled against his biological father. But breaking so strong an emotional bond is not easy for him, proving that in spite of his cynical plan to exploit his forthcoming moral reformation for political gain, Hal's affection for Sir John is genuine. He will have to spurn the old man several more times before he succeeds.

Falstaff is undeniably a thief and a con artist. He is also witty, egalitarian, wise, and very generous with his love. Like most good friends who spend much time together, he and Mistress Quickly periodically quarrel, only to forgive each other later. Hal's promise to pay Falstaff's debt to the Hostess may sound like a noble gesture but is really intended as an indirect insult to Falstaff. He exaggerates the fleeting, trivial enmity between Sir John and the Hostess in order to emphasize the moral gap between Sir John and himself. Hal is emotionally girding himself to exile the old man from his life.

After Hal departs, Falstaff returns to his sack, until waylaid by another old acquaintance whose presence nearby we did not suspect. A prostitute named Doll Tearsheat rises from her bed to insult the big man for many past offenses. But knowing that he is bound for war, she fondly embraces him. She claims not to care whether she sees him again or not. But at the Boar's Head Tavern words are often used to express feelings the opposite of what they outwardly mean. Insults become tokens of affection. Praise becomes insult. Again, the devaluation of words.

Distracted by a more pressing concern, Falstaff pulls away from Doll and goes to the window to bid farewell to Hal, passing by on horseback on the street below. The Prince rides towards the symbolic stone wall in the distance: towards King Henry, the war, and royal responsibility; away from play-acting, irresponsibility, and good fellowship. Departing into the sun, he yells back an affectionate nostalgic farewell to Falstaff, to "all-hallown summer," and to his own carefree youth. Lavagnino's splendid score reinforces this bittersweet parting.

At the royal castle King Henry informs his younger son of progress made in the war against the rebels. His eldest son, visible far in the background, appears to step between them. A slightly low camera angle places the room's stone arches high above the character's heads, reflecting the lofty burden of their responsibilities. The King shows contempt for his eldest son by addressing Hal indirectly, accusing him of betrayal, then turning his back on and walking away from him. The camera pans with Henry, removing Hal from the frame. The King walks past a tapestry depicting a monarch looking much like himself—all frozen majesty and abstract ideal. An icon.

Turning to face Hal after putting physical and emotional distance between them, Henry resumes his condemnation. The Prince, pictured from a distance, hesitantly moves towards his father. The King turns his back again and leaves the room, again rejecting his son. We track with the Prince in pursuit of his father, striding past stiff rows of machine-like subjects. Hal passes through doorways. The camera seems to pass through walls, reminding us of the magical nature of its and therefore our perspective. Were *we* at the castle, we would be a part of the humble, frozen, largely anonymous crowd of subjects. The camera closes on the Prince as he nears his goal, capturing both his resolute stride, but also a slight hitch in that stride, betraying his nervousness.

The castle's towering throne room dwarfs both the King on his elevated throne and the prodigal son standing far below him. Dismissed courtiers bow and depart. The Prince approaches Henry's throne, stopping respectfully one level below it. Henry describes his disobedient son as God's punishment for his own misdeeds, much as Hal chastised himself by targeting Falstaff's corrupt ways. The King descends from his throne to confront his son at close range, then turns away disgustedly in mid-insult. Hal intercepts him, maintaining vital face-to-face contact. Welles shows this closing of distance between the characters from extreme long range, emphasizing the tall, straight lines of the stone walls surrounding them. This is a world of abstract absolutes, very different from the messy world of Boar's Head. In some ways it is less fully human. But as an architectural embodiment of lofty ideals it is undeniably appealing, even awe-inspiring. It is to King Henry's mind, and to a part of Hal's mind, what the primordial setting of Dunsinane is to the mind of Macbeth.

The camera cuts closer to the confrontation. Silencing Hal, the King resumes his rebuke, then turns away again, as though unable to stomach the sight of his son. We witness as many rejections of the Prince of Wales by his father as of Falstaff by the Prince. Breaking strong ties is never easy. Among Henry's complaints is one that underscores the isolated, artificial nature of monarchy. Hal, the King alleges, has lowered public regard for himself by being too familiar with his subjects. This is the opposite of Falstaff's flagrant displays of his own faults to others. For Henry, image is paramount. Stepping out of the sunlight pouring down on him, the King descends further from his throne, figuratively mocking Hal's disgraceful fall from royal grace. The Prince of Wales is now "sick and blunted with community," no longer possessing a "sun-like majesty" in the eyes of his subjects.

After re-establishing distance between them, the King turns back to face his son while bringing his inventory of complaints up to date. In long shot the Prince stands alone near the throne he does not deserve to inherit. The sunlight shining down on him exposes his fidgety shame rather than imbues him with imperial grace. The King has stage managed this reversal of position in order to magnify that shame. But there is more to Henry's anger than royal outrage. After criticizing Hal for fraternizing too much with the general public, he complains there has *not* been enough fraternization between father and son. So the King's anger is prompted as much by private needs as it is by the dispassionate duties of King to country.

Father and son speak at each other over a great distance, emphasized by showing them in separate shots. Hal's voice cannot match the rhetorical power of the King's, and is therefore not very persuasive when he promises to reform. Unconvinced of that promise, Henry compares his son's irresponsible behavior to that of Richard II, from whom Henry stole the crown, and himself to Hotspur, who would now deny Hal that crown. Clearly the King admires Hotspur above his own heir. And though he stands far from his throne, Henry is pictured (from a two-dimensional perspective) with multiple rays of sunlight descending on him from above. He still embodies the royal authority that Hal must somehow appease.

Sensing that his father is on the verge of banishing him, Hal jumps down from his position of shame to offer a challenge. Tentatively at first, then with growing boldness. King Henry remains visually dominant, but the Prince at least gets his father to face him squarely. In separate shots we see the King looking noncommittal while the Prince, in a big close-up, fiercely condemns the rebellious Hotspur and promises to reverse roles with his upstart rival. His voice chokes briefly when he sees his father once again turn away. The possibility of a decisive rejection causes momentary panic. He did not anticipate failure when he spoke to Falstaff of his plan to stage his own moral reformation for political gain.

But the King is just being a king, acknowledging reconciliation not with laughter and a bear hug, as would Falstaff, but coldly, formally, indirectly. In an extreme long shot Henry walks away from his son while announcing, first, that the Earl of Westmoreland sets off for the war this very day and, second, that Hal is to follow in a week. By the highly theatrical pregnant pause before his signal of reconciliation, Henry punishes his wayward son for bad behavior even as he accepts Hal back into his good graces. In addition, Henry again demonstrates his (he believes) necessary emotional isolation as a monarch.

Disappearing into the shadows, Henry subsumes his role as father to his role as King. By the time he informs Hal, left alone on screen, "Our hands are full of business. Let's away," the King is a disembodied, godlike voice. The only *visible* indication of his favor are the double shafts of sunlight in the background. King and heir apparent are restored to each other. As the scene closes a chastened, silent Prince of Wales follows humbly in his father's royal wake.

Martial music from the opening credits returns as we return to Eastcheap, where the King's war sets everyone in motion. The camera looks up at a church bell chiming an alarm, then tilts down to show two separate columns of soldiers merging into one. Church and State too are in official alignment.

Scattered among the real soldiers are Falstaff's slacker cronies, lapping up the public celebration of wartime sacrifice and glory but also pausing to pursue purely private concerns, which aurally counterpoint the music and visually counterpoint the passing military parade. Nym displays some largeness of mind by questioning the reason for war. But Bardolph is preoccupied with haranguing Pistol to pay a gambling debt, while Pistol uses the war as a convenient excuse to ignore Bardolph's demand. He takes advantage of a public call to duty in order to evade a private obligation. The larger point of this satirical interlude is that no collective endeavor, however celebrated, remains untainted by private agendas. We've already seen that the war was inspired by Hotspur's desire to possess Henry's crown and Henry's desire to retain the crown he stole.

Camera angle and placement exaggerate speed and power as soldiers ride past a crowd of shouting, waving spectators, including excited children getting their first, false impression of war. Several pretty women wave and smile, presumably at soldiers off screen. But a new camera angle reveals the object of their affection to be Falstaff, who merrily waves back. Moving at a leisurely pace unlike the soldiers on horseback, he gallantly blows a parting kiss to Doll Tearsheat. His appearance in this scene triggers the displacement of martial music by music of a more lighthearted flavor.

Walking away from marching soldiers, Falstaff greets the Chief Justice, an old enemy who has already made a nasty remark about him. Their ensuing battle of words is no contest. Falstaff manages to be both superficially cordial and slyly insulting at the same time, while not allowing his foe to get a word in edgewise. His charms are not lost on Doll Tearsheat, who only with reluctance allows herself to be pulled back inside the tavern by the arms of a customer who probably pays more promptly for her services than Sir John ever did. Obviously Falstaff's appeal is more emotional than financial.

Leaving the speechless Chief Justice behind, Falstaff next encounters a pair of aristocratic heavyweights on horseback: Lord Westmoreland and a companion. Pictured in the foreground, they dwarf his figure in the background. He wisely and wittily concurs with their critique of the men he has conscripted, visible behind *him*, for service in the King's army. Better men, he claims, bought their way *out* of service. For "bought" read "bribed"— Falstaff always being in need of money. But if the wretched victims of his corrupt selection process are a sorry looking bunch, Falstaff is at least pictured *with* them rather than with his fellow aristocrats. A low-roofed building visible behind the conscripts contrasts their humble world with that of Westmoreland, which consists of high stone walls and uniformed men who look like real soldiers.

Following Westmoreland's departure, the Chief Justice returns for a rematch with Falstaff, bringing along a Bishop for reinforcement. Two stodgy figures of the power elite. Falstaff's parting inquiry of Westmoreland about Prince Hal's well-being is transformed by his new challengers into an insult directed back at Sir John. They accuse him of misleading the young heir apparent. He cleverly returns the insult back on them, and on Hal. "The young Prince has misled *me*." And there is some truth in his cleverness, considering Hal's plan to exploit his outlaw relationship with Falstaff as a stepping stone to public approval after he "reforms" himself.

From a low camera angle Falstaff is shown at a tactical disadvantage, hemmed in by two prominent foes, by the high stone walls with which they are affiliated, and even by the shadows of those same walls. Overmatched, he withdraws. But the Bishop and the Chief Justice dog him in a backtracking shot that highlights Sir John's bad limp. Falstaff falls back on a verbal attack that served him well in his previous battle with the Chief Justice. He contrasts the Justice's old age with his own youthfulness. It doesn't work this time, as both his foes pepper him with evidence of *his* old age and decrepitude. We've known since the Prolog that Falstaff is keenly aware of his mortality, and the inevitable loss of all things familiar and dear to him. So disturbing is the present inventory of his physical frailties that he tosses aside an apple he was about to eat. How often does *anything* distract Sir John from food or drink?

But words are Falstaff's magic. His ultimate defense. Stopping to confront the villains that pursue him like a pair of Grim Reapers, he cleverly transforms their descriptions of his frailty into tokens of infancy, thereby reducing their argument to nonsense. In addition, he reshapes their insult of his fading voice into a criticism of their slavish devotion to God and country. "I have lost it with hallowing and singing of anthems." In other words, with answering the institutional call to duty, of which the King's war is only the latest example.

Ironically, a reminder of that duty by one of his own allies liberates Falstaff from his pursuers. He happily answers Nym's summons to get on with the task of raising more soldiers for the King's army—a task to which Sir John is legally bound, by the way. And he emphasizes the institutional nature of that duty by referring to his rescuer as *Corporal* Nym. Outmaneuvered, the Bishop bestows an official if unenthusiastic blessing on Falstaff's official mission. Immediately taking advantage of that tepid approval, Sir John requests a thousand pound loan towards its accomplishment. Both Bishop and Chief Justice refuse to give him money, knowing they would never see its return. Alternating shots at the end of this confrontation show Falstaff backed by a crowd of civilian spectators while the Chief Justice and Bishop are backed by marching soldiers. Emotionally, they come from different worlds.

Falstaff gets no better results when he asks Bardolph to fetch him a bottle of sack. Bardolph demands money to pay for it. Falstaff has none. So with a frown and a shrug Sir John walks away, propping his cane over his shoulder in defiance of his game leg. The Chief Justice flings a last insult at him, "God send the Prince a better companion," which Falstaff easily parries: "God send the companion a better Prince." Punctuating his verbal victory, Sir John employs his versatile walking stick to tap the rump of a donkey carrying his enormous suit of battle armor. But the simple fact that he will soon need that armor signals a broader victory for the Chief Justice, the Bishop, and the King over Falstaff's peacetime sensibilities.

At the rebel army camp near Shrewsbury, Hotspur greets his subordinate, Vernon, arriving with news of the enemy. Vernon is alarmed at the size and solidarity of the King's army. Hotspur, walking briskly towards Vernon in a low angle backtracking shot that complements his mood, is by contrast all smiles and confidence. Until he moves into a medium long shot also showing Vernon and a row of soldiers behind him. Hotspur's voice and demeanor soften as he ponders the virtue of courageous action in the face of great risk. For a moment he even considers the danger to the men behind him. Spoken on a hilltop and against a clear sky, his monolog strikes us as conscientious and noble. Less bombastic and ironic than when he enthused about war back at his castle. But brief shots of Vernon and Worcester sharing a conspiratorial glance remind us that, however virtuously motivated Hotspur may be at this moment, the war he set in motion is fueled by the selfish ambitions of others besides himself. And the next scene chronicles one of the unfortunate consequences of Hotspur's call to arms.

Hotspur's speech concludes in a close-up of him alone. A direct cut counterpoints his handsome features and high-minded rhetoric with the plain features and mundane concerns voiced by Bardolph, announcing the impending arrival of Falstaff on a mission to conscript new soldiers at the house of Justice of the Peace Robert Shallow. With an equally plain face and a weak voice to match, Shallow is pleased by the cordiality of Sir John's formal greeting via Bardolph. It strokes the old man's vanity. And we *all* like our vanity stroked from time to time.

Shallow's brief dialog with an assistant named Davy exemplifies the difference between his concerns and those expressed by Hotspur in the previous scene. Henry Percy spoke of high ideals, but in the end was blind to the fate of soldiers whose lives are put at risk by those ideals. Shallow advises Davy to "use these men well," referring to the new military conscripts, lest they find cause and means for retaliation. It is an attitude of enlightened self-interest such as Falstaff often displays.

Sir John arrives at Shallow's residence. He is pleased to get out of the rain. Glancing around, he quickly assesses and compliments the material evidence of his host's prosperity. One can almost hear him thinking of ways to profit from his friend's good fortune. Reading those unspoken thoughts, Shallow maneuvers to counteract it. "Barren, barren, barren," he insists. The Justice of the Peace may be an old fool in many respects, but he's no idiot.

The potential conscripts Shallow has gathered for inspection are wretchedly unqualified for military duty. With a brief pause in his speech and a slight change in his tone of voice, Falstaff humorously concludes as much. When Shallow exits the room in search of his official list of conscripts, Sir John makes fun of *him* as well, noting the irony of his old friend, once a "lecherous ... monkey," becoming a prosperous, respectable squire. But his brief recollection of Shallow's past evokes nostalgia as well as humor. The bustling camera movement that accompanied his arrival settles down to a static, quiet image of Sir John telling Nym about Shallow's rambunctious youth. Falstaff loves an audience, *any* audience, even an audience of one. Though he and Shallow separately made it clear they intend to exploit each other, there is warmth in Sir John's voice as he describes old times and old acquaintances. He repeats and expands upon Shallow's earlier recollection, from the Prolog, of a past adventure at a place called Clement's Inn. It is a common point of reference for them, however much their friendship may at present be compromised by mutual exploitation.

Justice Shallow returns with his precious official list and takes his official seat at an official, elevated table. Shallow is a vain man, taking a bit too much pride in both his minor government post and the exaggerated adventures of his youth. His is a bargain basement version of the throne room at Pomfret Castle. But he is also often a kind and well-meaning man. The potential conscripts gather for review below him. Back-to-back shots from behind Shallow and from behind the conscripts convey the Justice's pre-eminence — an impression quickly neutralized when he interrupts an astonished Falstaff with a shout of "Silence!", then humbly explains that he was merely calling to his cousin, whose name is Silence, and not commanding Falstaff to *be* silent. Sir John, not Robert Shallow, is the ranking authority here. But unlike King Henry, Sir John is familiar and jovial with his social inferiors. He even transforms the misunderstanding with Shallow into a joke at the King's expense by remarking on how fitting it is that Silence should be in the service of peace (Shallow being Justice of the Peace) — his indirect point being that peace has no articulate advocate in the current political climate. Of course Shallow does not catch Sir John's double meaning, and quickly segues back to one of *his* favorite topics — exaggerated recollections of his past. Less inclined to dwell in that past, Falstaff deftly re-directs everyone's attention back to the official matter at hand.

Conscripting men into the army to face possible mutilation or death is an unpleasant task executed by Falstaff with grim humor, making the best of a bad situation. He seems almost offended that Shallow is amused by his first joke. The various parties involved in this mandated undertaking are frequently shown in separate shots, emphasizing their different perspectives of it. Protests from the potential conscripts are ignored. The judgement "Prick him," with its humiliating sexual connotation, is passed again and again, with few exceptions. Bardolph adds farcical injury to insult by shoving each new conscript out of the room, out of our sight, and to his unhappy fate, denoted by the crashing sound of an off screen pratfall. Even the stuttering of poor Silence contributes to this scene's weirdly farcical veneer. I suspect Welles intended us to feel uncomfortable at the humor of these grim proceedings.

Falstaff is corrupt, swiftly exempting from military service two new conscripts who slip him bribes, in spite of the fact that, as Shallow remarks, they are the two men most qualified for combat. Responding to Shallow's challenge, Sir John verbally inflates the assets of the three remaining and obviously less qualified conscripts who are still bound for the army. They pass helplessly in and out of the camera frame as he voices clever yet absurd reasons for pricking them. Contorting language to suit his purpose of the moment, Falstaff grandly declares, "Give me the spare men and spare me the great ones." His witty turn of phrase allows him to deflect the moral guilt of sending feeble men to their likely deaths. But Falstaff did not set the war in motion. He is as much a pawn of higher powers as are the conscripts he pricks. He is a coward. But he is a *wise* coward who recognizes the evil of what he is compelled to do. And perhaps the "great" men whose company he wishes to be spared are the Hotspurs, King Henrys, Worcesters, and in the end even the Hals who force Sir John to inflict war on the "spare" men he prefers.

Falstaff bids "Fare you well, gentle gentlemen" as he exits the building. "Gentlemen" is an ironic description of the conscripts, considering their low social rank and lack of sophistication. But by repeating and emphasizing the "gentle" in "gentlemen," he makes a valid if cleverly veiled point that none of these men are suited for war. In contrast to the high-born leaders who instigated that war, they *are* gentle men.

In extreme long shot we watch Falstaff recede into the rain, waving his cane around like a conductor's baton. He uses it to that effect throughout the scene, conducting with theatrical flair a composition imposed on him by King Henry. He instructs Bardolph to provide coats for the conscript. A compassionate gesture, but one he blithely reverses a moment later, rather cruelly but accurately reasoning, "they'll find linen enough on every hedge," referring to the clothing of dead soldiers. A static camera shows his motley crew of new conscripts slogging through the rain towards their violent fates. Shallow and Silence stand on a balcony watching Falstaff and his troops depart. "God send us peace," Shallow calls out in his feeble but sincere voice. Powerless to stop it, and not above profiteering from it, neither he nor Falstaff *desire* war. Hotspur and the Prince of Wales do.

The image of horsemen galloping through King Henry's military encampment counterpoints Shallow's prayer for peace. The horsemen ride past loaded catapults. A strong wind blows dirt in the same direction, metaphorically embodying the emotional tide of war irresistibly sweeping them along. The horsemen fly past Falstaff, who stands over a huge pot of soup with a ladle in his hand. He looks perturbed at their dusty disruption of his meal. Obviously *his* priorities have not changed.

King Henry and Worcester meet at the top of a hill to negotiate peace. The King is visually backed by an empty suit of armor — a sort of mechanical man such as we saw behind Hotspur while he bathed and ranted about war. Worcester is similarly backed by a row of armored soldiers carrying tall spears. Both men deny any desire for war, yet cannot bargain their way out of it. The howl of the wind swirling around them is a virtual war chant. *They* are the mechanical men. That ominous wind is an aesthetic device harkening back to Welles's *Macbeth* and *Touch of Evil*, which likewise feature characters who fail to resist the violent urges within themselves.

Falstaff, observing the negotiations from a discrete distance, supplies ironic commentary. "Rebellion lay in his way, and he found it" questions the sincerity of Worcester's claim not to want war. Stretching out behind Sir John is a line of armed soldiers and military banners, visually reinforcing his ironic words and conveying Worcester's true desires. Verbal counterpoint is provided by the Prince of Wales, who crosses behind Falstaff while commanding him to be quiet. Ironically, the word he employs to do so is "peace." But unlike Falstaff's, the Prince's irony is unconscious, reflecting back on himself.

The camera follows the Prince to his father's side. Addressing Worcester, Hal feigns peaceful intentions by heaping false praise on Hotspur at his own expense, then offers to settle the dispute by engaging Hotspur in single combat, thereby sparing the opposing armies from a general slaughter. It is a political ploy, designed less to save lives than to resuscitate Hal's tainted public image. King Henry, perhaps doubting his son's ability to defeat Hotspur in combat, intercedes with an offer of general amnesty for his foes if they stop their rebellion.

A shot of Hal standing behind Henry while the King makes his offer of amnesty to Worcester visually suggests a divided front between father and son. The Prince of Wales does not want a peaceful settlement. Only through combat can he establish, in the minds of the King and of his future subjects, his superiority to Hotspur. After Worcester departs, the Prince remarks, "It will not be accepted, on my life," which sounds more like a passionate wish than an objective assessment. King Henry's reply, "Then God befriend us as our cause is just," is a self-serving remark disguised as something nobler. In effect, the King absolves himself of guilt for starting the war, ignoring the part his own violent rebellion against Richard II played in fomenting the rebellion that now opposes him. The burden of war is conveniently heaped on Hotspur's shoulders alone.

Counterpointing King Henry's offer of a peaceful settlement, Worcester and his companions ride out of camp at a furious pace enhanced by Welles's camera angle and choice of lens. A mournful lament played on solo trumpet foreshadows the failure of their ostensibly peaceful mission. This musical lament clashes with the martial fanfare heard earlier. As we observe Worcester recede rapidly into the distance, our attention shifts to a huge crossbow loaded with four long, sharp, black spears at foreground right. They look like the barrels of a battleship turret, or a missile battery. The prospects for peace are dim. There are too many emotional, intellectual, and material forces blowing the other way.

The next scene begins with a shot of Worcester's group approaching from a great distance. The camera cranes down to reveal a forest of long, pointed spears in the foreground. Hotspur's army camp is as primed for battle as is the King's. The trumpet lament, carried over from the previous scene, is reinforced by the desolate moan of the wind.

Hotspur rushes forward through a formation of soldiers, eager to learn the results of Worcester's mission. But if the King's offer of amnesty had any chance of preserving peace, Worcester extinguishes that chance by concealing the offer from Hotspur. For reasons of his own, Worcester all but guarantees a war by informing Hotspur that the King's hostility is intransigent. He plays Lady Macbeth to Hotspur's Macbeth, dispelling doubts and eliminating options. The mere fact that Hotspur, at this juncture, *has* doubts about the war speaks well of him. One quick shot shows Worcester conferring with Hotspur in the distance while Vernon appears much larger in the foreground. A short time earlier, as they rode into camp, Worcester instructed Vernon not to reveal the King's amnesty offer. At this precise moment in time Vernon possesses the rare power to perhaps alter the course of history, and save many lives in the process. But he fails to act. The trumpet laments *his* failure as well as the failures of more prominent characters.

Misinformed about the King's unyielding hostility, Hotspur tells his soldiers to make ready for battle, strikes a theatrically noble pose, draws his sword, and sanctifies the coming battle with more poetry. He describes the men he will lead into battle as "fellows, soldiers, friends," not the hapless pawns in a royal game of power that they are. "Let each man do his best" focuses their attention on honor and duty instead of fear, mutilation, and death. His speech is self-serving as well an inspirational. Yet there is a quality of isolation and loneliness about his leadership in this scene, visually enhanced by the treeless landscape and by the physical distance between himself and his soldiers. His situation is not unlike that of the King he would depose.

Worcester is a *selective* liar, withholding information about King Henry's peace offer yet now stepping forward to tell Hotspur of Prince Hal's offer to fight him one-on-one. This reinforces Hotspur's determination to pursue the war, as a matter of personal honor. Worcester, desiring war for his own reasons, plays Iago spurring on Hotspur's Othello to avenge his wife's infidelity. Stepping aside to be alone, but with part of his army visible in the distance, Hotspur expresses a solemn wish that he and Hal *could* settle the conflict by themselves, sparing others. It is an impressive moment of moral doubt for a character who back at his castle exhibited an almost infantile enthusiasm for war. But like the dirt blown around him by the wind, he proves a slave to both his strict notions of honor and his desire for revenge.

Hotspur's fleeting moment of self-doubt is juxtaposed, by direct cut, with what at first glance appears to be a like-minded moment for the Prince of Wales, dressed in battle armor and standing alone in the foreground of the scene's first shot. The gray, ghostly outline of a portion of his father's army is visible far behind him. Falstaff, approaching from their direction, expresses a fanciful wish that the threat of war simply disappear, as if by magic. But Hal shares neither that wish nor Hotspur's moral qualms. Deserting Falstaff and walking out of the camera frame, he curtly replies, "thou owest God a death." Sir John, looking much less suited to his armor than does the Prince, challenges Hal's biting remark by reminding him of man's instinct for self-preservation. But men possesses *many* instincts—some contradicting others. Well aware of this fact, Falstaff adds, rather contemptuously of himself, that "honor pricks be on." Like the involuntary pricking of his reluctant conscripts.

To the amusement of at least one anonymous soldier observing from nearby (they are not *all* passive statues), Sir John closes again with the Prince and attacks the very concept of honor, defining it as an intellectual ornament, an illusion, useless against the slings and arrows of outrageous fortune. He makes his point in the face of the windblown dirt that seems to push other men towards war. Falstaff concludes his argument on a humorous, self-deprecating note. "And so ends my catechism." The master of wordplay knows too much about the trickery of language to embrace even his own words without qualification. But beneath his satirical jests lies a serious attempt to educate his surrogate son, and perhaps alter the tragic course of history. He believes what he says, at least on this occasion. And the fact that Hal has no glib retort suggests that Falstaff's little arrow finds its target. But a direct cut to the next scene makes it clear that mobilization for war continues unabated. Words could not save peace.

Soldiers in heavy armor are lowered onto their horses by means of ropes thrown over tree branches. They have become machines of war. Recovered from his brief attack of self-doubt, Hotspur speaks cheerfully and confidently again of settling matters with the Prince of Wales by way of combat. A direct cut returns us to King Henry's camp, where similar preparations are underway.

Falstaff's ascent to his horse is a fiasco, reducing the mobilization process to a joke. His enormous armored bulk causes the rope to break, sending him crashing to the ground in a clatter of metal. And there he sits like an overgrown child, while his smaller, lighter comrades ride past on horseback. Is it possible that Falstaff, like the Marx Brothers in *Duck Soup*, can achieve an aesthetic victory over war by means of parody? No. A direct cut to the next scene juxtaposes his comic antics with a hellish vision of battle.

A line of machine-like soldiers on horseback advances through a mist, their long lances pointing straight ahead. Muted drums propel them forward. Opposing them, in the next shot, is a similar row of soldiers. Individual human faces are scarcely visible. Mostly we see lances and horses' heads snorting visibly in the cold air, like armored tanks expelling exhaust. At this early stage of the battle we see only the mechanical and animal *masks* of war. And those masks are exciting to watch, generating anticipation in those of us who witness the battle from a safe distance. It doesn't matter much that we cannot easily distinguish one army from the other.

In addition to mounted troops, masses of foot soldiers advance on each other. Most of them are indistinguishable because of their helmets. The exception is Falstaff, who despite his head-to-toe armor is recognizable from his sheer bulk. Pointing the way to the front with his sword, he lumbers along among his comrades, looking like an antiquated World War One tank in a Desert Storm battle.

By filming the foot soldiers at various distances from the camera, and separately from the mounted troops, Welles creates the illusion of more combatants then there really are. And these fragmented images, abetted by ground fog, confuse us about which soldiers belong to which side, where they are in relation to each other, and in what direction they are moving.

Drums grow louder and the pace of action quickens, except for Falstaff, who lags behind his comrades. The drums are displaced by the same heroic background music we heard during the film's opening credits. Hotspur, Hal, and the King's vision of war as a noble enterprise dominates—initially. But soon rapid editing, camera movement, and varying shooting speeds rip the glory into chaos. In some shots the movement of horses and soldiers is so fast that their images blur.

Falstaff cowers behind tree branches as battle is joined. Simultaneously our perception of the battle changes. The moment blows are exchanged and men start to die, the music changes from heroic to apocalyptic. Brutal hammer blows of sound meld with eerie, melancholy, other-worldly vocalizations by a women's chorus. They could be the abstracted lamentations of the wives, mothers, and daughters of the men being slaughtered. This is a battle far removed from anything envisioned by the men who instigated, pontificated about, and hope to profit by it.

Rapid-fire vignettes depict brief, savage encounters. Images of swords, arrows, battleaxes, clubs, and horses mingle seemingly at random as order within both armies disintegrates. Armored knights are pulled down off their horses and pummeled to the ground. Iron meets flesh, spilling blood. Soldiers flail away at each other with fists. Battle descends earthward and becomes gruesomely intimate. The camera moves in for a closer look. No single hostile encounter dominates our attention because so many appear on screen at the same time. Everything overlaps. The only constants are general savagery and Falstaff's singular avoidance of it.

Gradually the pace of battle thickens and slows. The wet battlefield turns to mud under churning hooves and feet. The mud interferes with footing and leverage. Combatants collapse to the ground in clattering heaps. There is neither order nor honor here. In one close-up we see the entwined legs, but not the faces, of killer and victim, forming a grotesque parody of lovers. Which is not inappropriate considering the sexual passion that Hotspur diverted into his enthusiasm for war.

Surviving horse soldiers of the victorious army ride away from the battlefield, leaving their dead and dying comrades behind. The camera cranes up over the scene of destruction. Bodies are barely distinguishable from the earth to which they are returning, until a closer shot reveals the wounded still struggling for life in the muck. That image is immediately contrasted with a shot of the victorious army, accompanied by a return of the sanitary martial music heard before the battle was joined. Among the anonymous armored riders is the Prince of Wales, who removes his helmet and reveals his human identity in order to reprimand Falstaff for bragging about his phony heroic deeds during the battle.

Sir John falsely claims to have killed Hotspur, who happens to be sitting on a horse directly behind him. After a brief exchange of valorous-sounding challenges, the rivals for Henry's throne do battle, fully armored again. Falstaff discretely returns to the cover of foliage.

Apocalyptic music returns to accompany another exceptionally savage battle. The two combatants quickly knock each other off their respective horses, then do battle on the ground with swords and shields. The collision of metal is sharp and heavy. Rapid editing magnifies our impression of the violence and confusion. Falstaff cheers on his surrogate son, gesticulating in imitation of the Prince's thrusts and parries. He is like an audience at a war movie, participating vicariously in the violence yet safely removed from its consequences. But his semi-detached thrill ends when the action gets too close for comfort. He is inadvertently knocked to the ground by one of the combatants—which one we cannot tell, adding to the confusion of the battle. Prince Hal is the next to fall, stricken by a heavy blow from Hotspur. He comes perilously close to losing this fight, until a quick thrust of his sword up through a chink in Hotspur's chest armor reverses the upstart's tactical advantage and decides the contest.

Hal removes his helmet, aesthetically restoring his humanity. Instead of self-righteousness in his moment of triumph, we see exhaustion, surprise, maybe even disgust in his facial expression. He gently removes his victim's helmet, restoring Hotspur's humanity as well, and allowing the dying man to speak his piece.

The brutal clash of armies depicted earlier was visually eloquent but verbally inarticulate. This time Welles grants Shakespeare's hyper-articulate language its due. Accompanied by the same trumpet dirge that previously lamented the failure of high officials to preserve peace, Hotspur expresses his dying regrets in a philosophical manner. With a bitter, self-conscious irony that seldom accompanies the experience of acute pain and imminent death (the magic of Shakespeare is that he speaks from perspectives both immediate and detached), Hotspur confesses that even on the brink of death he clings more to "these proud titles thou hast won of me" than to "brittle life." Honor still pricks him even when he recognizes it as an illusion, and himself a fool. Like Othello in the aftermath of his great crime, Hotspur understands his folly after the fact.

Hotspur is about to transmit some sage advice to the Prince of Wales when death suddenly overtakes him. Throughout his death scene the camera cuts closer to each of the characters, conveying their greater understanding of each other. Hal offers a brief but heartfelt eulogy for Hotspur. And in that eulogy is evidence that he too, if only for a moment, sees the folly of excessive pride and ambition. Like Hamlet contemplating the skull of a long dead family servant, Hal notes the tragic irony of human life and death.

Leaving Hotspur, the Prince notices the apparently lifeless body of Falstaff, and commences another solemn eulogy. "I could have better spared a better man" simultaneously acknowledges the big man's faults and Hal's great affection for him. Ironic contradiction, like Hotspur's great spirit contained within a puny grave, or Yorick's great wit reduced to a moldering, lipless skull. But in Falstaff's case comic reversal triumphs over tragic irony. From beneath his death mask (helmet) comes his warm, visible, all-too human breath. Angry at being deceived, the Prince threatens to disembowel his resurrected mentor. Now *that's* irony. If his abandoned eulogy were a true indication of his *whole* mind, wouldn't Hal joyfully welcome Sir John back to the land of the living in spite of the old man's deception? Deceit is, after all, merely one of Falstaff's many faults which Hal claimed to overlook. Instead, anger trumps joy as the Prince of Wales peevishly walks away from the friend who was magically restored to him.

Falstaff requires the aid of two men to get his armored carcass back on its feet, at which point he utters his famous vindication of cowardice. "The better part of valor is discretion." But when he comes across the body of Hotspur, he ignores his own advice in an odd way. "I'll swear I killed him" is a very *in*discreet lie, told for material gain. His scheme is overheard by someone hiding in the bushes. Fortunately for Sir John it is only his loyal page. No danger of betrayal there.

Victory is declared, to the accompaniment of celebratory, orderly music very different from what we heard at the height of the battle. The remnants of Hotspur's army, dressed in light colored uniforms, surrender to the King's darkly dressed loyalists. The same color scheme applied to Hal versus Hotspur, rendering their dispute morally ambiguous as well. King Henry removes his black, crown-topped helmet to solemnize the victory, show mercy to the common soldiers of his enemy, and condemn Worcester to death. The camera, looking down on the defeated Worcester from close behind the King's head, visually reinforces the discrepancy in their powers and the harshness of Henry's judgement.

Hal approaches his father and the camera across a battlefield littered with the dead and dying. He pays them little regard, perhaps because he cannot emotionally afford to do so. His brother, John, suggests they search the battlefield to learn the fates of their friends. But it is an unconvincing expression of concern. Falstaff arrives with Hotspur's body slung over his shoulder. An undignified sight. But as Falstaff would be the first to say, there is no dignity in death. And what of the undignified deaths of the anonymous conscripts? Sir John's treatment of one dead aristocrat is no more callous than Prince Hal and Prince Johns' callous disregard for the dying soldiers lying on the ground nearby.

Hal is initially amused at Sir John's arrival with Hotspur's body, as though he were wondering what scheme the old man could be up to now. But Falstaff's phony claim to have killed Hotspur is a threat to Hal's identical claim, especially after King Henry arrives on the scene to assess the situation. Falstaff lies for material gain. Hal speaks the truth in order to gain respect from his father and his future subjects. Separate shots of the three characters involved in this confrontation tell a tale of widely divergent points of view. Falstaff appears nonchalant. He wants the King to think that dispatching Hotspur was a routine matter for so valiant a warrior as himself. Hal, looking at his father, silently protests that claim. But he does not, possibly out of a lingering loyalty to his old mentor, openly challenge Falstaff's lie. The King, glancing from Falstaff, to Hal, to Hotspur's body, and finally back to Hal, also remains silent. Maintaining the same outward detachment he did back at the castle, when he reconciled with the Prince, he simply walks away. Certainly he is not fooled by Sir John's absurd claim. But he may be disappointed in his son's unwillingness to discredit and disavow the old reprobate. Glancing at each other, Hal appears resentful while Falstaff is sheepishly amused. None of the three characters fully understands the other two at this moment.

Overcome by physical and emotional burdens, including yet another disappointment in his eldest son, the King slumps in the saddle after mounting his horse. A tight shot of him includes long lances upraised in the background, yielding a two-dimensional impression that they have pierced his body and gravely wounded him. A metaphorical token of the immense burden of leadership. But with assistance from a few loyal subjects, he regains royal composure, then loudly and poetically proclaims victory over Hotspur's rebels. Then he departs with a contingent of soldiers. In his wake, and probably at his command, Falstaff is ordered to accompany Prince John of Lancaster into battle against the as yet undefeated army of Northumberland. The King is maneuvering to separate Hal from a bad influence.

In their absence Falstaff insults both Prince John and the King, contrasting them with Hal, to whom he has taught an outlook on life very different from theirs. Within a circle of amused soldiers he shares a toast of sack with the Prince while expounding at length on both its virtues and Hal's. Familiar background music recalls the distant world of the Boar's Head Tavern, and contrasts the bleak, treeless landscape of the battlefield. But Hal reacts ambivalently to Sir John's appeal to roguish solidarity. Smiles and frowns compete for his mouth as his heart and mind shuttle back and forth between Falstaff and the King, and between warring inclinations within himself. Finally, without a word of farewell this time, unlike his earlier departure from Falstaff back at the tavern, he walks away in the direction of the departed King Henry.

Sir John, failing to recognize the seriousness of Hal's withdrawal, continues to sermonize on the virtues of self-indulgence. Hal looks back at Falstaff holding out another cup of sack for him and recommending addiction to it as part of his general philosophy of life. In an extreme long shot encompassing all relevant parties, the Prince of Wales discards the cup in his hand and follows in the wake of King Henry's contingent, visible now as a distant cloud of dust. Hal walks like a man in a trance, unable to resist the call to honor. Falstaff's grin fades. For a moment, but *only* for a moment, he begins to comprehend the growing gap between himself and Hal.

Ralph Richardson's narration sums up the end of the rebellion against King Henry. The narrator's voice is, as it was earlier, emotionally detached. But not so the imagery and background music that accompany it. Soldiers with spears march from foreground left to background right across the screen. Above and ahead of them, etched against a cloudy sky brighter on the horizon than overhead, we see a row of makeshift gallows dangling anonymous corpses. The same grim picture of royal power that we saw earlier in the movie, and previously in *Macbeth*. The route of the marching soldiers and the variable brightness of the sky emphasize the depth of this image, and thereby the immensity of the world in which the major characters play out their struggle for control and contentment.

King Henry's institutional triumph, via the hangman's noose, is juxtaposed with a portrait of his personal infirmity at the beginning of the next scene. Shown from a distance in his massive London castle, with a blanket warming his feeble legs, he looks like old Charlie Kane being pushed around in his wheelchair by a servant. The same mournful music that earlier lamented his use of the gallows to suppress rebellion now echoes the ravages of time on his aging body.

Westmoreland and other sycophants attend the King, exchanging mundane pleasantries. But Henry is preoccupied with his absent, eldest son. He turns halfway around in his chair to inquire about the Prince of Wales. How different is this impression of royal power from the movie's first image of Henry, seated on his throne, illuminated by shafts of sunlight, giving audience to subjects respectfully positioned in front of him. The simple act of turning in his chair to address his subjects puts him, from our perspective, at an aesthetic disadvantage, as it did Falstaff while debating Hal and Poins about the robbery at Gad's Hill.

Henry learns from Prince John that Hal has taken up again with his low-bred, outlaw cronies. There is resentment in John's voice — not surprising considering his father's greater interest in his older brother. Henry too is unhappy, obviously disappointed in Hal. And from John's description of Hal's recent behavior, we can presume the Prince of Wales is again estranged from his stern father. *No* one is content in this cold-hearted family, despite a recent military triumph over their enemies.

In solitary close-up the King ponders the shame brought upon him by his eldest son and by the prospect that after his death his kingdom too will suffer greatly under Hal's rule. Westmoreland assures him, accurately as it turns out, though perhaps more from a desire to curry favor than from insight, that Hal will eventually give up his corrupt ways. The King is convinced otherwise, perhaps because his own sense of guilt about other matters, such as the way he obtained the crown from Richard II, inclines him towards pessimism and self-punishment. Reaching out for the comfort of his royal crown, he collapses to the floor and is carried to his bed by several attending friars, whose white hoods and robes dehumanize their appearance, like the armor worn by soldiers. Hal is the only human contact the King craves. His relations in every other direction are rooted solely in duty, authority and obedience.

Henry calls for his crown to be set beside him in bed, like a frightened child clinging to a security blanket, or Charlie Kane to a glass paperweight that reminds him of happier times. But because he is full of contradictory feelings, the King walks away from that security blanket as soon as he gets it, leaving his attending subjects in order to be alone. As he was at the start of the scene, he is now pictured in extreme long shot, dwarfed by the walls and trappings of his castle. The symbols of his royal power mock his powerlessness in the face of guilt, sorrow, and fear of approaching death. He calls for music to be played, softly and at a distance. He is like a film director setting the scene for his own lament, trying to control the conditions of his life, as we all do at times. He gazes out a window again, hoping to see his prodigal son returning home.

Welles supplies counterpoint to the King's stage direction by briefly cutting away to Westmoreland and Prince John, speaking confidentially to each other. Into recent public reports of freakish natural phenomena they read signs of the King's impending death. Their voices are solemn and respectful. But their faces, shown in double profile, appear predatory, like the heads of perched vultures waiting for their prey to die. Image contradicts sound. Perhaps Falstaff's unflattering assessment of Hal's younger brother was based on more than mere annoyance.

The camera returns to King Henry, again looking fragile and vulnerable from a distance. At closer range we hear him bemoan his troubles. Like Macbeth, he is plagued with insomnia. Ironically, Welles throws a shadow over John Gielgud's sleepless eyes during this shot, focusing our attention on his mouth. It is a moving performance, arousing our pity yet preserving detachment. King Henry is a very human character, mixing nobility with pettiness. He bitterly contrasts his plight with that of his "vile" subjects, whom he envisions sleeping soundly without a care in the world. But does he ever contemplate the unquiet sleep of the families of the conscripts killed in his bloody war? Or the never-ending sleep of the dead conscripts themselves? "Then happy low, lie down" is an arrogant, presumptuous statement. "Uneasy lies the head that wears the crown," on the other hand, carries more weight because it is a subject about which Henry knows a great deal. And he says it during an extreme long shot which again emphasizes his isolation from his subjects. Like Falstaff's remark about discretion being the better part of valor, Henry's bitter observation about the terrible burden of leadership is a character-defining remark.

A close-up of the Prince of Wales complaining of weariness carries his father's funereal mood into the next scene, as does the complementary stillness of a lake visible in the background, and the overlap of melancholy music. But the next shot brings Poins into the equation, and reverses our initial impression. Poins injects a less reflective mood into the scene by making fun of Hal's complaint. The Prince reluctantly follows his companion's lighthearted lead. He is still torn between two worlds.

Bardolph and Falstaff's young page arrive, carrying a letter from Sir John to Hal. Poins brazenly confiscates the letter and reads it out loud, until he reaches the part where Sir John warns Hal not to trust Poins. And from what we saw of Poins's behavior back at the Boar's Head Tavern, Falstaff is justified in questioning his character. Hal confiscates the letter from Poins and reads the rest of it out loud, for his own amusement and to cause Poins embarrassment. What began as a demonstration of Poins's power (appropriating a letter addressed to the Prince) has now backfired. One of those little reversals of fortune that Welles loved so well to depict in his films. For the Prince, however, the letter is *good* news, jogging him out of his melancholy torpor and reconciling him again with Falstaff. Their parting on the battlefield was not, as it then appeared to be, the final chapter in their friendship. Sir John's good fortune is Poins's *mis*fortune.

Hal bribes Bardolph and the page not to inform Falstaff that he is coming to the Tavern. Perhaps he intends to play another prank on his mentor. The somber background music has faded, no longer contradicting the Prince's improved spirits. But as Bardolph and the page depart, the camera cuts to an extreme long shot, reducing them to tiny specks in a very large landscape. Tall trees overshadow them. Somber music creeps back into our ears. The next shot shows the Prince stepping away from Poins and debating with himself whether he should feel ashamed of wanting a drink, which by the way was Sir John's parting recommendation in their last scene together. The unspoken part of Hal's self-condemnation is, "while my father lies gravely ill." He cannot ignore one father in favor of the other.

Poins, returning to the Prince's side, tactlessly gives voice to Hal's unspoken thought, foolishly taking his master's tolerance for granted. The Prince fixes him with a glare and voices contempt for him. He shares Falstaff's low opinion of the man. But he grows accustomed to the dog-like devotion of his parasitic companion. After sternly reminding Poins of his low rank in the royal firmament, Hal mollifies him with a jest, walks away, then commands Poins to follow him. "I am your shadow, mylord. I follow you." There is a hint of treachery in Poins's creepy exhibition of untrustworthy servility reminiscent of Westmoreland and Prince John in the previous scene. Were he more daring and intelligent, Poins could be another Iago. But he is merely a lackey. Placing his arm around Poins's shoulder, the Prince displays his favor again. But their relationship is not based on friendship or love, as between Hal and Falstaff. It is more like the relationship of a remora to a shark.

The image of Hal with his arm around Poins overlaps a close-up of Falstaff at the Boar's Head Tavern. He appears downhearted. And just as we initially assumed that Hal's weariness, at the start of the previous scene, was an echo of his father's, we now assume that Falstaff's is linked to Hal. The overlap of background music from the previous scene encourages such an impression. But it is misleading. Maybe, instead, Sir John is preoccupied with his own mortality, as Peto comments. Again, no. A jest by Bardolph answered by a Falstaffian pun supplies the correct answer. Sir John's worry is more prosaic and immediate — a severe lack of funds. Unlike Hamlet, Othello, and Macbeth, he does not drive himself to distraction over life's *big* questions. Falstaff's lament over money is a parody of the high-minded concerns of his higher-ranking Shakespearean brothers.

From far in the background approaches a figure shrouded in black. The Grim Reaper? Of course not. It is only Doll Tearsheat, draped in Falstaff's giant cape and hat, come to claim her fee for services rendered. Several of Sir John's cronies depart after hearing that he is broke. But Doll is more confrontational. She and Falstaff exchange sexual insults. Neither intends to do serious emotional damage to the other because neither places much value on the words they fling back and forth. Unfazed, Sir John adjourns to an indoor privy.

Mistress Quickly functions like a mother in these minor domestic squabbles within her tavern family. She takes whatever meager payment Falstaff is able to give her, shares a little with Doll, and generously offers employment to Bardolph in the wake of Sir John's dismissal of him. Insults being the coin of friendship at the Boar's Head, she pokes fun at the sexual pretensions of both Doll and Falstaff by describing them as "rheumatic as two dry toasts." Yet a moment later she comforts an obviously sick Doll, reassuring her that "a good heart's better than gold." Each Boar's Head resident plays a *variety* of parts in the lives of his or her companions, shifting roles from scene to scene and even from moment to moment. It is a big, dynamic, sometimes chaotic family, but with a shared tolerance for the relatively small transgressions they inflict on each other.

Pistol's arrival at the Tavern triggers a new round of playful discord. The would-be dandy bizarrely misinterprets a request to buy Falstaff a drink as an invitation to have sex with Mistress Quickly and Doll Tearsheat. One selfish request is transformed into another. The women are not amused. Sir John, knowing that Pistol's boldness is all show and no substance, sends the man packing with a bold exhibition of swordplay. Returning from his successful rout of the enemy, Sir John brushes himself off in such a theatrical manner, to demonstrate the arduousness of his task and the easy manner in which he accomplished it, that we laugh *with* rather than at him.

Sir John's dubious heroism transforms him, in Doll's estimation, from a "fat muddy rascal" and "muddy conger" to a "sweet little rogue" and a "whoreson little valiant villain." High praise indeed, coming from her sharp tongue. But Falstaff's triumph is soon tempered by old age and ill health when he tries to bend over to inspect his allegedly injured groin. The surprising swiftness of his assault on Pistol, which was shown in a rapid series of shots, has left him exhausted. Doll pampers him as he sits on her bed. We view him from an oblique rear angle, from which his disheveled white hair and thick, indistinct voice accentuate our impression of his fragility. He looks almost childlike in his dotage. Doll promises him sex as a reward for his gallantry. The sexual insults exchanged between them earlier are now forgotten. A mere passing tiff between dear friends.

Acting on her invitation, Falstaff impulsively pulls Doll down on the bed and on top of him. But as youthful as that maneuver makes him seem, he just as quickly turns old and impotent again. And preoccupied with his mortality. For a moment he succumbs to grim thoughts he has held at bay throughout the movie, but which lurked just beneath the surface of his boisterous wit and sense of play. He requests a bawdy song to lift his spirits, and perhaps his weak flesh as well. Instead, the background score supplies somber music to match his brooding thoughts. "Thou't forget me when I'm gone," he tells Doll. Think of the black smoke, the residue of one man's lifetime, dissipating into the sky at the end of *Citizen Kane*. Doll assures her lover otherwise, then reassures him that in *her* mind he is far more virile than much younger men. *She* now plays the comforting, maternal role to Sir John that the Hostess played to *her* earlier in the scene. Falstaff, being wise, suspects the truth of the matter — that he *has* lost his virility and probably *will* be forgotten.

Hiding in a loft above the bed occupied by Doll and Falstaff, the Prince of Wales and Poins eavesdrop on the action below them. They are, like us, an audience reacting to events from a comfortable emotional distance. Observing his mentor in an emotionally vulnerable and revealing moment, Hal does not respond generously, as the music encourages *us* to do. "Is it not strange that desire should so many years outlive performance," he casually comments to Poins just before Sir John speaks of impotence in more heartfelt terms. This is neither the first nor last time that Hal and Falstaff fail to comprehend the depth of each other's feelings.

As if on cue, Doll and Falstaff discuss the Prince and Poins in unflattering terms immediately following Hal's joke about Sir John's impotence. Hypocritically, considering his own callousness, the Prince takes offense at Sir John's accurate description of him as "shallow." Craning his body over the edge of the loft, Hal betrays his eagerness to hear the rest of Falstaff's opinion of him. He is no less vain than Poins.

The eavesdropping pair reveal themselves to the couple on the bed. Alternating subjective camera shots capture the fun of that discovery. An affectionate insult directed at the Prince by Falstaff, this time deliberately, easily reconciles them. Laughing, Hal jumps into bed with Sir John and Doll. Poins makes it a merry foursome, but not before unsuccessfully urging the Prince to take revenge for Falstaff's earlier insult. What Poins *really* wants is for Hal to avenge the insult Falstaff directed at *Poins*, because Poins is too afraid to challenge the old man himself.

Mostly in fun now, Hal accuses Falstaff of being aware all along of his presence in the loft, and therefore of *deliberately* insulting him. To support this claim he reverses his argument, offered many scenes ago, that Falstaff did *not* recognize Hal and Poins as the men who robbed him at Gad's Hill. Like Falstaff, the Prince has no problem being inconsistent in order to gain a tactical edge. But both men do so largely in jest.

Falstaff verbally squeezes out of the tight spot in which Hal puts him, only to be pinched again by the tag team of Hal and Poins. Accused of insulting Doll, the Hostess, and Bardolph behind their backs, Sir John defuses the tension by repeating that alleged insult in such exaggerated terms that it is rendered inoffensive and harmless. Once more the Houdini of words escapes entrapment.

Untangling himself from the crowd on the bed while still verbally sparring with two of them, Falstaff retreats to the background. In the foreground the Prince and Doll get affectionate with each other while positioned suggestively between Poins's legs. So much for Doll's claim to love Sir John "better than I love e'er a scurvy young boy of them all." And it's only been a minute! Falstaff does not comment directly on his lover's transfer of sexual attention to a younger, more virile man. Instead he mockingly solicits pity for himself by complaining of the effects of old age. In other words, he rejects pity even as he requests it. Nevertheless, the sight of Doll and the Prince cavorting together must be galling for him. Viewed from a distance, he looks small and impotent compared to the amorous couple in the foreground.

Adding insult to injury, Falstaff's young page emerges from the privy with a pot containing the old man's urine. They exchange insults: Sir John remarking on the boy's short stature; the page commenting on Falstaff's questionable state of health. It's all said in good fun, but on some level Sir John's ego takes a beating in this scene. Poverty, old age, impotence, and disease have taken a toll on him, of which he is too well aware. And unlike Robert Shallow he has not yet taken refuge from his present troubles by withdrawing into exaggerated memories of his past vitality.

Falstaff rebounds with his usual wit, justifiably taking credit for inspiring as much of it in others as he dispenses himself. The camera pans with him as he says this, isolating him from the three characters on the bed. Then it cuts to a shot of those characters without him. The somber background music that Sir John's mood seems to have overcome now aligns itself with Hal's darkening mood as he quietly expresses shame for enjoying himself while his father lies ill elsewhere. Poins, laughing, is incapable of sympathizing with Hal's mixed feelings. Doll, who moments earlier fondly embraced the Prince, has fallen asleep on his chest and is now oblivious to his needs. This scene as a whole is a symphony of shifting perceptions and relationships. There is isolation and loneliness even within the comparatively congenial family of the Boar's Head Tavern.

In an intimate shot of Hal, Poins, and Doll, the first two fall out with each other while the third is unconscious of the other two. The part of Hal that conforms to the King's puritanism tries to distance itself from the likes of Poins and Falstaff, whom it unfairly lumps together. "Thou thinkest me as far in the devil's book as thou and Falstaff" he complains to his lackey. Falstaff, still verbally dueling with Hal but in an inattentive manner, unwittingly contributes to his growing rift with the Prince. "Be certain that either wise bearing or ignorant carriage is caught, as men take diseases of one another ... Let men take heed of their company" is meant by Sir John to imply that Poins is a bad influence on the Prince. Proving Sir John's point, Hal poses a question to Poins, who by his answer reveals his low regard for Hal's moral character. Or maybe it is merely Poins's spiteful revenge for Hal's nasty comments about *him*. Their brief confrontation is told in big, alternating close-ups. From a slightly more distant perspective we see Falstaff come between them and try to dispel their hostility with his good humor.

For a moment the Prince occupies a visually inferior position in his battle with Poins. Reacting to the sting of Poins's insult, which questions the sincerity of his concern for the King, Hal leaves the bed, walks out of the camera frame, and crosses the room to be alone. He continues the argument, but this time with himself. "Every man would think me a hypocrite indeed," he says softly. Does that mean he fears *being* a hypocrite, or being *perceived* as a hypocrite by his future subjects? Political acumen contends with filial love. "Let the end try the man" seems to confirm our suspicion of his cold-heartedness.

Overlapping and counterpointing Hal's monolog is Falstaff's good humor. He enters a shot of Hal, approaching from behind. Ignoring his mentor, the Prince walks out of the frame again, and then out of the room. Light streaming into the room through a narrow doorway renders Hal's departing figure a black silhouette, adding a visual exclamation point to the hostility and decisiveness of his exit. Sir John's attempt to wean the Prince away from Poins has inadvertently alienated the Prince from Sir John as well. Worried, Falstaff pursues the Prince. Doll Tearsheat, rising sleepily from her bed, is unaware of what has transpired between them. Poins, however, races past Falstaff in an effort to catch up to and make amends with the Prince first. But his motives are very different from Sir John's.

Descending from the tavern rafters, the camera drops us into a crowded scene of laughter, dancing, eating, drinking, and music. Through this vibrant tableau of good cheer passes first Hal, partaking in none of it, and then Falstaff, *trying* not to partake in it as he pursues the Prince. One of the revelers hooks her arm in his and reels him into the dance. He cannot help but enjoy it, until concern over Hal, and his own physical infirmities, force him to withdraw. An attack of gout is in turn attacked by Sir John with sharp wit ("I shall turn disease into a commodity") as he follows Hal out to the stables. Slipping on his gloves, he intends to follow the Prince, who has already mounted a horse. But Falstaff is too slow and Hal desires no company.

Wearing a long, flowing cape and seated on a lively white horse, the Prince of Wales cuts a romantic figure of youthful vitality as he pauses to wave a fond farewell to his old mentor. Behind him, contrasting that fondness, are a dim twilight sky and the black, sinister stone wall in the distance. In more than one respect it is towards that darkness the Prince now rides, leaving behind the bright conviviality and irresponsibility of his youth. A youth Falstaff emotionally never left behind but which physically is rapidly deserting *him*. Ironically, what turns out to be Hal's final farewell to Falstaff's joyful realm ends on a more hopeful note than some of his earlier, not-so-final farewells. Neither man recognizes this parting for the sea change it becomes.

Reassured by Hal's cordial farewell, a reinvigorated Falstaff announces his own departure to scam some much needed money out of old Robert Shallow. But as he walks gingerly (the gout again?) from the tavern, Doll Tearsheat, tearing herself away from several lusty customers and again demonstrating her persistent if not always consistent affection for Sir John, loudly expresses concern for his fragile health. Turning to face her while pictured against the looming blackness of the distant stone wall, he begs her not to remind him of his mortality, which clearly is never far from his thoughts these days. Doll's well-intentioned display of concern has the unintentional effect of exacerbating his melancholy, just as Sir John's well-intentioned warning to Hal about Poins drove the Prince away from his old mentor. Falstaff bids Doll farewell as though for the last time, which it turns out to be, and walks out of the stationary camera frame. By not following him with the camera, Welles focuses our attention on the *character's* movement, intensifying our impression of his frailty and of the sadness of two old friends parting, not knowing if they will ever see each other again. A reaction shot of Doll waving goodbye reminds us that she too is unwell.

Like life itself, *Chimes at Midnight* is a series of starts and stops, splits and reconciliations, greetings and farewells. Just when we think something permanent has occurred in a particular relationship, it is reversed. Hal's parting from Sir John on the battlefield seemed more definitive than their more recent parting. Events will prove otherwise. But underlying all of these fitful, confusing events is Falstaff's slow, inevitable slide towards death. The one facet of human existence for which there are no reversals—except by way of a faulty perception, as happens in the next scene.

We view the Prince of Wales from behind as he returns to his father's castle with boisterous good cheer—perhaps because he feels he is doing the right thing at last. The Prince is pictured against the backdrop of an elaborately patterned interior wall, with white-robed friars standing at its base, embodying the rigidly formal, emotionally sterile future that awaits him as King of England. Locating his brother, Hal jokes with him by way of a greeting. Westmoreland steps forward to inform Hal that the King is gravely ill, rendering Hal's jest inappropriate.

Hal enters his father's bedchamber alone. The camera initially observes him from a distance, framing father and son between the heavy stone sides of a doorway. A similar visual effect is employed in *Touch of Evil*, when we first see Susan Vargas lying unconscious on a hotel bed after being assaulted and kidnaped by the Grandi gang. All three characters are trapped, though of course in different ways.

The King's face and figure are barely visible in his large royal bed. Kneeling respectfully at his father's side, Hal protests the burdensome promise of the royal crown lying beside the King's head. Ironically, Henry ordered the crown placed there because he perceived it as a *comfort* rather than a burden. The Prince comments in general terms on the burden of *all* such crowns on their temporary owners. And he says this in a tight shot that includes himself and the crown but not his father, suggesting that he is thinking of his own impending reign as king. Perhaps he protests the royal burden *too much*.

Hal assumes that his father is dead. A new camera angle brings Henry back into the picture. Making the sign of the cross and complemented by a religious chant seeping into the room from far away, the Prince eulogizes his father, promising a proper show of grief. But he is quick to follow "Thy due from me" with "My due from thee is this imperial crown." For a son supposedly consumed by sorrow, Hal displays remarkable presence of mind.

With his eyes riveted on the crown he moments earlier condemned as a burden, the Prince of Wales takes it in his hands and stands up. A change in camera shots eliminates the presumably dead king from view, reflecting Hal's greater interest in his father's royal legacy than in the loss of his father. Pledging to hold on tight to that legacy, and using God's name to validate that grip on power, the Prince edges away from his father's deathbed, almost like a thief making away with a treasure. Outside the room he kneels, playing the pious penitent, but with the crown held firmly in his hands.

Cut to a shot of Falstaff, Shallow, and Silence seated in front of a blazing fireplace in Shallow's house. They reminisce about the good old days. Falstaff repeats his line from the Prolog, about hearing the chimes at midnight. By the lap dissolve transition from the previous scene to this one we see clearly the different paths taken by Falstaff and his surrogate son: one to his dotage and dubious recollections of the past; the other to the responsibilities and hypocrisies of young adulthood in the present. Our return to the action of the Prolog also sheds new light on what we saw many scenes ago. We realize now that Sir John's visit to his old friend, Robert Shallow, is motivated by more than nostalgia. He seeks money from his dotty companion.

Falstaff is not altogether pleased with Shallow's wallowing in recollections of the past. He looks disgusted when Shallow leans against him while droning on and on about old times. He looks even less comfortable when Shallow and Silence, seated on either side of him, discuss the inevitability of death. The steaming cup of sack in his hand is Falstaff's only consolation in the funereal moment of silence that follows. But bits of comedy temper the gloom as the bizarre conversation between Shallow and Silence, pursued over Sir John's prominent stomach, continues. Shallow's sudden verbal outbursts startle Sir John. And his comments on the deaths of old acquaintances are mixed with amusingly contrary and irrelevant topics. All of which disrupts Falstaff's attempts to drink from his cup. He mumbles the word "dead" as a phony echo of sympathy with Shallow's latest obituary for a mutual acquaintance. With the goal of obtaining money in mind, Sir John will tolerate the same depressing talk from Shallow that he begged Doll Tearsheat not to inflict on him two scenes ago.

Much of this scene occurs in a single, static shot. Like the nocturnal conversation between George and Fanny Minafer in the Amberson mansion kitchen, this scene has a slice-of-life quality. Conversation rambles, starting and stopping and changing direction fitfully. Both scenes are wonderful representations of ordinary, everyday, mundane communication between friends or family members with inevitably different points of view. Joseph K and Miss Burstner seemed on the verge of attaining such casual familiarity with each other in *The Trial*, until fear drove them apart.

We return to the Prince of Wales as we left him, except that he now stands rather than kneels, and Henry's crown is on his head instead of in his hands. Plus he is surrounded and presumably legitimized by clergymen. But this image of the new King is premature. The most surprising reversal of the movie occurs when King Henry rallies from presumed death and calls out from his bed for Prince John and Worcester, who rush to his side, excusing their previous absence by explaining that they had left him in the care of the Prince of

Wales. That information, plus the absence of his royal crown, reinvigorates the King with great resentment of his eldest son. He jumps out of bed and pursues a solitary course through the lofty corridors that dwarf his small, thin figure. Avoiding others, he complains of Hal's unseemly haste to displace him (a private concern) and of Hal's potential corruption of royal government with the appointment of common ruffians to high office (a public worry). As both a father and a King he feels betrayed, and alone. He passes by a heavily barred window similar to one we saw at Dunsinane in Welles's *Macbeth*. He is a prisoner in his own castle. A low camera angle and shadows double the prison bar effect.

Wandering into his throne room (another tangible security blanket, like his crown — objects a dying man can cling to), the King finds Hal wearing his crown and standing near the throne, bathed in the same sunlight that once illuminated Henry. Shocked at seeing his father alive, Hal addresses him respectfully, verbally rejoicing in the King's recovery. But Henry, overcome by the *visible* evidence of his son's callous *dis*respect, collapses to the floor. Hal then enters the same shot, kneeling at his father's feet, kissing his father's hand, and bowing his crowned head before his father's bare head.

Harsh lighting etches the figures of father and son as they debate the topic of betrayal versus loyalty. The weary King wants to know why Hal took the crown from his bed. Hal, removing that crown from his own head and returning it to his father, employs the same verbal sleight-of-hand we often hear from Falstaff. He tries to convince his father that he took the crown only to do battle with the unfair burden of leadership it placed on Henry. Spoken mostly in whispers, Hal's performance is subdued and convincing, so unlike the mostly over-the-top, self-consciously ironic performances of Sir John. Hal battles for his own future in the same way Shakespeare's Marc Antony employed false humility to turn the Roman mob against Brutus and Cassius. And because Henry is desperate to be convinced of his son's devotion, he suspends disbelief. He even praises the Prince's rhetorical skills of persuasion, so necessary in a monarch. Seeking to justify Hal's hasty action in his own mind, Henry credits divine intervention for *placing* the crown in the Prince's hands and thereby forcing Hal to *win* his father's love and respect by arguing his case so eloquently. There is both paternal self-deception and Machiavellian admiration in King Henry's approval of his son's self-defense.

Members of the royal court watch the throne room drama from a respectful distance. Hal, perhaps playing to that audience for the sake of his future as King, helps his feeble father climb to the elevated throne. The King, perhaps deliberately helping his son create a favorable public impression of filial devotion, does his best to cooperate. From far overhead we briefly observe their joint effort. The two royal figures appear meager, fragile, and eminently human on that cold, massive altar to power, surrounded by towering walls and a sinister, dark archway looming over their heads. In spite of their cynical manipulations of public opinion, it is difficult not to pity them when they are shown like this.

Nearing death, and still beyond the hearing range of their audience outside the throne room, King Henry passes on last minute advice to his heir. Distant, pious chanting counterpoints his confession that he employed unethical means to take the crown from Richard II. He foresees a more stable foundation for Hal's reign, however, thanks to the inevitable forgetfulness of their subjects over the course of time. But the cynical core of his advice is a recommendation that Hal involve the country in foreign wars as a means of diverting any lingering public hostility away from himself. The King's motive for offering such advice may be a genuine concern for his son's future, but it raises the specter of more horrendous battle scenes such as the one we witnessed earlier.

Melancholy background music gradually displaces the local chanting, encouraging us to sympathize with the dying King and his apparently grieving son. Henry begs forgiveness for usurping Richard's crown, yet encourages Hal to hang on to it by equally immoral means. Diluting neither the tragedy nor the irony of this scene, Welles encourages us to deal with moral/emotional contradiction as an irreducible fact of human life. It certainly makes for powerful film drama, especially as performed by John Gielgud and Keith Baxter.

Following Henry's death, members of the court slowly filter into the throne room, kneel before their new King, and formally swear their loyalty to him. The physical distance between the King and his subjects is pronounced. From his elevated position Hal declares in a firm voice that he will transform their sorrow into happiness, and his own vanity into "formal majesty." In a precarious and roundabout way, the plan he revealed to us early in the film, about staging his moral reformation in a manner that would impress his subjects, now comes to fruition.

The first pronouncement of King Henry V occurs while he is bathed in sunlight, looking every inch a monarch, and a young, vital one at that. But visible behind him, like a ghost from the past as well as a specter of the inevitable future, slumps his father's corpse, now shrouded in darkness. Hal has inherited his father's royal legacy, but he also inherits his father's mortality. It is a powerful juxtaposition of youth and old age, life and death, rhetorical virtue and silent vice. And one of Welles's finest visual portraits of human contradiction. The unavailability of John Gielgud to play this scene may have been one reason why Welles placed his double in obscure shadow. But the dramatic effect fully justifies the disguise.

During Hal's first address to his subjects the camera cuts away briefly to an extreme long shot. From that distance his figure and voice are less impressive, as were Charlie Kane's when viewed from a box seat far above him as he spoke at a political rally in *Citizen Kane*. But Kane's public downfall was imminent. Hal's is far in the future.

We return to a closer shot of the new King. With solemn formality he takes the crown from his father's dead hands. He raises it over his own head while keeping his back to the audience so that their gaze remains on the crown and its implied majesty, to which he aspires but in their eyes has yet to earn.

Cut to the decidedly *in*formal and unrehearsed affairs of the common man. Shallow and his cousin Silence dance a jig to entertain themselves. Falstaff watches their performance from the background, keeping his distance out of boredom, or even disgust. Shallow prattles on again about his youthful, madcap adventures at Clements Inn, which holds as treasured a place in his memory as Rosebud did for Charlie Kane. "I would have done anything too, and roundly too," he brags in a thin voice while demonstrating his *in*ability to do much *now*. Exhausted from dancing, he requires help from Silence merely to return to his chair. Falstaff retreats even further, to a bench far in the background, from this unpleasant preview of his own inevitable fate.

Shallow slumps helplessly to the floor. Silence gently strokes the top of his head. Davy arrives to help get Shallow up on his feet. The old man is grateful to both younger men. Obviously Shallow's little kingdom is brightened by the same system of mutual support, mixed of course with occasional fractiousness, as we saw at the Boar's Head Tavern.

Much of this scene is shot from a low angle and at a considerable distance from the characters, rendering them very small and calling our attention to the rickety support structure of the building's roof, which is a reflection of both Shallow's and Sir John's ancient bodies. The lack of camera movement highlights the feebleness of Shallow's movements. The camera's position does not change as we shift attention to Falstaff, far in the distance.

His voice is incongruously large for his tiny figure as he pokes fun at Shallow's inflated memories, of which, he contends, "every third word" is "a lie." Not yet reduced to living in the past, he nevertheless recognizes himself in his characterization of Shallow. He is more aware of his own faults than is anyone else in the movie. And that broad self-awareness is what distinguishes him from most of the other characters Welles played in his own movies.

Transforming a weakness into a strength, Falstaff ponders aloud the potential value of Shallow's irritating lies as entertainment for the Prince of Wales, when re-told and no doubt embellished (every *second* word a lie?) by Falstaff, who clings to the youth and vitality of Hal as passionately as Shallow clings to recollections of the past.

Pistol's arrival with big news from the royal court draws a semi-interested Falstaff from the background to the middle ground in this continuing shot. He is joined by Shallow and Silence. In his excessively flamboyant way Pistol tries to tell Sir John of King Henry's death and Prince Hal's ascent to the throne. Not understanding Pistol's garbled message (another example of faulty communication in a Welles movie, though one with comic rather than tragic consequences), Falstaff impatiently raps him on the arm with his cane. Pistol retreats to the foreground, just as Falstaff retreated from Shallow earlier in the scene. Similar need, different motives, opposite directions of flight. From a safer distance, Pistol repeats his news in clearer terms, this time drawing a *very* interested Falstaff to and even past him. Towering over the camera, Sir John is revitalized with energy.

Rushing out of Shallow's house and across a wintery landscape, Falstaff rashly promises gifts of high office to his friends and threatens retribution to his enemies. But the secret of Sir John's innocence is that he never attains the kind of power wielded and abused by the likes of Charlie Kane, Arthur Bannister, Macbeth, Hank Quinlan, and the Advocate. Wildly optimistic in his joy, Sir John exults, "the laws of England are at my commandment." Every *third* word a lie? Perhaps now *every* word. But this time Sir John lies to *himself*. He cavorts merrily out of the camera frame, in marked contrast to his movement in the film's Prolog, where he *limped* across a similar landscape. The wintery setting calls to mind two other deceptively cheerful scenes. In *The Magnificent Ambersons* the major characters enjoyed each other's company while riding through snow in Eugene Morgan's newfangled automobile. It was the last time they experienced so congenial a gathering. And in *Citizen Kane* young Charlie Kane played happily in the snow outside his mother's boarding house, unaware that inside three adults were plotting his future unhappiness.

Church bells pealing in celebration form a bridge between Falstaff rejoicing in the countryside and King Henry V riding in triumph through the streets of London. From various camera angles we catch only fleeting, distant glimpses of His Majesty, approximating what the common people see. Close-ups of their cheering faces imply that Hal was correct in predicting that his subjects would revere him more after his reformation. But in certain shots of the new monarch and his cheering subjects the visual intrusion of tall pennant poles held aloft by soldiers yields an impression of prison bars. Hal, like his late father, is a prisoner of the royal magic show no less than are his subjects.

Pistol pushes through the crowd to catch a glimpse of the new King. He is captivated by the ritual, as he was earlier by Henry IV's call to war. He exemplifies the uncritical mind. In his wake follows the slower, wiser, usually more skeptical Falstaff. But on this occasion too many intense passions flood his mind to permit critical detachment. They include fatherly pride, the anticipation of financial salvation, and the vicarious thrill of reliving his youth through his triumphant surrogate son.

Our first clear and relatively close view of the new King occurs as he leaves the cheering peasants behind and passes through the gateway of the cathedral where he will be coronated.

His elaborate crown, uniformed horse, and frozen, sober demeanor transform him into a living statue of royal dignity. Hardly a trace of the old Hal remains visible. Inside the cathedral the ritual of coronation is even more rigid and elaborate than was the celebration outdoors. Soldiers, members of the royal court, and clergymen gather in formal attire and with their various accouterments: smoke and incense, helmets and lances, banners and exalted music.

In the streets outside, Pistol pushes aside two soldiers' lances in order to see the celebration. Inside the cathedral Falstaff does the same. Both men break through the ritual's metaphorical prison imagery. Assuming he will have great influence with the new King, Sir John promises much to his companion, Robert Shallow, whom he owes for a previous loan. He briefly questions the appropriateness of his rough country attire. But by means of his usual wit, which this time he employs to deceive himself rather than to entertain others, he rationalizes his slovenly attire. By rushing directly to the King without stopping to change his clothes he demonstrates, or so he deludes himself, the sincerity of his devotion. Robert Shallow enthusiastically concurs, for the obvious reason that he expects a future payoff. Only a couple scenes ago Sir John *questioned* Shallow's judgement. But because it now props up Falstaff's fantasy, Shallow's opinion is credible to him. It is heartbreaking to see Sir John play the fool. Both he and Shallow believe their time in the sun has not yet run out, and that the best is yet to come.

Inside the cathedral proper where everyone else stands at rigid attention, only the King and Falstaff are in motion, except for clergymen walking ahead of the new King and kept discreetly off camera by Welles until later. The camera tracks with Sir John as he passes behind rows of soldiers blocking his way. From his point of view we catch only glimpses of Hal, scepter in hand, walking in procession. Then the new King disappears from view.

Pushing through the barricade of soldiers, Sir John shouts out, "God save thee, my sweet boy!" They are the words of a loving father, not a humble subject. The King stops in his tracks, halting the procession. But he refuses to turn around and acknowledge Sir John's rude disruption. Positioned behind the King, we share this rebuff with Sir John. Whispering so as not to disrupt the ceremony himself, Westmoreland chastises Falstaff. Yet not so long ago we caught a glimpse of Westmoreland's greed for royal power. Which crime is less forgivable — Westmoreland's phony show of reverence or Sir John's tactless but sincere display of affection?

Ignoring Westmoreland, Falstaff advances towards the King, calling out to Hal as "My Jove!" and half declaring, half pleading, "I speak to thee, my heart." In other words, he speaks to his own younger self, or to the son who would replace and comfort him in his old age. But the King has a different agenda. Keeping his back turned on his former mentor, thereby maintaining regal detachment, Hal declares coldly, "I know thee not, old man." It is a rejection not only of Falstaff but of the Falstaff in himself. Part of what made Hal human.

As he finally turns to face the intruder in his brave new realm, the camera cuts to a solo shot of Hal, eliminating Falstaff from view as ruthlessly as Hal cuts him off from his royal favor. From a low camera angle the King looks unassailably regal in his crown, scepter, and robes, visually aligned with the arched ceiling and lofty banners that aesthetically enhance his status. With no trace of the jesting that softened many of his earlier insults to Falstaff, the King humiliates his former friend by describing him as an old fool, a jester, a mere bad dream of immorality from which the King has thankfully awakened.

Unable to comprehend the suddenness and severity of the change in their relationship, Falstaff laughs and advances a few more steps to engage Hal in their usual battle of wits. But the King's stern voice stops him. Sir John is robbed of his greatest, perhaps his

Chimes at Midnight. Prince Hal (Keith Baxter), now King Henry V, adopts the formal trappings and exalted demeanor of his late father during his coronation. He has expunged nearly all traces of his former mentor, Falstaff, and the informal, low-born world of the Boar's Head Tavern.

only defense. *Words.* Speaking loudly now so that his other subjects will hear and be impressed, the King rejects his formerly corrupt ways and all acquaintances who shared in them. Like a punch to the gut, the words "I banish thee!" drop Falstaff to his knees. In a quavering voice eerily reminiscent of his late father's, Henry V spells out the harsh terms of Falstaff's exile. Then in a softer voice signaling a measure of pity calculated to impress his *other* subjects, he leaves opens to Falstaff a narrow avenue to reconciliation.

The King summons his Chief Justice to execute his decree, reversing Falstaff's anticipation of a personal triumph over that same official. But losing a power struggle to the Chief Justice is to Falstaff nothing compared to losing the affection of his beloved son. Hal and Sir John exchange a final look. Is there a glimmer of shame, of nostalgia and affection, in the younger man's expression? In two big close-ups Falstaff's huge, white-bearded face recovers a little of its former dignity. Without uttering a single, forbidden word, he exerts a powerful emotional pull on his former friend. His chin quivers. The barest hint of a smile crosses his lips. Background music, counterpointing the local, ceremonial music heard moments earlier, echoes Sir John's mute appeal. But the King turns and walks away. *Far away.* There will be no reconciliation this time. Falstaff's expression changes back to one of stunned sadness.

The coronation resumes as Falstaff walks slowly in the opposite direction. Spotting Robert Shallow at a distance, Sir John wearily acknowledges his thousand pound debt to his old friend. Something he would never have done in the past. Shallow closes the distance between them, but only to demand prompt payment, not to console his old comrade. Sir John rationalizes that the King's rejection was merely for public show, and that their reconciliation in private is assured. But he speaks with little conviction. Dejected, he walks slowly out of the camera frame. Shallow follows in feeble but determined pursuit, again demanding repayment of his loan. From a new camera angle the two men again appear far apart: Shallow in the foreground and Falstaff in the distance, his tiny figure reduced to insignificance by the massive stone wall that surrounds the cathedral.

Hope does not spring eternal, but in Falstaff it is a difficult thing to kill. The camera cuts closer to Sir John as his spirits momentarily revive. "I will be as good as my word" is followed by a more assertive repetition of his theory that the King's banishment was just for show, to be revoked later. He confidently invites Shallow to dine with him. Instead, Shallow too deserts him, as do several other old cronies who were waiting for him on the other side of the stone wall. Falstaff's good word was never very trustworthy. But it was entertaining enough to keep his audience enthralled. Now it is neither. A new camera angle shows him again diminished by the stone wall, even as he continues to mutter to himself that the King will send for him. Then in dead silence he hobbles slowly out through a gateway the wall, to be met by only his faithful page, played by Orson Welles's own daughter, Beatrice. A girl masquerading as a boy, displaying love and devotion to a real father masquerading as someone else. More Wellesian sleight-of-hand.

Falstaff's receding, diminishing figure is counterpointed by a reverse angle image of several high officials emerging from the cathedral, growing larger as they approach the camera. They are very pleased with the King's banishment of Sir John, and apparently confident of their own status within the royal firmament. The Bishop, Westmoreland, Prince John, and the Chief Justice pontificate smugly on the wisdom and compassion of their new King, whose calculated performance seems to have paid off.

From off screen Doll Tearsheat yells out, "Thou damned, tripe-visaged rascal!" She seems to be addressing the powerful group on screen, until a change in shots shows her struggling with soldiers blocking her path as she searches for Falstaff. *They* are the targets of her wrath. But in a larger sense the high officials we saw in the previous shot are equally deserving targets. Bardolph and Sir John's loyal page express concern for their exiled leader, indirectly challenging the sentence against him.

A quick dissolve to the next scene shows us more of the King's "good"judgement. On the battlements of his castle Hal informs the assembled nobles of his intention to conquer France by means war. He wastes no time acting on the advice of his late father. Westmoreland, whose loyalty to the new King remains suspect, is hypocritically the first to hoist a banner and declare support for Hal's call to arms. Hal now occupies a world in which no one dares challenge him face-to-face, as Falstaff did so freely.

Turning to the common masses gathered below his castle walls but kept at a respectful distance by a barricade of soldiers, whose tall spears again create a prison bar effect between leader and led, the King rallies their support for his war. Pictured against a sky in which the sun and clouds contend for dominance (Naremore, p.223), a now confident and secure Hal allows a sliver of compassion for his old mentor to shine through his Machiavellian demeanor. Contrary to the wishes of his advisers, he pardons Falstaff. Unfortunately, that reversal of judgment comes too late. "In those days they had time enough for everything," remarked the narrator at the beginning of *The Magnificent Ambersons*. But that is no longer true for Hal and Falstaff, as it was no longer true for George and Isabel or for Eugene and Isabel by the end of Welles's 1942 film.

The King's belated compassion is contrasted, via a direct cut to the next scene, with the callousness of the messenger he sends to deliver the good news to Falstaff. Poins strolls casually, almost contemptuously through the main hall of the Boar's Head Tavern, which was once his home. Many scenes ago Hal sent him to *dismiss* the King's messenger. Now he *is* the that messenger. His smugness stems from the fact that he has displaced Sir John as Hal's ally. Munching on some food, he saunters out to the stable where he finds Falstaff's page, Mistress Quickly, and a few of Sir John's other loyal friends. He greets no one, as though they were beneath his notice. But *their* silence proceeds from a different cause. The lack of background music at the start of this scene adds to our sense of the tavern's emptiness. The vitality of former days is gone.

From the presence of an enormous wooden coffin in the stable, Poins surmises that Falstaff is dead. The casket dwarfs the King's emissary as he stands beside it, just as in life its occupant dwarfed Poins in so many other respects. Each in his one way, Sir John's friends eulogize their fallen leader. Mistress Quickly's account of the great man's passing is both heartfelt and eloquent. She speaks like a mother mourning her dead child, despite perhaps being younger than Sir John. From her we learn that at the end of his life Falstaff regressed to infancy far more radically than did Robert Shallow. His battle to remain young at heart ended with his realization that Hal's rejection was final and complete. Which, ironically, turned out not to be the case. He became preoccupied with simple, immediate things, like his own fingers. Until the final moment, when he called out to God, or was it Hal, whom he previously referred to as Jove? Mistress Quickly did her best to distract him from sober thoughts. Yet she clings to her own cherished myths as an antidote to grief, consigning Sir John's spirit to the care of the legendary King Arthur—an impossibly idealized icon of English royalty. Falstaff's death is tragic, like all deaths. But it is not pathetic in the way Charlie Kane's was. Kane died alone. Falstaff was at least comforted by a friend who loved him.

Bardolph/Peto, the page, and the Hostess are shown in separate shots as they speak about Sir John. Though united in sorrow, each describes the loss somewhat differently, as did the more widely dispersed acquaintances of Charlie Kane. With his usual flair for contrast, Welles demonstrates those differences in a shot that visually incorporates all of the mourners, though at varying distances from the camera. Even at a moment of emotional solidarity, there is contention. The Hostess disputes Bardolph's claim that Falstaff called out for women with his last breath. But on second thought she half concedes the point by manipulating words to re-define Bardolph's meaning into something more acceptable to herself. Which is a kind of tribute to Sir John—the master of rhetorical prestidigitation.

Bardolph and Peto push the cart bearing Falstaff's giant coffin out through the tavern gate. The page repeats one of the master's witticisms, at Bardolph's expense. Bardolph is sentimentally touched rather than insulted by that recollection, adding to its effect by noting that wit was the only form of compensation he ever received in the service of Sir John. His tone of voice implies that such wit was worth more than its weight in gold. Welles himself once remarked, "Even if the good old days had never existed, the fact that we can *conceive* of such a world is, in fact, an affirmation of the human spirit" (Welles/Bogdanovich, p.100). Falstaff's mourners remember the best about him and tend to forget the worst. But in his usual contradictory manner, Welles follows up this harmless example of nostalgic distortion with a more famous, historical example perhaps not quite so harmless.

The camera rises above the tavern gate to picture Falstaff's huge coffin now dwarfed by the stone wall in the distance. From a different camera angle the coffin and its mourners are diminished by clouds in a sky that dominates the top four-fifths of the camera frame. Man as an individual is small and transitory compared to both his collective institutions (the distance wall) and Nature (the sky). But that visual discrepency is counterbalanced by the emergence of a musical lament on the soundtrack, complementing and amplifying the devotion of Sir John's loyal friends. The music is similar to what we heard at the death of King Henry IV. Though attended by only a handful of peasants, Sir John Falstaff is dispatched with all the gravity of a Shakespearean king.

From a high camera angle we watch with Mistress Quickly, standing within the protective frame of her tavern's gate (her home), as she watches Falstaff's casket recede slowly into a vast landscape. Ralph Richardson's off screen narration adds verbal counterpoint to the imagery and the music by paying tribute to King Henry V. Figuratively stepping back from the small event we witness on screen, he offers a broader view of history. In a detached and presumably objective voice he speaks high praise for the new King. But in a manner reminiscent of Falstaff, his choice of words slyly undercuts that praise. "Determined to put on him the shape of a new man" suggests a false front, manufactured for political reasons, rather than a genuine reformation. "A captain of such prudence and policy that he never entertained anything before it forecast the main chances that it might happen" suggests a complete lack of spontaneity. And to describe "left no offense unpunished nor friendship unrewarded" as "humane" borders on sarcasm, since such behavior implies both ruthless intolerance and bribery. All of which throws into question the narrator's concluding description of King Henry V, "a majesty was he that both lived and died a pattern in princehood, a lodestar in honor, and famous to all the world alway." To live and die "a pattern" sounds more machine-like than human, while "lodestar in honor" and "famous to the world alway" sound suspiciously like the products of collective myth, which the film as a whole tends to debunk. In a roundabout way, Falstaff gets the last word in his running debate with Hal.

As the movie's end credits roll by we hear a pounding, ceremonial drumbeat while watching an orderly gathering of nobles, clerics, and soldiers standing beneath black banners and the stained glass window of a cathedral. They are attending a funeral of State—probably King Henry IV's. Small movements of heads and bodies repeat themselves over and over as a single strip of film footage runs forwards and backwards. Individuals are reduced to mechanical puppets by the trickery of film. Locked into patterns they cannot escape. This film loop at the end of *Chimes at Midnight* might be a metaphor for the thoughtless habits of numerous characters in Welles's movies: Charlie Kane's compulsion to collect things and people; George Minafer's blind possessiveness of his mother, at the expense of her happiness; Elsa Bannister's compulsive need for financial security; Macbeth's unchecked ambition and paranoia; Othello's unshakeable belief in Desdemona's infidelity, which he absorbed from the liar Iago: Hank Quinlan's desperate need to punish criminals regardless of means; Joseph K's unconscious little hypocrisies; and King Henry IV's puritanical obsession with superficial displays of virtue. Then again, maybe the film loop is merely a technical consequence of Welles's strained finances. Something he employed to fill up the screen during the final credits. Or maybe it's *both*— necessity and creativity operating hand in hand.

At the very least, the coldly formal, public mourning of a famous public figure compares unfavorably to the spontaneous and genuine grief exhibited by a handful of Falstaff's loyal friends at his historically unrecorded and insignificant funeral procession.

By bracketing his chronicle of the witty, fun-loving, active Falstaff with a Prolog depicting him in a more passive, reflective mood and an ending depicting his meager funeral procession, Welles places a frame of human tragedy around a core of human comedy. Aesthetically the effect is reminiscent of a scene in *The Magnificent Ambersons*, where we accompany Eugene from the cold, dark, and wind of a winter's night to the warm, bright, crowded hospitality of the Amberson mansion, on the occasion of the last Christmas ball ever to be staged there. For one magical evening we defy the sadness of the past (Eugene's lost opportunity for romance with Isabel) and dream of bright possibilities in the present. Until disappointment, death, and regret overtake us.

For a brief, shining moment (roughly a hundred minutes screen time), a deeply flawed but warmly tolerant character named Sir John Falstaff embodies the broadness of vision and intensity of feeling that Orson Welles strove to convey to his audience through the magic of his cinematic paint box. He is the whole that no single witness to Charlie Kane's life could re-create in his or her interview with Thompson. He is both the detached narrator and the vibrant on-screen characters in *The Magnificent Ambersons*. He is what Michael O'Hara might someday become, long after his bittersweet experiences in *The Lady from Shanghai*. He is the point of mutual understanding that Hank Quinlan and Miguel Vargas, who have much more in common then they realize, fail to achieve in *Touch of Evil*. He is what Josef K perhaps became in his last moments in *The Trial*. He is the elusive conjunction between the passion of youth and the wisdom of old age. But he is also a fragile human being, who tragically falls further and harder from that visionary pinnacle than any other character Welles's portrayed. And in the end, an embrace that took in the whole world was reduced to playing with his own fingers and toes.

The movies of Orson Welles, whether sponsored by film studios or produced independently, embraced rather than homogenized the contradictions within human nature. Vice and virtue, comedy and tragedy, walk side by side, sometimes stride for stride. Occasionally indistinguishable, and often wholly ignorant of each other — except in the imagination of Orson Welles, where with the help of a little technological wizardry we strive to see and hear and understand ev erything at once. Like Don Quixote's, it's an impossible quest, as Welles would probably be the first to admit. But with Orson Welles as our guide, definitely worth the effort.

Selected Bibliography

Anderegg, Michael. *Orson Welles, Shakespeare, and Popular Culture*. New York: Columbia University Press, 1999.
Bazin, Andre. *Orson Welles: A Critical View*. New York: Harper & Row, 1979.
Brady, Frank. *Citizen Welles: A Biography of Orson Welles*. New York: Doubleday, 1990.
Callenbach, Ernest. "The Trial." *Film Quarterly*, Vol. 16, No. 4 (Summer 1963), pp. 40–43.
Carringer, Robert L. *The Magnificent Ambersons: A Reconstruction*. Berkeley: University of California Press, 1993.
_____. *The Making of Citizen Kane*. Berkeley: University of California Press, 1985.
Comito, Terry, ed. *Touch of Evil–Orson Welles, Director*. New Brunswick, NJ: Rutgers University Press, 1987.
Conrad, Peter. *Orson Welles: The Stories of His Life*. London: Faber and Faber, 2003.
Cowie, Peter. *The Cinema of Orson Welles*. New York: Da Capo, 1989.
Crowl, Samuel. "The Long Goodbye: Welles and Falstaff." *Shakespeare Quarterly*, Vol. 31, No. 3, (Autumn 1980), pp. 369–380.
Heylin, Clinton. *Despite the System: Orson Welles Versus the Hollywood Studios*. Chicago: Chicago Review Press, 2005.
Higham, Charles. *The Films of Orson Welles*. Berkeley: University of California Press, 1970.
Houston, Beverle. "Power and Dis-Integration in the Films of Orson Welles." *Film Quarterly*, Vol. 35, No. 4 (Summer 1982), pp. 2–12.
Johnson, William. "Orson Welles: Of Time and Loss." *Film Quarterly*, Vol. 21, No. 1 (Fall 1967), pp. 13–24.
Lebo, Harlan. *Citizen Kane: The Fiftieth-Anniversary Album*. New York: Doubleday, 1990.
Lev, Peter. "Three Adaptations of *The Trial*." *Literature and Film Quarterly*, Vol. 12, No. 3 (1984), pp. 180–185.
McBride, Joseph. *Orson Welles*. New York: Viking, 1973.
Naremore, James. *The Magic World of Orson Welles*. Dallas: Southern Methodist University, 1989.
Orwell, George. "New Words." *George Orwell: The Collected Essays, Journalism & Letters*, Vol. 2, pp. 3–12. Boston: David R. Godine, 2000.
Slavitt, David R. "New Films in Review." *Yale Review*, Vol. 52, No. 4 (Summer 1963), pp. 627–629.
Thomson, David. *Rosebud: The Story of Orson Welles*. New York: Alfred A. Knopf, 1996.
Welles, Orson, and Bogdanovich, Peter. *This is Orson Welles*. New York: HarperCollins, 1992.

Index

"Adagio in G Minor for Organ and Strings" (Albinoni) 180, 189, 192, 194-195, 199, 212, 214, 216
Albinoni, Tomasso 180, 189, 192, 199, 212, 214, 216
Anderegg, Michael vii, 213, 236
Antheil, George 105
The Apartment (1960 film) 195

The Barber of Seville (opera) 45
Barry Lyndon (1975 film) 51
Baxter, Keith 223, 257, 260
Bazin, Alfred 48
Bogdanovich, Peter 56, 61, 81, 98, 104, 106, 113, 118, 120, 124, 132, 145, 179–182, 204, 216, 221, 263
Brady, Frank 138, 179
Bride of Frankenstein (1935 film) 48

The Cabinet of Dr. Caligari (1919 film) 181
Cagney, James 141 266 267
Calleia, Joseph 156, 164, 172
Callenbach, Ernest 179, 215
Carringer, Robert vii, 20, 50, 61, 64, 72, 83, 89, 93–94, 97–100, 102–103
Chimes at Midnight (1966 film) viii, 1, 29, 98, 161, 208, 217–264
Chopin, Frederic 10
Citizen Kane (1941 film) viii, 1–2, 5–61, 63, 65–66, 81, 103–105, 108, 112, 121, 128–129, 141, 143, 145, 158, 161–163, 178, 180, 187, 191, 195, 213, 217–219, 225, 251, 257–258
Citizen Welles: A Biography of Orson Welles (Brady) 138
A Clockwork Orange (1971 film) 1, 213
Cohn, Harry 104–105, 132
Coleridge, Samuel Taylor 7
Collet, Jean 138
Columbia Studios 104
Comito, Terry 138, 146
Commingore, Dorothy 44, 50, 52, 55
Conrad, Joseph 2
Conrad, Peter vii, 48
Costello, Dolores 86
Cotten, Joseph 86, 140, 217
Cowie, Peter 179, 181, 184, 215
Crowl, Samuel 235, 268
Crowther, Bosley 179

Despite the System: Orson Welles Versus the Hollywood Studios (Heylin) vii
Dietrich, Marlene 146, 172
Dr. Strangelove (1964 film) 190, 200, 213, 227
Don Quixote (unfinished film) viii
Duck Soup (1933 film) 245

Elgar, Edward 10

F for Fake (1972 film) viii, 60, 213
Ford, Henry 83
"Funeral March" from *Sonata No.2 in B flat Minor*, Op. 35 (Chopin) 10

Gielgud, John 249, 257
Grant, Cary 105

Hardy, Oliver 218
Haufler, Max 197
Hayworth, Rita 105, 126, 135
Hearst, William Randolph 33
Heart of Darkness (novella) 2
Herrmann, Bernard 5–7, 11–13, 16, 18, 21, 24, 30–31, 33, 44, 49, 55, 59–61, 63, 67, 78, 80–81, 93, 96–97
Heston, Charlton 156
Heylin, Clinton vii
Higham, Charles 179, 215, 269
Hitchcock, Alfred 121, 151, 192
Hitler, Adolf 8
Holt, Tim 92
Holtzmann, Thomas 202
Homer 110
Houdini, Harry 252
Houston, Beverle 154

If I Die Before I Wake (novel) 104
The Immortal Story (1968 film) vii

Johnson, William 171
Julius Caesar (play) 193, 234

Kafka, Franz 179
King, Sherwood 104

King Kong (1933 film) 51
Kubrick, Stanley vii, viii, 1, 51, 173, 190, 192, 200, 213, 227

The Lady from Shanghai (1946 film) viii, 2, 104–135, 144, 147, 182, 198–199, 208, 214, 227, 264
Lang, Fritz 132, 195
Laurel, Stan 218
Lavagnino Angelo Francesco 218
Lebo, Harlan 49
Ledrut, Jean 186, 270
Leigh, Janet 151, 167
Leigh, Vivien 50
Lev, Peter 215
Little Caesar (1930 film) 141

Macbeth (1948 film) viii, 81–82, 132, 145, 159, 165, 218–219, 242, 248, 256
The Magic World of Orson Welles (Naremore) 136
The Magnificent Ambersons (1942 film) viii, 20, 29, 31, 61–105, 107–108, 112, 137, 144, 173, 221, 225–226, 230, 258, 262, 264
The Magnificent Ambersons: A Reconstruction (Carringer) vii, 61, 72, 89, 93–94, 97, 99–100, 102–103
The Making of Citizen Kane (Carringer) 20, 50
Mancini, Henry 136, 147, 168–169, 175, 178
Mankiewicz, Herman 21
Martinelli, Elsa 202
Marx Brothers 245
McBride, Joseph 37, 59, 102, 178–179, 215
Mendelssohn, Felix 10
Metropolis (1926 film) 132, 195
A Midsummer Night's Dream (play) 225
Milian, Victor 156
Mr. Arkadin (1955 film) 159
Moby Dick (novel) 134
Morocco (1930 film) 130, 271

Naremore, James 75, 136–137, 177, 179–180, 188, 210, 215, 219, 222, 225, 262
"New Words" (essay) 2
New York Times 24

The Odyssey (poem) 110
Olivier, Laurence 227
"Orson Welles: Of Time and Loss" (Johnson) 171
Orson Welles: One Man Band (1995 film) 1
Orson Welles, Shakespeare, and Popular Culture (Anderegg) vii
Orson Welles: The Stories of His Life (Conrad) vii, 48
Orwell, George 2
Othello (1952 film) viii, 2, 21, 50, 118, 133, 218–219, 224

Perkins, Anthony 151, 197, 202
"Pomp and Circumstance" March No. 1 in D, Op. 39 (Elgar) 10
"Power and Disintegration in the films of Orson Welles" (Houston) 154
Psycho (1960 film) 151, 165, 192

Reed, Carol 176
Richardson, Ralph 219, 248, 263

RKO Studios 2, 20, 51
Robinson, Edward G. 141
Rodway, Norman 227
Roemheld, Heinz 104–106, 108, 111, 117–118, 130–131, 134 272
Roosevelt, Theodore 26
Rosebud: The Story of Orson Welles (Thomson) 172

Sanford, Erskine 129
The Scarlet Empress (1934 film) 130
Schmidlin, Rick 136, 138
Shakespeare, William vii, 193, 218, 225, 228, 233, 246, 256, 263
The Shanghai Express (1932 film) 130, 146
Shannon, Harry 162
Slavitt, David R. 179
Sternberg, Josef von 130, 146
The Stranger (1946 film) viii, 87, 213, 226
A Streetcar Named Desire (1951 film) 50
Sunset Boulevard (1950 film) 146

Tamiroff, Akim 167
Tarkington, Booth 62, 67, 103
Taylor, John Russell 179
The Third Man (1949 film) 157, 176, 191, 208
Thomson, David 172, 179
Touch of Evil (1958 film) viii, 2, 21, 29, 116, 123, 136–178, 187, 204, 217–218, 221, 223, 225–226, 228–229, 242, 254, 264
"Touch of Evil, or Orson Welles and the Thirst for Transcendence" (Collet) 138
Touch of Evil — Orson Welles, Director (ed. Comito) 138, 273
The Trial (1962 film) viii, 2, 6, 118, 123, 128, 132, 145, 147, 157, 163, 179–217, 226–227, 234, 255, 264

Universal Studios 136, 143, 166

Waldteufel, Emil 61
Weaver, Dennis 151, 166
Webb, Roy 93, 102
"Wedding March" from *Incidental Music to "A Midsummer Night's Dream"* (Mendelssohn) 10
Welles, Beatrice 261
Welles, Orson vii, viii, 1–3, 7, 10, 14–16, 19–21, 24, 28–29, 32–33, 35, 44, 46–50, 52–56, 60–68, 70, 75, 78–81, 85, 87, 93, 95, 97–106, 108, 111–113, 116–124, 126–130, 132–136, 139–140, 143–146, 149–151, 154, 156, 158–160, 163, 165–167, 169, 171–173, 176–182, 187, 191–192, 194–195, 197, 201, 204–205, 208, 210, 213, 216–219, 221, 223, 225–227, 230, 234–235, 237, 242, 245–246, 249, 256–259, 261–264
Whale, James 48
Wiene, Robert 181
Wilder, Billy 195
Wise, Robert 93
The Wizard of Oz (1939 film) 213

www.ingramcontent.com/pod-product-compliance
Lightning Source LLC
Chambersburg PA
CBHW081546300426
44116CB00015B/2771